PAT MACPHERSON

REFLECTING ON THE BELL JAR

London and New York

First published in 1991
by Routledge
11 New Fetter Lane, London EC4P 4EE

Simultaneously published in the USA and Canada
by Routledge
a division of Routledge, Chapman and Hall Inc.
29 West 35th St reet, New York, NY 10001

Typeset by LaserScript Limited, Mitcham, Surrey.
Printed in Great Britain
by Cox & Wyman Ltd, Reading

British Library Cataloguing in Publication Data

Macpherson, Pat *1951–*
Reflecting on the bell jar. – (Heroines?).
1. Poetry in English. American writers. Plath, Sylvia,
1932–1963
I. Title II. Series
811.54

Library of Congress Cataloging in Publication Data

Macpherson, Pat, 1951–
Reflecting on The bell jar/Pat Macpherson.
p. cm. – (Heroines?)
Includes bibliographical references.
1. Plath, Sylvia. Bell jar. 2. Feminism and literature – United
States – History – 20th century. 3. Heroines in literature.
I. Title. II. Series.
PS3566.L27B436 1991
811'.54 – dc20 90-49425
CIP

ISBN 0–415–04393–X

WITHDRAWN
REFLECTING ON THE BELL JAR

Boo ... to be returned on o ...
he last date below.

SPECIA ...

In the 1950s America was in u... grip of Cold War para...
McCarthyism. Communism and 'gender maladjustme...
twin threats to the social ideals of family and security. Yet
previous readings of Plath and her heroine have ignored much
of the social context of this era.

Reflecting on The Bell Jar acknowledges this repressive post-war
regime of social hygiene. Pat Macpherson's reading takes into
account the fundamental rearrangement of the social contract
between citizen and state, built on the newly made connections
between national security and mental health. She investigates
the trial of the Rosenbergs and its connections with the electro-
therapy Plath and her heroine both experience. Macpherson
also evaluates the coercive effects of society's self-imposed
inquisitional attitude of surveillance, and explores its role in
forming female identity. Esther Greenwood, says Macpherson,
is the first heroine of our own era of popularized therapeutic
culture.

As challenging and thought-provoking as the novel itself,
Reflecting on The Bell Jar provides a new approach to one of
feminism's most difficult heroines. It will be fascinating reading
for students of women's studies, literature and cultural studies,
and for all those intrigued by the writings of Sylvia Plath.

HEROINES?

Certain fictional women have become part of western mythology. They are the stars of novels, films, radio and TV programmes, which have caught the imagination of generations of women. What is the secret of their magnetism?

This new feminist series about literary heroines investigates their lasting appeal. Each writer explores her chosen heroine's relationships with other characters in the novel, with her own author, with readers past and present, and lastly with herself. These characters all touch chords of reality for us. By their very 'ordinariness' they demonstrate that, in the most general feminist sense, all women are heroines.

For general readers as well as students, these concise, elegantly-written books will delight all lovers – and even haters – of the original classics.

Titles in the series include:

Mary Evans *Reflecting on Anna Karenina*

Pat Macpherson *Reflecting on Jane Eyre*

Rebecca O'Rourke *Reflecting on The Well of Loneliness*

Bernice Chitnis *Reflecting on Nana*

Marion Shaw and Sabine Vanacker *Reflecting on Miss Marple*

FOR MARY EVANS AND DON MACPHERSON,
MY KIND OF COLLABORATORS

CONTENTS

ACKNOWLEDGEMENTS

MARY EVANS set Sylvia Plath's *Letters Home* as one of the Texts and Problems in Feminism in her course at the University of Kent at Canterbury in the spring of 1982, and launched a conversation that continues today. This book is only a part of that dialogue, my attempt to research and interpret the details of post-war American middle-class life that made Sylvia Plath typical of her time and place.

Bronwyn Duffy, Mary Evans and Don Macpherson read the manuscript with great care, and taught me new meanings and methods of revision. My conversations with them clarified my prose and sustained my spirits during a project that grew more ambitious and difficult than was convenient. Molly Layton's suggestions for Chapter three, and our many conversations about mothers and daughters, feminism and family therapy, were clarifying and sustaining to me. Conversations with Shirley Brown and Kristine Long about feminist teaching and adolescence – including our own – are deeply embedded in this book. Conversations with Della Black Barol revised many of my oldest ideas about mothers and daughters. Students who discussed *The Bell Jar* in three classes at Germantown Friends School in Philadelphia gave me insight into the crucial questions of the novel for middle-class adolescents today. My conversation with Ruth Mortimer, Curator of Rare Books at Smith College, revised several of my assumptions about Plath and Smith. And the Institute for Media Analysis sponsored the conference, 'Anticommunism and the US: History and Consequences', in

Acknowledgements

November 1988 at Harvard University, which raised many questions and perspectives useful for my work, and assembled an inspiring group of radicals with hair-raising stories to tell.

The publisher is grateful to Faber and Faber Limited for allowing permission to quote from *The Bell Jar* by Sylvia Plath.

INTRODUCTION

Cold War Paranoia – Theirs and Ours

'WE DON'T need an interpreter here', the hero of *The Manchurian Candidate* explains when his Korean sidekick shows up in New York looking for a job after the war. 'We all speak the same language.' He does accept Chunjin's mute services as cook, houseboy and bodyguard, however. This cold warrior's version of our national state of security is a paranoid's dream-come-true, his version now the only version. Objectivity has never felt the need for interpretation. By the mid-1950s 'the norm', a single-dimensional conformity based on image, seemed to have achieved the status of official language. Dissent within and about the norm was muted. Those speaking a different language were by definition Alien, subject to surveillance by the national security state.

The 'Hoover in every home' of post-war America was not, I would argue, the humble vacuum cleaner. J. Edgar Hoover, as Director of the FBI and chief among cold war propagandists, was the real engineer of social hygiene. By rhetorically linking national, family and mental health, the most successful surveillance was internalized, the Hoover taken in to the citizen's psychic household.

In *Loyalties* (1989), Carl Bernstein reveals how Red-baiting paranoia seeps in. When he was nine, his mother testified before the House UnAmerican Activities Committee (HUAC), newspapers published her photo, and headlines exposed her as a Communist. 'The suggestion of espionage hung over the story like the asphixiating cloud of the epic itself', Bernstein explains

1

(*Vanity Fair* 1989). He thought it meant his mother was going to be killed for her politics, following in Ethel Rosenberg's footsteps. Worse still, 'Somewhere subconsciously there was always the fear that I would stumble onto something', for instance 'that my mother and father might have become ensnared in espionage' (*Vanity Fair* 1989). He had internalized three linked features of cold war ideology: the HUAC tribunal's moral that Communists are spies, the mass media's conviction-by-exposure (guilty if charged), and the Justice Department's heavy-handed moral that national security demanded the execution of the Rosenbergs.

That execution begins Esther Greenwood's narration in *The Bell Jar*. She is in New York in June of 1953, and 'that's all there was to read about in the papers' (*1*).* The Rosenbergs' guilt and punishment were debated then, and ever since. They were convicted of giving away the secret of the atomic bomb to the Russians. Arthur Miller argues that their trial and execution were 'at worst . . . a frame-up' and at best 'a bleeding sacrifice on the altar of cold war politics' (Schneir and Schneir 1983: back cover). The Rosenbergs were scapegoated as spies, Communists, traitors in our midst, with their Jewishness and Ethel Rosenberg's strong womanhood seen as part of the Alien nature of this Enemy Within.

The Rosenberg case was only the most extreme of McCarthyism's prosecutions. All McCarthyist tribunals depended on secret surveillance of citizenry and public exposure through the mass media. Fear of such surveillance, and such prosecution-by-public-accusation, created a paranoia in dissenting and neutral citizens alike, a paranoia about the lengths to which Their paranoia was undermining Our democratic institutions and Our basic civil rights. 'You're a Communist nowadays if you sign peace appeals', Sylvia Plath wrote a friend in 1950. 'People don't seem to see that this negative Anti-Communist attitude is destroying all the freedom of thought we've ever had. . . . Everything they don't agree with is Communist' (Wagner-Martin 1987:59). Sylvia Plath's beloved

*All quotations from *The Bell Jar* are cited by page number only.

high-school English teacher was called before the town board to account for his pacificism, and in 1953 one of her Smith College professors was the first academic to testify before the HUAC, naming names of Communists at Harvard in the 1930s (Schrecker 1986: 194).

But 'If power were never anything but repressive, if it never did anything but to say no, do you really think one would be brought to obey it?' (Benjamin 1988:4) Foucault's question turns our analysis to the question of how one comes to obey what one first resisted. This is the story of *The Bell Jar*, of Esther Greenwood's paranoid relationship to the repressive norms of the 1950s. Not only does the novel 'point up the controlling presence of the medical, corporate or legal collective gaze at the woman' – so inquisitional, so often punishing in the McCarthy era – but also *The Bell Jar* is Esther Greenwood's 'look *back* at a collective inquiring gaze' (Walker 1987: 209) – a heroine's contest with the terms defining her life and self.

When pop-Freudianism wed functionalism in post-war mass culture, a monstrous norm of Family was hatched. Taking Freudian ideas about how children acquire gender identity, and avoiding any claims of the unconscious, the sociologist Talcott Parsons created a pragmatic model of the nuclear family functioning by means of sex roles, females 'expressive' both by nature and nurture, males 'instrumental'. 'By the late 1940s', Benita Eisler argues, the therapeutic culture had arrived at 'a definition of mental health as social adjustment' to roles (Eisler 1986:34), and the Norm was born.

TV and film and magazines screened both the norm (family fulfilment, scientific objectivity) and the Other (adulterous women, effeminate men, commie robots from Outer Space). *Image as norm* was disseminated through the sophisticated visual language of a mass communication system unprecedented in history.

The cruellest assumption, to my mind, was the paradox that one's role came naturally, and failure to be fulfilled was sign of sickness. So each citizen was set self-policing to enact a 'fulfilled' conformity convincing to others if always fraudulent to oneself. Paranoia proceeds naturally enough from this basic psychic dishonesty, seeking only external screens on which to project the denied self and call it the Other. This, I would argue, is the real 'enemy within' that Hoover called forth as Communism. Each citizen, if repression really worked, was self-divided into conformist front and denied demon Other – and anxiously seeking release from such tension whether by stoning scapegoats like the Rosenbergs, or confessing and being punished for crimes of deviance and dissent.

No one toured these Hoovered halls of paranoia-gone-patriotic-and-psychiatric more thoroughly than Anne Parsons, whose life paralleled that of Sylvia Plath and her heroine of *The Bell Jar.* Anne Parsons' story, however, is ruled by the singular killing irony of a feminist having Talcott Parsons, the father of functionalism, for a father. Like Sylvia Plath, Anne Parsons was a career woman who had a nervous breakdown trying to fulfil the (expressive) feminine mystique and the promise of her (instrumental) education in the same life. Like Plath she was a pacifist alarmed at the growth of the military-industrial complex and its role in international cold war confrontations. Like Plath she was frightened by public apathy. In her 'diary of a mental patient' she recorded her 'panic' about missiles, about biological and chemical warfare and the absence of 'any resistance' to them – and was told, she reported, 'I was resisting insight into my feminine instinct' (Breines 1986:830). She realized that her therapy redefined her political paranoia as gender maladjustment. She realized the insidiousness of the repressive norm infecting therapy, and realized 'that one of the troubles with a confession is that it gives too much power to the priests who then tend to use it for their own ends' (Breines 1986:836). Then the worst happened: she failed her therapy at McLean, a private mental hospital. (Plath passed her therapy at McLean, and went back to Smith College 'whole and well'.) Parsons was told she had 'serious neurotic difficulties not treatable by means of psychoanalysis' (Breines: 1986:826). After much resistance to the therapeutic culture's link between her social deviance and her incurable mental pathology, Parsons eventually broke down and accepted the blame: 'It was my life that failed,' she wrote her parents (Breines 1986:838). She committed suicide in 1964, Sylvia Plath in 1963.

Esther Greenwood does not, in the end of *The Bell Jar*, commit suicide. She is cured, pronounced 'whole and well'. She rolls forth triumphantly, 'patched, retreaded, and approved for the road' back to college. My *Reflecting on The Bell Jar* seeks to understand how and why she takes on and takes in the norm, transforming it to suit her own desires, and being transformed by it at the same time.

Chapter One

COMING APART IN THE ATOMIC AGE

ESTHER'S story begins with her month in New York as one of twelve Guest Editors at the fictional equivalent of *Mademoiselle*, the Magazine for Smart Young Women. Her career dreams as Fiction Editor and writer are put to the test there, and so are her glamour dreams about fashioning her femininity. The magazine becomes for Esther a kind of tribunal, a College Board on female identity questions of career and – or is it *or*? – femininity. The tribunal is conceived as a test of her social role success and her mental health at once, in a colossally powerful equation first established in the 1950s. Esther's ability to play all the roles assigned her is understood to be a test of her maturity. Her social maturity as a 'hatted and heeled' mademoiselle is the sign of her psychic maturity as a developmentally 'whole' and medically 'well' citizen-patient of therapeutic culture.

Esther fails *Mlle*'s test and falls apart. When she goes home and fails to be cured by the tribunal of doctors supervising housewives' health, she suspects she is being punished by shock treatments. She attempts suicide and is 'sentenced' to a mental hospital, more shock treatments, and therapy. The mental hospital's tribunal is her last – passed – test.

Esther, like millions of her fellow citizens in the 1950s, burrows inward to find and repair the sub-atomic psychic fissure responsible for her nervous condition. Identifying the cause and treatment of her maladjustment is the business of a growth industry of experts, from teen magazines to psychiatrists.

6

Meanwhile, outside this fall-out shelter of adjustment-oriented popular discourse, the nuclear fall-out of new forces set loose in the atomic age spread its invisible threat everywhere. The post-war world was made by the Bomb. 'Not only the weapon which could destroy civilisation,' Raymond Williams points out, the Bomb was 'the shadow under which a new authoritarian war economy would grow and expand' (Williams 1984:85). Most insidiously, the Bomb was chief weapon in the cold war arsenal of totalitarian *rhetoric* dividing Us from Them along some very repressive and punishing lines.

McCarthyist tribunals gave public face to much larger and more pervasive post-war processes threatening democracy: the institutionalized surveillance of citizenry, a military-industrial corporate economy fronted by a consumer democracy and sold by a rapidly expanding commercialized mass media, and the evaporation of liberal public debate about these issues.

Esther Greenwood's liberal idealism turns from schoolgirl squeak to complete silence in the course of her stay in New York.

> I knew something was wrong with me that summer, because all I could think about was the Rosenbergs and how stupid I'd been to buy all those uncomfortable, expensive clothes, hanging limp as fish in my closet, and how all the little successes I'd totted up so happily at college fizzled to nothing outside the slick marble and plate-glass fronts along Madison Avenue. (2)

The clothes, the college successes for a career launch, and the fate of the Rosenbergs: Esther searches for the connections.

Slick fronts are what Esther finds in New York – in cold war witch-hunting politics, in advertising and mass media, and in the magazine's glossed-over contradiction between education for career and full-time wife-and-motherhood. Accountability on these fronts is even harder to get a handle on than her own sanity. The slick marble and plate-glass fronts along Madison Avenue do not offer any real finger-holds for small-town good-girlism.

FASHIONING FEMININITY: THE FEMALE BODY POLITIC

How to become a successful mademoiselle? Study 'the Magazine for Smart Young Women', as *Mlle* subtitled itself. Esther can as always do better than that: she writes and edits the magazine, and perhaps most important, her photo appears in its August college issue, irrefutable sign that this 'hatted and heeled' mademoiselle has passed the test. Underneath and inside Esther Greenwood has already fallen apart when her picture is being taken. But this only emphasizes the post-war paradox: the distance between image-as-success and internal-dissent-as-hidden-failure. 'Faking normalcy was the name of the game' (Eisler 1986:86) as Benita Eisler (Smith class of 1958) explains her generation.

> In the fifties, *image* began to be exploited on a scale undreamed of in the earlier days of advertising and public relations. . . . The Age of Television – and the billions of dollars riding on its sales potential – was required to exploit [the] sincere dishonesty
> (Eisler 1986:91)

of the image as the norm.

Fashioning femininity through image is the business of Esther's magazine. The creation of appearance is the pre-test for femininity, the securing of dates the real test. As with career, Esther comes to see commerce at work behind the scenes. Woman-as-consumer *produces* herself: this is the moment of self-commodification. Woman-as-desirable-commodity *sells* herself as date-bait: this is the moment of self-commercialization. Typically Esther resolves to make the meat market's cold calculus into a challenge only *her* precocity can solve.

Esther is ideally situated for this project, having all the magazine's resources at hand, and loads of free cosmetics and fashion tips thrown in. Beauty is democratically within each consumer's reach through the magazine. In 1950 Mary McCarthy analysed women's magazines, called 'the slicks', and found there the post-war process beginning to define both citizenship and adolescence chiefly through consumption. 'The rhetoric of fashion as democracy, as an inherent right or manufacturer's guarantee' (McCarthy 1951: 177) shapes female readers' identities within a norm of 'choice' among fashions. The key is no longer high fashion bought by the few, but mass-produced slicks and goods accessible to all.

The dark underside of this self-improvement road to female identity, reassuringly sign-posted though it is, is that the more thorough the instructions and illustrations, the more thorough the surveillance and regulation of the female body. 'Are your legs in a fit state for public display? Nylon stockings show up every little blemish. . . . Something must be done at all costs!' (Carter 1984:205). The camera eye and the advice columns direct each reader's eye to survey her own body for every little blemish well nigh everywhere. All must be remedied for public display. Big Brother is Watching You is not the worst news for women. They have been set watching themselves in the mirrors, according to meticulous standards of female appearance they learn as femininity itself. Esther's colleague Hilda, Fashion Editor extraordinaire, provokes Esther's horrified fascination as such a slave to image. A veritable 'mannequin' moving down Madison Avenue, Hilda 'stared at her reflection in the glossed shop windows as if to make sure, moment by moment, that she continued to exist' (*110–11*).

Hilda follows fashion dictates like a storm-trooper, as Betsy enthusiastically tells Esther, filling her in on the fur show:

> "It was wonderful," Betsy smiled. "They showed us how to make an all-purpose neckerchief out of mink tails and a gold chain, the sort of chain you can get an exact copy of at Woolworth's for a dollar ninety-eight, and Hilda nipped down to the wholesale fur warehouses right afterward and bought a bunch of mink tails at a big discount and dropped in at Woolworth's and then stitched the whole thing together coming up on the bus." (*30–1*)

Betsy could be writing her advice column as she speaks; hers is the official agenda-setting voice of the magazine. Advertising initiates the search (the fur show has a commercial motive); Betsy's advice column explains how-to-do-it-yourself using a real subject, Hilda; and the fashion photo – *the image* – is the product, the successful result that the story captions: 'Sure enough,' Esther observes, 'she was wearing an expensive-looking scarf of furry tails fastened on one side by a dangling gilt chain' (*31*).

'First a small shopping expedition', suggests one of the slicks in Mary McCarthy's essay. 'Then give your mind a good going-over, stiffen it with some well-starched prose, apply a gloss of poetry, two coats at least' (McCarthy 1951: 183–4). Linking commerce to appetite and culture to duty, the injunction is to shop first, then work. Mental housekeeping, like cleaning, ironing and furniture polishing, is a matter of maintaining oneself in a fit state for public display. In the slicks, McCarthy explains, 'Literature and the arts are offered as a tonic to the flabby personality . . . a vital agent in the general toning-up process' (McCarthy 1951:185). To take literature more seriously, as reader or writer, deviates from the norm of the slicks and femininity at once. Education and brains threaten femininity, as Mary McCarthy's Vassar grads realize in her novel *The Group*.

'It's trying to get an education and a man at the same time that's the number-one problem and strain on any girl', as *Mlle* in 1957 described this tension (Bailey 1988:44). In 1961 *Mlle* felt it necessary to explain cause and effect:

> It's a sad, difficult business, for the girls have lost much of their own femininity in the course of their liberation, and they know it. For femininity is a gift a woman receives in large measure from a man who feels himself to be a man – and, of course, vice versa.
>
> (Bailey 1988:105)

What's the difference between the magazine-as-mirror and the man-as-mirror through which femininity is secured?

One dating manual proposes a novel partnership between the fashion magazine and the date, in which the date becomes the means to self-improvement, instead of its goal. Dating creates the competitive motivation necessary to cultivate femininity to its fullest developed state. To put your best foot forward, drop 'Freddy' your steady, because with him there's

> no competition and no impression to be made. . . . If you didn't have Freddy, you'd be spending a lot more time in front of the mirror – deciding how to bring out your best features. You'd be poring over fashion magazines and exploring shop windows to find out what the perfect style is for you. Without Freddy, you'd be putting your best foot forward and there wouldn't be an old sneaker on it.
>
> (Bailey 1988:55)

The mirror, the magazine and the shop window are at least static images one can study, preparing oneself at home in advance. The date is a moving image whose plot is sexual politics. The female is always vulnerable, always negotiating between success-as-seduction and success-as-chastity. On each and every date, the Catch-22 of femininity is put to the test. 'The American virgin [is] dressed to seduce' (Plath 1983:9), as Sylvia Plath described herself in her journal at age eighteen.

Standing in her bathroom, 'smoothing, perfuming, powdering' herself for her date, Plath contemplated themes of nature and artifice, innocence and femme-fatality, the primitive and modern, trying to uncover the 'feeling of expectancy' lurking 'beneath the surface of my understanding, waiting for me to grasp it . . . when I consider the prolonged adolescence of our species' (Plath 1983:11–12). Ten years of adolescence (as the Kinsey Reports make clear by 1953) make a mockery of virginity as a natural or innocent state of mind or body. One look in the bathroom mirror and closet reveals the stock of beauty products and prescriptions necessary to create her calculatingly innocent look of all-natural seductive virginity.

Marilyn Monroe, who perfected the art of seductive innocence to extremes of both comedy and tragedy, explained the tricky relationship between her mirror/photo image and the calculation that must be *hidden behind* it:

> When the photographers come, it's like looking in a mirror. They think they arrange me to suit themselves, but I use them to put over myself. It's necessary to the movie business, but I often hate it. I never show it, though. It could ruin me.
>
> (McCann 1988:72)

(Fashion Tip: one of the secrets of Monroe's success was wearing her bra to bed every night to keep her breasts in a fit state for public display.)

'You must apply yourself relentlessly to the task of making nature over so that you can take your place without self-consciousness in the race for a husband' (Bailey 1988:71), a 1950 manual advises us with the direct address that makes it clear we are receiving a homework assignment due the very next day. Exactly how this relentless making up of self can be achieved without self-consciousness is the task awaiting each American virgin at puberty. To Plath it felt like a 'monumental grotesque joke' (Plath 1983:12).

Central to this process is of course the magazine, whose advice columns and fashion photos provide the recipes for turning the raw into the cooked. 'It takes extra care in dressing and making up the raw material you were blessed with to do its best selling job for that personality of yours,' the *Ladies' Home Journal* advice column explained (Bailey 1988:72). Luckily science and industry have provided advanced formula products for the task. 'All that is necessary . . . is to select the proper cosmetic for the proper occasion', which is where 'advice' comes in. Two 1950s advice manuals set the agenda with a certain blunt, if bullying, charm, *Get a Husband* and *How to Woo, Win and Keep Your Man*:

> The modern world has given you a billion-dollar cosmetic industry, diet experts, specialized stylists and brand-new psychological knowledge; all to storm the barricades of bachelorhood.

* * *

> Science has placed the magic of Cinderella into the hands of today's women. . . . All that is necessary for the aspirant to beauty is to select the proper cosmetic for the proper occasion.
> (Bailey 1988:72)

Plath describes herself 'bent over the washbowl in unthinking ritual, washing the proscribed areas, worshipping the glittering chromium . . . ' And, the kicker: 'And you are the moving epitome of all this. Of you, by you, for you' (Plath 1983:13). She is the butt of the joke, the 'epitome' of the culture's commodification of seductive virginity, thoroughly addicted to its prescriptions, lavishly made up using its products, and certified clean using its sterile standards of hygiene. But her self-consciousness yields only self-blame, dooming her to an alienated double perspective she keeps secret, closeted behind her bathroom mirror.

Addressing herself only is perhaps Plath's limitation in trying to solve the riddle of femininity in her journal. Her solitary self-consciousness reflects on itself as the source of her internalized strictures of femininity. Plath's contemporary, Shirley Jackson, shows how the group enforces the code of femininity, through ritual.

'Are you a virgin?' is the interrogation question asked by her college peers of Natalie, the mental-breakdown heroine of Shirley Jackson's 1951 novel, *Hangsaman.* In an initiation ceremony suitably set in the girls' shared bathroom,

> She gave her name (*was* it her name?) and then, when asked if she were a virgin – and this question, gaining adherents from the unkind and the merely curious, was being asked now by three or four voices at once, and even, Natalie saw from the high point of the stool, being echoed by the traitor freshmen themselves – said briefly, "I won't answer."
>
> Jackson 1951:78)

Peer pressure takes on daunting new dimensions in the McCarthy era when trials for deviancy enforced the norm. Raped, secretly, this heroine's violation of the virgin norm makes her both inadmissibly guilty and innocent at once, a mind-twisting caricature of the paradox of seductive virginity if there ever was one. But as with McCarthy's victims, any real crime disappears and co-operation with the tribunal becomes the only issue:

> What a silly routine, Natalie thought, not realizing, sitting there alone on the stool in the center of the ring of girls, how she was

jeopardizing her own future in college, her own future for four years and perhaps for the rest of her life; how even worse than the actual being a bad sport was the state of mind which led her into defiance of this norm, this ring of placid, masked girls, with their calm futures ahead and their regular pasts proven beyond a doubt; how one person, stepping however aside from their meaningless, echoing standards, set perhaps by violent movement before their recollection, and handed down to them by other placid creatures, might lose a seat among them by questions, by rebellion, by anything except a cheerful smile and the resolution to hurt other people.

(Jackson 1951:79)

'It makes no difference whether you really were guilty of that first offense or not. Once you get talked about, you must be careful never again to make the mistake that caused the gossip' (Duvall 1956:129). These are the *Facts of Life and Love for Teen-Agers*, as Evelyn Duvall explains them in her 1956 best-seller. The consequences of nonconformity are social alienation.

Conformity to the American virgin dating norm, on the other hand, has its dangers as well. 'Seduction' meant some petting as payment for the date. When Nancy Hunter Steiner tells of her summer as Sylvia Plath's room-mate in 1955, she reveals – while denying – this underlying commercial deal of the date:

Our shopgirl mentality prompted us, early in the summer, to strike a bargain – to agree that we would accept any and all dates that included an invitation to dinner or the theater, even if we found the men themselves uninteresting. We had a gluttonous appetite for the attractions of the city and little money to indulge it. We had made the pledge in a moment of high good spirits, and I did not believe that either of us was quite mercenary enough to make a habit of premeditated avarice. Still, we did not expect the men we met that summer to be important to us; Syl had practically decided to marry Jeff McGuire and I was half-engaged to a boy back home. We felt safely immune and unassailable. We flirted and charmed our way through a dozen brief encounters, enjoying the imagined stir we created as we bounced from one diversion to the next, presenting a united front to all pursuers.

(Steiner 1973:78–9)

Steiner's version of virginal seductiveness serves to keep her innocence technically intact. 'Safely immune' from sexual desire themselves, all innocent of any 'gluttonous appetite' for sex or money or social status, the usual currency of dates, these shopgirls from Smith are hungry only for culture. So when Plath says she has been raped by the sinister Irwin she has been dating, after many warnings from her friend, Nancy Hunter Steiner can only tactfully imply that Sylvia's post-coital haemorrhaging looked to her like 'a large incriminating pool' around her body on her bed. Later, 'I found her on the bathroom floor in a pool of blood that spread like a giant wound across the regular, hexagonal white tile' (Steiner 1973:86). This seductive virgin's slick wheeling and dealing is brutally punished, and she and her formerly all-white bathroom are left soiled with her own blood. This sordid episode alienates the victim from her best friend, leaving her to bury the 'secret rape' under monumental amounts of guilt and anger. Again the *Facts of Life and Love for Teen-Agers* points out the moral:

> Getting into trouble is not a pleasant experience for a girl. At best it is disillusioning, often painful, and a poor introduction into womanhood. At worst it can wreck her whole life and make her feel so like 'damaged goods' that she never afterward can love and be loved by a man worthy of her devotion. Society tries to safeguard girls from such circumstances by rules and regulations designed for their protection. When a girl defies these safeguards she places herself in a highly vulnerable position. Better by far is willing conformity to the standards of one's culture, based upon one's intelligent awareness of why such restrictions are important.
>
> (Duvall 1956:65–6)

Esther Greenwood in *The Bell Jar* contemplates the *Reader's Digest* 'Defense of Chastity' her mother sent her at college, written by 'a married woman lawyer with children' warning that

> the best men wanted to be pure for their wives, and even if they weren't pure, they wanted to be the ones to teach their wives about sex. Of course they would try to persuade a girl to have sex and say they would marry her later, but as soon as she gave in, they would lose all respect for her and start saying that if she did

that with them she would do that with other men and they would end up by making her life miserable. (*89*)

The double standard stands firm as the basis of the marital contract, 'purity' the wife's coin that buys her husband's 'respect'. Esther's dates with Constantin and Marco reveal to her that this currency of female flesh, whether given or withheld, structures men's expectations and so predetermines the morality and commerce of the date. Constantin dates Esther to pay back his American hostess, buying her 'a bite to eat' (*56*) and gallantly ignoring her seductive intentions; sex would only increase his debt instead of clearing it. So poor Esther cannot even *her* score with her boyfriend by losing her virginity, one-upping his waitress with her UN simultaneous interpreter. Marco's diamond tie-pin catches Esther's interest more than he does as her blind date; but she finds she is expected to pay for his gift of it with sex – in the mud, her dress ripped, 'slut' hissed in her ear. ' "Sluts, all sluts." Marco seemed to be talking to himself. "Yes or no, it is all the same" ' (*122*). Her view does not register in this woman-hater's monologue, which is but a worst-case-scenario of any date's power politics.

'Now the one thing this article [on dating chastely] didn't seem to me to consider was how a girl felt' (*89*). *Esther's* view has no public articulation whatsoever, and so cannot be made to 'exist' at all. Her experience of womanhood shows her to be *subject to* the double standard, against her own will. 'I resented virginity, and the so-called "purity" of women, and reacted violently to any suggestion about it. It had always shamed me that men judged women by such a standard' (White 1985:153). Agnes Smedley's heroine Marie Rogers in *Daughter of Earth* (1929) at nineteen like Esther wants to escape virginity's apparent complicity with the double standard. But the fact that it 'shames' her to be so judged shows how insidiously 'purity' clings to her own sense of femininity, even as it is being 'violently' resisted. As with Esther's violent resistance to Marco's attempted rape, her 'yes or no, it is all the same' in this contest. Protest does not register. Words seem immaterial for her challenge to the double standard. Words fail Esther.

When she finds a man who is not a predator and happily ends up in his bed, Esther thinks she can score points and protest the game at the same time. Esther grandiosely speculates that sleeping with a Russian speaker like Constantin is equivalent to a European grand tour in the cosmopolitan datebook and a defiantly liberal gesture in cold war relations. Once Esther's extravagant expectations are raised, the crash quickly 'punishes' them. Esther feels betrayed by his showing no interest in having sex with her:

> As I stared down at Constantin the way you stare down at a bright, unattainable pebble at the bottom of a deep well, his eyelids lifted and he looked through me, and his eyes were full of love. I watched dumbly as a shutter of recognition clicked across the blur of tenderness and the wide pupils went glossy and depthless as patent leather. (*94*)

Constantin's failure of interest in Esther and Marco's failure of respect for Esther are complementary commentaries on Esther's femininity that cast doubt on both her desirability and virtue. The American virgin, having failed to seduce, has only herself to blame. 'Just such problems as these constitute the fork in the emotional adjustment or maladjustment roads for many an individual' (Bailey 1988:133) threatens one marriage expert. Esther has nothing to show for herself after her dates in New York, nothing at all.

THE FICTION EDITOR AT THE MAGAZINE FOR SMART YOUNG WOMEN

The magazine is the grand central station of Esther's dilemmas, where her glossy career-girl dreams meet cold war realities of women's place in the economy. First women are consumers, clothes-buying as college girls (as *Mlle*'s 350-page college issue of August 1953 amply illustrates), then appliance-buying as housewives (the graduate-level *Good Housekeeping*). Only secondarily are women career girls, subordinate to men, housekeepers and receptionists and secretaries for the service economy. *Mlle*'s March 1953 issue asks the question, 'Can You

Live on Your First Pay Check?' and answers it in September 1953 with a chart of '21 jobs for the liberal arts graduate': from copy writer to junior underwriter, including airline stewardess, museum aide, department store trainee – running the gamut of the oxford-shirt class of pink-collar labour. 'We share a common gripe against employers', admit two of Plath's fellow guest editors in *Mlle*'s August 1953 issue, speaking for all twenty of the group. 'We find that the people who hire us respect us more for the jobs we've held (yes, even our baby-sitting jobs – and we've all been baby-sitters) than they respect us for our college educations' (*Mlle*, August 1953:253–4). Prepped to high-dive from her elite education into the waters of Madison Avenue, Esther sees that a plastic wading pool of paper-shuffling hostess jobs awaits her twenty storeys below. And – the really annoying part – *Mlle*'s own sales job actually talked her up the ladder. Esther, super-saleswoman guest editor, is hardly in a position to back down off the College Board now.

Her solution is to reinforce her illusions. Esther-the-ingenue views the Fiction Office as the place where achievement is rewarded, power is dispersed to the deserving, careers are fostered, the knowing meet each other and transcend the rules the less talented have to play by. Esther sees herself as the exception, an identity that is the real diploma from her elite women's college. Ironically this is precisely what Margaret Shook identifies as 'the product of a communal imagination' at Smith in the 1950s. Esther Greenwood is 'the image we had of what we were, or rather what we thought we were, in moods of comic awareness' (Shook 1988:117).

Esther's salvation from fashion foolishness is in her brainy and ironic sensibility as a writer. She after all is apprenticed to the Fiction Editor, the 'head' office where intellectual and literary decisions are made, in comparison to which the Fashion Editor is but a mindless (female-as-all-body) follower of fad. Fiction of course transcends the commercial concerns of Fashion, just as male/mind transcends female/body, just as Art, created by 'the god-eyed tall-minded ones' (as Plath calls great male poets in her journal (Plath 1983:76)), transcends mere earthlings' cloddish subjection to gravity. Having her own stories accepted for prizes and publication, and then her own exemplary English major's career endorsed by the award of the guest editorship, Esther Greenwood sees her future as star writer and editor already forecast, and with it her own subjection to gravity (and the female world) momentarily cancelled.

Sylvia Plath's caption for a photo of the guest editors, posed as a star for *Mlle*'s August 1953 college issue, shows her expectation that the experience is a springboard with considerable bounce, catapulting stargazers into the very stars 'for jobs and futures', and taking men's oxford shirts off their backs in a fashion statement of unambiguous sexual politics:

> We're stargazers this season, bewitched by an atmosphere of evening blue. Foremost in the fashion constellation we spot *Mlle*'s own tartan, the astronomic versatility of sweaters, and men, men, men – we've even taken the shirts off their backs!!! Focusing our telescope on college news around the globe, we debate and deliberate. Issues illuminated: academic freedom, the sorority controversy, our much labeled (and libeled) generation. From our favorite fields, stars of the first magnitude shed a bright influence on our plans for jobs and futures. Although horoscopes for our ultimate orbits aren't yet in, we Guest Eds. are counting on a favorable forecast with this sendoff from *Mlle*, the star of the campus. (*283–5*)

This alarmingly exuberant voice of *Mlle* is the voice of the *other* guest editors in *The Bell Jar*, exemplified by Betsy's bubble-brained blurbery about Hilda's scarf – but never Esther's. So projected and so denied, this voice 'made' Plath's adolescent writing career, but she does not let it speak through her heroine's mouth in *The Bell Jar*.

In her scrapbook about her month at *Mlle*, Sylvia Plath writes in the same 'feminine burbling' (Plath 1983:69) about the same astronomic ambition as her *Mlle* blurb. There seems to be no difference between the official and unofficial versions of her month *and her self* at the magazine.

> After being one of the two national winners of *Mlle*'s fiction contest ($500!) last August, I felt I was coming home again when I won a guest editorship representing Smith & took a train to

NYC for a salaried month working – hatted and heeled – in *Mlle*'s airconditioned Madison Ave. offices. . . . Fantastic, fabulous, and all other inadequate adjectives go to describe the four gala and chaotic weeks I worked as guest managing Ed . . . living in luxury at the Barbizon, I edited, met celebrities, was feted and feasted by a galaxy of UN delegates, simultaneous interpreters & artists . . . an almost unbelievable merry-go-round month – this Smith Cinderella met idols: Vance Bourjaily, Paul Engle, Elizabeth Bowen – wrote article via correspondence with 5 handsome young male poet teachers. (*283*)

Plath's two blurbs show how language is the currency she uses to create her self as a 'hatted and heeled' mademoiselle. Her command of language allows her to translate the rawness and chaos of her experience into the coherent social images of achievement, success, profitability. At the same time, language is the medium through which the social world shapes and positions her. The voice of *Mlle* speaks her as much as she speaks it. Much of her image of herself actually comes from the pages of the magazine.

The Bell Jar denies such alarming interactions between Esther's identity and the magazine. The other guest editors foolishly enact *Mlle* types, while Esther's ironic distance serves to present us with her integrity. She is innocent of such vulgar influence, and such manipulations of image for reward. To acknowledge the *real* power of *Mlle* magazine would make our heroine the complicit creator of her own calculatedly commercial writer's career and female self, sashaying along in too knowing a choice of hat and heels, all too at 'home' on Madison Avenue. Sylvia Plath's investment in the innocence of Esther Greenwood obscures the most intimate sources of her breakdown, those that explain why Esther is defenceless against her sense of invasion and self-betrayal when it finally breaks through.

The vulgar process of assigning commercial value to literary merit is the magazine production process itself. In the Fiction Editor's office, our heroine is disillusioned to learn how stories and interviews are selected and produced and paid for. The terms of success do not seem to be exactly those of High Art.

The sophisticate sneers that of course commerce calls the tune. The schoolgirl whines that her teachers did not warn her that after graduation, 'all the little successes totted up so happily at college [would fizzle] to nothing outside the slick marble and plate-glass fronts along Madison Avenue' (2).

For Esther Greenwood, keeping Art separate from commerce is a battle for psychic survival. The *purity* of Art provides the whole precarious rationale for her adult identity as that most serious of writers, a poet. She came by the idea honestly as an English major invested in the New Criticism isolating art from all social context, where T.S. Eliot as God Himself defended the lonely peaks of High Art. What she learns as Fiction Editor threatens her very self. Denial has to run neck-and-neck with disappointment to stay ahead of disillusionment.

Again the best explanation for Esther's dilemma can be found in Sylvia Plath's direct analysis of her own experience, in an article in Punch magazine, April 1963, called 'America! America!' Settled in England at age twenty-nine with her husband and two children, Plath explains to the English how America's democratic meritocracy was mediated by its guidance counsellors in public schools. Academic excellence was not enough for college; one had to be 'All-Round', which meant subjecting oneself to the mindless prescriptions of teen culture. As with working her way into Mlle magazine, Plath in explaining her own 'rabid teenage pragmatism' explains Esther Greenwood as *The Bell Jar* does not. As Plath would have it, Esther Greenwood would never stoop so low. For herself, Plath gaily admits that once the system betrayed her, her revenge was to buy in and fake it, since that was the way the goodies were being handed out.

> By the time we (future cop and electronic brain alike) exploded into our prosperous, postwar high school, full-time guidance counselors jogged our elbows at ever-diminishing intervals to discuss motives, hopes, school subjects, jobs – and colleges. . . .
> The girls' guidance counselor diagnosed my problem straight off. I was just too dangerously brainy. My high, pure string of straight A's might, without proper extracurricular tempering, snap me into the void. More and more, the colleges wanted

All-Round Students. I had, by that time, studied Machiavelli in Current Events class. I grabbed my cue.

Now this guidance counselor owned, unknown to me, a white-haired identical twin I kept meeting in supermarkets and at the dentist's. To this twin, I confided my widening circle of activities – chewing orange sections at the quarters of girls' basketball games (I had made the team), painting mammoth L'il Abners and Daisy Maes for class dances, pasting up dummies of the school newspaper at midnight while my already dissipated co-editor read out the jokes at the bottom of the columns of *The New Yorker*. The blank, oddly muffled expression of my guidance counselor's twin in the street did not deter me, nor did the apparent amnesia of her whitely efficient double in the school office. I became a rabid teenage pragmatist.

(Plath 1980:54)

The real betrayal hidden at the centre of this comedy of manners is the societal betrayal of educated women forced to scale themselves down into what Betty Friedan called 'the feminine mystique' in her book published the same year as Plath's article. This is the obvious tragedy of Esther Greenwood, and others too numerous to mention.

Reinforcing and obscuring this societal betrayal is however that other, more insidious and impervious process popularized in the 1950s: personalizing the political, and victimizing the social critic. Sylvia Plath in recounting her betrayal by the system of democratic meritocracy makes the joke at her own expense, and her unwilling conformity to teen identity a kind of self-chosen self-betrayal. Not coincidentally, Plath's writing of Esther Greenwood's story enacts this same narrowing of focus from the structural to the individual 'problem'.

First the guidance counsellor betrays her by telling her that the highest and 'purest' academic achievement – all A's – is not enough for college: chewing orange sections, pasting up dummies, being 'popular' and participating in teenage rituals have been added to the achievements necessary. The intellectual meritocracy has been 'already dissipated' like her co-editor reading the cartoons, not the High Art content, of *The New Yorker*. But this is not the worst of it.

Precocious student that she is, she leaps the new hurdles as earnestly as the old (if there is another team to be made, we can be sure that in record time, 'I had made the team'), and eagerly awaits her prize. Second betrayal: her guidance counsellor gazes blankly at her newly fulfilled requirements, mysteriously refusing to *recognize her* – recognize her *as* the sum of her prescribed achievements. Doubly, in the guidance counsellor's office her 'apparent amnesia' again blankly cancels Sylvia's new record, repeating the non-recognition that obliterates moment-arily the approval-seeking-and-receiving structure of her psychic and social identity.

Thirdly coils the worst betrayal, possible self-betrayal. By going through the motions of rabid teenage pragmatism, pretending a belonging she did not feel in a teen culture she did not respect, she loses the 'high, pure' intellectual's relationship to culture, while not securing the rewards of buying in to – and being bought by – mass culture. She shifts to accommodate, reproduce the Daisie Mae dumb broad version of femininity decorating school dances, the clean-living athlete all-American girl version bouncing around the gym, and the one-of-the-guys camaraderie of the newsroom. All these are diminishments of her stature, yet she undertakes such self-belittling and fraud in order to win the prize her A's have already paid for. When she does not win, when the guidance counsellor does not register her as the winner, she feels betrayed but blame shifts hauntingly away from corrupt authorities, who recognize no accountability for her frustration, and lurks accusingly around her own complicity in constructing an all-American girl 'front' with cold-blooded calculation. Sylvia Plath's fury when a professor called her work 'factitious' suggests her own denials about producing just such artificial goods for a market she considered herself superior to catering to. Lowering herself to commerce when rejected for her pure art, only to find her offerings indifferently received, she might yet find more comfort in a reading of self-betrayal than in wholesale disillusionment with the pure literary and the corrupt commercial worlds both. If the problem can be limited to her own fraudulence, a cure can be found in her own self-purging. This is the cold war strategy of 'containment' that *The Bell Jar* enacts on the 'problem' of Esther Greenwood.

Esther's New York experience replays the plot of Plath's uncanny twin-guidance-counsellor double-cross. Esther encounters the shift from 'pure' meritocracy to 'extra-curricular' commercial values, in the shift from school to job, as she explains herself:

> The one thing I was good at was winning scholarships and prizes, and that era was coming to an end.
>   I felt like a racehorse in a world without racetracks or a champion college footballer suddenly confronted by Wall Street and a business suit, his days of glory shrunk to a little gold cup on his mantel with a date engraved on it like the date on a tombstone. (*84*)

The social worlds of college and commerce are not playing by the same rules.

At the same time, Esther's relationship to other women repeats the 'unknown twin' mystery of the guidance counsellor – another problem of 'separate spheres' in the social world. The 'whitely efficient double in the school office' is the sterilized-by-career woman, the all-job-nothing-else choice, the social 'void' that Sylvia Plath's dangerous brains might snap her into in Manhattan. The 'blank, oddly muffled' ghost in the super-market is the mind-numbed housewife, the all-childcare-nothing-else choice, apparently devoid of brains, commerce and meritocratic prizes alike, which she encounters once home in the suburbs.

In New York when Esther tries to pin down the great expectations of two professional women, Jay Cee the Fiction Editor and Philomena Guinea the writer, the guidance-counsellor double-cross can be detected directing her fate behind the scenes. These shifting mentors and shifting value systems begin to drive the schoolgirl to distraction.

In just the manner of Plath's guidance counsellor, Jay Cee grills Esther on her ambitions after college, and Esther finds herself unable to summon up her 'old, bright salesmanship' of self, and is told she is unprepared for the editorial job she assumed was waiting for her:

"You ought to read French and German," Jay Cee said mercilessly, "and probably several other languages as well, Spanish and Italian – better still, Russian. Hundreds of girls flood into New York every June thinking they'll be editors. You need to offer something more than the run-of-the-mill person. You better learn some languages."

. . . "I'll see what I can do," I told Jay Cee. "I probably might just fit in one of those double-barrelled accelerated courses in elementary German they've rigged up."

. . . What I didn't say was that each time I picked up a German dictionary or a German book, the very sight of those dense, black, barbed-wire letters made my mind shut like a clam. (*36–7*)

Jay Cee at this moment mysteriously reminds Esther of her physics and chemistry teacher Mr Manzi. His mimeographed book 'to explain physics to college girls' was 'four hundred pages long with no drawings or photographs, only diagrams and formulas. . . . What I couldn't stand was this shrinking everything into letters and numbers' (*38*). Jay Cee's requirement of languages like German and Russian, which look more like letter formulas than literature to Esther, and her use of the commercial competition calculus that does not seem to register Esther's writing ability, are indeed a kind of 'shrinking everything' Esther has 'to offer' the world 'into letters and numbers' of market value.

Esther enacts a revenge on Mr Manzi that makes a pantomime of his pantomime of teaching and hers of learning his calculus. Esther wiggles out of the required second half after winning straight A's for the first half of his course by memorizing formulas whose applications and meanings she never comprehended. She attends the class with the fraud that 'I would take [it] for no materialistic reason like credit and an A, but for the sheer beauty of chemistry itself' (*39*). There Esther sat, apparently listening to his lectures while writing villanelles and sonnets. As commentator on science, perhaps academia itself, Esther would appear to have the last laugh here. 'Seeing Mr Manzi standing on thin air in back of Jay Cee's head, like something conjured up' (*41*), makes the same mockery of Jay Cee's lecture and Esther's good-girl front. But as with the guidance counsellor, Esther makes herself into 'an awful liar'

25

who disguises any rebellion or critique, and earns herself 'a sweet little conspiring smile' (*38*) from the teacher at the expense of her own self-betrayal.

Jay Cee's own work as editor leaves Esther reading the pile of story manuscripts while she goes to lunch with two famous writers. Again the business calculus determines the terms of the 'literary exchange', transforming reputation into market value, stories into cash.

> The man had just sold six short stories to the *New Yorker* and six to Jay Cee. This surprised me, as I didn't know magazines bought stories in lots of six, and I was staggered by the thought of the amount of money six stories would probably bring in. Jay Cee said she had to be very careful at this lunch, because the lady writer wrote stories too, but she had never had any in the *New Yorker* and Jay Cee had only taken one from her in five years. Jay Cee had to flatter the more famous man at the same time she was careful not to hurt the less famous lady. (*42*)

Implied but unanalysed is any connection between gender and literary/market success, between *New Yorker* and *Mademoiselle* stories and policies, between buying in bulk and literary merit, and between Jay Cee's coinage of (female) flattery and the vulgar (male) market of fame. These connections recur in Esther's doubling vision after Jay Cee leaves for her lunch, when Esther first imagines herself in Jay Cee's chair as 'Ee Gee, the famous editor' (*42*), and then imagines Jay Cee as an improvement over her mother, who 'was always on me to learn shorthand after college, so I'd have practical skill as well as a college degree. "Even the apostles were tentmakers," she'd say' (*43*). Jay Cee's advice on Esther's market value echoes her mother's: 'My mother kept telling me nobody wanted a plain English major. But an English major who knew shorthand was something else again. Everybody would want her' (*83*). English degrees are a dime a dozen; shorthand *sells*. Esther fears her life of letters is being commuted into 'those little shorthand symbols in the book my mother showed me [which] seemed just as bad as let *t* equal time and let *s* equal the total distance' (*83*) in Mr Manzi's book of formulas for college girls. Jay Cee, her mother, Mr Manzi, like Plath's guidance counsellor, gaze blankly at the skills of the English major, threatening Esther with obliteration, and lecture on about the formulas for success she shows no aptitude or interest in.

Esther intimates the practical as a threat to her literary identity. Underneath lurks the matrophobic fear of becoming her mother, an embittered secretarial teacher doubly betrayed, first by a husband who died and left her without insurance (man as provider fails twice), then by the market assigning her to the female drudgework sector of business and education.

'I hope you enjoy that, it cost forty-one cents a pound', says her mother's mother of her Sunday roast, turning the taste in Esther's mouth to copper with her first forkful (28). The family economy – that 'enjoyment' is an expensive luxury bought by a mother's self-sacrifice – is played out by mother and daughter in the labour market economy: Esther's 'apostle' career as writer is paid for by her mother's 'tent-making' career as teacher of secretaries. The market seems to have the same moral: mothers (underpaid service sector) pay for exceptional daughters (professional women with glamour-jobs, but without children demanding mother's sacrificial services). Is there no freedom from this market and its calculus of a mother's interest and the daughter's debt of enjoyment?

Philomena Guinea, Esther's scholarship patron, next leaps to Esther's mind in this chain of mother-mentors who seem to be adding up the bill for Esther's degree and suggesting repayment schemes on their investment. Philomena Guinea is a 'wealthy novelist' (43), with all that that and her Anglo-money name imply in Esther's art vs. commerce, pure vs. corrupt adolescent scorecard of moral idealism. Esther scorns her novels as over-written romantic tripe, which significantly 'earned Philomena Guinea, who later told me she had been very stupid at college, millions and millions of dollars' (44). The college library, observing Esther's literary standards, does not carry this alumna patron's novels.

Esther repays Mrs Guinea with her standard counterfeit coin: 'I wrote . . . how all knowledge was opening up before me and perhaps one day I would be able to write great books the way she did' (*44*). Esther's short-sighted revenge is to 'attend' without actually listening, as she did with Mr Manzi's lectures: 'I shut his voice out of my ears and sat back . . . and wrote page after page of villanelles and sonnets' (*40*). Unwittingly she explains how her system of denial works. She admits then 'shuts out' the fact that her Pure Art identity depends on her fraudulent front, that she depends on her mentors and their system of commercial value = real value. Secretly minting her own high-art currency is Esther's idea of investment in her own future – and innocence. She can afford to be deaf to all stockbrokers who can only trade on others' money: she makes her own.

Having thus deposited all her eggs into what any reader can see is the highly impractical and disaster-prone basket of Pure Art, Esther trips homeward 'to write', an accident just waiting to happen. In this stressful and self-destructive fashion Esther is just able to hold the line of Innocence to the cruel demands of Experience during her days as Fiction Editor at the magazine.

Sylvia Plath constructs the New York chapters as a test of Esther Greenwood's schoolgirl innocence about Madison Avenue commerce. In putting together the magazine, and in deconstructing her blind dates, Esther realizes that free enterprise is governed by who controls the money, not by who has the talent, and women's bodies are of more exchange value in the market than women's minds. Given the real terms in which the magazine and the social world actually transact business, Esther's good-girlism doesn't even pay her own way around town.

THE ROSENBERGS AND THE TEXT OF THE SENTENCE

On 19 June 1953 crowds jammed West 17th St in New York with banners reading 'We are innocent', as Julius and Ethel Rosenberg were electrocuted for treason, the only Americans so distinguished in the twentieth century. They were convicted for passing the secret of the atomic bomb to the Russians.

The Bell Jar begins with the electrocution of the Rosenbergs. What post-war American adolescent could make up as momentous, as publicized, as conspiratorial a persecution scenario as the case of the 'atomic bomb spies'? What more fully orchestrated prosecution of self-proclaimed innocence – and what more cosmically consequential a crime – could any angst-ridden adolescent invent on the verge of her very own nervous breakdown?

'It had nothing to do with me,' Esther says, 'but I couldn't help wondering what it would be like, being burned alive all along your nerves' (*1*). Esther's curiosity on this point is satisfied soon enough, when later in the summer she is given electro-shock treatment for her depression.

Why does Esther Greenwood identify with the Rosenbergs? Why does Sylvia Plath begin her novel with their execution? These questions launched my own reflections on *The Bell Jar*. By studying the ways in which the text of the Rosenbergs' sentence was written in America's cold war politics, I began to see the process by which the text of our heroine's sentence was subject to the same – but in her case, largely invisible – forces.

The year 1950, when the Rosenberg case first surfaced, was 'a season of fear', according to two students of the story, Walter and Miriam Schneir, researchers and authors of *Invitation to an Inquest*.

> Nineteen fifty was the year Americans learned of the decision to build a bomb a thousand times more powerful than the one that destroyed Hiroshima; the year a bloody 'police action' in Korea threatened to escalate into World War III; the year McCarthyism became a force in the land; the year the press referred openly and often approvingly to the possibility of mass roundups of subversives for incarceration in already prepared detention camps; the year school officials soberly drew up plans for protecting pupils from Soviet A-bombs by teaching them to crouch beneath their wooden desks – each child wearing around his neck a metal name tag as a kind of atomic age amulet. Paradoxically, 1950 was also a year of full employment and economic boom.
>
> (Schneir and Schneir 1983:76)

'My nightmare is the H-bomb. What's yours?' Marilyn Monroe asked (McCann 1988:66). Accountability for the bomb, and the fear, was the issue. The Rosenberg case began in 1949 when J. Edgar Hoover sent FBI agents out to find whoever had given the Russians 'the basic secrets of nuclear fission' (Schneir and

Schneir 1983:425) – presuming the Russians were too backward to have developed their own bomb. Jean-Paul Sartre accused America of being so 'sick with fear . . . you are afraid of the shadow of your own bomb. . . . By killing the Rosenbergs you have quite simply tried to halt the progress of science by human sacrifice' (Schneir and Schneir 1983:254).

The prosecutor of the Rosenberg case for the US Government, Irving Saypol, announced after the jury's guilty verdict, 'The case is a necessary by-product of the atomic age. Let us hope that it will serve to supply the democracies of the world with some significant lessons' (Schneir and Schneir 1983:167). Those lessons were drawn by Saypol in the course of the trial, with the considerable aid of the judge in the case, Irving Kaufman.

US Attorney Saypol introduced his prosecution with the accountability of the Rosenbergs, not just for the bomb but for world survival:

> We will prove that the Rosenbergs devised and put into operation, with the aid of Soviet . . . agents in the country, an elaborate scheme which enabled them to steal through David Greenglass this one weapon, that might well hold the key to the survival of this nation and means the peace of the world, the atomic bomb.
>
> (Schneir and Schneir 1983:120)

David Greenglass, Ethel Rosenberg's brother, had worked as a mechanic at the Los Alamos bomb project, and his crude drawing of the bomb was the government's key evidence, his testimony saving him from prosecution himself.

Behind the Rosenbergs lurked the Communists. Saypol began his case with Them: 'The evidence will show that the loyalty and allegiance of the Rosenbergs and Sobell were not to our country, but that it was to Communism, Communism in this country and Communism throughout the world' (Schneir and Schneir 1983:120). The link is 'the enemy within', J. Edgar Hoover's term for American Communists, automatically granted spy status. Saypol called the Rosenbergs 'perhaps the sharpest secret eyes of our enemies' (Schneir and Schneir 1983:167). This is paranoia's constant search, to find and link domestic aliens (Jews, Communists) to the enemy Other. And, as the jury foreman of the non-Jewish jury realized, the trial's Jewish judge and Jewish prosecutors (especially, I would add, Roy Cohn) completed any paranoid's persecution scenario: 'I felt good that this was strictly a Jewish show. It was Jew against Jew. It wasn't the Christians hanging the Jews' (von Hoffman 1988:108). In the spirit of the age, democracy gone paranoid (or rather, paranoia gone democratic), he sees to the heart of paranoia's secret pact with self-hatred. Let Jews (and homophobic homosexuals and fascistic patriots) convict each other of crimes against the national security state.

It was Judge Kaufman, however, who literally wrote the text of the sentence, the rationale for electrocuting the Rosenbergs:

> I believe your conduct in putting into the hands of the Russians the A-bomb years before our best scientists predicted Russia would perfect the bomb has already caused, in my opinion, the Communist aggression in Korea, with the resultant casualties exceeding fifty thousand and who knows but that millions more of innocent people may pay the price of your treason.
>
> (Schneir and Schneir 1983:170)

'The mere fact that such statements' as Kaufman's about the Rosenbergs' responsibility for the Russians' bomb and the Korean War 'should have found their place in the text of the sentence, raised the gravest doubts in our minds as to its soundness and motivation' (Schneir and Schneir 1983: 257), wrote Jacques Monod in the *Bulletin of Atomic Scientists* (October 1953). As a Frenchman he appealed to American scientists' 'permanent pact with objectivity and truth' (Schneir and Schneir 1983:256) to decry the false conviction of the Rosenbergs for an impossible crime. Monod points out that a leader of the Los Alamos project, 'Urey himself clearly stated in a letter to President Eisenhower that he considered it impossible, saying "a man of Greenglass' capacity is wholly incapable of transmitting the physics, chemistry and mathematics of the atomic bomb to anyone" ' (Schneir and Schneir 1983:257). Monod finds a parallel in 'our own Dreyfus case, when a handful of intellectuals had risen against a technically correct decision of justice, against the Army hierarchy, against public opinion and government which were a prey to nationalist fury' (Schneir and Schneir 1983:258). 'Nationalist fury' is indeed the text of the Rosenberg sentence, as Judge Kaufman's rhetoric reveals.

Kaufman's speech shifts the threat of 'atomic bomb attack' from any American accountability (for Hiroshima, for Nagasaki, for creating both the A- and the H-bombs), to Russian accountability for the imminence of World War III well begun with 50,000 deaths in Korea. Someone is responsible for the end of the American monopoly of the bomb and with it mastery of world politics. Someone gave away 'this nation's most deadly and closely guarded secret weapon' and with it the security of the nation:

> In the light of the circumstances, I feel that I must pass such a sentence on the principals in this diabolical conspiracy to destroy a God-fearing nation, which will demonstrate with finality that this nation's security must remain inviolate.
>
> (Schneir and Schneir 1983:170)

Kaufman's sentence necessarily begins with the basic Us Versus Them imperative of cold war prosecution:

> The issue of punishment in this case is presented in a unique framework of history. It is so difficult to make people realize that this country is engaged in a life and death struggle with a completely different system.
>
> (Schneir and Schneir 1983:169)

Lucky for the Rosenbergs, they received democracy's promise of a fair trial. Russia would not have obliged. 'Yet they made a choice of devoting themselves to the Russian ideology of denial of God, denial of the sanctity of the individual and aggression against free men everywhere instead of serving the cause of liberty and freedom' (Schneir and Schneir 1983:170).

When Kaufman applies his framework of 'life and death struggle with a completely different system' to the case of the Rosenbergs' 'choice' of 'slavish devotion to a foreign ideology' (Schneir and Schneir 1983:170), the necessity of Their death to preserve Our life is built into the sentence. Kaufman's rhetoric depends on – but does not name – the disease metaphor for Communism, to explain the death threat Their pathological system carries against Our health. Our bodily security must be defended against Their invasive germ warfare, carried by 'secret . . . forces among our own people' (Schneir and Schneir 1983:169) such as the Rosenbergs, who become more Them than Us in this formulation.

'They're taking us over – cell by cell!' shouts one alarmist in the 1956 film, *Invasion of the Body Snatchers,* handily connecting Communism, Martian invasion and pathology: 'It's a malignant disease spreading through the whole country.' The disease metaphor was anti-Communism's most effective weapon in the war for America's hearts and minds. Even the liberal Adlai Stevenson called Communism 'a disease which may have killed more people than cancer' (Sayre 1982:201). Worse yet, Stevenson voiced the virulent strain of paranoia, by asserting that Communism intended 'total conquest, not merely of the earth, but of the human mind' (Sayre 1982:201). Stevenson's rhetoric refers to – but does not name – the brainwashing methods thought necessary to a foreign ideology with no more persuasive means to gain and retain its adherents. Kaufman too by referring to 'slavish devotion to a foreign ideology' suggests slaves to Alien Control, the human mind programmed by that enemy of democracy, ideology.

Harry Gold takes us into the psyche of paranoia. He testified as a self-confessed atom spy for the Rosenberg case, claiming he was the link between Klaus Fuchs (convicted British spy) and the Rosenbergs. In 1956 when he testified before the Senate Internal Security subcommittee, Gold said that working as a spy with Russian agents had reduced

> my identity and my desire to be an individual. I was becoming someone who could be told what to do and who would do it. . . . I came to realize . . . that I had completely lost my free

will; I had actually turned over my complete personality, my complete soul, and everything. I wasn't living the life of a normal person. I wasn't married.

(Schneir and Schneir 1983:365)

The connection between Communism and brainwashing (and bachelorhood!) and between contamination and purge, is explicit in the text of Gold's self-sentencing: 'I must be punished, and punished well, for the terribly frightening things that have been done' (Schneir and Schneir 1983:370). Paranoia's only comfort is conspiracy exposed. McCarthyism gave form and forum for Harry Gold's redemption, as he gratefully acknowledged:

> The manner in which all of the pieces of the giant jig-saw puzzle, of which I was a part, are falling ever so gloriously into place – to reveal the whole picture – has added a tremendous zest and sense of achievement to my life.
>
> (Schneir and Schneir 1983:370)

Exposure before the tribunal comes as his relief, by 'indisputably establish[ing] the authenticity and enormity of my crime' (Schneir and Schneir 1983:370). Better to know the source and consequence of one's alienation, than live in the purgatory of doubt that the paranoid state reserves for those who have not yet been accused.

Just the momentary suspicion that the Rosenbergs *could* have been framed by the FBI, with or without whatever assistance by the Justice Department and Judge Kaufman, might well be enough to send a shudder of paranoia through the nerves of a thoughtful nineteen-year-old like Esther Greenwood. The 'conspiracy so immense' that J. Edgar Hoover termed cold war Communism would be *inverted* in the case of a frame-up, with branches of the government and a veritable secret police in charge of national security conspiring to scapegoat dissenters with the aid of a headline-hungry press and an apathetic public.

'There is no yelling, no horror, no great rebellion', Plath wrote in her journal on 19 June 1953.

That is the appalling thing. The execution will take place tonight; it is too bad that it could not be televised . . . so much more realistic and beneficial than the run-of-the-mill crime program. Two real people being executed. No matter. The largest emotional reaction over the United States will be a rather large, democratic, infinitely bored and casual and complacent yawn.

(Plath 1983:81)

One particular yawn struck Sylvia Plath that day, from one of her fellow guest editors at *Mlle* magazine for the month:

The tall beautiful catlike girl who wore an original hat to work every day rose to one elbow from where she had been napping on the divan in the conference room, yawned, and said with beautiful bored nastiness: "I'm so glad they are going to die." She gazed vaguely and very smugly around the room, closed her enormous green eyes, and went back to sleep.

(Plath 1983:80)

The cat-like girl becomes Hilda in *The Bell Jar*, Plath's symbol for McCarthyism's captive citizen, all too significantly apprenticed to the Fashion Editor.

"I'm so glad they're going to die."
Hilda arched her cat-limbs in a yawn, buried her head in her arms on the conference table and went back to sleep. A wisp of bilious green straw perched on her brow like a tropical bird.
Bile green. They were promoting it for fall, only Hilda, as usual, was half a year ahead of time. . . .
Fashion blurbs, silver and full of nothing, sent up their fishy bubbles in my brain. They surfaced with a hollow pop.
I'm so glad they're going to die. (*110*)

Hilda's fashion-blurb about the Rosenberg execution reminds Esther of the play she had seen the night before,

where the heroine was possessed by a dybbuk, and when the dybbuk spoke from her mouth its voice sounded so cavernous and deep you couldn't tell whether it was a man or a woman. Well, Hilda's voice sounded just like the voice of that dybbuk. (*111*)

Hilda's dybbuk (a Yiddish type of devil) gives voice to the forces of darkness gathering around the guest editors and beginning to *speak through* some of them. Hilda is Plath's creature born from the unlikely marriage of McCarthyism and *Mlle*. Hilda speaks as a slave to fashionable fascism without 'a human string in the cat's cradle of her heart':

> "It's awful such people should be alive."
> She yawned then, and her pale orange mouth opened on a large darkness. Fascinated, I stared at the blind cave behind her face until the two lips met and moved and the dybbuk spoke out of its hiding place, "I'm so glad they're going to die." (*110–11*)

Hilda unites the cattiness of competitive femininity with the witchiness of Arthur Miller's possessed Puritan anti-heroine of *The Crucible*, Abigail, who has the voice of the devil speaking through her when she says of an innocent man her testimony has condemned to death, 'Thank God he is [in jail], and bless the day he hangs and lets me sleep in peace again!' (Miller 1976:149–50). Hilda and Abigail put a post-war kind of premium on their beauty rest, as if to underline their authors' social criticism that conscience was snoring away under fantastically fashionable hats. The considerable irony of depicting McCarthyism – an all-male, all-American homophobic pissing match if there ever was one – as a problem of female bitchery seems to have been lost on both Arthur Miller and Sylvia Plath. In the context of the cold war, 'effeminacy' was the moral weakness threatening 'our boys' in Korea and at home. Using this logic, more, not less, dog-like behaviour was the solution.

Miller's play about McCarthyism, originally intriguingly entitled *Those Familiar Spirits* (1952), was actually performed on Broadway in June of 1953, when Sylvia Plath (and Esther Greenwood) were in town. On the night the Rosenbergs died, 'the audience, upon John Proctor's execution, stood up and remained silent for a couple of minutes, with heads bowed' (Miller 1987:347). In searching for his own metaphor for McCarthyism, Arthur Miller researched the Salem witch trials, and elaborated his own conspiracy theory of hysterical adolescent females, initiated into diabolism by a West Indian slave woman, and later manipulated by power-hungry men of chilling impersonality.

Miller establishes the well-spring of witchery in Tituba, woman, black, West Indian, slave, conjuror: a whole series of Others contrasting with Puritanism's very white and very male rationality and spirituality and hierarchy. Renouncing Abigail, the teen witch he slept with, is the key to John Proctor's salvation, and showing Abigail to be the unworthy female Other disrupter of community is the key to Arthur Miller's moral about contagion and purge. *The Crucible* locates the riddle of McCarthyism's sources in the riddle of women-in-nature, symbolized by Tituba and the girls dancing naked in the forest. While ostensibly criticizing witch-hunts, the play actually seems to demonstrate the necessity for *purging amoral female nature* from encroaching on man's civilized space. *The Crucible* implicates femininity in the bodily guilt of illicit sexuality and asserts masculinity as the purge of conscience necessary to the diseased body politic. The crucible is Proctor's trial and test of conscience, and Proctor himself is the vessel in which the high-temperature purge of community occurs.

Even in this liberal public space created by Arthur Miller to contest McCarthyism, *morality is gendered.* To be a heroine of the 1950s, Esther must re-solve gender itself. She must reconcile herself as both moral subject (heroine and narrator of her own story) and amoral object (her femininity is defined by her body). To be whole, she must re-solve *The Crucible*'s riddle of the nature of femininity (Is it amoral?) and riddle of the nature of conscience, of moral agency (Is it male?). Imagine Arthur Miller's mind mating itself to Marilyn Monroe's body, and Esther's vaulting ambition can be understood. The approved solution to Esther's problem, of course, is to marry the brains and brawn, and cultivate only the bosom on which the husbandly head nightly rests.

The gendered morality of cold war politics can be seen in another part of the text of the Rosenbergs' sentence, in a letter written by President Eisenhower. He uses the woman as the reason why he cannot sign the stay of execution. He describes his thinking in a letter dated 16 June to his son John serving in Korea:

> To address myself . . . to the Rosenberg case for a minute, I must say that it goes against the grain to avoid interfering in the case where a woman is to receive capital punishment. Over against this, however, must be placed one or two facts that have greater significance. The first of these is that in this instance it is the woman who is the strong and recalcitrant character, the man is the weak one. She has obviously been the leader in everything they did in the spy ring. The second thing is that if there would be any commuting of the woman's sentence without the man's then from here on the Soviets would simply recruit their spies from among women.
>
> (Schneir and Schneir 1983:242)

Rather than going 'against the grain' of chivalry, his decision merely shows its cost: public execution of the deviant woman. Ike's view of the necessity for example-setting punishment of 'the strong and recalcitrant character' puts witch-hunting in its normative context, where the woman's unnatural strength is associated with pathology and foreign invasion of the otherwise secure Family. Ethel Rosenberg as wife-and-mother is supposed to be the source of security at the very centre of our national security. Judge Kaufman pointed out this domestic treason when he sentenced the Rosenbergs: 'Love for their cause dominated their lives – it was even greater than their love for their children' (Schneir and Schneir 1983:170–1). In just such ways, as J. Edgar Hoover said, Communism spread its 'evil and malignant way of life . . . that eventually will destroy the sanctity of the home' (May 1988:260–1). As in *The Crucible*, men of conscience rally to purge the diseased state by accusing the deviant woman who has betrayed family and community at once.

Given this state of siege, Esther's deepening disillusionment and dissent are never spoken, except as her nervous breakdown itself. Then the muted female body speaks its paranoia as paralysis of the will. Esther's silent reaction to the text of Hilda's sentence on the Rosenbergs shows how McCarthyism enforced its normative tyranny. Only a few drops of sweat were to show for each victim's secret self-policing in the face of Hilda's democratic yawn of disdain for the deviant.

Ellen Schrecker analyses the secret of McCarthyism's success, in her study of McCarthyism and the universities, *No Ivory Tower*.

> McCarthyism was amazingly effective. It produced one of the most severe episodes of political repression the United States ever experienced. It was a peculiarly American style of repression – nonviolent and consensual. Only two people were killed; only a few hundred went to jail. Its mildness may well have contributed to its efficacy. So, too, did its structure. Here, it helps to view McCarthyism as a process rather than a movement. It took place in two stages. First, the objectionable groups and individuals were identified – during a committee hearing, for example, or an FBI investigation; then, they were punished, usually by being fired. The bifurcated nature of this process diffused responsibility and made it easier for each participant to dissociate his or her action from the larger whole. Rarely did any single institution handle both stages of McCarthyism. In most cases, it was a government agency which identified the culprits and a private employer which fired them.
>
> (Schrecker 1986:9)

The Rosenberg case exposed the extremities of repression. J. Edgar Hoover set the FBI to investigate and interrogate the defendants, actually shaping the case by the Justice Department. The jury, judge, Supreme Court and President, all were implicated in sentencing the Rosenbergs to as fiery an execution as the law provided.

McCarthyism's two-part process, when internalized, neatly enacts the normative tyranny of the 1950s within the individual psychic state. First a tribunal articulates the norm to be enforced. In Esther's case the College Board becomes for her a jury of her peers judging her femininity. Her mentors seem to line up to judge her school graduation and job market requirements. Brows furrow, eyebrows are raised.

> I felt very low. I had been unmasked only that morning by Jay Cee herself, and I felt now that all the uncomfortable suspicions

I had about myself were coming true, and I couldn't hide the truth much longer. (*31*)

Once home in the suburbs, a second tribunal, this one medical, evaluates her condition and undertakes her treatment and cure. The suburban psychiatrist (mis)applies shock treatment when her depression fails to respond to pills. Esther interprets it as punishment and wonders 'what terrible thing it was that I had done' (*161*). Is there a gendered moral to her case? The female body is always political, but never more so than in the post-war American return to the Home.

Chapter Two

THE MOTHERLY BREATH OF THE SUBURBS

A FTER Esther scatters her *Mlle* career-girl wardrobe over Manhattan from the roof of the Amazon hotel – perhaps her most articulate commentary on her guest-editorship – she goes home to see the other life on offer to her: suburban wife-and-mother. In no time at all she has explored the four corners of that box: the social organization of the suburb, the power relations of marriage, the medicalization of childbirth, and when all else fails, the final solution of psychiatry, defining and enforcing norms for women in relation to family. Her experience of anomie, thoroughly explained by her recognition of the oppressively reinforcing interconnections among these four social institutions, is none the less diagnosed as her own problem by Dr Gordon the psychiatrist, and treated first with pills and then with shock treatment. Her suicide attempt can be read as her critique, as a refusal, as Dr Gordon's failure to adjust her.

Esther's life at Home with Mother is the stage-set for her breakdown. While withholding all direct analysis of cause, the narrative implicitly connects Esther's constricting vision with the claustrophobia-inducing concentric circles of containment-oriented, security-minded suburban regional planning. Lewis Mumford (quoted by Ada Louise Huxtable in the *New York Times Book Review*, 26 November 1989, p. 25) called the suburbs 'an asylum for the preservation of illusion', and in the 1950s, Mom stood at the centre of the illusion of security – and its breakdown.

Zipping from New York to suburban train station, the commuter is driven home in the station-wagon, the wife-and-mother having democratically replaced all domestic staff with her own All-Round personality. Esther's movement is that of the college-educated woman upon marriage.

> I stepped from the air-conditioned compartment onto the station platform, and the motherly breath of the suburbs enfolded me. It smelt of lawn sprinklers and station wagons and tennis rackets and dogs and babies.
>   A summer calm laid its soothing hand over everything, like death. (*126–7*)

Her mother at the wheel, driving her homeward into the heart of suburban domesticity, seems to be locking the doors and throwing away the key when she announces that Esther has not won her way into a writing seminar in Boston for the summer.

> All through June the writing course had stretched before me like a bright, safe bridge over the dull gulf of the summer. Now I saw it totter and dissolve, and a body in a white blouse and green skirt plummet into the gap. (*127*)

The structure of school and the fuel of winning her way is the structure and fuel of Esther's psyche itself. In the suburbs this structure disappears, leaving 'large unfenced acres of time' (Plath 1983:51) devoted solely to domestic maintenance and child-raising, with not one of the familiar supports of 'achievement' possible. Esther's feeling the suburban summer world as a gulf and gap points to its threat to her psychic as much as social identity.

Plath's journal in 1952 uses the bell jar to describe the elaborately structured, rewarded and time-managed atmosphere of her schooling, internalized as her psychic structure itself, which is then threatened with disaster when all external structure is removed:

> The responsibility, the awful responsibility of managing (profitably) 12 hours a day for 10 weeks, is rather overwhelming when there is nothing, no one, to insert an exact routine into

the large unfenced acres of time. . . . It is like lifting a bell jar off
a securely clockworklike functioning community, and seeing all
the little busy people stop, gasp, blow up and float in the inrush
(or rather outrush) of the rarefied scheduled atmosphere.

> (Plath 1983:50-1)

The bell jar here is the 'superficial and artificial' pressure to
achieve in the competitive enterprise systems of school,
magazine and literary world. Lift that motivational support,
drive educated women into the 'dead summer world' of
suburban child-rearing, and not just poor old Esther but 'all the
little busy people stop, gasp, blow up . . .'

> The thought of spending two weeks with two children in a close
> dark hole was too horrible to think of and we knew we had to do
> something. Now that we women have started we will no longer
> be content to be dull uninformed housewives.
>
> (May 1988:208)

Nuclear war threatened a potentially explosive excess of
togetherness in the family bomb shelter and rationalized the
formation of the Women's Strike for Peace in 1963, as these
words testify. But they also testify to the pressures women felt
within the nuclear family in the suburbs, where they were in
charge of security and civil defence through sound citizen-
building. Dr Spock in 1945 explained this cold war
maternalism: 'Useful, well-adjusted citizens are the most
valuable possession a country has, and good mother care during
early childhood is the surest way to produce them. It doesn't
make sense to let mothers go to work' (Spock 1945:460). Such
responsibility for making the family work in the 'close dark
hole' of the 'togetherness' norm is enough to induce
claustrophobia – of which mothers themselves became the
causes in the therapeutic and popular culture stereotypes of the
smothering mother.

By assigning herself the blame for failing as a student, Esther
can assign herself the appropriate punishment: a summer stuck
in the suburbs, her days spent unable to read or write, her
nightly entertainment a sleepless watch over her Medusa-

mother's pincurls, 'glittering like a row of little bayonets' (*137*) in the other twin bed next to her.

Esther feels shame at having failed her college achievement test, and suggests that the suburbs are the prison to which women are sentenced – or sentence themselves:

> I felt it was very important not to be recognized.
> The gray, padded car roof closed over my head like the roof of a prison van, and the white, shining, identical clapboard houses with their interstices of well-groomed green proceeded past, one bar after another in a large but escape-proof cage.
> I had never spent a summer in the suburbs before. (*127–8*)

The horror at the heart of this darkness can be read in two ways at once: as Esther's self-punishing withdrawal from the social world due to the breakdown of her capacity for making meaning in her life, and as American society's punishing relegation of middle-class women to the domestic sphere, breaking down their capacities to make meaning from their education in relation to the larger social world – destroying the 'bright, safe bridge' of some career dream built to transport one's self from college to housewife. This is the reason 'why America produced the most vigorous feminist movement in the world', Barbara Ehrenreich points out: 'We were one of the only countries in which the middle class (which is wealthy by world standards) customarily employed its own women as domestic servants' (Ehrenreich 1989:40).

Adlai Stevenson delivered the liberal version of this message to women at Sylvia Plath's commencement from Smith in 1955, as Nancy Hunter Steiner explains almost twenty years later:

> We had chosen Adlai Stevenson from a long list of names to give the address, and we listened, properly dignified and attentive, as he described the lives that lay before us. If they were not exactly the lives we had visualized, at least they would make use of the educations we had received. Our unanimous vocation, as Governor Stevenson saw it, was to be wives and mothers – thoughtful, discriminating wives and mothers who would use what we had learned in government and history and sociology courses to influence our husbands and children in the direction

> of rationality. Men, he claimed, are under tremendous pressure to adopt the narrow view; we would help them to resist it and we would raise children who were reasonable, independent, and courageous. The speech was eloquent and impressive and we loved it even if it seemed to hurl us back to the satellite role we had escaped for four years – second-class citizens in a man's world where our only possible achievement was a vicarious one.
>
> (Steiner 1973:108–9)

Steiner, like her classmates, hides her disappointment in this message, with all the social grace to be expected of a 'thoughtful, discriminating' professional wife. Having *chosen* the hero of liberalism – 'Abe Lincoln' to Plath – to deliver them from Smith to the world, gratitude impels them to 'love it', even as they are instead 'hurled back' to domestic servitude. Considerable anger and ingratitude, violence of disillusionment, charge Steiner's description of moving 'back' into second-class citizenship and second-hand achievement – all kept to herself, presumably, as she applauded Stevenson's eloquence.

Mrs Dale Carnegie delivers a more conservative and bullying version of the same message in *Better Homes and Gardens*, April of 1955 – women's 'pretty heads' in the service of the family.

> The two big steps that women must take are to help their husbands decide where they are going and use their pretty heads to help get them there. . . . Let's face it, girls. That wonderful guy in your house – and in mine – is building your house, your happiness and the opportunities that will come to your children. . . . Split levels may be fine and exciting when you're planning your house. But there is simply no room for split level thinking – or doing – when Mr. and Mrs. set their sights on a happy home, a host of friends and a bright future through success in HIS job.
>
> (Hine 1987: 30–1)

All of American science, technology, industry were committed to 'make easier the life of our housewives', Richard Nixon explained to Nikita Kruschev in 1959 at the American exhibition of kitchens in Moscow.

> To us, diversity, the right to choose, . . . is the most important thing. We don't have one decision made at the top by one government official. . . . We have many different manufacturers and many different kinds of washing machines so that the housewives have a choice.
>
> (May 1988:17)

Such male provision of female choice makes consumerism both a privilege and a civic duty supporting the economy and democracy as one and the same thing. Middle-class women's lack of choice of adult role is masked by their privileged position as chief executive consumer of the household. The fact that the culture had to use the hard-sell to inculcate this message suggests that it was not entirely satisfactory as a commencement address. The fact that the women publicly applauded while privately horrified suggests both the power behind the speech to determine the structure of women's lives, and the private costs yet to surface from their attempt to live those lives.

The Bell Jar and Sylvia Plath's journals from 1950 to 1953 examine both those cultural expectations as they were articulated by family and friends, and the private critique of them Sylvia Plath worked out with prescient feminist insight, 'ricocheting' as she called it (Plath 1983:13) between rebellious self-assertion and shame-ridden self-doubt – between a late-1960s strong-minded liberationism and a mid-1950s suicidally deviant alienation.

Buddy Willard has the thankless role in *The Bell Jar* of articulating the ramifications of Esther's shrinkage from girlfriend to wife. He does this with a completely unselfconscious conviction of male superiority, necessarily accompanied by an equally complete lack of interest in and understanding of women, including Esther. His marriage offer – 'How would you like to be Mrs Buddy Willard?' – tidily frames his expectations into her prospects. 'I also remembered Buddy Willard saying in a sinister, knowing way that after I had children I would feel differently, I wouldn't want to write poems any more' (*94*). Buddy's smug knowingness makes her wife-and-motherhood seem like a *fait accompli.* Her imagination completes the story as a sci-fi horror film: 'So I began to think maybe it was true that when you were married and had children it was like being brainwashed, and afterward you went about numb as a slave in some private, totalitarian state' (*94*). As for marital sex, for a sneak preview, Buddy drops his fishnet underpants, explaining, 'They're cool, and my mother says they wash easily' (*75*).

> Then he just stood there in front of me and I kept on staring at him. The only thing I could think of was turkey neck and turkey gizzards and I felt very depressed. (*75*)

What's wrong with Mr Right?

> I didn't know what to say. My mother and my grandmother had started hinting around to me a lot lately about what a fine, clean boy Buddy Willard was, coming from such a fine, clean family, and how everybody at church thought he was a model person, so kind to his parents and to older people, as well as so athletic and so handsome and so intelligent. (*75*)

Buddy is the all-American ideal, a 'big, broad-shouldered bonehead' type like the football hero of the movie Esther saw in New York that put her 'in terrible danger of puking' (46). You've seen the movie, now live the life. She sees the scriptedness of Buddy's lines, her mother's and grandmother's rapt approval of Buddy's good-guy image, and the inevitability of the plot-line from 'roses and kisses and restaurant dinners' to the domestic 'flatten[ing] out underneath his feet like Mrs Willard's kitchen mat' (93–4). Half her objections are to her own apparently irrevocable reduction into domestic drudge – 'a dreary and wasted life for a girl with fifteen years of straight A's' (93) – and half are to other women's apparent willingness to undergo this metamorphosis called marriage – 'cook and clean and wash was just what Buddy Willard's mother did from morning till night, and she was the wife of a university professor and had been a private school teacher herself' (93). At the movie with her fellow guest editors, she sees romance glowing on their faces while the shadow of slavery to the totalitarian state lurks like the real moral of the story for 'stupid moonbrains' (46):

> At about this point I began to feel peculiar. I looked round me
> at all the rows of rapt little heads with the same silver glow on
> them at the front and the same black shadow on them at the
> back, and they looked like nothing more or less than a lot of
> stupid moonbrains. (*46*)

The Happy Ending was promised but left undocumented by this
Big Screen romance. Esther has the question posed by all
female adolescents: If 'a happy marriage was the happiest
condition', as Elizabeth Barrett Browning said she 'vaguely
believed', ' – *where were the happy marriages?*' (Browning 1978:6).
The Willards are the intact family in *The Bell Jar*, Mr Willard
playing 'the arrow into the future' and Mrs Willard 'the place
the arrow shoots off from' (*79*), if Mrs Willard's model of
marriage can be taken as the achieved reality of their relationship. The only thing missing is a daughter, and Mr Willard
graciously offers the part of daughter-in-law to Esther. Again the
Big Question reads more like a final door-slamming answer in
Esther's book. Her hysterical inability to speak brings tears at
the father's suggestion, and 'the awful impulse to laugh' at the
son's marriage proposal (*97; 102*).

In 1961–2, settled in England with her husband, two children
and writing career, Sylvia Plath can satirize the absurdity of this
suburban kitchen-mat marriage offer. In the early 1950s it was
no laughing matter for Sylvia Plath in her journal to try to come
to terms with the either/or-ness of motherhood and career,
purity and sexuality, domesticity and education. Page after
tormented page, year after year, boyfriend after boyfriend, *A*
after *A* after *A*, she tries every means to a new solution, seeking
the way through to the exceptional fate she has earned with
every prize, every published poem, with her elite education,
with her mother's ambition and self-sacrifice breathed into her
every achievement. Plath – along with the rest of educated
American womanhood since World War II – was determined to
exempt herself from such punishing choice. Her solution is
manic over-achievement. The structural problem of separate
spheres remains.

In her journal, Plath's ideas and feelings about female
identity and marriage (inextricable by definition) form a

continuum from the summer of 1950, when she was seventeen and on her way to Smith, to the summer of 1953 when she attempted suicide and the journal breaks off. The pressure increases to resolve the irreconcilables of her own nature – her creativity, sexual desires, intellectual ambitions, and emotional hungers – *and*, as she writes, 'to have my whole circle of action, thought and feeling rigidly circumscribed by my inescapable femininity' (Plath 1983:30).

In the summer of 1950 she equates femininity with her mother, and feels trapped. Nothing like having one's 'freshly washed hair up on curlers' to make one ponder the nature and artifice of femininity as some kind of 'monumental grotesque joke' (Plath 1983:12). 'I felt suddenly breathless, stifled. I was trapped, with the tantalizing little square of night above me, and the warm, feminine atmosphere of the house enveloping me in its thick, feathery, smothering embrace' (Plath 1983:12). The maturing female body can look like her fate itself to a girl at puberty, a house – and a mother – she cannot escape. 'The Tidy House that is no more a Tidy House' describes the change into motherhood anticipated by three girls in a study by Carolyn Steedman, *The Tidy House* (1982:148). These girls – more clearly than Plath – perceive that motherhood involves both a literal loss of control, autonomy and physical integrity for women, and a cultural devaluation and objectification into domestic drudges indistinguishable from untidy houses.

Later that same summer Sylvia Plath tries to embrace maternity as a solution to her loneliness and lust: 'Isn't it better to give in to the pleasant cycles of reproduction, the easy, comforting presence of a man around the house?' (Plath 1983:14). Marriage, at least, would hurl her over the double standard for the unmarried, which has her 'sitting here, swimming, drowning, sick with longing' (Plath 1983:15) for sex and freedom: 'I can only lean enviously against the boundary and hate, hate hate the boys who can dispel sexual hunger freely, without misgiving, and be whole, while I drag out from date to date in soggy desire, always unfulfilled. The whole thing sickens me' (Plath 1983:15).

'But women have lust, too. Why should they be relegated to

the position of custodian of emotions, watcher of the infants, feeder of soul, body and pride of man?' (Plath 1983:29). Plath's feminist query the next summer occurs when her boyfriend tells her he slept with a waitress he worked with because Sylvia did not come to see him (Wagner-Martin 1987:74). She's furious, not least because a middle-class man and working-class woman get to enjoy non-marital sex as she does not, by propriety. 'Some slutty waitress' (*78*) Esther Greenwood calls the woman that Buddy sleeps with, and with that word assumes the double standard and its degradation of women through sex, and loses the feminist anger of Plath in her journal.

Before she has a steady boyfriend, Plath's self-counselling is resigned rather than frantic, speculation is general, philosophical.

> After a while I suppose I'll get used to the idea of marriage and children. If only it doesn't swallow up my desire to express myself . . . if only my art, my writing isn't just a mere sublimation of my sexual desires which will run dry once I get married.
>
> (Plath 1983:15)

Plath identifies the sticking-point here, the Freudianism at the centre of femininity in the 1950s: maternity *is* female desire, all else is sublimation.

Marriage and motherhood loom as the monstrous maternal maw, threatening to swallow up her unmaternal self, desire to express herself, and sexual desires. This totalitarian state of kitchen-mat-wifehood is the fate of Mrs Willard in *The Bell Jar*. Such an alarming possibility is mentioned as a probability by Plath's boyfriend Dick Norton, the prototype for Buddy Willard in *The Bell Jar*. Plath quotes Norton as telling her: 'I am afraid the demands of wifehood and motherhood would preoccupy you too much to allow you to do the painting and writing you want' (Plath 1983:44). There is a crazy-making aspect to negotiating these marital expectations, which include her own ambivalences, as well as Dick Norton's idea of a doctor's wife, and both mothers' enthusiasm about the couple, which seems to support *his* version of wifehood. 'He alternately denies and accepts me, as I silently do him' (Plath 1983:44–5), Plath writes, making clear how powerful the Other is in confirming or negating our own sense of ourselves – all within a social structure where identity comes primarily through job. The eligible woman is recognized by her education, accepted as a professional for the equal-partners companionate marriage. Then her professional identity is denied in the domestic sphere. Her sexual equality is denied before marriage, accepted after. Now you see her, now you don't. On her part, such acceptance and denial of him is done 'silently', totally subverting all her potential power to shape *his* identity-through-relationship. They're not arguing, after all, about what a man is or does or wants or needs or gets in marriage. The burden is all on her to resist, redefine and convince – without, of course, being 'strong and assertive'. 'So [Dick] accuses me of "struggling for dominance"? Sorry, wrong number. . . . It is only *balance* that I ask for. Not the *continual* subordination of one person's desires and interests to the continual advancement of another's! That would be too grossly unfair' (Plath 1983:43). This grossly unfair continual subordination of the wife-and-mother to Family was defined as femininity itself in the 1950s.

Yet marriage is the only solution to the problems of a legitimate sexuality and social security, Plath concludes after numbering her reasons 1, 2, 3: 'So, resolved: I shall proceed to obtain a mate through the customary procedure: namely, marriage' (Plath 1983:36). Comically pragmatic in adopting convention, Plath then tragically tries to apply this conventional wisdom to her own psychic housekeeping:

> The self-love I can hide or reweld by the biblical saw of "losing myself and finding myself." For instance, I could hold my nose, close my eyes, and jump blindly into the waters of some man's insides, submerging myself until his purpose becomes my purpose, his life, my life, and so on. One fine day I would float to the surface, quite drowned, and supremely happy with my newfound selfless self.
>
> (Plath 1983:36)

A general plan is one thing, a specific man and his proposal quite another:

> The most saddening thing is to admit that I am not in love. I can
> only love (if that means self-denial – or does it mean
> self-fulfillment? Or both?) by giving up my love, of self and
> ambitions. Why, why, can't I combine ambition for myself with
> another?
>
> (Plath 1983:39)

The meaning of love is a cultural meaning, a prescription for
womanhood itself. Does a woman's love mean self-denial or
self-fulfilment? At a transitional moment in American history,
Plath's generation of women were caught between their
mothers' kamikaze missions – 'I have none of the selfless love
of my mother,' Plath recognizes (Plath 1983:34) – and the self-
fulfilment model that has reigned supreme since the 1960s.

The terms of self-fulfilment, from the right hairdo to the
right man to the right toaster, are amply illustrated in the pages
of women's magazines. 'Picture me then', Plath instructs her
mother in one of her letters home, literally constructing her
self by writing as if from the pages of such magazines. The
mother is their reader vicariously envying the happy
experience enacted by women protectively encapsulated in the
photographs and stories. 'I'd taste her enjoyment as if it had
been my own', as Aurelia Plath (Plath 1975:38) explains. Each
is the witness necessary to the other's self-fulfilment. Imitating
media representations of happiness, and trying to read our
own pleasure off of audience response, make self-fulfilment
something of a second-hand experience at best, mediated by
external expectations and singularly lacking in space for
unselfconscious spontaneity, for real choice of any sort.

Plath's *Letters Home* show how she used strictly conventional
types of socially awarded achievements as forms into which she
poured her great talents and her great neediness, to initiate
the recognition on which her very self depended so
precariously.

The breaking-point occurs between daughter and mother,
when the daughter balks at relinquishing her careerist
self-fulfilment identity, with its structure of approval from and
vicarious fulfilment for the mother too. Esther breaks down at
the prospect of adopting the mother's identity of selfless

sacrifice for the Family. Daughterly careerism pays back the mother for her own lost career – but it also betrays motherhood, rejecting and devaluing it. Daughterly maternalism sacrifices all the mother's sacrifices but passes the culturally approved loyalty test of femininity-*as*-motherly-sacrifice – daughters learning martyrdom at their mothers' already bent knees.

'Matrophobia' grows here at this mother–daughter breaking-point, as Adrienne Rich explains:

> "Matrophobia" as the poet Lynn Sukenick has termed it is the fear not of one's mother or of motherhood but of *becoming one's mother*. . . .
>   Matrophobia can be seen as a womanly splitting of the self, in the desire to become purged once and for all of our mothers' bondage, to become individuated and free. The mother stands for the victim in ourselves, the unfree woman, the martyr. Our personalities seem dangerously to blur and overlap with our mothers'; and, in a desperate attempt to know where mother ends and daughter begins, we perform radical surgery.
>
> (Rich 1977:237–8)

'The motherly breath of the suburbs' seems to inhale Esther herself. Like Plath in summer after summer at home, 'I felt suddenly breathless, stifled. I was trapped, with the tantalizing little square of night above me, and the warm, feminine atmosphere of the house enveloping me in its thick, feathery, smothering embrace' (Plath 1983:12). Esther's 'radical surgery' is performed with razors and pills. Her suicide attempts try to purge her domestic depression and its infinitely slower death by martyred self-suppression, its creeping paralysis of self-will, its slow draining of all meaning from the life in relation to the larger world.

But women cannot save themselves from each other, Esther learns. It takes a man and his machine. Suicidal breakdown delivers Esther from 'mother's clutch' (Plath 1983:280) into the hands of the experts, the men in charge. They promise to complete the purge that Esther bungled. Resented saviours, their manly objectivity seems the only cure for the spreading contamination of female hysteria.

Having rejected Buddy Willard's invitation to the Happy

Family, Esther finds him waiting for her in the hospitals to which she is sent. There he bears on his broad shoulders the burden of all paternalism controlling the professions, especially science and medicine, as they justify conventionality using large doses of clinical rationality. After Esther's anomie, such certitude has its attractions.

> [His] mind, she was certain, would be flat and level, laid out with measured instruments in the broad, even sunlight. There would be geometric concrete walls and square, substantial buildings with clocks on them, everywhere perfectly in time, perfectly synchronized. The air would be thick with their accurate ticking.
>
> (Plath 1980:301)

Plath's bell jar image from her journal haunts this passage from 'Sunday Morning at the Mintons'. Plath's story, published in Mlle in 1952, celebrates the triumphant flight of female imagination over such male flat-footed certitude. But ten years later in *The Bell Jar*, by setting such men as Buddy Willard in their institutional contexts of hospital and happy family, Plath shows the social power that makes his cartoonish balloon-speeches into the punishing particulars of female patienthood, whether obstetrical or psychiatric. 'It is so', proclaims the silver hair in its boyish crewcut, the clear blue eyes, the pink cheeks (97). 'If you think so', rebelliously thinks the dutiful daughter. 'I think we understand each other' (97) he finishes, turning misrecognition into male knowledge with a satisfied sigh.

The photo of the wife-and-kids on the psychiatrist's desk does all the talking for Doctor Gordon during Esther's sessions with him. When that fails to enable Esther to snap out of it, he applies 'his private shock machine. Once I was locked up they could use that on me all the time' (*179*) she accurately predicts – and furiously undertakes yet another frustrated suicide attempt, in classic female fashion. Electro-shock treatments, like delivery-room anaesthetics, like tranquillizers, were popularized in the 1950s with largely the same rationale for largely the same clientele. Buddy assures Esther that the woman giving birth really didn't know what she was doing because she was in a kind of twilight sleep . . . on a drug that would make her forget she'd had any pain.

I thought it sounded just like the sort of drug a man would invent. Here was a woman in terrible pain, obviously feeling every bit of it or she wouldn't groan like that, and she would go straight home and start another baby, because the drug would make her forget how bad the pain had been, when all the time, in some secret part of her, that long, blind, doorless and windowless corridor of pain was waiting to open up and shut her in again. (72)

'That's what I heard – that's what everybody tells you – that it's to make you forget' (Warren 1987:133) explained 'Rita', a woman given shock treatments. Carol Warren's study *Madwives* (1987) re-examines the medical records and interviews of a group of women in a California hospital in the 1950s, and draws firm connections between the isolation of suburban housewives and depression, and between husbands and hospitals and technology co-ordinating an oppressive social control of women. Another woman explained the desired result: after shock treatments 'I wasn't depressed or despondent. . . . Now, I don't feel anything' (Warren 1987:135). 'Rita' said her shock treatments 'made me forget some things, but not enough. I haven't had enough, I guess' (Warren 1987:133). Medical technology refined the behavioural control of women patients under the principle of adjustment toward normalcy. More than one woman interpreted her treatment and even her depression as her punishment for deviancy, for failure to fulfil her role – or, even more shameful, for failing to *want* to fulfil her role. Taking the blame for breakdown is halfway back to normalcy, accepting one's responsibility to adjust oneself.

One mother's story of breakdown and institutionalization is told in Deborah Luepnitz's *The Family Interpreted: Feminist Theory in Clinical Practice* (1988), and outlines the pressure of isolated child-raising intensified by male institutional control. Deborah Luepnitz describes the family therapy session itself:

Margo began to tell the story of her hospitalization. She said that of course she loved all of her children, but that it had been very hard to have them so close together. She especially had wanted to wait a while after Kip was born, because she was tired from having two little ones and Kip had been sick as a baby.

Mrs McGinn: Maybe it sounds selfish, but I just didn't want to take care of anybody for a while. I was worn out.

Gus had apparently understood this, and had gone to their parish priest to explain that Kip was sick, their financial situation was poor, and his wife felt overwhelmed, and asked if it were possible to use contraception. The priest gave him an emphatic 'no.' Margo said she knew how devoted Gus was, but that nonetheless she was crushed that he would show more respect for the Church's wishes than for her own. She soon became pregnant again.

Mrs McGinn: I felt like a nonperson. I don't know how else to say it.

Deborah Luepnitz: Can you try to tell us how that was for you?

Mrs McGinn: A person with no rights. Like something you wind up and it cleans up everyone's mess and cooks and has babies and gets up at dawn and does it over again. Now I feel like shit saying this. You know I love them, but I really couldn't manage. And one day, when Cindy was two, I just stopped coping. Gus found me crying and I just couldn't stop. I couldn't take care of the kids anymore. I couldn't even take care of myself. They put me in a mental asylum, which is probably where I belonged.

Mr McGinn: It wasn't exactly a –

Mrs McGinn: Yes, it was. It was exactly. Do you think it was like this place? There were shock treatments, and terrible drugs, and cloth . . . [crying].

Howard: What kind of cloth, Mom?

Mrs McGinn: Cloth restraints.

(Luepnitz 1988:251)

Esther's gruesome tour of the hospital with Buddy the medical student, her poorly played imitation of a volunteer nurse on the maternity ward at the local hospital, and her painfully mishandled shock treatments at Doctor Gordon's suburban clinic for depressed housewives, gradually move Esther toward the experience of involuntary institutionalization, the ultimate female subjection to male control of knowledge and technology. Plath remembered the film The Snake Pit, and feared the tunnels under the hospital, through which the patients get wheeled to that intimate mating of their nerves with Dr

Frankenstein's lightning machine, the marriage of their accumulated pain with all the wisdom of male science.

Chapter Three

'YOU DON'T BLAME ME FOR HATING MY MOTHER, DO YOU?'

'YOU DON'T blame me for hating my mother, do you?' asks he hero of The Manchurian Candidate – and indeed, we cannot. Raymond's mother has evidently had her heart removed, along with her patriotism and conscience, in one of those 1950s sci-fi brain-takeovers by the Communists. A spy who plots a Presidential candidate's assassination, she manipulates her son with hard-edged Oedipal possessiveness, kissing him right on the mouth when the patricidal trap has been set. Like Oedipus, Raymond is fated to kill the king. As with Sophocles' Oedipus, and Freud's for that matter, it's not his idea. He is innocent of the intention. As 'the Manchurian Candidate' he was secretly brainwashed by the Communists when a prisoner of war in Korea, programmed to kill on command when he sees the 'Red Queen' card, 'in so many ways reminiscent of Raymond's dearly loved and hated mother' (Condon 1959:49) as the novel patiently explains to those unsophisticated in Freudian theory.

Raymond's 'cherished monologue' of mother-blame is built 'upon the beloved memory of his long-dead, betrayed father, who had been cast off by that bitch before Raymond could begin to love him' (Condon 1959:25), in the novel's rather unflattering formulation of the son's filial devotion. This 'cherished monologue' casts the absent father as the only rescue for the child about to be eaten alive by the monstrous maternal maw. It is the plot shared by sci-fi films and popularized psychotherapy, the plot of the 1950s suburban family under siege to the togetherness norm.

Talcott Parsons' influential version of the family has since been re-viewed by feminism (Boss and Thorne 1989). Michael Rogin re-views films in 'Kiss Me Deadly: Communism, motherhood, and cold war movies' (1984). The common theme is that the origins of self-betrayal can be traced to Alien Mothers, and rescue is provided by stiff-necked Paternal Experts – scientists, G-men and shrinks.

'I've been talking to a psychiatrist for two years about how much I dislike my mother', Tony Randall says in *Pillow Talk* (1959). 'He doesn't like her either.' But what if we are women? The plot of mother-blame in *The Bell Jar* answers this question in hair-raising detail. Against their own will, mother and daughter are infected by the self-hatred at the centre of 1950s femininity. For the daughters, unlike the sons, mother-blame is not any kind of solution but rather a cause of self-destruction. Killing the mother does not purge the *daughter*'s body politic. Only revising the valuation of the mother can save the daughter. This is the key to the case of Esther Greenwood.

Rather than reading *The Bell Jar* in the culturally approved fashion diagnosing the mother's failures, I read the novel as a daughter's case of matrophobia. Esther's fear and hatred of her mother entrap her within a misogynist version of motherhood that is potentially lethal. The novel's description of the social sources and psychological consequences of matrophobia make it required reading in the literature on female adolescence. Encountering the fear of becoming one's mother is the central experience of female adolescence, in my book, and denying-while-projecting the fear and hatred of mothers the central experience of the American middle class in the 1950s. Esther Greenwood spoke for her generation, just as Sylvia Plath intended and dreamed she would.

The mainspring of Esther Greenwood's talking cure – and the only piece we are given – is Esther's realization that she hates her mother:

"I hate her," I said, and waited for the blow to fall.

But Dr Nolan only smiled at me as if something had pleased her very, very much, and said, "I suppose you do." (*229*)

Esther, that prize pupil, reads her 'correct' diagnosis as the cure itself in her psychiatrist's eyes: the 'bad' mother (scrimping and stinting her daughter on a teacher's salary) is the problem, the 'good' mother (a professional) the solution.

We don't blame Esther for hating her mother, do we?

> My mother was the worst. She never scolded me, but kept begging me, with a sorrowful face, to tell her what she had done wrong. She said she was sure the doctors thought she had done something wrong because they asked her a lot of questions about my toilet training, and I had been perfectly trained at a very early age and given her no trouble whatsoever. (*228*)

The therapeutic model sets up the search for cause within the family, within the childhood past. The move to the suburbs in the 1950s socially reproduced this cutting-off from extended family, neighbourhood and the social context of the past – all in one willed move. Using such a model of the nuclear family, we never have far to search for suspects. The father is of course missing. The son is found innocent (as in *The Manchurian Candidate*), if he can be found at all. In *The Bell Jar* the son is played by Buddy Willard, who is always Innocence itself. That leaves the mother and daughter under psychiatric scrutiny. The mother rightly fears her hidden 'wrong' is buried somewhere in the daughter's pain, to be dug up in therapy, exposed to a horde of doctors, a psychiatric tribunal on the crimes of motherhood. The daughter participates in therapy at the price of disloyalty to her mother. And she can look forward to her own future fate as the Accused in the court of mother-blame.

This is the crazy-making moment between mother and daughter, left alone together to fight over accountability for the helplessness and pain between them. They mirror back and forth their longing for and loss of each other, and their guilt and blame for it. Therapy in the 1950s did little to explain and much to reinforce 'the loss of the daughter to the mother, the mother to the daughter, . . . the essential female tragedy', in

Adrienne Rich's words (Rich 1977:240). Fighting for innocence when guilty doubt defines the self only reinforces self-division and its projection on to the Other.

This victim's story is told by Aurelia Plath in *Letters Home* and Sylvia Plath in her journals. Each casts herself in the role of Righteous Innocent. Between mother and daughter that can make for a pretty fierce and stubborn naïvety. The Plaths' story has a simple plot: Daddy dies. It's the moral that's tricky. The heroines are tested by the trials of male tyranny and incompetence. The man fails – the father dies, the Colossus is a fraud. Yet the triumph remains his. The blame and shame and bag-carrying are all left to the wife, the mother, the daughter. They angrily fight over accountability, but never directly, always in elaborate code heavily punctuated by silence and denial.

Their story reveals how women recreate in themselves the gender system that oppresses them, in which 'freedom and desire remain an unchallenged male domain, leaving women to be righteous but de-eroticized, intimate and caring, but pleasureless', as Jessica Benjamin explains in *The Bonds of Love* (1988:92). Nowhere is this grim story told in more painful detail than in the writing of Sylvia Plath. The combination of cultural misogyny and learned self-hatred is more deadly than any rational feminist analysis can resolve.

In the passage quoted above from *The Bell Jar*, Sylvia Plath is half satirizing psychiatry's blame-the-mother moralism for looking for First Cause in some child's stool. Yet at the same time Plath satirizes – even blames – Mrs Greenwood for her naïve acceptance of such psychiatric authority at her own expense – and at Esther's. Earlier when Esther has seen the ineffectual Dr Gordon, Mrs Greenwood's response is so passive, so female, so helpless in its bitterness at her situation, that Esther sees her mother's face (*and her own fate*) as bitter fruit, 'anxious and sallow as a slice of lemon' (*147*). 'Well, what did he say?' her mother asks, symbolically dependent on The Man's/The Doctor's word. Esther has already seen the doctor's complete lack of understanding of women; all he remembers of Esther's college is 'a pretty bunch of girls', a WAC station he attended during the war.

Esther sees her mother – so imperviously well-intentioned, so stupid about male power, so unsophisticated about mental illness – as *subjecting her to* Male Medicine, a Nurse Nancy, following Doctor's orders. Mrs Greenwood delivers her to the shock treatments in their neighbour Dodo Conway's station-wagon, doles out the prescribed sleeping pills, and chauffeurs her to the private hospital in Mrs Guinea's limousine, having arranged Esther's 'scholarship' there with well-targeted telegrams that elicited Mrs Guinea's support. After Esther's first shock treatment, 'Sitting in the front seat, between Dodo and my mother, I felt dumb and subdued' (*163*). Reduced to mental vacuity, Esther feels punished, and her mother and Dodo look like unwitting accomplices in her persecution, especially when her mother says, 'I knew you'd decide to be all right again' when Esther refuses further shock treatments. 'I knew my baby wasn't like . . . those awful dead people at that hospital' (*163*) she explains, blaming 'those' for their failure of will and excepting her baby when she shows she'll 'be good' (*203*) again. Excepting Esther is her means of accepting Esther back into the old story. Deviancy is indeed a punishable offence in Mrs Greenwood's unwitting account. Esther later feels her mother blames her for having a breakdown:

> A daughter in an asylum! I had done that to her. Still, she had obviously decided to forgive me.
> "We'll take up where we left off, Esther," she had said, with her sweet, martyr's smile. "We'll act as if all this were a bad dream."
> (*267*)

Plath accurately targets the 'niceness' code of female gentility in Mrs Greenwood, showing how the massive territory of the mother's denial is the 'landscape' of the daughter's reality. 'Maybe forgetfulness, like a kind snow, should numb and cover' the figures in this bad-dream world, Esther speculates, acknowledging her mother's mental-health strategy. 'But they were part of me. They were my landscape' (*267*). To remember, to explore, to face these demons is the business of Esther's therapy with Dr Nolan, her 'good' mother, through whom she is reborn. To forget the past, not to know the war, to ignore the not-niceties pounding on the door, is the business of the wife and mother maintaining the togetherness norm in the sub-urban frontier of the post-war American dream.

Besides incarcerating and electrocuting her for having a nervous breakdown, Esther finds her mother guilty of crimes against Esther's father, by putting on the smiling face even in the face of his death.

> My mother hadn't cried. . . . She had just smiled and said what a merciful thing it was for him he had died, because if he had lived he would have been crippled and an invalid for life, and he couldn't have stood that, he would rather have died than had that happen. (*188–9*)

This is taking the silver-lining imperative rather too far. The mother's denial covers the father's grave like plastic flowers, leaving the daughter truly lost to the reality of her father, and explaining in part why 'his death had always seemed unreal to me' (*186*): because his life and self had been mythologized by a mother–daughter pair of fiction-making professionals.

But they were not working alone. Worshipping the absent father was encouraged, even required by such experts as Dr Spock. As *For Her Own Good* explains, the mother 'had the dramatic responsibility of creating a *mythical* father to preside over the family. No matter what the real father had been like, this ghostly father figure had to be a strong and positive image of manhood' (Ehrenreich and English 1979:250). Otherwise the mother would fail to engineer her children through the stages in 'sex role socialization' that completed the job of the Oedipus and Electra Complexes. The mythical 1950s family, born from a 'melding of psychoanalytic theory with sociological role theory', played Freud's tragic Oedipal drama as a situation comedy with resolution at the end of every half hour. Plot was predictable, 'an orderly series of functional necessities' (Ehrenreich and English 1979:248–9) that parents directed and children performed as sex roles. When Talcott Parsons' new science of functionalism was applied, like a management training course, to the 1950s Freudian family, Mom's psychic housekeeper duties were no longer left to

chance. 'Father Knows Best' was a law *she* enforced, *her* failures
engraved on the child's botched psyche.

'The Disquieting Muses', Plath's poem addressed directly to
her mother about the 'disfigured and unsightly kin' her mother
has refused to admit, is made to be read from the daughter's
point of view as an accusation in which the mother's denial
creates the daughter's disturbed reality. As the mother tells her
stories 'whose witches always, always/Got baked into gingerbread' (Plath 1981:75), as 'the schoolgirls danced . . . singing
the glowworm song', as her mother floats 'in bluest air . . . with
a million/Flowers and bluebirds that never were', the daughter
'could/Not lift a foot', 'Tone-deaf and yes, unteachable', 'I
faced my traveling companions', those disquieting muses 'with
heads like darning-eggs' and 'gowns of stone'. The blame and
shame are assigned: 'And this is the kingdom you bore me
to,/Mother, mother'. And then the good daughter twists the
knife using that brave soap-bubbles smile learned from
you-know-who: 'But no frown of mine/Will betray the company
I keep'. The daughter has learned to use her mother's denials
against her, announcing their cost to her and then bravely
swallowing the martyr's pill.

'I think it was a remarkable poem but I was hurt by it', Aurelia
Plath said in a videotaped interview about 'The Disquieting
Muses'. 'She manipulated what I said . . .' (*Voices and Visions*
1988). Unwitting still, the mother's literal-mindedness in the
court of mother-blame blinds her to the daughter's 'reality' of
the symbolic, the uncanny, where speaks all that hurts, manipulates and – worst crime – is ungrateful. Of *The Bell Jar* itself
Aurelia Plath wrote in 1970, 'As this book stands by itself, it
represents the basest ingratitude. That was not the basis of
Sylvia's personality' (Plath 1971:295, biographical note). 'Sylvia
loved' the real people represented by characters in the novel;
'each person had given freely of time, thought, affection, and,
in one case, financial help during those agonizing six months of
breakdown in 1953' (Plath 1971:295). The mother's currency
system of daughterly 'love' in return for motherly 'help' is
monstrously violated by the novel; to explain this, Aurelia Plath

referred to her daughter's explanation of the novel to her, in July 1962, as

> a pot boiler really, but I think it will show how isolated a person feels when he is suffering a breakdown. . . . I've tried to picture my world and the people in it as seen through the distorting lens of a bell jar.
>
> (Plath 1971:295)

Adding other reasons why the novel is a distortion, Aurelia Plath only succeeds in sounding like Mrs Greenwood trying to convince Esther that the pain she has ploughed up by having a nervous breakdown and then talking about it is best treated as a kind of bad fiction best forgotten: 'We'll act as if all this were a bad dream' (267). The next novel, Aurelia says Sylvia told her, 'will show that same world as seen through the eyes of health' (Plath 1971:295). The mother explains the daughter's view as sickness-induced; like a bad dream, it is neither real nor true. 'The eyes of health' see rightly, the world as the mother knows it.

The mother reads her daughter's journal in the same way. Aurelia Plath explains her 'consent to the release of this material' for publication:

> Much of the material in these pages relating to Sylvia Plath's therapy is of course very painful to me, and coming to the decision to approve its release has been difficult. I have no doubt that many readers will accept whatever negative thoughts she reveals here as the whole and absolute truth, despite their cancellation on other, more positive pages.
>
> (Plath 1983:265)

As with and in *The Bell Jar*, the mother's pain 'pays' for the daughter's published/public version of her pain. Psychiatry, like publication, is seen as a kind of tribunal reviewing the mother–daughter relation. The daughter's darkness – 'whatever negative thoughts' – is 'cancelled' – not balanced or enlightened or challenged – by 'other, more positive pages'. The mother's silver-lining imperative actually includes 'cancelling' the cloud, so complete is her faith in the power of her denial to order reality. How then is the daughter to be understood by such a mother?

Esther's suicide attempts can be read as 'messages' in which she writes the great unsayables between herself and her mother. 'I propped the message where my mother would see it the minute she came in' (*189*) Esther explains. Instead of a suicide note, however, she writes a lie about going for a walk, which diverts rescue for guilt-mounting days. Like her mother, she finds her dark side to be unspeakable, and offers a perky-faced lie instead. She covers and exposes her helplessness and anger in the same gesture, asking for and refusing help in classic adolescent fashion. The daughter's demanding refusal matches her mother's style of 'loving reproach'. Each implicitly accuses the other while blocking any giving or getting. Gridlock!

The story of Esther Greenwood's suicide-slide can be all too easily read as an indictment of the mother. Plath and her mother certainly struggled over – and resisted – that damning interpretation of *The Bell Jar*. But when framed by the tribunal on motherhood of the 1950s, the daughter's breakdown can be read in one way only: as a colossal failure of femininity to produce itself normally. 'Here is the real crux of the situation', as those infamous Freudian moralizers, Lundberg and Farnham, grade the mother–daughter homework assignment. The daughter's femininity is dependent on 'the mother's feelings for herself as a woman and acceptance of her feminine role'. She must find 'complete satisfaction, without conflict or anxiety' or the aid of any outside job or helper (Lundberg and Farnham 1947:228). The absence of maternal fulfilment is the pathology itself in the Freudian court.

Rather than blaming either mother or daughter for problems with maternity, *The Bell Jar* looks at the social sources for Esther Greenwood's fears and her silence about them.

The suicide sequence resembles a slide down which Esther feels herself pushed by a chain of motherly women – her mother, the heavy breeder Dodo Conway, her family doctor Teresa, nurses and suburban clubwomen – at the end of which is maternity itself, whether the maternity ward at the hospital where Esther is sent as volunteer, or the mental hospital ward where crazy women knit and gossip and read tatty copies of *Vogue* with intense interest (*213*). Esther feels she is being set up for maternity, that motherhood *is* a set-up, a brainwashing.

> I also remembered Buddy Willard saying in a sinister, knowing way that after I had children I would feel differently, I wouldn't want to write poems any more. So I began to think maybe it was true that when you were married and had children it was like being brainwashed, and afterward you went about numb as a slave in some private, totalitarian state. (*94*)

She can feel no maternal instinct beckoning from within, yet mothers graze cow-like all around her, mindless and content. Is she next?

Women conspire to send her toward her mother's fate, in Esther's not-entirely-paranoid version of the suicide squeeze from college girl into domestic drudge. Volunteer for Maternity is 'What all the Junior League women wanted to do'. As an exceptional woman, does Esther get an exemption from this army of recruits? Or does her failure to 'want' maternity signal a fatally flawed femininity that speaks volumes in the Freudian casebook? 'Why was I so unmaternal and apart? Why couldn't I dream of devoting myself to baby after fat puling baby like Dodo Conway?' (*250*) With this question haunting her, Esther's mother's advice looks sinister:

> My mother said the cure for thinking too much about yourself was helping somebody who was worse off than you, so Teresa had arranged for me to sign on as a volunteer at our local hospital. It was difficult to be a volunteer at this hospital, because that's what all the Junior League women wanted to do, but luckily for me, a lot of them were away on vacation.
>
> I had hoped they would send me to a ward with some really gruesome cases, . . . But the head of the volunteers, a society lady at our church, took one look at me and said, "You're on maternity."
>
> . . . But before I came to the door of the first room I noticed that a lot of the flowers [to be delivered] were droopy and brown at the edges. I thought it would be discouraging for a woman who'd just had a baby to see somebody plonk down a big bouquet of dead flowers in front of her. (*182*)

Esther's message to new mothers is the dead bouquet, representing the killing-off of the promise of their education, of all further intellectual and public power – of all further 'growth' as a person. Like Friedan in *The Feminine Mystique*, Esther assumes that 'a stunting or evasion of growth . . . is perpetuated by the feminine mystique' and that all stimulation occurs in the public world of phallic activities like 'splitting atoms, penetrating outer space, creating art that illuminates human destiny, pioneering on the frontiers of society' (Friedan 1963:77;66). Art, like human beings, like destiny itself, is viable only in the public sphere – of men. The tasks, creatures and fates in the domestic sphere are stunted – and female. The 'really gruesome cases' that frighten Esther are mothers.

The dead foetuses in jars that Esther saw on her hospital tour with Buddy represent both women as patients, subject to Male Medicine's persecutory experimentation, and women as mothers, frozen in their development as humans. Esther sees four cadavers cut up and then a woman giving birth, given pain-killers and then cut up and sewn up. 'You oughtn't to see this,' Esther is told. 'You'll never want to have a baby if you do. They oughtn't to let women watch' (*71*). The 'secret' of motherhood – its pain, all the pain-killers to hide the pain, its female helplessness under men's instrumentality – is kept from women until it's too late. Not too late for Esther, always the exception. She reads the message from 'the baby in the last bottle . . . the size of a normal baby . . . he seemed to be looking at me and smiling a little piggy smile' (*69*).

Esther's first shock treatment feels like a kind of punishing, forced delivery: 'a great jolt drubbed me till I thought my bones would break and the sap fly out of me like a split plant' (*161*). The doctor is wordless and mechanical like his machine. The nurse is the grotesque mother. 'Dumpy and muscular', she offends femininity; 'in her smudge-fronted uniform' she is unclean, suspect; with her 'large, conspiratorial grin' and witchy hiss, she betrays other women while pretending Esther is her ally; with her wall-eye and thick spectacles, Esther cannot tell which eyes are false and which real, which one crooked and which straight – what to trust in her motherly intentions for Esther.

> As she leaned over . . . her fat breast muggled my face like a cloud or a pillow. A vague, medicinal stench emanated from her flesh.
>
> "Don't worry," the nurse grinned down at me. "Their first time everybody's scared to death." (*160*)

Suffocation from the somehow sinister maternal breast is only the first half of Esther's matrophobic nightmare, the part shared with movie fans of sci-fi, melodrama and cold war films alike. As in *The Manchurian Candidate*, the inhuman monster dominates the big screen, threatening to destroy civilization – including our very subjectivity – as we know it. As the male scientist warns about the nuclear fall-out mutant ants in *Them!* (1954), 'Unless the queens are destroyed, *man* as the dominant species on this planet will probably be destroyed.' In *Invasion of the Body Snatchers* (1956), the victims' 'bodies [are] host to an alien form of life' which like the devouring mother secretly mutates them in the process of satisfying its inhuman appetite. The invasion occurs during sleep, when the psyche is defenceless, trustingly child-like. The hero announces his worst horror: 'A moment's sleep and the girl I loved was an inhuman enemy bent on my destruction.' He warns the audience directly at the close of the film: 'You fools, you're in danger. . . . They're HERE already! You're next! You're next! You're next!'

For the heroine, of course, the second part of the matrophobic nightmare is to awaken *as* 'the inhuman enemy', the Alien Mother. 'You're next!' the little piggy foetus smiles at Esther. You fall asleep – or get anaesthetized or shocked – and wake up one of them! – those pincurled, knitting, gossiping, flabby, sharp-faced clubwomen 'chattering like parrots' (*183*) when happy, 'cross and loud and full of complaint' in less attractive moments (*184*). No wonder Esther doesn't want to fall asleep that summer, with her pincurled mother snoring away in the 'twin' bed next to her like her fated tomorrow. The shared bedroom, the wards and dorms full of women, the hairpins and bathrobes underpinning women's domestic realm – so comforting to others, so uncannily threatening to Esther.

'So many women, the house stank of them. . . . A stink of women: Lysol, cologne, rose water and glycerine, cocoa butter on the nipples so they won't crack, lipstick red on all 3 mouths' – her own, her mother's, her grandmother's, Plath writes in retrospective matrophobia in her journal in 1959 (Plath 1983:266). The painted mouth represents femininity as a self-wounding legacy of mother to daughter. In the mirror of the mother's dressing-table, the daughter watches her mother 'make up'. The cruellest twist for Esther comes when the mother's mouth is anxiously forced into a smile for the daughter, because the mirror's reflection only compounds the confusion of real and false faces between mother and daughter. Who is the lipstick for? Who is the smile for? One of Plath's 'mothers', the novelist Olive Higgins Prouty, who was her scholarship sponsor for Smith College and McLean hospital alike, portrays this mother–daughter moment in her novel *Stella Dallas*, made into a film with such a scene before the dressing-table mirror. 'The scene ends', as Linda Williams describes it, 'with mother and daughter before the mirror tacitly relating to one another through the medium of the feminine mask – each putting on a good face for the other' (Williams 1987:311).

The art of cosmetology – of putting on, of making up – is a matter of easily learned technique. The art of cosmetic surgery – destroying the face beneath the mask by mastering self-denial – takes more training and an even steadier hand. Esther is a modern woman who sees her mother's martyrdom as archaic. Self-denial has made a monster out of her, and Esther has made sure she herself has never succumbed to a self-denying impulse in her life. What monstrous image does the daughter of such a mother see in her mirror? What makes Esther break the mirror in the hospital after her suicide attempt?

In the all-female wards, Esther sees women learn self-hatred in the mirrors of each other, without benefit of male technology, impersonality or rationality. All is feeling, all is female, all is feline. How to escape? Can any woman be trusted to help her escape?

The nurse attaching the electrodes to Esther's skull is disconcertingly double, mother and electrocutioner, relief and torturer, escape and fate. The nurse's untrustworthy eyes, straight and skewed, are the mother's 'twin' legacy of recognition and denial. The real eye sees, and enables the precocious daughter to escape her mother's fate. The false eye makes up fairy-tales about daughters who are Cinderellas entitled to escape hearth-scrubbing, fictions that lie, imprison children in gingerbread houses.

Esther 'escapes' through the enabling therapy provided by the good mother, a professional woman who is *not* a mother, *not* ruled by duty and self-denying service. She enables Esther to become 'sexual' – a woman – by providing her with birth control and the permission to be sexually active without any reference to marriage, to becoming a mother. She also enables Esther to express her hatred for her mother – and so allows her to pay for her own normalcy and goodness using the cultural currency of the mother's failures. Yet this richly ambiguous and ambivalent territory is the fertile ground for feminism as well as matrophobia. In articulating rather than denying or deflecting the disappointments of women's lives, the daughter may find that questions of agency provide more future for her than the mother's story of victimization – and may explain more about her mother's life as well.

To be able to adopt the mother's point of view – and to give up the daughter's – can be the essential step in therapy: from child-victim to adult analyst. Such a shift in point of view enables feminism to lessen its investment in daughterly innocence and totalitarian states of persecution, and adopt less flattering but more empowering models of self-in-society that take into account the truly nasty side of the victim's story: her own participation.

But adopting the mother's point of view proves an elusive business. Motherhood itself is denied subjectivity by cultural definition. Instead, Mom and her motives are everywhere *object*ified, 'known', idealized or reviled. Motherhood is spoken about as a state, an Otherhood. Mothers speak through – and are heard through – our ideas *about* motherhood. In our Family Drama, mothers are the object of desire and fear, against whom we understand our selves and define Family. So understood, to whom can mothers speak their desire and fear?

To find and hear the voice of the woman *behind* the mother is, I think, the daughter's crucial adolescent task. To know the woman before and beyond the mother enables the daughter to realize that self is not vapourized when Motherhood moves in and seems to Take Over in body-snatcher fashion. Such a shift in the daughter's perspective, Doris Lessing writes, is

> a mysterious process, frightening because there is nothing whatsoever you can do about it, that takes you from fierce adolescence – as if parents and you stood at either side of a battlefield, hands full of weapons – to a place where you can stand where they did, in imagination, any time you want.
>
> (Lessing 1984:52)

Struggling to take on the mother's point of view is abandoned in favour of simple transference in both Esther's and Sylvia Plath's therapy. They cling to the earlier and easier task of finding the therapist a welcome replacement for the mother.

When the bad mother and the good mother act the parts in Esther's struggle for identity, the one wears the frown of self-denial and the other the smile of self-fulfilment. Esther's transference follows the shift in feminine identity between Plath's mother's generation and her own. But the characterizations of both mothers are sketchy in the novel, more often absent than present. A few symbolic conversations and gestures speak volumes for Esther's mother's exacting pay-your-way maternal resources and let's-be-nice code, and Esther's doctor's free-flowing generosity of empathy and workman-like deconstruction of Esther's mother-and-daughter accounting system. The novel draws the veil over Esther's therapy, her exploration and apparent escape from the matrophobic maze.

Plath's journals provide a fuller explanation of both the bad mother and the good therapist, and how a heroine can begin to move from victimhood to agency in relation to these two key figures.

Sylvia Plath's psychiatrist Dr Ruth Buescher (R.B.) can be spotted in the journal written in Boston in 1958–9, when Plath re-entered therapy with the same doctor she had at McLean after her breakdown in 1953. Plath quotes some of Buescher's

Maria

actual questions in therapy, and these provide interesting clues to Plath's dilemma from the outside. In fact Ruth Buescher's is the only clear representation of any other point of view in Plath's self-obsessed journal in its published form, suggesting the power of her influence to challenge if not change Plath's assumptions.

This journal outlines the story of how empowerment can occur through therapy. In a delightful inversion, *the feminist doctor challenges the patient's Freudian fatalisms.* The young female therapist may be the real heroine of this story, struggling to free a patient's enthralment to one of the most oppressive norms of femininity in American history. Buescher questions its two most conservative assumptions: the mother's devouring motives, and marriage-as-salvation for the daughter, through which her identity is achieved through the role of wife. Plath's male-rescue fantasy, for instance – 'He is a genius. I his wife' (Plath 1983:258) – runs the same reels as her mother's: 'I listened, fascinated, to his accounts of travel and colorful adventures, fully realizing that I was in the presence of a true genius in both the arts and sciences' (Plath 1975:6). Cut to Dr Buescher's question in therapy about *The Man*: 'Would you have the guts to admit you'd made a wrong choice?' (Plath 1983:269). Later she asks, 'Does Ted want you to get better?' (Plath 1983:271).

The therapy begins with the key, which is 'better than shock treatment', Plath writes: 'I give you permission to hate your mother.' She continues,

> So I feel terrific. In a smarmy matriarchy of togetherness it is hard to get a sanction to hate one's mother especially a sanction one believes in. I believe in R.B. because she is a clever woman who knows her business & I admire her. She is for me "a permissive mother figure." I can tell her anything, and she won't turn a hair or scold or withold her listening, which is a pleasant substitute for love.

> (Plath 1983:265–6)

Two major historical figures appear here: the smarmy togetherness imperative outlining the mother's identity in the 1950s, and the new improved role model, a clever woman of business who is nurturant of the daughter's career aspirations *and* emotional life (not either/or) *without* exacting love (gratitude, obedience, self-domination, depression) in return. Such a dutiful-daughterly love, defined and created by its context of the 1950s norm of Family, frames the terms of loyalty to her mother and pens her within her own matrophobia. Hers is but an extremely unflattering and stymied case of every daughter's buried self-hatred, home-grown out of realistic fear of her mother's fate.

The doctor is her liberation from this maze. She offers a recognition through listening that is 'the essential response, the constant companion of assertion' in the interactive model proposed by Jessica Benjamin in *The Bonds of Love* (1988:21). This recognition (and its lack) secures the most intimate psychic moorings of the gender system. 'The desire to be recognized as a subject' means that 'the child wants recognition of her will, of her desire, of her act' from mother and father, 'in a long series of struggles to achieve a sense of agency, to be recognized in one's desire' (Benjamin 1988:101–2). In a culture which robs motherhood of such subjectivity, of any autonomous desire or will, the daughter can see no self in the mother, and so cannot see her own self in motherhood. Esther Greenwood never names the woman who is her mother, and sees only death and oblivion of her own recognized self in motherhood.

Sylvia Plath, on the other hand, in therapy with R.B. begins to see the woman-as-subject who has lived her mother's life, and begins to recognize a desire to be a mother in herself. Her insights are cast in so culturally conventional a form, however, that they threaten to reinforce rather than liberate her from the prison-house of hateful and entrapping gender types. Plath sees her mother *through* her old fear of suffocation and her hatred of the self-sacrificing martyr. She cannot see *around* her mother's 'mask, her fate, and most of her affliction' to the woman who lived the life (Munro 1990:26). Alice Munro explains her own shift to see her mother with

> Her mask, her fate, and most of her affliction taken away. How relieved I was, and happy. But I now recall that I was

74

disconcerted as well. I would have to say that I felt slightly cheated. Yes. Offended, tricked, cheated, by this welcome turnaround, this reprieve. My mother moving rather carelessly out of her old prison, showing options and powers I never dreamed she had, changes more than herself. She changes the bitter lump of love I have carried all this time into a phantom – something useless and uncalled for, like a phantom pregnancy.
(Munro 1990:26)

Plath sees 'the mother working for bread like no poor woman should have to and being a good mother on top of it', the mother as subject, the mother as both worker and nurturer. But Plath then objectifies her as 'one sweet ulcerous ball. She pinched', Plath begins again, then grammatically erases her mother as subject of the sentence: 'Scraped. Wore the same old coat. But the children had new school clothes' (Plath 1983: 266). She imagines only a mother's motives of self-sacrifice for her children, no other self.

So too with motherhood for herself. When she finally imagines it, it is an all-or-nothing, life-or-death proposition: 'for a woman to be deprived of the Great Experience her body is formed to partake of, to nourish, is a great and wasting Death' (Plath 1983:308). Plath reveals her pragmatic goal for her therapy, and her fury at being denied her prize: 'I have come, with great pain and effort, to the point where my desires and emotions and thoughts center around what the normal woman's center around, and what do I find? Barrenness' (Plath 1983:310). Her desire, finally found, is only fated to be its own punishment: 'If I could not have children . . . I would be dead' (Plath 1983:310). And then of course the man-trapping necessity, the last bulwark of her femininity: 'How can I keep Ted wedded to a barren woman?' (Plath 1983:311).

'Keeping Ted wedded' translates her desire (for him, for love, for sex, for children) into a pragmatic project of control and disguise worthy of her mother. Finding 'barrenness' at the centre, where the 'normal woman' finds fertility, calls into question both her own natural femininity, found wanting, *and* the usefulness of therapy to bring her self around, 'with great pain and effort, to the point where my desires and emotions and thoughts center around what the normal woman's center around' – maternity. Her project of willing herself into normalcy is punished by failure to reproduce the ideal 'naturally', authentically. She is found out as a fraud.

The functional role of therapy popularized in the 1950s – to adjust one to one's role – was perhaps most successful in focusing blame on the individual psyche that did not respond normally to the project. To fail therapy was the mark of true – uncorrectable – deviancy. Her mother's moral-of-the-story surfaces in Plath's conclusion that therapy results in exposure of the Alien Mother, fraudulent and destructive.

To find such a monster at the end of the therapeutic trail is the patient's feared result, not presumably the desired goal of any therapist. But given the norms of 1950s femininity, therapy was quite a trap-laden trick for female therapist and female patient.

Any successful analysis involves an adult's re-vision of the past and its influences on the present – not a recreation merely, which perpetuates the child's helpless flailing, but a re-understanding and re-valuation. Only through adult eyes can one see the parents' flawed selves, and from there see the crucial fact that while a child is indeed 'stuck', an adult has the power to move. (Plath never moved.) Adults can shift point of view, analyse and even change situations. This reveals one's power to 'unstick' the child from its eternal helplessness, rescue it into the protection of the adult self, powerful, knowing, nurturant. There is no evidence that Plath was able to revise any conclusion about herself, about her mother, about motherhood as a trap-door that suddenly reveals an abyss, barrenness, a lifetime of unmet need cruelly read as one's own 'lack'.

Sylvia Plath's six months of therapy ended with her leaving Boston for a summer cross-country trip, followed by a stay at Yadoo in the fall and then her move back to England in December. She became pregnant early in the summer. Her journal that fall reviews old mother–daughter tangles in the new light of her own incipient motherhood. She resolves:

> I need the reality of other people, work, to fulfill myself. Must never become a mere mother and housewife. Challenge of baby when I am so unformed and unproductive as a writer. A fear for the meaning and purpose of my life. I will hate a child that substitutes itself for my own purpose: so I must make my own.
>
> (Plath 1983:327)

She resolves, in other words, not to do what her mother did: 'My mother had sacrificed her life for me. A sacrifice I didn't want' (Plath 1983:268).

By realizing that motherhood and career are not an either/or choice for herself Plath unblocks half her own stalemate; so does Esther by the end of *The Bell Jar*. Esther first imagined her problem of life plan using the metaphor of a fig tree she's in, unable to choose which one fig she'll eat for her life's fulfilment. The figs wither as she's still trying to make up her mind. *The Bell Jar*'s resolution suggests at the end that she'll work toward career and let marriage take care of itself, meanwhile enjoying a sex life using her new diaphragm and attendant identity as her 'own woman'.

But the mother remains behind in the daughter's new story, burdened with the old baggage of both. This, I would argue, is the matrophobia story unrevised, the pregnant daughter trying to load and leave the mother with her own unsolved pain. Plath in effect tries to 'mummify' the mother by writing her, freezing her threat 'in print so that everything I write now doesn't get sucked in its maw' (Plath 1983:318). She writes what she calls the Mummy story, a story that has since disappeared.

She calls it 'A ten-page diatribe against the Dark Mother. The Mummy. Mother of Shadows' (Plath 1983:316). She plans 'Twenty-page chapters out of nightmare land. . . . If only I can get some horror into this mother story' (Plath 1983:316). Three days later she writes, 'The Mummy story dubious. Is it simply feminine frills, is there any terror in it? Would [there] be more if it were real? Set with real externals? As it is, it is the monologue of a madwoman' (Plath 1983:317). The daughter's mother-blame story is indeed a monologue, and a highly repetitive one at that, and it is not so much about as by 'a madwoman', the 'mad' grown daughter unable to release herself from her own 'diatribe' of rage.

The next day Plath reports she 'finished the Mummy story . . . then was electrified . . . to read in Jung case history confirmations of certain images in my story' (Plath 1983:317). Paternal expert to the rescue of the patient drowning in her own subjectivity! Using Jung to 'confirm' her 'instinctive images with perfectly valid psychological analysis' is not however the needed re-solution to her Mummy story, only an impressively authorized retelling. What she reports she finds in Jung is another child's fearful view of a mother:

> The child who dreamt of a loving, beautiful mother as a witch or animal: the mother going mad in later life, grunting like pigs, barking like dogs, growling like bears, in a fit of lycanthropy. The word "chessboard" used in an identical situation: of a supposedly loving but ambitious mother who manipulated the child on the "chessboard of her egotism"; I had used "chessboard of her desire." Then the image of the eating mother, or grandmother: all mouth, as in Red Riding Hood (and I had used the image of the wolf). All this relates in a most meaningful way my instinctive images with perfectly valid psychological analysis. However, I am the victim, rather than the analyst. My "fiction" is only a naked recreation of what I felt, as a child and later, must be true.
>
> (Plath 1983:317–18)

Plath's conclusion insists on her child's position in relation to the mother: 'However, I am the victim, rather than the analyst.' She is not doctor but patient. She is not adult revising the past but child simply reliving it. She is not objective but only subjectively recreating her child's reality. And she is not mother but child, 'the victim' who is innocent of all agency, all analysis, all accountability for the past. Casting herself as Little Red Riding Hood (which Plath did for a Hallowe'en party, with Ted her wolf) leaves appetite for others and reserves an anorectic innocence for herself.

'Ted is my salvation,' she inauspiciously concludes soon after the Mummy story is finished. 'Ted is the ideal, the one possible person' (Plath 1983:320–1). She turns from the dead-end with the mother (who can never be completely mummified and killed in the daughter), to 'rescue' by the Right Man from the Mother: the classic escape-attempt from female adolescence into one's 'own woman'hood. The illusion is that the mother blocks the exit. The illusion is that only the Man, like God Himself, can create Woman. The culturally enforced illusion is that the daughter needs to be *purged* of the devouring mother, by being 'born again' from the Prince's kiss. Sylvia Plath invested her very self in this illusion of the daughter's redemption and cure by The One Possible Person: 'waking into a new world, with no name, being born again, and not of woman' (Plath 1983:113). 'Keeping Ted wedded' was Plath's escape attempt from matrophobia, from her never-ending nightmare vision of the mother's manless misery in the domestic dead-end dead-head world of women.

Chapter Four

'I AM NOT NOW A HOMOSEXUAL AND I HAVE NEVER BEEN A HOMOSEXUAL.'

'I AM not now a homosexual and I have never been a homosexual. I never in any way attempted to seduce Sylvia Plath' (*Guardian* 1987). Jane V. Anderson, a psychiatrist at Harvard, sued the Plath estate in 1987, claiming she was the basis for *The Bell Jar*'s lesbian suicide character, and disclaiming the lesbianism, the seduction, and the suicide. Esther calls Joan Giddings her 'double' when she shows up at the mental hospital, 'specially designed to follow and torment me' (*231*), her identity 'close enough so that her thoughts and feelings seemed a wry, black image of my own' (*246*). As if taking her cue from the character Joan in the novel, Anderson uncannily reappears as Sylvia Plath's dark double. Twenty-four years after Plath's suicide, Anderson surfaces to publicly revive and revise The Bell Jar's 'lesbian threat' scenario. But she ends up merely replaying it: lesbianism is called up only to be denounced and denied – neck wrung, body buried. What is the nature of the lesbian threat for Jane Anderson? Esther Greenwood? Sylvia Plath?

The lesbian threat is the dark double haunting heterosexuality as health itself in female adolescence: buried but not, apparently, quite dead. As if exhumed from a time capsule, Jane Anderson in her public suit articulated the nature of the lesbian threat, both its power and pathology, as experienced by collegiate women of the 1950s. Much like Esther Greenwood, Jane Anderson finds Joan's seduction attempt 'sickening beyond words and extremely objectionable' (*Time* 1987).

'Sickening' echoes Esther's blunt rejection of Joan: 'I don't like you. You make me puke' (*248*).

Homosexuality as disease is the necessary Other in the organic medical model of mental health. If heterosexuality is the natural culmination of psychic development signalling adulthood and the end of adolescence, homosexuality is the corrupt and sickly wrong turn, a dead-end developmentally, a fixation forever in the sexual insecurities of adolescence (fate worse than death). Lesbianism threatens the whole project of female adolescence: to secure gender identity irreversibly, by heterosexual initiation into womanhood.

If – as feminism has claimed since Esther Greenwood's time – womanhood is *not* secured by heterosexuality, and heterosexuality is *not* the key to mental health, our heroine Esther Greenwood is in trouble as she exits the mental hospital 'patched, retreaded and approved for the road' (*275*). If heterosexuality is not secure but open to reversal, if adulthood is not set but disturbed by history and revision, our still-living heroine Jane Anderson has reason to find lesbianism a still-living threat in 1987. And if our Freudian model of development is not absolute but disturbed by feminist revision, the psychiatrist Jane Anderson of Harvard Medical School has a reason to feel the lesbian threat as an attack on her professional, as well as personal, identity. 'Sickening beyond words and extremely objectionable', lesbianism must be made to show its diseased parts in the court of psychiatric authority, where pathology knows its place, its name, and can be controlled by diagnosis and treatment by experts. In particular the film/video version of *The Bell Jar* threatens, because its images speak beyond words. Seeing, to an alarming extent in mass culture, Is Believing.

The videotape of the film of *The Bell Jar* was Jane V. Anderson's 'worst nightmare' come true, sending her into therapy in 'extreme anxiety', and into the courts to restore her reputation as a psychiatrist at Harvard. 'It was the fulfillment of my worst nightmare that a movie version of *The Bell Jar* would be available to anyone anywhere in this country.' Jane Anderson 'saw' the lesbianism in the film as she had not in the novel, where 'It had not registered with me' (*Guardian* 1987). Films, like nightmares, expose horrors without strict regard for reality or reputation. Repression is impotent as the nightmare unreels. Anderson suffered 'flashbacks' after seeing the film, likening them to those of Vietnam veterans, in which 'colored, visual images of various components of the painful aspects' of McLean 'start and stop in a way I did not have control over' (*New York Times* 1987). Her nightmare included a loss of control of her own image, its revision into lesbianism, and its contagion-like spread nation-wide, made 'available to anyone anywhere in this country' in the promiscuity of mass marketing.

Of course Anderson's law suit causes her *own* public exposure as the video could not. She says she both is and is not Joan Giddings, announcing and denying her 'lesbian character' at the same time. If her 'worst nightmare' is having her closet door ripped open and a video camera thrust inside, why does she call a public tribunal for the purpose of denying homosexual tendencies?

A McCarthyist model of conviction-through-allegation underlies Jane V. Anderson's worst nightmare. Her denial takes its form from Joseph McCarthy's witch-hunting question, 'Are you now or have you ever been a member of the Communist Party?' But as with Communism, so with homosexuality: mere association is enough to convict *in the public eye*. TV-cameras were McCarthy's necessary medium for exposure, the visual image magically convicting even as the witness verbally denied all charges.

The video's threat to Anderson's version of herself seemed to demand a 'vindication' in another public eye where she could exert more control, where her professional credentials could influence public interpretation of her – and of lesbianism – as they could not in the mass movie culture's image of the seductive lesbian. Such insistence on control of interpretation – by a psychiatrist, no less – is one key to the social construction of mental health normalized in the 1950s. Another key is her worst nightmare identity issue, lesbianism exposed in the court of popular Freudianism. A third is the nightmare inversion of rational analyst/irrational patient, in which Anderson herself is uncannily cast as the female patient convicted by her own unconscious homosexual tendencies popping into view. Her idea of vindication, then, reasserts herself as psychiatrist who controls interpretation of the raw material. She considered her out-of-court settlement of $150,000 'a vindication of me' (*Guardian* 1987).

The version that Anderson's case contests is a version of lesbianism itself. The film's lesbian, unlike the novel's, is beautiful and sophisticated, and in the film two lengthy seduction scenes show Esther's strong attraction to Joan. The film reflects a 1980s feminist revision of the lesbian image, no longer the horsey-and-hungry dyke of the novel, but a 'normal' female indistinguishable in appearance from Esther's femininity. The dissemination of *this* image of lesbianism, unmarked by any sign of deviance, and alarmingly 'available to anyone anywhere in this country', represents the successful challenge feminism has made to Freudianism on the battleground of mass culture. Anderson's suit may be about her professional version (of lesbianism as sickening) overturning the lower court of mass culture (lesbianism for the masses), with the higher court of psychiatric opinion, the law, experts.

Anderson's assumptions are shared by the crude subtext of Esther Greenwood's mental health recovery process in *The Bell Jar*. She too is vindicated by a tribunal evaluating her normalcy, pronouncing her 'whole and well' (*247*), the two basic signifiers of 1950s mental health as a function of unarrested and undiseased development. Esther's encounter with lesbianism overtly on offer ('I like you', says Joan, stretched out on Esther's bed with a silly smile (*249*)) is considered resolved when the lesbian commits suicide and is buried under a blanket of snow. 'I wondered what I thought I was burying' (*273*), Esther hints, the coy analysand suggesting a topic for her next session. Plath's 'public hanging' of the lesbian threat in *The Bell Jar* rivals Jane Anderson's court case in its unwitting exposure of the crude homophobia underpinning – indeed, hemming and doublebinding – women's normal identity as heterosexual.

Joan's lesbian threat catapults Esther out of her safe hiding place in the women's ward, anxious to prove she is her 'own woman' (*251*) by sleeping with a man: no irony intended. Esther is obsessing herself with the catatonic Miss Norris when 'the big, horsey girl in jodhpurs' (*219*) gallops into the next stall and redirects Esther's flagging energies from self-erasure to self-definition. 'Hour after hour I had been keeping watch by Miss Norris's bedside, refusing . . . diversion . . . simply to brood over the pale, speechless circlet of her lips' (*218*). The anorectic refusal mode of an advanced case of spinsterism presents Esther with an alternative to the chattering parrothood of femininity offered by the bridge players.

Such refusal, however, is what all the women have in common, whether it's the wife who refused to serve her mother-in-law, the mother who went mad before her debutante daughters' coming out, the student daughter who refused to read or write or sleep or wash her hair, or the secretary who refused to service her boss's emotional demands. Once the wife began acting like one, 'dish[ing] out everybody's food like a little mother, . . . they sent her home and nobody wanted to take her place' (*204*). Managing the once-refused domestic routine is the sign of normalcy, all editorial comment considered part of the pathology of resistance. Where exactly does this leave Esther with her refusal of Achieving Daughterhood?

Joan introduces choice for Esther, the choice of the 'third sex', alternative to celibacy or heterosexual subordination to the first sex. Joan arrives to play her double in identity crisis, with all the same elements – same neighbourhood, same college, same role models like the Willards, same suicide attempt. Joan announces that reading Esther's suicide story in the newspaper actually inspired her to try it herself. 'For the first time it occurred to me Joan and I might have something in common' (*225*), Esther confesses, reconsidering her former 'cool distance' (*220*). Joan's arrival brings her out of her disconnected daze, arouses her curiosity and reactivates her search for connection, or at least identification, with others, Esther's rather limited form of female friendship.

'Refusal' is the broken-down Esther's solution to the problems of her life, refusing her past, her visitors, her mother, her old identity. Then one day a nurse educates her in her privileged but fragile class position. 'Either I got better, or I fell down, down, like a burning, then burnt-out star, from Belsize, to Caplan, to Wymark and finally, after Doctor Nolan and Mrs Guinea had given me up, to the state place next door' (235). This realization, accompanied by insulin shock and electro-shock therapy, seems to jump-start Esther's old achievement motor, and Joan's parallel course provides a competitor to run against. Up she climbs through the elaborate hierarchy of mentally healthy behaviour, from no longer wearing her pyjamas during the day, to social interaction, to initiating sexual intercourse with a misogynist, her trump card 'validating' her womanhood and mental health to Freudian specifications.

Hate men? That's Joan's lesbian business, despising a man like Buddy Willard, who 'thought he knew everything about women' (246). This of course had been Esther's complaint about Buddy, entirely accurate as feminist critique of patriar-chal presumption. Then Joan came along and shouldered the burden of man-hater and feminist, leaving Esther free of those damning associations with penis-envy. Esther's – and Plath's – crude use of doubles as deniability- dummies (Hilda's the bitch; Doreen's the nymphomaniac; Joan's the lesbian) shows how naïvely pragmatic their version of psychic housekeeping could be. The cattiness of competitive femininity in adolescence, so richly documented in the writing of Sylvia Plath, is measure of the vast instability of femininity as identity. Other women threaten and must be discounted before the One Right Man can come to the rescue.

Joan's lesbianism is made doubly threatening because Esther 'sees' it unclosed and unapologized for when she walks in on Joan and DeeDee in bed (just as Jane Anderson felt most threatened when she saw it on the big screen). And then it is uncriticized by her psychiatrist.

> "I don't see what women see in other women," I'd told Doctor Nolan in my interview that noon. "What does a woman see in a woman that she can't see in a man?"
> Doctor Nolan paused. Then she said, "Tenderness."
> That shut me up. (246–7)

Failing to secure psychiatric reinforcement for her defences (too bad Jane Anderson wasn't practising then), Esther falls back on dismissive stereotypes. When Joan tells Esther, 'I like you better than Buddy' (247), Esther's response is to conjure up collegiate lesbian stereotypes such as 'a stumpy old classical scholar with a cropped Dutch cut' (247), before telling Joan, 'You make me puke' and 'leaving Joan lying, lumpy as an old horse, across my bed' (248), and heading *straight* for the doctor for birth control, 'buying my freedom' (249), then straight to the Widener library 'to find the proper sort of man' (251) to complete her identity statement in no uncertain terms. Joan, later receiving the bleeding bride from the gallantly 'impersonal' Irwin, does not understand what happened and believes Esther's lie (about her period) because 'My going to bed with Irwin was utterly incomprehensible to her' (260). While meant as a commentary on lesbian dim-wittedness, Esther's deceit actually defends the boundary between the two sexualities, making her heterosexuality impenetrable, so to speak, to lesbianism. Joan finds heterosexuality 'utterly incomprehensible' and Esther finds lesbian sex unimaginable: 'I could never really imagine what they would be actually doing' (247).

But it is Esther's intercourse, as an act of sexual desire, much less a convincing proof of heterosexual identity, that needs explanation. The incident actually confirms Joan's point about men's ignorance of women, and Dr Nolan's about women's tenderness. Irwin is a cold and calculating jerk, the intercourse is painful and results in Esther's violent haemorrhaging, the blood is mopped by a naïve female friend. Esther's mother's moral about the Bungling Husband is proved as well, to the moral if not sexual satisfaction of the abandoned wife. Is this Esther's point too? 'How does this experience change her?' Sylvia Plath asked in her journal when planning the novel – a question she leaves unanswered. Here Plath's limitations as novelist resemble Esther's as heroine. Like schoolgirls they treat experience as a test – 'Would I pass, keep myself intact?' (Plath 1983:306) Pencils sharpened, girls? Never dull.

Esther's initiation replays the plot of the impersonal male expert's instrumentality and the female victim's 'It's-only-my-blood' self-sacrifice as her 'part of a great tradition' (*258*). Irwin is expert on several scores: a 'full professor', a 'boy genius' (*256–7*), 'somebody quite experienced to make up for my lack of it' (*257*), and 'a kind of impersonal, priestlike official, as in the tales of tribal rites' (*257*). This is the moral of the gender system interconnecting Esther's experience of medicine, sexual relations and mental health: Esther's body is 'fixed' by an impersonal male.

'Ever since I'd learned about the corruption of Buddy Willard my virginity weighed like a millstone around my neck' (*257*). As a competitive rejoinder to male privilege and presumption, Esther's satisfaction comes from scoring her point (sexual 'equality') and demystifying the game (a lustless and loveless operation endured but not enjoyed). She defies her mother yet ends up sharing her martyred, pleasureless femininity. She defines herself as part of her generation: sexually active outside marriage, rebelliously unromantic about sex, using birth control so pregnancy is no longer the coercive 'big stick' enforcing dependence in marriage. Freedom from the 'millstone' of chastity and the 'big stick' of unwanted pregnancy are two of the most basic rights on the feminist bill of rights, with freedom from economic dependence on a man a necessary third. Esther heroically claims all three.

But being her 'own woman' within the gender system of the 1950s still rests on her unrevised assumption that femininity is awarded by a man's attention, and that women without men become – or are – horsey, lumpy, stumpy, 'gargoyles': the spinster and the lesbian virtually identical in dumpy deviation from the eye-batting norm. 'Not to be bitter', Plath counsels herself at Cambridge among the dons. 'Save me from that, that final wry sour lemon acid in the veins of single clever lonely women' (Plath 1983:125). At the same time her dependence on men does not seem to empower her either. 'Is it some dread lack which makes my alternatives so deadly? Some feeble dependence on men which makes me throw myself on their protection and care and tenderness?' (Plath 1983:140) she asks, again accepting the cultural norm of female 'lack'.

In her journal in 1959, Sylvia Plath is married and pregnant with her first child when she contemplates the character of the lesbian poet May Swenson: 'Independent, self-possessed M.S. Ageless. Bird-watching before breakfast. What does she find for herself? Chess games. My old admiration for the strong, if lesbian, woman. The relief of limitation as a price for balance and surety' (Plath 1983:327). How did *she* escape the debt-ridden state of femininity, so in need of credit from a man? Lesbianism is supposed to be stunting, self-limitation causing its own unhappiness if not self-destruction. How can she be strong and self-possessed, balanced and sure, when she is lacking the necessary for fulfilment, the man and child who fertilize woman's 'growth'? Plath's search for evidence of lesbian sterility finds only her own unaccountable lack of fulfilment. She resolves to 'work to be a person worthy' of her male partner, her debits nagging her into achievement. Always behind, pedalling furiously to keep herself up.

'She was what came from higher education – a lonely, unfulfilled middle-aged spinster' (Hall 1951:112). *The Well of Loneliness* (1951, first published 1928) bluntly states the Career Woman stereotype, in this case the heroine's tutor. Perhaps Radclyffe Hall's lesbian horsewoman heroine provided Plath with a role model for Joan Giddings. Certainly Joan is designed to show the de-feminization caused by academic abstraction and athletics: 'A physics major and the college hockey champion. . . . She was as big as a horse, too' (*65*). Esther rushes to differentiate herself, though she like Joan lacks 'second dates', key indicators of 1950s femininity-failure; what did He see in the first date that scared him off? 'I didn't think I deserved it', Esther defends herself. 'After all, I wasn't crippled in any way, I just studied too hard, I didn't know when to stop' (*64*). As Plath later described her own 'problem', 'I was just too dangerously brainy' (Plath 1980:54).

Helene Deutsch's *The Psychology of Women* (1944) explains the danger in brains: 'All observations point to the fact that the intellectual woman is masculinized; in her, warm intuitive knowledge has yielded to cold unproductive thinking' (Deutsch 1944:291). When the mental health thermometer detects Arctic frigidity where bosomy intuition should be, diagnosis suggests dreaded Oedipal irregularities in need of psychiatric correction. Deutsch's ideas of femininity are of course not merely fashion tips but prescriptions for psychic processes that sound very much like homework assignments, especially to the ears of precocious students of psychology:

> Thus the task of adolescence is not only to master the Oedipus complex, but also to continue the work begun during prepuberty and early puberty, that is, to give adult forms to the old, much deeper, and much more primitive ties with the mother, and to end all bisexual wavering in favor of a definite heterosexual orientation.
>
> (Hirsch 1989:101)

Libidos aimed and ready, girls?

The Bell Jar's three psychiatrists suggest Plath's own norms of mental health and gender. The stupid man fails to understand his female patient. Esther's smart woman heals her without seducing her. Joan's suspiciously 'shrewd, single lady' (*252*) brainwashes her into following her footsteps into psychiatry, as in an older-lesbian seduction and replication plot: That's how they reproduce themselves! As a physics major and lesbian Joan has already announced her unfeminine interests; then Plath underscores the connections between Joan's cold thinking and her careerism through Joan's psychiatrist: she 'had an abstract quality that appealed to Joan, but it gave me the polar chills' (*252*). Esther's shrink is, in contrast, 'a cross between Myrna Loy and my mother. She wore a white blouse and a full skirt gathered at the waist by a wide leather belt, and stylish, crescent-shaped spectacles' (*210*). No hint of the mannish Girl Scout leader here, with those threatening 'flat brown leather shoes with fringed tongues lapping down over the front that are supposed to be so sporty' (*212*). Dr Nolan is Esther's idea of a smart woman, both spectacled and stylish, and scientific enough to be unmaternal, safe: untentacled, unseductive, no tongues lapping down over her clean white blouse.

'I would guess that she was late to mature, and frigid' (Kenner 1979:41–2). Plath, this is, as the critic Hugh Kenner read her through *The Colossus*. 'I have you typed, baby. You'll be a prude at forty' (*164*). Esther, this is, as one of her blind dates analysed her kisses. The Freudian frigidity vs. femininity problem was the real threat for collegiate women, the strongest motivation to renounce brains for intuition, career for normalcy. *The Bell Jar* enacts this Freudian moralism all too crudely on Esther and Joan in relation to their sexuality. Plath promotes Esther when she passes the test of definite hetero-sexual orientation, her sexuality the key to being psychiatrically 'approved for the road' (*275*) by the experts. Plath destroys Joan through self-strangulation, convicting her sexually of twistedness, and therapeutically of a developmental dead-end, suicide her own recognition of failure.

Jane Anderson in 1987 explained the threat she seemed to represent to Plath: 'I think she perceived me as someone who found the strength and could tolerate the isolation' of being a career woman in the 1950s (*Gazette* 1987). Anderson went on to medical school from Smith, rather than putting a husband through medical school as the tradition had it. 'She wanted to get rid of me and what I represented' (*Gazette* 1987) as Anderson reads her role in *The Bell Jar*. Her threat was not lesbianism, but successful careerism. Certainly Jane Anderson's scaling the peaks of male power in Harvard Medical School and psychiatry are as instrumentally and scientifically successful as one could be in the world of *The Bell Jar*, a woman could not prove herself any more competitive than that.

The lesbian character from this angle looks like a dis-crediting cover for the real threat, being 'alone in our giftedness', as Anderson described herself and Plath growing up (*Gazette* 1987). The strength to tolerate the isolation of Career Woman as Plath and her culture understood that – *the Woman Alone* – was Jane Anderson's life success and Sylvia Plath's life's failure, in Anderson's implied reading.

For Plath, brains were always so dangerous as to threaten everything else. 'Dangerous brains', 'without proper extra-curricular tempering' (dates, marriage, children) 'might snap me into the void' (Plath 1980:54), as Plath wrote about her education. Her solution is the opposite of Anderson's single-minded path into the void of brainland, no husband, children or apple pies in sight. Plath went for All-Round perfection, which meant appealing to the standards of those all round her, teachers and husband and big-name poets and grant-givers and magazine editors and mother and mentors. 'I grabbed my cue', she says (Plath 1980:54), from the test itself, from those administering the test, and strove to pass according to their standards. What good girls this produces: 'The best little third graders in the world', as a member of her generation described herself (Eisler 1986:182). So Esther in the last sentence of *The Bell Jar* grabs her cue from the psychiatric tribunal at the doorway out of the mental hospital, 'guiding myself by them, as by a magical thread' (*275*).

Once married, Plath looks back into this void:

> How did I ever live in those barren, desperate days of dating, experimenting, hearing Mother warn me I was too critical, that I set my sights too high and would be an old maid. Well, perhaps I would have been if Ted hadn't been born. I am, at bottom, simple, credulous, feminine and loving to be mastered, cared for.
>
> (Plath 1983:212)

The clichés spring forth thick and fast: 'that passionate and spiritual love is the only thing on earth worth having', 'I feel, miraculously, I have the impossible, the wonderful – I am perfectly at one with Ted, body and soul, as the ridiculous song says' (Plath 1983:212). Through journal entry and letter, the same theme is endlessly constructed through the opposition of the 'barren, desperate' manless woman and the 'feminine and loving to be mastered' wife. 'Too critical' is diagnosed as the problem, 'simple, credulous' the solution, the passivity and subordination 'loved' as her part in the deal.

What was actually involved in making this fabulous marriage deal is tellingly detailed in Plath's journal about the night she met – and marked – Ted Hughes at the party for a new Cambridge literary review published that day. Her perception of the role of gender in the *St Botolph's Review*, which had published Hughes' poetry and criticized her own, led to her precocious 'solution' to this problem of male published poet vs.

female-as-body. Plath's journal's narrative begins with Plath's pique that her poetry has been criticized. Next she describes how she secured Hughes' attention by quoting from his poem just published. Then she elicits Hughes' consolation for the criticism of her poetry, Hughes 'saying Dan knew I was beautiful, he wouldn't have written it about a cripple' (the compliment to her body compensates for one to her poetry?), 'and my yelling protest in which the words "sleep with the editor" occurred with startling frequency' (Plath 1983:112–13). How to get published if a woman? She *protests* her body as the currency. 'And then it came to the fact that I was all there, wasn't I, and I stamped and screamed yes . . .' which means bodily there, granting access: 'And when he kissed my neck I bit him long and hard on the cheek, and when we came out of the room, blood was running down his face' (Plath 1983:113). She exacts her fee, publicly marking 'the only one there huge enough for me' (Plath 1983:112) as hers, his access matched by her access – to body but through body to publication. 'It is as if Ted were my representative in the world of men' (Plath 1983:293) Plath writes a few years later, and in terms of the London literary world, a male marker assured access of a kind not available to the cripple, the poetess hobbled by the 'ess' around her ankle.

Plath's pragmatism as a poet and wife has been amply noted, but her pragmatism about her own psychic housekeeping demands further attention, revealing as it does the relationship between social world (*St Botolph's Review* as a microcosm of the literary world) and a woman's most intimate reading of her own body and mind.

We come back to the symbolism of the shock treatments once again, male instrumentality seeming to have the last word over the woman's mute body. But Plath thinks of a way to make her word, and her experience, into the means of literary access to the male review. 'I thought about the shock treatment description last night' (Plath 1983:113) – meaning either at or after the party, Plath writes in her journal the next day. After describing the party and how she met Hughes, already designated 'the one man' for her (Plath 1983:113), she plots her next move in her next paragraph. 'I shall write a detailed description of shock treatment, tight, blasting short descriptions with not one smudge of coy sentimentality, and when I get enough I shall send them to David Ross', the editor of *St Botolph's Review*. 'There will be no hurry, because I am too desperately vengeful now' (Plath 1983:113), she wisely counsels herself. The manly material of shock treatment, tightly blasted forth in manly style, would surely gain admittance where female sentiment and (penis-envying) desperation are barred. The story itself, as she goes on to shape it, is the story of a woman symbolically killed by madness, 'the deadly sleep of her madness', and after 'electrocution [is] brought in, and the inevitable going down the subterranean hall, waking to a new world, with no name, being born again, and not of woman' (Plath 1983:113).

Not of woman: the erasure of her woman's life, and her mother's whence she came, and her rebirth like Athena from Zeus's brow – thunderbolts and all – is all too directly designed to appeal to 'the god-eyed tall-minded ones' guarding the gates of literary heaven. Purge the mind, purge the body, of the 'smudge' of femininity, and join the rarefied discourse of poetry. Adrienne Rich explains the idea of their time: 'I still believed that poets were inspired by some transcendent authority and spoke from some extraordinary height.' This involved 'trying to think and act as if poetry – and the possibility of making poems – were a truly universal – that is, gender-neutral – realm' (Heilbrun 1989:66). While confiding her strategy as a writer in regard to this particular impasse, Plath reveals an interpretation of her shock treatments that *The Bell Jar* hasn't the nerve to say. Plath's journal suggests that the purge of the shock treatments is a purge of the 'smudge' of womanhood itself, in its twin faces of 'coy sentimentality' and 'desperate vengeance'.

In the gendered world of *The Bell Jar*, Esther's 'purge' can be seen as a pragmatic 'solution' to her numerous problems with womanhood, including matrophobia, the lesbian threat, the 'big stick' of pregnancy, the even bigger stick of subordination and shaming of women in heterosexuality, and the limitations of being a literary woman in the world of literary men.

Esther's purge takes its meaning from the unpurged women around her, 'stewing in [their] own sour air' (*209*) of embittered femininity, imprisoned by unfulfilled female desire (no men want them), trapped by the female body unsaved, unrescued, *untransformed*. When Esther returns from her first successful 'purge' by electro-shock, she likens Joan to a horse and DeeDee a cat. Both are actually potentially powerful images of desire and will and sensuality – as Plath went on to show about the woman/horse in her ever-so-sexy poem 'Ariel' – but this possibility is precisely the threat, embodied as the lesbian threat of female desire, announcing its bestial tastes unselfconsciously. Esther reduces these images to negatives, lacks: all body, no mind, all animal, no humanity, and all too definitively rejected by men. 'I thought how sad it was Joan looked so horsey', Esther says, and then turns to dismiss Joan's partner: 'And DeeDee's husband was obviously living with some mistress or other and turning her sour as an old fusty cat' (*243*). Lesbian Otherness is underscored when she likens Joan to 'a Martian, or a particularly warty toad' (*246*) – take your pick.

Esther, ever the exception, has found a way to insure her exceptional female fate, her escape from all the fusty feline envy, her catty comments to the contrary. She interprets electro-shock as having purged her of the sour claustrophobia of the feline cat-box, the body stinking with its own unmet needs. 'All the heat and fear had purged itself' (*242*) when Esther is reborn. 'The bell jar hung, suspended, a few feet above my head. I was open to the circulating air' (*242*). Her 'head' cleared of feline 'heat', she has access to literary circulation, aspiration, inspiration, the rarefied 'air' outside the domestic box.

Plath's adolescent description of her own sexual desire, unsatisfied on dates, is overcast with images of sickness and drowning, a pathology of unfulfilled female desire, in contrast to 'the boys who can dispel sexual hunger freely, without misgiving, and be whole, while I drag out from date to date in soggy desire, always unfulfilled. The whole thing sickens me' (Plath 1983:15). In *The Bell Jar*, Esther's reaction to Doreen's breast-popping dance with the cowboy deejay is similarly one of female-sickness in need of a purge. Esther is purged by a bath, restoring her to the purity of a baby. Doreen is only half-purged by 'a jet of brown vomit', right at Esther's feet outside her door. When she passes out, Esther abandons her there, 'an ugly, concrete testimony to my own dirty nature' (24–5).

Esther's need of a 'purge' in order to feel her self 'growing pure again' (22) defines her central identity process. First is her ambitious immersion in experience – in the magazine, in the shark pool of Manhattan, in female friendships, in dating, in the suburban world of women as mothers, in psychotherapy, in mental hospital life. Then the impasse is encountered, revealing her limited control over the terms of achievement and reward. Drastic measures – often bloody and self-destructive – seem necessary to reassert her exceptional status, as others settle for compromise, for sticky kisses, for being kitchen mats, for equine careerism, for myopic spinsterism.

The violent purges of self Esther undergoes again and again in *The Bell Jar* culminate in The Big Purge, heterosexual initiation defining her as her 'own woman', and burying at once the lesbian and suicide threat. A student of mine once identified the crux of female adolescence as the moment when 'everything that was wrong with her life was to be made right by a man'. Heterosexual initiation is the 'crucible' in which all womanly lacks and wrongs and impurities are superheated and purified by the Right Man.

Sylvia Plath's heroine emerges from her nervous breakdown cleansed, cured and unencumbered. The claims of her mother, her boyfriend and her lesbian girlfriend have all been purged. As in her mentor Olive Higgins Prouty's novel *Now, Voyager*, Esther is a dutiful daughter who 'finally finds escape from the domination of her mother through doors opened by a nervous breakdown' (Robinson 1984:15). With her psychiatrist's encouragement and medical access to birth control, and Mrs Guinea's money, Esther becomes a sexually liberated woman who declares herself free from the spell of Buddy Willard and marriage as her necessary goal. 'Sex without the probability of marriage expressed the outermost limits of existential heroism', as Benita Eisler describes the norm at

Smith in the 1950s (Eisler 1986:137). When Buddy asks, apropos of Joan's and Esther's suicide attempts after dating him, 'Do you think there's something in me that *drives* women crazy?', Esther bursts out laughing, remembers Dr Nolan's assurance that Joan alone was responsible for her own suicide, and answers, 'You had nothing to do with us, Buddy' (*270*). Taking charge of her own nervous breakdown and recovery is on the face of it a kind of feminist agency, a declaration of independence from the interests of men. The female psychiatrists and sponsors and supporting cast of nurses and patients underline this point.

But Esther's claim for female agency, against female victimhood at men's hands, literally *denies the problem* when Esther says that Buddy had nothing to do with it. *The Bell Jar* actually shows every aspect of the gendered social system 'in' the disingenuous Buddy 'that drives women crazy'. Plath means to give us Esther as heroine. But the deeply despised details of female life and character littering Esther's triumphant exit from the women's ward are not the stuff of feminist heroism but of disguised self-hatred.

'She's mad because she's a woman', a boy tells the heroine of *Cat's Eye*, Margaret Atwood's novel. 'This is something I hadn't heard for years, not since high school [in the 1950s]. Once it was a shaming thing to say, and crushing to have it said about you, by a man. It implied oddness, deformity, malfunction' (Atwood 1988:362–3). In the world of *The Bell Jar*, feminist anger turns inward and becomes female 'mad'ness, self-hatred of the casualty of femininity.

Such 'rebirth' as Esther's through shock treatment and analysis and heterosexual initiation, unaccompanied by her own re-vision of the meaning of gender relations, wipes the slate clean only to prepare it for the exact same message. Feminism demands re-vision, as Adrienne Rich – Plath's contemporary – wrote:

> Re-vision – the act of looking back, of seeing with fresh eyes, of entering an old text from a new critical direction – is for women more than a chapter in cultural history: it is an act of survival.

Until we can understand the assumptions in which we are
drenched we cannot know ourselves.

(Rich 1979:35)

Esther's rebirth, at the cost of Joan's suicide, simply retells the
old mother–daughter sacrificial victim story, with no shift in
point of view signalling new female agency born of feminist
re-vision. The despised woman in *The Bell Jar* has her neck
wrung and her body buried. She's bound to haunt.

BIBLIOGRAPHY

Atwood, M. (1988) *Cat's Eye*, New York: Doubleday.

Bailey, B. (1988) *From Front Porch to Back Seat: Courtship in Twentieth-Century America*, Baltimore, Md and London: Johns Hopkins University Press.

Benjamin, J. (1988) *The Bonds of Love: Psychoanalysis, Feminism, and the Problem of Domination*, New York: Pantheon.

Bernstein, C. (1989) *Loyalties*, New York: Simon & Schuster.

Boss, P. and Thorne, B. (1989) 'Family sociology and family therapy: a feminist linkage', in M. McGoldrick, C. Anderson and F. Walsh (eds) *Women in Families: A Framework for Family Therapy*, New York: Norton.

Breines, W. (1986) 'Alone in the 1950s: Anne Parsons and the feminine mystique', in *Theory and Society* 15:805–43, Dordrecht, the Netherlands: Martinus Nijhoff Publishers.

Browning, E. (1978) *Aurora Leigh*, London: Women's Press.

Carter, E. (1984) 'Alice in the consumer wonderland', in A. McRobbie and M. Nava (eds) *Gender and Generation*, London: Macmillan.

Condon, R. (1959) *The Manchurian Candidate*, New York: McGraw-Hill.

Deutsch, H. (1944) *The Psychology of Women* vol. 1, New York: Grune & Stratton.

Duvall, E. (1956) *Facts of Life and Love for Teen-Agers*, New York: Popular Library.

Ehrenreich, B. (1989) *Fear of Falling: The Inner Life of the Middle Class*, New York: Pantheon.

Bibliography

Ehrenreich, B. and English, D. (1979) *For Her Own Good: 150 Years of the Experts' Advice to Women*, Garden City, NY: Anchor Books.

Eisler, B. (1986) *Private Lives: Men and Women of the Fifties*, New York: Franklin Watts.

Friedan, B. (1963) *The Feminine Mystique*, New York: Norton.

Gazette, 3 February 1987.

Guardian, 3 February 1987.

Hall, R. (1951) *The Well of Loneliness*, Garden City, New York: Permabooks.

Heilbrun, C. (1989) *Writing a Woman's Life*, New York: Ballantine.

Hine, T. (1987) *Populuxe*, New York: Knopf.

Hirsch, M. (1989) *The Mother/Daughter Plot*, Bloomington, Ind: Indiana University Press.

Jackson, S. (1951) *Hangsaman*, New York: Farrar, Straus & Young.

Kenner, H. (1979) 'Sincerity kills', in G. Lane (ed.) *Sylvia Plath: New Views on the Poetry*, Baltimore, Md and London: Johns Hopkins University Press.

Lessing, D. (1984) 'Impertinent daughters', in *Granta* 14, Harmondsworth: Granta Publications.

Luepnitz, D. (1988) *The Family Interpreted: Feminist Theory in Clinical Practice*, New York: Basic Books.

Lundberg, F. and Farnham, M. (1947) *Modern Woman: The Lost Sex*, New York: Harper Brothers.

McCann, G. (1988) *Marilyn Monroe*, New Brunswick, NJ: Rutgers University Press.

McCarthy, M. (1951) 'Up the ladder from *Charm* to *Vogue*', in *On the Contrary*, New York: Noonday Press, Farrar, Straus & Co. *Mademoiselle*, August 1953.

May, E. (1988) *Homeward Bound: American Families in the Cold War Era*, New York: Basic Books.

Miller, A. (1976) *The Crucible*, New York: Penguin.

Miller, A. (1987) *Timebends*, New York: Grove Press.

Munro, A. (1990) *Friend of My Youth*, New York: Knopf.

New York Times, 28 January 1987.

Plath, S. (1971) *The Bell Jar*, New York: Harper & Row.

Bibliography

Plath, S. (1975) *Letters Home*, New York: Harper & Row.

Plath, S. (1980) *Johnny Panic and the Bible of Dreams*, New York: Harper & Row.

Plath, S. (1981) *The Collected Poems*, New York: Harper & Row.

Plath, S. (1983) *The Journals of Sylvia Plath*, New York: Ballantine.

Rich, A. (1977) *Of Woman Born: Motherhood as Experience and Institution*, New York: Bantam.

Robinson, C. (1984) *Now, Voyager* (screenplay), Madison, Wis: University of Wisconsin Press.

Rogin, M. (1984) 'Kiss Me Deadly: Communism, motherhood, and cold war movies', in *Representations* 6, Spring 1984, Regents of the University of California.

Sayre, N. (1982) *Running Time: Films of the Cold War*, New York: Dial Press.

Schneir, W. and Schneir, M. (1983) *Invitation to an Inquest*, New York: Pantheon.

Schrecker, E. (1986) *No Ivory Tower: McCarthyism and the Universities*, New York: Oxford University Press.

Shook, M. (1988) 'Sylvia Plath: the poet and the college', in L. Wagner (ed.) *Sylvia Plath: The Critical Heritage*, London and New York: Routledge.

Spock, B. (1945) *The Common Sense Book of Baby and Child Care*, New York: Duell, Sloan & Pearce.

Steedman, C. (1982) *The Tidy House: Little Girls Writing*, London: Virago.

Steiner, N. (1973) *A Closer Look at Ariel: A Memory of Sylvia Plath*, New York: Popular Library.

Time, 9 February 1987.

Vanity Fair, March 1989.

Voices and Visions: Sylvia Plath (1988) videotape dir. and prod. by L. Pitkethly, Annenberg CPB Project, Washington, DC.

von Hoffman, N. (1988) *Citizen Cohn*, New York: Bantam.

Wagner-Martin, L. (1987) *Sylvia Plath: A Biography*, New York: Simon and Schuster.

Walker, J. (1987) 'Hollywood, Freud and the representation of women: regulation and contradiction, 1945–early 60s', in C. Gledhill (ed.) *Home is Where the Heart is: Studies in Melodrama and the Woman's Film*, London: British Film Institute.

Warren, C. (1987) *Madwives: Schizophrenic Women in the 1950s*, New Brunswick, NJ and London: Rutgers University Press.

White, B. (1985) *Growing Up Female: Adolescent Girlhood in American Fiction*, Westport, Conn. and London: Greenwood Press.

Williams, L. (1987) '"Something else besides a mother": *Stella Dallas* and the maternal melodrama', in C. Gledhill (ed.) *Home is Where the Heart is: Studies in Melodrama and the Woman's Film*, London: British Film Institute.

Williams, R. (1984) *Orwell*, London: Fontana.

EVIDENCE-BASED SCHOOL
LEADERSHIP AND
MANAGEMENT

Sara Miller McCune founded SAGE Publishing in 1965 to support the dissemination of usable knowledge and educate a global community. SAGE publishes more than 1000 journals and over 800 new books each year, spanning a wide range of subject areas. Our growing selection of library products includes archives, data, case studies and video. SAGE remains majority owned by our founder and after her lifetime will become owned by a charitable trust that secures the company's continued independence.

Los Angeles | London | New Delhi | Singapore | Washington DC | Melbourne

EVIDENCE-BASED SCHOOL LEADERSHIP AND MANAGEMENT

A Practical Guide

GARY JONES

Los Angeles | London | New Delhi
Singapore | Washington DC | Melbourne

Los Angeles | London | New Delhi
Singapore | Washington DC | Melbourne

SAGE Publications Ltd
1 Oliver's Yard
55 City Road
London EC1Y 1SP

SAGE Publications Inc.
2455 Teller Road
Thousand Oaks, California 91320

SAGE Publications India Pvt Ltd
B 1/I 1 Mohan Cooperative Industrial Area
Mathura Road
New Delhi 110 044

SAGE Publications Asia-Pacific Pte Ltd
3 Church Street
#10-04 Samsung Hub
Singapore 049483

Editor: James Clark
Editorial assistant: Diana Alves
Production editor: Nicola Carrier
Copyeditor: Elaine Leek
Proofreader: Lynda Watson
Indexer: Gary Kirby
Marketing manager: Dilhara Attygalle
Cover design: Naomi Robinson
Typeset by: C&M Digitals (P) Ltd, Chennai, India
Printed in the UK

Library of Congress Control Number: 2018935960
British Library Cataloguing in Publication data

A catalogue record for this book is available from
the British Library

ISBN 978-1-5264-1167-9
ISBN 978-1-5264-1168-6 (pbk)

At SAGE we take sustainability seriously. Most of our products are printed in the UK using responsibly sourced
papers and boards. When we print overseas we ensure sustainable papers are used as measured by the PREPS
grading system. We undertake an annual audit to monitor our sustainability.

CONTENTS

ABOUT THE AUTHOR

Dr **Gary Jones** has been involved in education for over thirty years and has extensive experience as a senior leader. Gary has a doctorate in educational management from the University of Bristol, with his dissertation focusing on the use of school development plans in primary schools. Gary has written extensively about educational leadership in his blog *Evidence Based Educational Leadership:* https://evidencebasededucationalleadership.blogspot.com

Gary is a Fellow of the Center for Evidence-Based Management and is also an associate of the Expansive Education Network based at the University of Winchester, where he supports teachers engaging in evidence-based practice.

In recent years Gary has spoken about evidence-based school leadership at a number of conferences both in the United Kingdom and abroad – including Sydney, Melbourne, New York, Washington DC and Gothenburg.

ACKNOWLEDGEMENTS

To my editor, James Clark for his patience and guidance, along with everyone at Sage who has helped put the book into production.

To my family Fina, Philippa and Milly who provided endless encouragement and support.

Finally – if this book has any merits it is down to others, if it has any faults it is the responsibility of the author.

FOREWORD

When it comes to evidence-informed practice, Dr Gary Jones is a phenomenon. An ardent and assiduous blogger, unrelenting member of the twitterati and researchED stalwart, Gary's efforts in getting the message across to educators and policy-makers that research use is the future for schools have in some cases been (to quote one tweet) 'literally life changing'. With this book Gary has begun to flesh out and develop his ideas into a manifesto for change. And a timely manifesto it is too. As you are likely to be aware – indeed it is probably the reason that led you to pick up this book in the first place – evidence-informed practice in education is a hot topic, not only in England but worldwide. It is also fair to say that the current focus on evidence-informed teaching is justified. Recent studies have shown for instance that, when done well, collaborative research use by teachers can improve their confidence, resilience and pedagogy, enhance the professional discourse that occurs in schools and enable effective practice not only to be developed, but also shared and acted on widely. Vitally, however, effective engagement with research evidence by teachers has been shown to impact positively on student outcomes (most notably at Key Stage 2).

Despite these benefits, the current focus on encouraging teachers to engage with research evidence and, of course, the moral argument that teachers should always try to ensure they are abreast of and employ what is currently known to be effective, we are not yet at the point where we have an evidence-informed schools system (either here or elsewhere in the world). The reasons for this are manifold and include well-rehearsed arguments regarding: the use, value and applicability of much research; teachers' ability to access research – not only because much of what academics and universities produce is stored behind paywalls, but also because of the language in which it is written; mismatches in research priorities (with academic interests not always coinciding with those of teachers, schools and policy-makers); and the generalisability of much education research, which often is qualitative in nature or focuses on small numbers of cases. These issues are not insurmountable however, and Gary's book does a sterling job in helping teachers and school leaders navigate through many of them. In particular and vitally, it provides an accessible way for educators to understand and engage critically with research and other pertinent evidence. Most helpfully perhaps, Gary has provided crucial guidance on how we can understand research quality and what warrants for action we can truly make from different forms of research.

Gary's work also goes beyond what much of the literature in this area focuses on, however. Knowing the vital but often indirect importance of school leadership for pupil outcomes, as well as having an acute understanding of the many ways leaders can improve on how they make decisions, Gary highlights that, more than just evidence-informed practice, school leaders should be fostering, encouraging and engaging in evidence-informed decision-making more generally. This book therefore serves to broaden the evidence-informed horizon in ways many others have currently failed to do. Considering leadership in the round therefore, the implications of Gary's work are that, whatever our position in school and whatever responsibilities we have in addition to teaching, we should be continuously considering whether and how we can engage with colleagues more effectively through engaging with pertinent and high-quality research-evidence.

Of course, only time will tell if those who believe in the power of research use can ensure evidence-informed decision-making will end up as the norm, but as more and more schools become academies or become part of multi-academy trusts, it seems sensible that with the freedom to make decisions and innovate that this entails, schools should attempt to do so as effectively as possible. I commend Gary for the way he has gone about writing this book, the intention behind it and its helpfulness and accessibility. It has been a joy to see it come to fruition and I hope you enjoy reading it as much as I have.

Professor Chris Brown
University of Portsmouth

INTRODUCTION

I shall begin this book with a 'trigger warning'. If you are reading this book with the expectation that it will provide a comprehensive summary of the research evidence on either school leadership or effective teaching and learning, then you will be disappointed. My aims are somewhat different. I want to:

1. Provide guidance to school leaders – at whatever level – as to how they can go about evidence-based decision-making.
2. Encourage school leaders to use evidence-based practice beyond the classroom, and show how it can be applied to all aspects of the work in a school.

3. Provide school leaders with access to a range of techniques and approaches which can help them engage more critically with multiple sources of evidence.
4. Provoke discussion as to what it looks like to lead an evidence-based school.

As such, this book is informed by the following rationale, which has been developed from the work of Brown and Zhang (2017) and Neeleman (2017):

- Around the world, school leaders have both increasing levels of autonomy and range of responsibilities in decision-making along-side growing pressure to bring about increases in both the efficiency and effectiveness of schools. Furthermore, there is an increasing evidence base as to 'what works', not just in education but also in leadership and management.
- However, there is a research–practice/knowing–doing gap result-ing in leadership and management decisions in schools not being informed by the best available evidence – be it research, stake-holder views, organisational data and practitioner expertise.
- Accordingly, school leaders should adopt a structured approach to evidence-based school leadership and management – which incorporates all domains of the role of the leaders – be it educa-tional, the school as organisation, and staff.
- By using research and other sources of evidence this should pro-vide school leaders with increased levels of knowledge and understanding of the educational, organisational and staffing domains of the school.
- This learning will impact upon school leaders' professional judge-ment, and the awareness of the availability of teaching and leadership strategies in the classroom and other settings.
- This should lead to improved decision-making resulting in an increased likelihood of improved pupils' outcomes (cognitive and emotive), staff well-being and organisational sustainability.

Who is the intended audience of this book?

This booked is aimed at anyone who has an interest in either school leadership or evidence-based practice. Aspiring leaders may find the book helpful, as it provides an introduction to some of the key issues associated with evidence-based practice. Heads of department may also find the book useful as it describes a number of simple techniques which are relevant to day-to-day leadership and management. School research leads and champions will find the book useful as it provides a primer into how to help colleagues critically appraise research evidence. School business managers will gain insights into how evidence-based practice in schools is not limited to matters relating to teaching and learning, and extends to all aspects of the schools, including support services. Senior leaders will find that the book contains insights into how to close the gap between the 'rhetoric' and the 'reality' of evidence-based practice. Governors and trustees will also find value in the book as it shows how decision-making can often fall foul of cognitive biases, and suggests techniques that may minimise the impact of such biases. Finally, hopefully anyone who is interested in making evidence-based decisions will find something of value somewhere between the covers of the book.

How did this book come about?

This book has its origins in my blog *Evidence Based School Leadership* (https://evidencebasededucationalleadership.blogspot. com) which I began to write in the spring of 2014. Initially, the product of a 'professional disappointment' (code for not getting a senior position and a subsequent change in lifestyle) the blog was intended to provide a voice for my interest in educational leadership and management research, an interest which goes back to the formative stages of my career and masters and doctoral level study at the University of Bristol. At first, the blog was also heavily influenced by nearly 30 years of experience of working in education, where I had often seen the negative consequences of the latest teaching/managerial fad or an unwillingness to engage with the 'data' to understand performance at a system level. Unfortunately, teacher and headteacher professionalism had acted as an insufficient bulwark to these negative consequences. Indeed, my experience was that prevailing 'professional' cultures may well have contributed to the non-use of evidence, with professional 'interests' being prioritised over the needs of pupils, parents and other stakeholders.

Nevertheless, two events soon led to the blog taking a slightly different direction. First, by chance I read an article by Furnham (2014) which introduced me to work of Rob Briner, Eric Barends and Denisse Rousseau and the Center for Evidence-Based Management. This resulted in a summer of reading about the development of evidence-based practice (Barends et al., 2014) and evidence-based medicine in particular, for example, Sackett et al. (1996). Second, at the end of the year I attended a researchED one-day event, designed to support school research champions. It became immediately apparent that although there was interest and enthusiasm for the use of research in schools, there was little or no awareness about the broader evidence-based practice movement. As a result, from January 2015 the blog became focused on techniques and approaches drawn from evidence-based practice, in general, and evidence-based medicine in particular, that could be used to support both school leaders and school research leads and champions.

Since the beginning of 2015, I have written over 140 posts which have had some focus on the use of research and evidence within schools. Indeed, it is the writing of these posts that has strongly influenced the contents of this book. Nevertheless, there is no doubt that over the period of time spent writing this book my thinking about evidence-based school leadership has changed, shifting from a focus on 'what works', to a far greater awareness of how to develop the knowledge, skills and judgement to make contextual decisions about what is likely to work in a particular school, given the nature of the pupils, staff, stakeholders and available resources

Outline and content of the book

Chapter 1 begins with a discussion of the ethical case for evidence-based school leadership. This is followed by an examination of a number of additional arguments in support of evidence-based school leadership, which include: the maintaining and upholding of professional standards; reducing occurrences of unnecessary ineptitude by school leaders; making schools less vulnerable to educational fads, fashions, 'rusty' evidence and bullshit. The chapter goes on to consider the impact cognitive biases have on the decision-making process and how evidence-based practice may act as a partial counterweight to such biases. Finally, given changes in the context in which schools operate, be it increased levels of autonomy or changes in the demands for accountability, the chapter discusses why evidence-based school leadership is particularly timely.

Chapter 2 provides a comprehensive definition of evidence-based practice. This leads on to a discussion of some of the commonly held misconceptions about evidence-based practice. Next, there is an examination of some of the key terms, for example, conscientious, judicious and explicit, which are embedded in the working definition of evidence-based school leadership. The chapter concludes with a discussion of the limitations of evidence-based practice.

Chapter 3 looks at the scope of evidence-based school leadership and management. This leads on to an analysis of: what is meant by the term 'problem of practice'; how these problems of practice can be identified and prioritised; and which problems of practice are best suited to an evidence-based approach. This is followed by discussion of a number of techniques, drawn from medicine and organisational science, to help evidence-based school leaders frame and develop well-formulated questions. The chapter then looks at techniques associated with the formulation of answerable questions, which can be integrated into the day-to-day work of the school.

Chapter 4 examines the nature of various sources of scientific research, school data, practitioner expertise and stakeholder evidence, and also includes a discussion of the difference between tacit and explicit knowledge. This is followed by a review of the challenges associated with the use of the best available evidence and what criteria might be used to help identify that evidence. Subsequently guidance will be provided on how to develop an evidence search strategy for all four sources of evidence and is accompanied by a brief examination of how to distinguish between 'good, bad and ugly evidence' found on the Internet. Attention will then be given to understanding the components of both practitioners and stakeholders of theories of action. The chapter will then consider some of the internal and external data and evidence that is available about most schools. Finally, the chapter will look at a technique known as 'open to learning' conversations as a mechanism for acquiring stakeholder evidence.

Chapter 5 sets out to try to help evidence-based practitioners know when to trust expert advice, and will make use of a framework developed by Willingham (2012). This is followed by a discussion of the notion of a hierarchy of evidence, and leads on to a review of the nature of both systematic reviews and randomised controlled trials. The chapter then draws upon the work of Wallace and Wray (2016) to examine components of an argument – the claim and associated warrant – and how these can be used to appraise the quality of research. Consideration is then given to how to make the most of research, the use of abstracts and the writing of critical appraisals of research. The chapter concludes by presenting a comprehensive framework to help evidence-based school leaders judge the usefulness of research evidence.

Chapter 6 provides a brief introduction into becoming a critical reader of quantitative educational research evidence and covers topics such as: what is meant by an 'effect size'; how effect sizes are calculated; how to interpret the 'size' of an effect size; meta-analyses and their limitations. The chapter then looks at correlation and how this is often misunderstood. Next, the chapter briefly explains the terms: p-values, confidence intervals, statistical significance and highlights some of the challenges in ensuring they are interpreted correctly. The chapter concludes with a checklist of questions to be asked when seeking to interpret the quality of quantitative educational research findings.

Chapter 7 moves on to consider ways of appraising different sources of evidence. In particular the chapter looks at the challenge for evidence-based school leaders associated with using 'organisational/ school facts' to inform decision-making. Discussion then focuses on problems associated with appraising stakeholder feedback and in particular how to know when you are receiving good advice. The chapter also looks at what to do when you, as you no doubt often will, disagree with others. The chapter ends with a discussion of experience and intuition, and explores the limits of expertise, and whether intuition can be used as a trusted source of evidence.

Chapter 8 looks at the challenge of aggregating different sources of evidence. Initially, simple tables are used to aggregate research evidence, followed by more sophisticated examples found in systematic reviews. This leads on to a discussion of how the different sources of evidence – be it school data, stakeholders' views, practitioner expertise and research – can be combined. This is followed by a discussion of how logic models can help classify and organise the available evidence. The chapter concludes with a review of several approaches the evidence-based school leader can use when judging both the quality of the aggregation and the synthesis of the evidence.

Chapter 9 examines the challenges of integrating evidence into the decision-making process. Drawing upon the work of Peter Drucker, the chapter will consider a simple rule of thumb to be used when making a decision on whether to act or not. In doing so, this will lead to a brief discussion of the costs and benefits associated with educational intervention. Following on from this is an examination of some key issues associated with the decision-making; for example, the strength or otherwise of recommendations. Next, the chapter considers the impact of cognitive biases on the decision-making and strategies, and identifies strategies, such as the 'premortem', that could be adopted to minimise their impact. The last part of the chapter will begin to explore the issues associated with implementing the decision – such as the scale of implementation – and the Plan–Do–Study–Act (PDSA) cycle. Finally, attention will then focus on some of the many challenges associated with trying to implement successfully an intervention or innovation on a large scale, which will be particularly relevant to multi-academy trusts.

Chapter 10 explores the issues associated with trying to evaluate the outcome(s) of the decision that has been taken. In doing this, the chapter looks at the distinction between merit (does it work?) and worth (even if it worked, was it worth it?). The chapter then looks at a technique known as After-Action-Review, to help the busy evidence-based school leader learn from outcomes of decisions. The chapter also explores issues associated with learning from failure and how best a school can do that. There is also a brief discussion of contribution analysis and how that can be used to help evaluate decision outcomes. Finally, a checklist will be provided to help school leaders assess their performance as evidence-based practitioners.

Chapter 11 explores the difference between the rhetoric and the reality of leading the research- and evidence-based school (Coldwell et al., 2017). Next the chapter looks at a number of mechanisms that can be used to promote the capability, opportunity and motivation to use evidence. The chapter then makes extensive use of the work of Brown (2015) to help draw up a checklist that school leaders can take to help create a research and evidence-based culture within their school, with various elements being explored in some detail. Finally, the question is posed – is your school ready for evidence-based practice?

Chapter 12 brings the book to a close with a number of observations, suggestions and recommendations for individuals and organisations involved in evidence-based education – suggestions, observations and recommendations which hopefully will help close the gap between the rhetoric of evidence-based education and the reality of day-to-day life in schools.

How to read this book

The chapters in this book can either be read consecutively or as stand-alone chapters, with this depending upon your existing knowledge and understanding of evidence-based practice. Whatever way you choose to read this book, each chapter follows the same basic structure.

1. All chapters begin with a basic overview as to what is to be covered in that chapter.
2. Where at all possible, worked examples have been provided to show you how to apply some of the techniques associated with evidence-based school leadership.
3. The end of each chapter has a list of key points which summarise the contents of the chapter.

Finally, by no means should this book be seen as a definitive statement as to how to go about evidence-based school leadership. In the context of education there are still many questions to be addressed and which were highlighted in a recent UCL Institute of Education debate on evidence-informed practice (IOE, 2018). Some of the questions raised in the debate include:

- Do we really know 'what works' in education?
- Can we ever really find out 'what works' in education?
- What is the role of values in determining 'what works'?
- How do we, or indeed should we, maintain a 'broad church' of what is meant by reliable and valid educational research?
- How can educators determine whether 'what works' is something that is worth doing in the first place?

This book does not answer these questions, but should be seen as an attempt to bring together a diverse range of influences and resources to help school leaders make evidence-based decisions. If, in reading this book, you are able to find some small insight or technique into how to make decisions based on evidence rather than prejudice, fact rather than bullshit, knowledge rather than ignorance, then it will have done its job.

References

Barends, E., Rousseau, D. and Briner, R. (2014) *Evidence-Based Management:the Basic Principles*. Amsterdam: Center for Evidence-Based Management.

Brown, C. (2015) *Leading the Use of Research and Evidence in Schools*. London: IOE Press.

Brown, C. and Zhang, D. (2017) 'How can school leaders establish evidence-informed schools', *Educational Management Administration & Leadership*, 45 (3): 382–401.

Coldwell, M., Greany, T., Higgins, S., Brown, C., Maxwell, B., Stoll, L., Willis, B. and Burns, H. (2017) *Evidence-Informed Teaching: an Evaluation of Progress in England. Research Report*. London: Department for Education.

Furnham, A. (2014) 'On your head: a magic bullet for motivating staff', *The Sunday Times*, Sunday 13 July 2014.

IOE (2018) 'What works? examining the evidence on evidence-informed practice'. Blog post, 29 January 2018. https://ioelondonblog.wordpress.com/2018/01/29/what-works-examining-the-evidence-on-evidence-informed-practice/#comments (accessed 30 January 2018).

Neeleman, A.-M. (2017) *Grasping the Scope of School Autonomy: a Classification Scheme for School Policy Practice*. Stratford-upon Avon: BELMAS.

Sackett, D., Rosenberg, W., Gray, J., Haynes, R. and Richardson, W. (1996) 'Evidence based medicine: what it is and what it isn't', *BMJ, 312* (7023): 71–2.

Wallace, M. and Wray, A. (2016) *Critical Reading and Writing for Postgraduates*, 3rd edn. London: Sage.

Willingham, D. (2012) *When Can You Trust the Experts: How to Tell Good Science from Bad in Education*. San Francisco, CA: John Wiley & Sons.

1

WHY DO WE NEED EVIDENCE-BASED SCHOOL LEADERSHIP?

Chapter outline

This chapter aims to provide a clear justification to why evidence-based school leadership is needed. In doing so the chapter will look at issues related to:

- the ethics of evidence-based school leadership;
- the relationship between evidence-based school leadership, fallibility and professional standards;
- the problems of fads and faddism within education;
- how facts become 'rusty';
- the increasing role of social media and how this can leave school leaders vulnerable to bullshit;
- the impact of cognitive biases on decision-making.

> The chapter then briefly explores why evidence-based school leadership is needed now. Finally, the chapter examines some of the potential benefits of evidence-based school leadership.
>
> Key words: *evidence-based practice, decision-making, ethics, cognitive biases, professional standards*

Imagine going to the doctor because you are not feeling well. Before you had a chance to describe your symptoms, the doctor writes out a prescription and says,

> 'Take two of these three times a day, and call me next week.'
> 'But – I haven't told you what's wrong,' you say, 'How do I know this will help me?'
> 'Why wouldn't it?' says the doctor. 'It worked for my last two patients.' (Christensen and Raynor, 2003)

Consider this hypothetical situation, which has been derived from Hill et al. (2016). You are the chair of the appointment panel who is looking to appoint a new headteacher for your school. The previous headteacher resigned after two years of GCSE results being well below expectations and a disappointing Ofsted inspection. At the end of the selection process you are left with two candidates, both of whom have quite different approaches to bringing about school improvement, and you have the 'casting vote' on the selection panel. Candidate A already has experience of successfully 'turning around' two schools similar to your school, and has two very clear priorities. First to improve pupil behaviour by introducing a 'zero tolerance' approach to behaviour management and suspending and expelling pupils who do not conform. Second, to improve GCSE results as fast as they possibly can by focusing resources on Year 10 and Year 11. They plan to do this by reducing class sizes, allocating the most effective teachers to classes in Year 10 and Year 11, and introducing revision classes during the Easter break. Candidate A is very well dressed, self-assured, extremely confident in their own abilities, and says they can get the job done in two years and will then leave.

Candidate B – who is a deputy headteacher at a school not known to you – takes a different view on what is needed to bring about school improvement. Candidate B's priority is to focus on improving pupil behaviour by ensuring the curriculum offer is appropriate for different pupils, intending to develop relevant pathways for poorly behaved or performing pupils and does not intend to use a zero tolerance behaviour policy. Candidate B also wants to prioritise the creation of an all-through school by acquiring a primary school and creating a post-16 A-level provision. Candidate B also proposes to improve teaching in all year groups by introducing a substantial programme of continuing professional development, although this will only be done once both pupil behaviour has improved and a new school leadership and management structure has been implemented. Nevertheless, Candidate B acknowledges it may be at least three years before there is a major improvement in GCSE results. Candidate B, whilst being a confident and effective communicator, is far less charismatic and comes across as being very humble.

In making your decision as to whom to appoint as headteacher, what will you rely on? Experience, intuition, performance in the selection process or the advice of external experts? On this occasion, you decide to rely upon the advice of the external consultant on your selection panel, who from the very beginning of the appointment recommended the appointment of a so-called 'super head' who has a track record of turning around schools. This advice is consistent with your own intuition and 'gut feeling', which suggests Candidate A might be the 'charismatic leader' needed by the school. However, you decide not to adopt an 'evidence-based' approach as to whether Candidate A's or Candidate B's plans for the school are most likely to provide long-term success for the school. Unfortunately, this may be a major mistake.

Research by Hill et al. (2016) suggests that if you do appoint Candidate A, although after two years there may be impressive improvements in GCSE results, this will come at a significant cost to the long-term future of the school. School revenues decline as a result of a fall in pupil numbers due to a significant number of exclusions. After two years, Candidate A leaves, and GCSE results fall below their previous levels, as younger pupils who have been taught by less effective members of teaching staff move through the year groups. Hard-working, dedicated and long-serving teaching staff leave the school as they become despondent that things will only get worse as there are no resources to invest into the improvement of teaching and learning.

The local community, whose hopes have been raised by the initial improvements in the school's GCSE results, lose confidence in the new headteacher.

On the other hand, Candidate B is in all likelihood the better appointment. Although GCSE results may not improve rapidly, they do improve and continue to improve in years three, four and five of Candidate B's tenure as headteacher. A revised curriculum offer meets the needs of all pupils within the school, resulting in improved pupil behaviour, relatively few exclusions and stable school revenues. Although a number of staff leave the school on the appointment of Candidate B, those staff that do remain are committed and believe in the continued improvement and success of the school. Along with steady improvement in GCSE results, the acquisition of the primary school and the development of the sixth form provision increases the local community's confidence in the school as parents can see their commitment to their children's education from ages 4 through 18 (Hill et al., 2016).

Disappointingly, in school leadership and management, ignoring the best evidence and making decisions by relying on personal experience, intuition or the popular ideas of so-called educational experts, consultants and others is a regular occurrence. As Lewis and Caldwell (2005) state, many leadership and strategic decisions are based on 'evidence that is ill-informed, outdated, and incorrect' (p. 182). So instead of basing a decision on evidence that is ill-informed, outdated and incorrect an alternative is evidence-based school leadership.

Evidence-based school leadership helps school leaders and managers of whatever level – aspiring leaders, heads of department, senior leaders, headteachers, chief executives, governing bodies and boards of trustees – develop practical answers to important school-based problems by making use of the best available evidence. Moreover, evidence-based school leadership helps school leaders and managers make 'decisions through the conscientious, explicit and judicious use of the best available evidence from multiple sources ... to increase the likelihood of favourable outcomes' (amended from Barends et al., 2014: 2).

Chapter 2 will provide the full version of Barends et al.'s (2014) definition of evidence-based management and will help increase understanding of the 'what' and the 'how' of evidence-based school leadership. In doing so, Chapter 2 will address the unnecessary distinction between evidence-based and 'evidence-informed'. Whereas, the remainder of this chapter will follow the advice of Sinek (2009) and 'start with why' and ask two questions: one, why is evidence-based school leadership needed; two, why is evidence-based school leadership needed now?

Evidence-based school leadership as an ethical endeavour

First and foremost, evidence-based leadership is an ethical endeavour and should be seen as a way of ensuring that those practices which can lead to favourable outcomes for pupils, staff, parents and the broader community are either continued with, or introduced to the school. Alternatively, evidence-based school leadership involves ensuring that those practices which lead to unfavourable outcomes for pupils, staff, parents and the broader community are withdrawn or never introduced. Writing about evidence-based practice in health, Gambrill (2006) cites Gray (2001) who states:

> When evidence is not used during clinical practice, important failures in clinical decision-making occur: ineffective interventions are introduced; interventions that do more harm than good are introduced; interventions that do more good than harm are not introduced; and interventions that are ineffective or do more harm than good are not discontinued (Gambrill, 2006: 351).

		Practices	
		Introduced	Withdrawn
Net impact	Benefits exceed costs	Quadrant 1 NO	Quadrant 2 YES
	Costs exceed benefits	Quadrant 3 YES	Quadrant 4 NO

Figure 1.1   The consequences of the non-use of evidence-based practice

Figure 1.1 illustrates the consequences of the non-use of evidence-based practice. In Q1 there are new practices that are warranted by a comprehensive range of evidence, which are not introduced to the school due to a lack of awareness of the evidence. In Q2 there are good practices that benefit pupils and/or staff, which are withdrawn without sufficient consideration as to whether the decision is warranted. In Q3 practices have been introduced for which there is little or no evidence, but where costs clearly outweigh the benefits. Finally, in Q4 we may have practices that continue to be used – and not withdrawn – despite the costs outweighing the benefits to pupils/staff.

On the other hand, if an evidence-based practice approach is adopted then practices or innovations that have the potential to bring about improvement in 'outcomes' are more likely to be introduced. Current practice, which may be causing harm where 'costs outweigh the benefits', may be withdrawn, or innovations that have negative consequences are less likely to be introduced (see Figure 1.2). In Q1 new practices with the potential to provide benefits that exceed the costs will be introduced. In Q2 existing practices where benefits exceed costs to pupils/staff are continued with and not withdrawn. In Q3 the introduction of interventions where costs exceed the benefits is avoided, whereas in Q4, using an evidence-based approach existing practices where costs exceed the benefits are withdrawn.

		Practices	
		Introduced	Withdrawn
Net impact	Benefits exceed costs	Quadrant 1 YES	Quadrant 2 NO
	Costs exceed benefits	Quadrant 3 NO	Quadrant 4 YES

Figure 1.2 The consequences of using an evidence-based approach to practice

Indeed, one way of thinking about evidence-based school leadership is to see it as a way of ensuring practices that are detrimental to pupils and the wider school are either withdrawn or never introduced. As Carl Hendrick states: 'my view is that there is an ethical imperative to provide the best possible classroom conditions in which the students in our charge can flourish. This means rejecting what wastes time and embracing that which makes the most of it' (Hendrick and MacPherson, 2017: 11).

Evidence-based school leadership and fallibility

However, it would be wrong to think that the evidence-based school leader is infallible and things will not go wrong. There will be occasions where the evidence-based school leader makes a decision that does not lead to favourable outcomes: what is hoped will work does not; benefits that are expected to appear fail to materialise; and costs, which are anticipated to be small, escalate. As such, the evidence-based school leader may fail in what they set out to do. However, not all failures are created equal with some failures being more acceptable than others.

To help understand 'failure' Gawande (2010) draws upon Samuel Gorovitz and Alasdair MacIntyre's 1976 essay 'Toward a theory of medical fallibility', which identifies three reasons for failure. First, there is ignorance, with there being a limited understanding of what works, for example, in teaching, learning and management. Second, there is ineptitude – where the knowledge exists about what to do in certain situations, be it headteachers or other school leadership who do not apply that knowledge competently. Third, there is necessary fallibility and some things we want to do are beyond our capacity. Complex systems – such as schools – are beyond all-encompassing generalisations due to the differences in the circumstances of each individual school and complex feedback systems. In these circumstances, the best possible judgement may turn out to be incorrect – even if it is based on the best available evidence from multiple sources.

The interesting question then is: what does this mean for the practice of school leadership and management? At a simple level, it would suggest that school leaders who do not make use of the best available evidence, and avoidable mistakes are made, are leaving themselves unnecessarily open to charges of ineptitude. Perhaps another and more gentle way of putting it is that school leadership and management, at whatever level, is difficult enough without leaders unnecessarily disadvantaging themselves by denying themselves access to the best available evidence of what works, for whom, to what extent, in what context and for how long.

Evidence-based school leadership and professional ethics

The preceding discussion on ignorance, necessary fallibility and ineptitude naturally leads to a discussion of professional codes of conduct and ethics. In the context of educational leadership and management within the English education system there are professional standards that either directly or indirectly make reference to the need for evidence-based school leadership and management. Examples of some of these professional standards are summarised in Table 1.1.

Table 1.1 Professional standards relevant to school leaders and managers

Role	Relevant professional standard(s)	Standards
Headteacher	Sustains wide, current knowledge and understanding of education and school systems locally, nationally and globally, and pursues continuous professional development Challenges educational orthodoxies in the best interests of achieving excellence, harnessing the findings of well evidenced research to frame self-regulating and self-improving schools	*National Standards of Excellence for Headteachers: Departmental advice for headteachers, governing boards and aspiring headteachers* (Department for Education, 2015)
School business manager	Engages with research to inform effective policy development and seeks to influence it	*National Association of School Business Managers Professional Standards, succeeded in November 2017 by the Institute of School Business Leadership*
Governor	Acts with honesty, frankness and objectivity taking decisions impartially, fairly and on merit using the best evidence and without discrimination or bias	*A Competency Framework for Governance: the knowledge, skills and behaviours needed for effective governance in maintained schools, academies and multi-academy trusts* (Department for Education, 2017)

As such, to reach and maintain those professional standards, it is difficult to see how school leaders, of whatever level or role, cannot actively engage in some form of evidence-based practice. To do otherwise would suggest these leaders are not being consistent with their own professional standards As Gambrill (2006) states:

Are these merely for window dressing, to impress interested parties that our intentions are good and therefore our outcomes are good, to convince others that we are doing the right things.

Or are these codes really meaningful? Is it ethical to agree to abide by the guidelines described in professional codes of ethics, for example, to draw upon practice-related research, and then simply not do so? (p. 351)

Evidence-based school leadership and fads and faddism

Regrettably school leadership and management is highly susceptible to crazes – fads and fashions that change as frequently as clothing styles. As Slavin (1989) states, 'educational innovation is famous for its cycle of early enthusiasm, widespread dissemination, subsequent disappointment, and eventual decline - the classic swing of the pendulum' (p. 752).

Examples of fads within education include the use of interactive whiteboards, BrainGym and learning styles. More recently there has been an explosion of interest in schools around growth mindsets, grit, resilience and character education. Helpfully, McGill (2016) provides a list of educational fads over the last 20 years, which include:

- Lesson outcomes
- Assessing pupil progress
- Chinese teaching
- Textbooks
- Sitting in rows
- Group work
- Zero tolerance
- Verbal feedback stamps
- Triple-marking
- Starters, middle and plenaries

However, fads in education are not confined to teaching and learning, they can also be found in leadership and management. Furnham (2015) identifies a number of fads and fashions in leadership and management going back to the 1950s and goes on to highlight a number of current management ideas which appear to be 'hot' such as employee engagement, leadership derailment, women in management, intrinsic motivation, outsourcing and heterogeneous teams and team-working. Whereas management ideas such as empowerment, total quality management, the learning organisation, benchmarking and emotional intelligence appear to be 'not hot'.

However, evidence-based school leaders can protect themselves from the worst excesses of some fads put forward by educational consultants, gurus and other experts by asking the following questions:

- What evidence is there that the new approach can provide productive outputs and outcomes? Are the arguments based on solid evidence from lots of schools followed over time?
- Has the approach worked in schools similar to our own that face similar challenges?
- Is the approach relevant to current priorities and strategies of our school or multi-academy trust?
- Is the advice specific enough to be implemented? Do we have enough information about implementation challenges and how to meet them within the context of our school?
- Is the advice practical for our school given our capabilities and resources?
- Can we reasonably assess the costs and prospective benefits? (Amended from Miller et al., 2004: 14)

Evidence-based school leadership and the half-life of facts

School leaders need to be constantly engaged in evidence-based school leadership practice, as evidence that might be used to support decisions can become 'rusty' (Hargreaves and Fullan, 2012). Evidence that we have relied on in the past may no longer be current or applicable; indeed advice based on 'old' research evidence may now be viewed as being no longer justified. For example, addressing low aspirations and confidence before teaching subject content does not appear to be consistent with the latest research (Coe et al., 2014). Arbesman (2012) argues that just like radioactive material, 'facts' have a half-life and decay over time. Arbesman states: 'Facts, in the aggregate, have half-lives: We can measure the amount of time for half of a subject's knowledge to be overturned. There is science that explores the rates at which new facts are created, new technologies develop, and even how facts spread' (p. 3).

To illustrate this point, Arbesman cites the work of Poynard et al. (2002), who demonstrate that in a particular field of medicine – cirrhosis and hepatitis – the half-life of facts in this field was approximately 45 years. In other words, half of what we thought we knew about cirrhosis and hepatitis was within 45 years shown to be incorrect.

Given that careers in education can last over 40 years, there is every chance that what school leaders learnt at the beginning of their careers about teaching, learning and the management of people may have been superseded by better, more plausible accounts and explanations. School leaders who are actively engaged in evidence-based school practice will provide both themselves and their schools some degree of protection from the continued use of ideas and interventions which are no longer supported by the evidence.

Evidence-based school leadership, social media and the post-truth world

Increasingly teachers and school leaders are using social media – be it Twitter, Facebook or blogs – as a source of professional development. However, in what some would describe as the post-truth world it is necessary to provide teachers and school leaders with the tools necessary to help them ensure that they do not fall victim to 'bullshit' (Ball, 2017). It should be noted that bullshit is not confined to social media and may often be heard, dare I say it, on a regular basis in school staff rooms and senior leadership team meetings.

Ball draws upon the work of Frankfurt (2009) to distinguish between lies, untruths and bullshit and summarises Frankfurt's argument as: 'to tell a lie, you need to care about some form of absolute truth or falsehood, and increasingly public life is run by people who don't care much either way – they care about their narrative' (Ball, 2017: 6).

Ball goes on to cite Frankfurt who concludes:

Someone who lies and someone who tells the truth are playing on opposite sides, so to speak, in the same game. Each responds to the facts as he understands them, although the response of the one is guided by the authority of the truth, while the response of the other defies that authority, and refuses to meet its demands.

The bullshitter ignores these demands altogether. He does not reject the authority of the truth, as the liar does, and oppose himself to it. He pays no attention to it at all, by virtue of this, bullshit is a greater enemy of the truth than lies are. (Ball, 2017: 6)

So how can evidence-based school leadership protect the school leader from being susceptible to bullshit? Ball suggests a number of strategies that can be adopted, which are integral to evidence-based school leadership and which are more fully explored in later chapters.

- *Burst your bubble*: the evidence-based school leader makes sure they meaningfully engage with people who have different views to themselves, with the aim of this engagement being to understand the views of others, rather than seeking to convince others as to the strength of their own arguments.
- *Learn some statistics*: evidence-based school leaders will find it useful to get to grips with concepts such as p-values, confidence intervals, effect sizes, statistical significance and correlation (see Chapter 6).
- *Treat narratives you believe in just as sceptically as those you don't*: just because a plausible and believable narrative is being promoted in social media does not mean that it is right. On such occasions, the evidence-based school leader needs just to step back and say – is there an alternative view or views on this? If so, what is it? Are there any elements of these alternative views which are robust?
- *Remember Hanlon's Razor*: Ball argues that in a world of bullshit there is a tendency for there to be a rise in conspiratorial thinking and that others are 'out to get us'. When evidence-based school leaders begin to think conspiratorially – it is always worth remembering Hanlon's Razor. This concept can be described in a number of ways, for example: 'Never attribute to malice that which is adequately explained by stupidity' or 'Don't assume bad intentions over neglect and misunderstanding'.
- *Use deliberative thinking*: evidence-based school leaders need to engage in deliberative thinking rather than thinking which is far more intuitive and instinctive. This naturally leads us to the final reason for evidence-based school leadership – cognitive biases – which are now explored in more detail.

Evidence-based school leadership and cognitive biases

Our final, though possibly most compelling, reason for the use of evidence-based practice relates to how cognitive biases can get in the way of our ability to objectively evaluate data, form balanced judgements and make effective decisions. Wilke and Mata (2012) define cognitive biases as 'systematic error(s) in judgment and decision-making common to all human beings which can be due to cognitive limitations, motivational factors, and/or adaptations to natural environments' (p. 531). For example, people are often described as being cognitive misers who demonstrate a strong preference to rely on fast, intuitive processing ('system 1') rather than on more demanding, deliberate thinking ('system 2') (Kahneman, 2011). One consequence of this preference is that it leads to something called attribute substitution: when people are faced with a challenging and difficult question they will intuitively answer a less difficult question.

Let's look at this example developed by Frederick (2005: 27) to illustrate the point:

> A bat and a ball cost $1.10 in total. The bat costs $1.00 more than the ball. How much does the ball cost?

The answer that intuitively and immediately comes to mind is '10 cents', which is incorrect. If the ball were to cost 10 cents, the bat would cost $1.10 (i.e., $1 more) and then the total cost would be $1.20. The correct answer is 5 cents (so that the bat costs $1.05) with a total of $1.10. The explanation for this mistake is that people replace the critical 'more than' statement with a simpler statement. That is, the bat costs $1 more than the ball is read as the bat costs $1. So instead of working out the sum, people intuitively breakdown $1.10, into $1 and 10 cents which is easier to do. In other words, because of the substitution people give the correct answer to the wrong question.

Benson (2016) has identified 175 cognitive biases and four general problems, which are probably all too familiar to school leaders, that cognitive biases help to solve. First, there is 'too much information' and individuals need to identify the most useful information. Second, there is 'not enough meaning' so individuals need to find ways of connecting different bits of information to develop stories and models of how the world operates. Third, individuals sometimes 'need to act fast' on the information becoming available to use, otherwise this may lead to inaction which may be extremely detrimental if not dangerous. Four, 'what should we remember?' There is so much information it is constantly necessary to work out what's best remembered and also what's best forgotten. Unfortunately, the use of these strategies and associated biases can lead to all sorts of distortions to the decision-making process.

Benson (2016) goes on to identify four drawbacks that arise from attempting to solve the above problems.

1. **We don't see everything.** Some of the information we filter out is actually useful and important.
2. **Our search for meaning can conjure illusions.** We sometimes imagine details that were filled in by our assumptions, and construct meaning and stories that aren't really there.
3. **Quick decisions can be seriously flawed.** Some of the quick reactions and decisions we jump to are unfair, self-serving, and counter-productive.
4. **Our memory reinforces errors.** Some of the stuff we remember for later just makes all of the above systems more biased, and more damaging to our thought processes. (Benson 2016, online)

So how can evidence-based practice help school leaders and managers to reduce the negative impact of cognitive biases? First, as Stafford (2015) notes, it is important to recognise that everyone is prone to cognitive biases, and it is not something which can be eliminated from individuals' thinking. Second, evidence-based practice promotes critical thinking, the examination of claims, the underpinning argument and supporting evidence. Third, processes associated with evidence-based practice provide a framework to support 'disciplined' decision-making. Fourth, the role of research in evidence-based practice should help mitigate against over-reliance on 'anecdotes' and 'case studies' and create conditions for the use of potentially more robust evidence.

Evidence-based school leadership – why now?

Although the term evidence-based management (EBMgt) is relatively new, in a systematic review of evidence-based management

Reay et al. (2009) identified 144 articles relating to evidence-based management, with the first article appearing as early as 1948. However, evidence-based management only began to come to prominence in the 1990s and early 2000s, with Professor Denise M. Rousseau giving a 2005 Presidential Address to the Academy of Management entitled 'Is there such a thing as "evidence-based management?"'. In 2006 the publication of Pfeffer and Sutton's (2006) treatise on the dangerous half-truths and total nonsense prevalent in much of the popular management literature followed, which had its intellectual roots in the evidence-based medicine movement Sackett et al. (1996).

Rousseau (2012) goes on to identify three factors that explain 'why the time is ripe for the emergence of evidence-based management' (p. xxiv):

- Since World War II, a large body of social science and management research has investigated the individual, social and organisational factors that impact managerial performance.
- The Internet offers broad access to scientific knowledge.
- Increasing awareness of the consequences from managerial decisions prompts widespread concerns with improving its quality.

(Rousseau, 2012: xxiv–xxv)

In the context of education, around the globe there is growing interest in the use of research evidence to improve the quality of teaching and learning (Brown, 2015). However, as Collins and Coleman (2017) note, this interest in the role of evidence in education is not new in both the United Kingdom and the United States, and can be traced back to the 1970s. More recently, there has been an increase in political interest in the use of evidence in schools. In the United States, December 2015 saw the passing of *The Every Student Succeeds Act* (ESSA), which provides a definition of the evidence required for a program or practice to be considered 'strong', 'moderate', or 'promising'. Prior to this in England, the Coalition government provided £125m of funding to set up the Education Endowment Foundation. So far the Education Endowment Foundation has committed more than £75m to fund 127 projects and has reached over 7,500 schools and 750,000 children and young people (EEF, 2016). In 2016/17 the Institute of Effective Education, based at the University of York, and the Education Endowment Foundation set up a network of 22 research schools. In addition, there has been an increase in teachers' interest in research and evidence, which is reflected in the rise of the researchED movement.

Nevertheless, within education, evidence-based practice has focused primarily around teaching and learning. However, over the last 30 years there have been significant changes in the roles of head-teachers and other school leaders as a result of a move towards site-based management (Wood, 2017). Since 1988 England has seen the introduction of the local management of schools, changes in funding systems, academies outside of LEA control, multi-academy trusts, free schools, studio schools, university technical colleges (UTCs) and university training schools (UTSs).

These changes have led to the introduction of a number of new roles within the leadership and management of schools, be it school business leaders, executive headteachers and chief executive officers, all of which have significant responsibilities outside the leading of teaching and learning. The role of school bursar has morphed into being a school business leader having responsibility for activities such as finance, human resources management, facilities, marketing, information technology, risk and management information services, with headteachers within these schools being ultimately accountable for the success or otherwise of these activities (Wood, 2017).

Increasingly there are job advertisements for the post of executive headteacher who directly leads two or more schools in the form of a partnership arrangement. In a NFER (2017) report on the role of executive head, four broad role descriptors were outlined; strategic leadership, financial and business management, educational leader-ship and management, and people leadership and management. Within the strategic leadership there is reference to ensuring and monitoring consistent and ongoing implementation across the school groups of key policies and strategies (e.g. finance, HR, IT and behaviour). Within finance and business management, there is refer-ence to providing financial leadership. Within people leadership and management there is reference to ensuring an effective approach to managing staff performance and staffing issues. Finally, within edu-cational leadership and management, there is reference to leading outstanding teachers and innovative practice to enhance learning.

As for chief executive officers of multi-academy trusts, given that there are a number of academy chains, where the academy trust chief executive officer may have responsibility for anywhere between two and seventy schools, evidence-based practice is going to have to extend beyond maintaining and developing high educational standards across all the academies of the academy chain. Indeed, in all likelihood the chief executive officer of a multi-academy trust will be leading a team of senior managers who have a focus on finance, human resources, estates and performance management.

Evidence-based school leadership – the potential

However, for many school leaders, evidence-based school leadership might be seen as just another management fad, with there being a queue of other policies in 'line' ready to take its place (Collins and Coleman, 2017). Nevertheless, while there may be some justification in those claims, it has yet to be shown whether evidence-based practice leads to school improvement. However, there are numerous reported benefits to practitioners engaging in evidence-based practice (Jones and CEBMa, 2016). First, high-performing school systems appear to facilitate the collaborative examination of research evidence in order to identify both likely problem areas (in relation to teaching and learning) and potential solutions to these problems (Supovitz, 2015). Second, there is also evidence that indicates that where research is used as a component of high-quality initial teacher education and continuous professional development, there is a positive correlation with changes in teacher, school and system performance. Third, there is also evidence of a range of positive teacher outcomes that arise from evidence-informed practice, including improvements in pedagogical knowledge and skills and greater teacher confidence in what works (Cordingley, 2015). In addition, Sheard and Sharples (2016) have published a proof of concept of the relationship between the use of research evidence and school improvement.

As such, evidence-based school leadership would appear to have the potential to provide both leaders and members of a school community with a number of benefits. This benefits school leaders by focusing attention on 'what works for who, in what context, for how, for how long, to what extent, and why'. This potentially saves evidence-based school leaders time and money by focusing on what works and eliminating what does not. Evidence-based leadership also helps protect schools from unsubstantiated management and teaching fads. Finally, evidence-based school leadership, when done well, improves relational trust within schools.

Summary and key points

- Put simply, evidence-based school leadership helps school leaders and managers – of whatever level – help make decisions through the conscientious, explicit and judicious use of the best available evidence from multiple sources to increase the likelihood of favourable outcomes.
- Fundamentally, evidence-based leadership is an ethical endeavour and should be seen as a way of ensuring that those practices which can lead to favourable outcomes for pupils, staff, parents and the broader community are either continued with, or introduced to the school.
- Alternatively, evidence-based school leadership involves ensuring that those practices which lead to unfavourable outcomes for pupils, staff, parents and the broader community are withdrawn or never introduced.
- Evidence-based school leaders recognise the potential for fallibility and the need to reduce unnecessary ineptitude through the use of the best available evidence.
- Evidence-based school leaders recognise that if school leadership is to be recognised as a profession it is necessary to maintain and uphold professional standards that emphasise the role of evidence-based practice.
- Evidence-based school leadership has the potential to protect schools from fads, faddism, the 'half-life of facts' and 'post-truth' agendas.
- The existence of cognitive biases requires school leaders to take action in order to reduce the impact of such biases on decision-making processes.
- Change in the way in which schools are organised and led – particularly in England – is increasing the need for evidence-based

school leadership, not just on teaching and learning but for all aspects of the work of the school.
- The increased use of evidence-based school leadership is particularly timely, given the pressures on schools to both improve and make better use of resources.

References

Arbesman, S. (2012) *The Half-Life of Facts: Why Everything We Know Has an Expiration Date*. Harmondsworth: Penguin.

Ball, J. (2017) *Post-Truth: How Bullshit Conquered the World*. London: Biteback Publishing.

Barends, E., Rousseau, D. and Briner, R. (2014) *Evidence-Based Management: the Basic Principles*. Amsterdam. Center for Evidence-Based Management.

Benson, B. (2016) 'Cognitive bias cheat sheet: because thinking is hard'. *Better Humans* 2017. https://betterhumans.coach.me/cognitive-bias-cheat-sheet-55a472476b18 (accessed 20 November 2017).

Brown, C. (2015) *Leading the Use of Research and Evidence in Schools*. London: IOE Press.

Christensen, C.M. and Raynor, M.E. (2003) 'Why hard-nosed executives should care about management theory', *Harvard Business Review, 81* (9): 66–75.

Coe, R., Aloisi, C., Higgins, S. and Major, L.E. (2014) 'What makes great teaching? Review of the underpinning research'. *Project Report*. London: Sutton Trust.

Collins, K. and Coleman, R. (2017) 'Evidence-informed policy and practice', in P. Earley and T. Greany (eds), *School Leadership and Education System Reform*. London: Bloomsbury.

Cordingley, P. (2015) 'The contribution of research to teachers' professional learning and development', *Oxford Review of Education, 41* (2): 234–52.

EEF (2016) *Annual Report 2015/16*. London: Education Endowment Foundation.

Frankfurt, H.G. (2009) *On Bullshit*. Princeton, NJ: Princeton University Press.

Frederick, S. (2005) 'Cognitive reflection and decision making', *Journal of Economic Perspectives, 19* (4): 25–42.

Furnham, A. (2015) 'Fads and fashions in management', *European Business Review*, 2017. www.europeanbusinessreview.com/fads-and-fashions-in-management/ (accessed 20 December 2017).

Gambrill, E. (2006) 'Evidence-based practice and policy: choices ahead', *Research on Social Work Practice, 16* (3): 338–57.

Gawande, A. (2010) *The Checklist Manifesto*. Harmondsworth: Penguin Books.

Gorovitz, S. and MacIntyre, A. (1976) Toward a theory of medical fallibility. *The Journal of Medicine and Philosophy, 1* (1), 51–71.

Gray, J. (2001) *Evidence-Based Healthcare: How to Make Health Policy and Management Decisions*. London: Churchill Livingstone.

Hargreaves, A. and Fullan, M. (2012) *Professional Capital: Transforming Teaching in Every School*. New York: Teachers College Press.

Hendrick, C. and MacPherson, R. (2017) *What Does This Look Like in the Classroom? Bridging the Gap between Research and Practice*. Melton: John Catt.

Hill, A., Mellon, L., Laker, B. and Goddard, J. (2016) 'The one type of leader who can turn around a failing school', *Harvard Business Review*, 20 October. Available at: https://hbr.org/2016/10/the-one-type-of-leader-who-can-turn-around-a-failing-school (accessed 29 April 2018).

Jones, G. and CEBMa. (2016) *Evidence Based Practice: a Handbook for Teachers and School Leaders*. Available at: http://evidencebasededucationalleader ship.blogspot.co.uk/2016/02/evidence-based-practice-handbook-for.html (accessed 29 April 2018).

Kahneman, D. (2011) *Thinking, Fast and Slow*. London: Macmillan.

Lewis, J. and Caldwell, B.J. (2005) *Evidence-Based Leadership*. London: Taylor & Francis.

McGill, R. (2016) 'Trends: Twenty years of educational fads'. *Teacher Toolkit*. www.teachertoolkit.me/2016/07/10/education-fads/ (accessed 29 April 2018).

Miller, D., Hartwick, J. and Le Breton-Miller, I. (2004) 'How to detect a management fad—and distinguish it from a classic', *Business Horizons*, *47* (4): 7–16.

NFER (2017) *Executive Headship: A Summary of the Executive Headteacher (EHT) Role, with Practical Questions and Exemplar Role Descriptors to Consider When Creating the Position*. Slough: National Foundation for Educational Research.

Pfeffer, J. and Sutton, R.I. (2006) *Hard Facts, Dangerous Half-Truths and Total Nonsense: Profitting from Evidence-Based Management*. Boston, MA: Harvard Business School Press.

Poynard, T., Munteanu, M., Ratziu, V., Benhamou, Y., Di Martino, V., Taieb, J. and Opolon, P. (2002) 'Truth survival in clinical research: an evidence-based requiem?', *Annals of Internal Medicine*, *136* (12): 888–95.

Reay, T., Berta, W. and Kohn, M.K. (2009) 'What's the evidence on evidence-based management?', *Academy of Management Perspectives*, *23* (4): 5–18.

Rousseau, D.M. (2012) 'Preface' in D. Rousseau (ed.), *The Oxford Handbook of Evidence-Based Management*. Oxford: Oxford University Press.

Sackett, D., Rosenberg, W., Gray, J., Haynes, R. and Richardson, W. (1996) 'Evidence based medicine: what it is and what it isn't', *BMJ*, *312* (7023): 71–2.

Sheard, M. and Sharples, J. (2016) 'School leaders' engagement with the concept of evidence-based practice as a management tool for school improvement', *Educational Management Administration & Leadership*, *44* (4): 668–87.

Sinek, S. (2009) *Start with Why: How Great Leaders Inspire Everyone to Take Action*. Harmondsworth: Penguin.

Slavin, R. (1989) 'Pet and the pendulum: faddism in education and how to stop it', *Phi Delta Kappan*, *70* (10): 752–8.

Stafford, T. (2015) 'Bias mitigation'. www.tomstafford.staff.shef.ac.uk/?p=342 (accessed 20 November 2017).

Supovitz, J. (2015) 'Teacher data use for improving teaching and learning', in C. Brown (ed.), *Leading the Use of Research and Evidence in Schools*. London: Bloomsbury Press.

Wilke, A. and Mata, R. (2012) 'Cognitive bias', in *Encyclopedia of Human Behaviour*, 1: 531–5.

Wood, E. (2017) 'The role of school based business leaders', in P. Earley and T. Greany (eds), *School Leadership and Education System Reform*. London: Bloomsbury.

2

WHAT IS EVIDENCE-BASED SCHOOL LEADERSHIP?

Chapter outline

This chapter begins by providing a comprehensive definition of evidence-based practice. This will then allow a discussion of some of the common misconceptions which are held about evidence-based practice. Next, the chapter will briefly explore the implications of evidence-based school leadership for how a school is led and managed. The chapter will then move on to explore some of the key terminology associated with evidence-based practice, such as evidence, decisions, conscientious, explicit, judicious and favourable outcomes. Finally, the chapter will give some consideration to the limitations of evidence-based practice.

Key words: *evidence-based practice, evidence, decision, conscientious, explicit, outcomes, judicious*

When looking for guidance for what is meant by the term evidence-based practice, a useful place to start is Hammersley-Fletcher et al. (2015), who define evidence-based teaching as 'teaching practice or school-level approaches that are based upon the results of evidence about interventions or strategies that are effective in helping pupils to progress' (p. 10). Alternatively, definitions that focus on evidence-informed practice could be used. For example, Hammersley-Fletcher et al. cite Nelson and O'Beirne, who define evidence-informed practice as 'how teachers can engage with multiple forms of knowledge, evidence and expertise to make decisions in contexts' (Nelson and O'Beirne, 2014, cited in Hammersley-Fletcher et al., 2015). In addition, Brown et al. (2017) adopt the definition of evidence-informed practice provided by England's Department for Education: 'A combination of practitioner expertise and knowledge of the best external research, and evaluation based evidence' (Department for Education, 2014, cited in Brown et al., 2017: 132).

However, as a group, these definitions of both evidence-based and evidence-informed practice have a number of limitations. First, as will be demonstrated later in the chapter, there is an unnecessary distinction between evidence-based practice and evidence-informed practice. Second, none of the above definitions provides any substantive guidance as to the skills required to be an evidence-based practitioner. Third, the way in which these definitions have often been interpreted has led to a narrow focus on teaching and learning rather than a broader perspective on the role of evidence in school leadership (see Chapter 3).

To help address these issues, this book will turn to the work of the Center of Evidence-Based Management and Barends et al. (2014) who define evidence-based practice as:

> making decisions through the conscientious, explicit and judicious use of the best available evidence from multiple sources by:
>
> - Asking: translating a practical issue or problem into answerable questions
> - Acquiring: systematically searching for and retrieving the evidence
> - Appraising: critically judging the trustworthiness of and relevance of the evidence
> - Aggregating: weighing and pulling together the evidence

- Applying: incorporating the best available evidence into the decision-making process
- Assessing: evaluating the outcomes of the decision taken to increase the likelihood of a favourable outcome.

(Barends et al., 2014: 2)

Barends et al. (2014) go on to argue that a distinguishing feature of evidence-based practice is that it brings together four sources of evidence: scientific research, organisational data, practitioner expertise and stakeholder evidence. For the purposes of this book these terms will be defined as:

- **Educational and other research:** Findings from published academic research.
- **School/college evidence:** Data, facts and figures gathered from the school/college.
- **Experiential evidence:** The professional experience and judgement of the practitioners making the decision.
- **Stakeholder evidence:** The expertise, values and concerns of people who may be affected by the decision.

The relationship between these four sources of evidence and decision-making is illustrated in Figure 2.1. Indeed, by combining all four

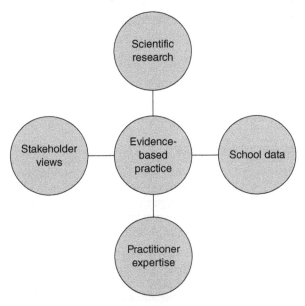

Figure 2.1   The four sources of evidence

sources of evidence, this increases the chances of making decisions that are 'wise' rather than merely 'informed' or 'blind to their impact' (Tierney, 2015).

A major benefit of using Barends et al.'s (2014) definition of evidence-based practice is that it directly addresses the misconception that evidence-based practice places little value on practitioner expertise and as such makes the term evidence-informed practice redundant. As Barends et al. (2014) note: 'this misconception directly contradicts our definition of evidence-based practice – that decisions should be made through the conscientious, explicit and judicious use of evidence from four sources, including evidence from practitioners' (p. 12). However, and as examined in Chapter 7, experiential evidence needs to be closely scrutinised for both its usefulness and accuracy. Nevertheless, the key point is evidence-based practice involves using multiple sources of evidence rather than any exclusively relying on scientific research evidence.

It is important to eliminate these misconceptions for three reasons: first, these misconceptions prevent school leaders making the most of the potential of evidence-based school leadership to improve outcomes for pupils; second, by conflating evidence-based school leadership with engaging in research, leaders and teachers are being mistakenly encouraged to be researchers rather than evidence-based practitioners seeking to make better decisions; third, not making good use of evidence-based school leadership can lead to increasingly scarce resources being wasted. A number of these misconceptions and subsequent counter-arguments are summarised in Table 2.1.

Table 2.1 Misconceptions associated with evidence-based practice

Misconception	Correction
Evidence-based practice ignores the practitioner's professional experience	This misconception directly contradicts the definition of evidence-based practice – that decisions should be made through the conscientious, explicit and judicious use of evidence from four sources, *including experiential evidence*
Evidence-based practice is the same as research-based practice	Evidence-based practice involves drawing upon evidence from a range of sources, be it 'academic research', practitioner experience, organisational/school data and the views of stakeholders. As such, research-based practice is a subset of evidence-based practice

Misconception	Correction
Evidence-based practice involves school leaders undertaking research	Evidence-based practice is not about attempting to create new and generalisable knowledge through the conduct of research. Rather evidence is about using the best available current evidence to make decisions in order to increase the likelihood of favourable outcomes
Evidence-based practice is all about numbers and statistics	Evidence-based practice involves seeking out and using the best available evidence from multiple sources. It is not exclusively about effect sizes, p-values and confidence intervals (see Chapter 6); it also includes the use of qualitative data and the views of stakeholders
Evidence-based school leaders need to make decisions quickly and don't have time for evidence-based practice	The need to make an immediate decision is generally the exception rather than the rule. Indeed, in a school certain decisions may only be implemented at certain points of the school year, and as such have a long lead-in time
Each school is unique, so the usefulness of scientific evidence is limited	Most management issues are *'repetitions of familiar problems cloaked in the guise of uniqueness'* (quote from Lowenstein, 2006; citing Drucker, 1966)
If you do not have high-quality evidence, you cannot do anything	The evidence-based school leader may have no other option but to work with the limited evidence at hand and supplement it through learning by doing by using the Plan–Do–Study–Act cycle(Langley et al., 2009)
Good-quality evidence gives you the answer to the problem	Evidence-based school leaders make decisions not based on conclusive, solid, up-to-date information, but on probabilities, indications and tentative conclusions. Evidence-based school leadership is not about 'certainties' but instead is about 'best bets'

Source: Based on Barends et al., 2014

Understanding the relationship between evidence-based practice and school leadership

Nevertheless, when school leaders and managers first embark on evidence-based practice the emphasis is often on accessing research evidence. Leaders and managers ask questions such as: How can I access research evidence? Where can I get research evidence from? How do I appraise research evidence? How do I find the time to search for evidence?

Given the competing demands on time-pressed school leaders, these questions are all very sensible. However, they are not the best place to start. Evidence-based practice is more than just acquiring the best available evidence to help make a decision, it is an approach that should influence all aspects of the school, be it the future vision of the school; how conversations take place; the context in which those conversations take place; developing and supporting colleagues who are keen to make the most of the best available evidence; and, ensuring that this evidence is shared amongst colleagues elsewhere in the school (Von Krogh et al., 2000). The implications of adopting an evidence-based practice approach to school leadership will be explored in more detail in Chapter 11.

Having provided both a comprehensive working definition of evidence-based school leadership and an initial examination of the consequences for school leadership, attention will now turn to providing detailed explanations of some of the key terms associated with evidence-based practice.

What do we mean by evidence?

Understanding the difference between data and evidence is a key component of becoming an evidence-based practitioner (Wilkinson, 2017). Data is information, and represents anything that you can find which helps you answer your problem of practice. However, as Booth et al. (2016) note, data is 'inert' until it is used to support a claim that answers a research question, or what for the purposes of this book is known as a 'problem of practice'. (Chapter 3 will discuss in more detail the nature of a problem of practice.)

When discussing 'evidence', this means 'information, facts or data supporting (or contradicting) a claim, assumption or hypothesis' (Barends et al., 2014). This evidence may come from the school, be it measures of performance or other observations of current school conditions. Evidence may also come from stakeholders – both within or outside of the school – be it pupils, teachers, support staff, senior leaders, members of the governing body, trustees of multi-academy trusts and the local education authority. Furthermore, professional experience is an important source of evidence. For example, past experience of running a department, key stage or school could suggest the strategy that is likely to be the most successful in dealing with a particular problem of practice. Evidence may also come from academic and scientific research in the form of articles in peer-reviewed journals or research reports. The source of the evidence does not matter, what matters is whether the evidence can be judged to be accurate, appropriate and relevant.

What do we mean by a decision?

Writing in the *Oxford Handbook of Evidence-Based Management*, Yates and Potworowski (2012) define a decision as: 'a commitment to a course of action that is intended to serve the interests and values of particular people' (p. 201). This definition makes a distinction between interests and values of the intended beneficiaries of the decision, as they are not always one and the same. For example, a struggling member of staff may wish to stay within the teaching profession as it is something they have always wished to do (due to their personal values). However, staying in the teaching profession may not be in the long-term interest of the member of staff as it may have a serious impact on his or her mental health.

Conscientious

The Oxford English Dictionary defines 'conscientious' as 'Obedient to conscience, (habitually) governed by a sense of duty, done according to conscience, scrupulous, painstaking; of or pertaining to conscience'. This definition has two broad implications for the conscientious evidence-based school leader. First, to be conscientious is to 'do the right thing'. Evidence-based school leaders have a strong sense of ethics, moral purpose and values. They want to do what is right for pupils, staff, parents and the community at large. Second, evidence-based school leaders want to 'do things right' – they want things to be done in the right way – and have a clear understanding of what that means for how a school is run and how evidence-based decisions are made.

As a consequence, evidence-based school leaders are hardworking, committing time and effort towards ensuring the right thing is done in the right way – evidence is used to be productive and get things done. Secondly, evidence-based school leaders are going to be careful, prudent and deliberative rather than impulsive, and are not going to rush to make decisions. Evidence-based school leaders will have both an 'eye for detail' and will actively seek-out evidence that is inconsistent with their current view of 'what works'. Third, evidence-based school leaders are going to be persistent; they recognise that becoming an 'expert' evidence-based school leader will take time and effort to acquire the appropriate knowledge, skills, experience, and ultimately wisdom.

Explicit

Cronbach and Suppes (1969) notion of 'disciplined inquiry' is extremely helpful in trying to unpack what is meant to be an 'explicit' evidence-based practitioner. As they state:

> disciplined inquiry has a quality that distinguishes it from other sources of opinion and belief. The disciplined inquiry is conducted and reported in such a way that the argument can be painstakingly examined. The report does not depend for its appeal on the eloquence of the writer or on any surface plausibility. (p. 15)

Being explicit is a central task of being an evidence-based school leader. Unless others – be it colleagues or other stakeholders – can examine the evidence used, the claims being made and how this has led to a particular decision, why would they trust decisions made by so-called evidence-based school leaders. And if they do not trust the decision, or indeed the decision-maker(s), why would they make the effort to successfully implement and execute the decision?

It is necessary, therefore, to ensure that the results of disciplined/evidence-based inquiry are communicated in such a way that they are both understandable and useful for its intended audience. The 'explicit' evidence-based school leader minimises the unnecessary use of terminology and explains things in a way that is both simple yet not simplistic. In addition, being an evidence-based school leader involves making sure the evidence used to support the decision is fully reported, so that it can be checked to ensure that the underlying evidence has not been misreported. Next, the evidence-based school leaders should explain their assumptions when interpreting the evidence and make sure any associated reasoning is made explicit (see Chapter 7 and the ladder of inference). Finally, this is all done in such a way as to encourage dialogue, with the evidence-based school leader making sure that others are given permission to disagree and challenge any recommendations and explore why they might indeed fail (see Chapter 9 and pre-mortems).

Judicious

In the context of evidence-based school leadership, being judicious has two meanings. First, the evidence-based school leader needs to be judicious in how they evaluate evidence of whatever kind, and which Chapters 5, 6 and 7 will explore in more detail. In particular, given the prevalence of fads and faddism within education, evidence-based school leaders needs to be judicious in distinguishing between the practical and the puerile (Anderson et al., 2001). Indeed, the evidence-based school leader needs to be able to distinguish between 'popularist science', which may be addressing a very important and practical issue, but is done with very little scientific rigor and which is often written by high profile teachers and leaders, and 'pragmatic science', which addresses both an important issue and is done with a high degree of methodological rigour, for example Education Endowment Foundation evaluation reports. In doing so, the evidence-based school leader will need to demonstrate elements of what De Hart Hurd (1998) describes as 'scientific literacy', which includes: being able to distinguish between experts and the uninformed, being able to tell 'theory from dogma', and 'data from folklore'.

Second, the evidence-based school leader needs to be judicious in turning the evidence into a decision. Badaracco (2016) is extremely helpful, in that he suggests five questions which are particularly valuable when the evidence, from whatever source or sources, is unclear, contradictory or, at best, incomplete. Evidence-based school leaders need to work through the following five questions before coming to a decision.

- What are the net consequences of all my options? What will be the impact on pupils, colleagues, peers and others' lives?
- What are my core obligations to my pupils, colleagues, peers and other stakeholders?
- What will work in the school and world as it is – rather than in the school and world that you would like it to be?
- Who are we? What are our core values and norms? What does the school stand for?
- What can I live with? Can you explain your decision with comfort to a close colleague or mentor? (adapted from Badaracco, 2016)

The evidence-based school leader will tackle these questions by making the most of the best available evidence. However, they realise that evidence does not give them the answer and they will have to answer these questions for themselves. Nevertheless, by being conscientious, explicit and judicious and by undertaking a disciplined process of evidence-based practice, the evidence-based school leader cannot be sure they have got the 'right answer' but at least they can be sure they have given themselves the best chance to do 'the right thing in the right way'.

The likelihood of favourable outcomes?

In seeking to understand the phrase 'the likelihood of favourable outcomes', it is necessary to look at each of the key terms in turn.

Likelihood

An underpinning assumption of evidence-based school leadership is that by bringing together the best available evidence this will increase the chances that whatever decision is made will provide favourable outcomes for the intended beneficiaries. However, evidence-based school leadership does not guarantee either favourable or improved outcomes, as often the quality of evidence is variable. Even if the evidence is of very high quality the process of summarising and bringing the evidence together may lead to some of the subtleties and nuances of the evidence being lost. As Higgins et al. (2013) note, the summarisation of evidence only intends to give 'an overall best bet'. It does not guarantee what worked in the past in other settings, will work in the specific context faced by the evidence-based school leader. On the other hand, it does not mean that things that have not worked elsewhere will not work in a different setting. All evidence-based school leadership can seek to do is increase 'chances' rather than delivering certainty. Accordingly, evidence-based school leadership is as much 'art' as a 'science'.

Favourable

One of the main assumptions of evidence-based practice is that if decision-makers use a range of evidence – research, practitioner experience, school data and stakeholder views – then they will make better decisions. In order to get round the issue of deciding what is a good decision or bad decision, Yates and Potworowski (2012) adopt the stance that 'effective decisions are ones that, in fact, serve the interests and values of the intended beneficiaries' (p. 204).

Outcomes

However, as Yates and Potworowski (2012) note, there are many ways in which a decision may impact on the intended beneficiary or beneficiaries, and it is important to recognise the distinction between outcomes and process, costs and benefits. In the context of evidence-based school leadership and practice this is particularly important, as Zhao (2017) argues that educational research has largely ignored the potential harms arising from what works. As such, it may not be that easy for the evidence-based school leader to identify the negative side effects associated with an intervention, which in turn makes it extremely difficult to act if, on balance, the benefits greatly outweigh the risks and costs.

Langley et al. (2009) argue that in a simple system it is relatively straightforward to see whether a change has led to an improvement 'by informally observing the system' (p. 94). However, Langley et al. go on to note that in more complex systems – which include classrooms, schools and educational systems – a range of measures will be required. Langley et al. provide a number of guidelines, which have been adapted for use in an educational setting:

- Ensure the interests of the intended beneficiaries of the decision – pupils, staff, parents, other stakeholders – are reflected in the measures.
- Collect data from before and after change. However, do not ignore a measure if data is not available from before a change took place, as it may provide a number of insights.
- Sometimes, and especially in education, it may not be possible to measure the impact of a decision for a number of years. It may be necessary to look for a range of intermediate or proxy measures of improvement (note this can cause a range of problems – see Coe, 2013).
- To measure both the costs and benefits of a decision outcome, multiple measures will be required, though Langley et al. suggest trying to keep the number of measures to six or fewer.

Langley et al. (2009: 96) then go on to identify three different levels of measure which have the potential to contribute to organisational and individual learning in the complex setting of a classroom, school or system.

- Outcome measures are measures of the performance of the system under study.
- Process measures are measures of whether an activity has been accomplished.
- Balancing measures: To achieve an improvement in some measures while degrading performance in others is usually not acceptable. In making changes to improve outcomes and process measures, we want to be sure any related measures are maintained or improved.

The issues associated with identifying favourable outcomes will be discussed in more detail in Chapters 8 and 9.

Limitations in applying evidence-based practice to education

As already noted, an essential task of an evidence-based practitioner is to continually challenge the assumptions underpinning his or her practice. Accordingly, it is necessary to be aware of both the criticisms and limitations of evidence-based practice. Very helpfully Hargreaves and Fullan (2012), Brown (2015) and Cain (2015) all provide extensive lists of some of the challenges and controversies associated with evidence-based practice within education. For example, Brown (2015) raises issues around: the nature and quality of evidence; whether evidence-based practice reduces teachers' professional autonomy; how can professionals' tacit knowledge be combined with scientific research; power differentials between practitioners, researchers and policy-makers; whether systematic reviews and randomised controlled trials are appropriate for education; whether teachers and school leaders have the capacity to engage with research; and, both the physical and intellectual accessibility of research.

Hopefully the rest of this book will either explicitly or implicitly address some if not all of these criticisms. For example, Chapters 5, 6 and 7 will go into some detail about how different sources of evidence can be appraised for their usefulness in addressing problems of practice. Chapter 11 will consider how evidence-based school leadership can increase the professional autonomy of both teachers and school leaders. Chapter 5 will look into the nature of both systematic reviews and randomised controlled trials and critically examine their usefulness for the evidence-based practitioner. Chapter 9 will look at some of the very real challenges of combining tacit and explicit knowledge in the decision-making process. Chapter 4 will look at how school leaders and teachers can easily increase their physical and intellectual access to educational research.

Summary and key points

- Evidence-based practice within education is not limited to teaching and learning and can be extended to all aspects of school leadership and management.
- Evidence-based practice involves a six-stage process:
  - Asking: translating a practical issue or problem into answerable questions
  - Acquiring: systematically searching for and retrieving the evidence
  - Appraising: critically judging the trustworthiness of and relevance of the evidence
  - Aggregating: weighing and pulling together the evidence
  - Applying: incorporating the best available evidence into the decision-making process
  - Assessing: evaluating the outcomes of the decision taken
- The four main sources of evidence used by evidence-based practitioners include: educational and other research, school/organisational data, practitioner expertise and stakeholder views.
- Practitioner expertise has a central role to play in evidence-based practice.
- Done properly evidence-based practice has fundamental implications for the leadership and management of the school and how conversations take place between colleagues.
- Evidence-based school leaders aim to 'do the right thing' and 'do things right'.

- Evidence-based school leaders ensure that their decision-making is conducted and reported in such a way that the argument can be painstakingly examined.
- Being judicious involves evidence-based school leaders being appropriately critical of evidence and at the same time displaying 'practical wisdom'.
- Nevertheless, there are a number of criticisms and limitations of the use of evidence-based practice within education, of which evidence-based school leaders should be aware.

References

Anderson, N., Herriot, P. and Hodgkinson, G. (2001) 'The practitioner–researcher divide in industrial, work and organizational (IWO) psychology: where are we now, and where do we go from here?', *Journal of Occupational and Organizational Psychology*, 74 (4): 391–411.

Badaracco, J.L. (2016) 'Managing yourself: how to tackle your toughest decisions', *Harvard Business Review*, 94 (9): 104–7.

Barends, E., Rousseau, D. and Briner, R. (2014) *Evidence-Based Management: the Basic Principles*. Amsterdam: Center for Evidence-Based Management.

Booth, W., Colob, G., Williams, J., Bizup, J. and Fitzgerald, W. (2016) *The Craft of Research*, 4th edn. Chicago, IL: The University of Chicago Press.

Brown, C. (2015) *Evidence-Informed Policy and Practice in Education: a Sociological Grounding*. London: Bloomsbury Publishing.

Brown, C., Stoll, L. and Godfrey, D. (2017) 'Leading for innovation and evidence-informed improvement', in P. Earley and T. Greany (eds), *School Leadership and Education System Reform*. London: Bloomsbury.

Cain, T. (2015) 'Teachers' engagement with published research: addressing the knowledge problem', *The Curriculum Journal*, 26 (3): 488–509.

Coe, R. (2013) *Inaugural Lecture of Professor Robert Coe Director of CEM and Professor of Education at the School of Education*. University of Durham.

Cronbach, L.J. and Suppes, P. (eds) (1969) *Research for Tomorrow's Schools: Disciplined Inquiry for Education*. New York: MacMillan.

De Hart Hurd, P. (1998) 'Scientific literacy: new minds for a changing world', *Science Education*, 82 (3): 407–16.

Hammersley-Fletcher, L., Lewin, C., Davies, C., Duggan, J., Rowley, H. and Spink, E. (2015) *Evidence-Based Teaching: Advancing Capability and Capacity for Enquiry in Schools: Interim Report*. London: National College for Teaching and Leadership.

Hargreaves, A. and Fullan, M. (2012) *Professional Capital: Transforming Teaching in Every School*. New York: Teachers College Press.

Higgins, S., Katsipataki, M., Kokotsaki, D., Coe, R., Eliot Major, L. and Coleman, R. (2013) *Teaching and Learning Toolkit: Technical Appendices*. London: Sutton Trust Education Endowment Foundation.

Langley, G.J., Moen, R., Nolan, K.M., Nolan, T.W., Norman, C.L. and Provost, L.P. (2009) *The Improvement Guide: a Practical Approach to Enhancing Organizational Performance.* San Francisco, CA: John Wiley & Sons.

Lowenstein, R. (2006, January 22). 'When business has questions, Drucker still has answers', *New York Times, Bu* 7.

Nelson, J. and O'Beirne, C. (2014) *Using Evidence in the Classroom: What Works and Why?* Slough: National Foundation for Educational Research.

Tierney, S. (2015) 'Four Aces for Improving the Quality of Teaching #rEdScot'. *@LeadingLearner.* https://leadinglearner.me/2015/08/29/four-aces-for-improving-the-quality-of-teaching-redscot/ (accessed 21 February 2018).

Von Krogh, G., Ichijo, K. and Nonaka, I. (2000) *Enabling Knowledge Creation: How to Unlock the Mystery of Tacit Knowledge and Release the Power of Innovation.* Oxford: Oxford University Press.

Wilkinson, D. (2017) 'What's the difference between data and evidence? Evidence-based practice'. *The Oxford Review.* www.oxford-review.com/data-v-evidence/ (accessed 1 May 2018).

Yates, J.F. and Potworowski, G.A. (2012) 'Evidence-based decision management', in *The Oxford Handbook of Evidence-Based Management.* Oxford: Oxford University Press.

Zhao, Y. (2017) 'What works may hurt: side effects in education', *Journal of Educational Change, 18* (1): 1–19.

3

ASKING WELL-FORMULATED QUESTIONS

Chapter outline

In this chapter issues associated with the scope of evidence-based school leadership and management are explored. Consideration is given to: what is meant by the term 'problem of practice'; how these problems of practice can be identified and prioritised; and which problems of practice are best suited to an evidence-based approach? Problems of practice will then be turned into well-formulated and answerable questions by using techniques such as PICOT, CIMO and SPICE. Finally, attention will focus on how these techniques can be embedded into the day-to-day work of the school.

Key words: *problem of practice, well-formulated questions, urgent, important, PICOT, CIMO, SPICE*

When considering how to make the most of the potential of evidence-based practice, school leaders will, quite rightly, have teaching and learning at the forefront of their minds. However, as already indicated in Chapter 1, evidence-based school leadership is not limited to teaching and learning and applies to all aspects of the role of the school leader. To help get to grips with the range of problems to which evidence-based practice could be applied, Neeleman (2017) has identified three main domains and 16 sub-domains associated with the work of the school leader and manager (see Table 3.1).

Table 3.1   Grasping the scope of school autonomy: a classification scheme for school policy practice

Domain	Sub-domains			
Education	Pedagogical approaches	Educational programmes	Systemic pathways	Learning environments and methods for teaching, learning and assessment
The school as an organisation	Mission, vision, identity culture and image	Organisational structures	Organisation of education	Quality assurance
	Student care and support	Stakeholder relationships	Financial resources	Facilities and accommodation
Staff	Professional autonomy and culture	Teaching and school-related assignments	Staffing policy: assessment and payment	Recruitment and employment

Source: Neeleman (2017)

Although supporting the development of evidence-based teaching and learning is an extremely important aspect of the work of the school leader, it does not mean that the use of evidence-based practice should be limited to matters associated with pedagogy educational programmes. Evidence-based practice can, and should, be extended to all aspects of the work of the school, including finance, facilities and accommodation, staffing, recruitment, employment and school culture.

At any one time, across these 16 sub-domains, there will be a number of different demands on school leaders' time and attention. As such, the question arises: how do school leaders identify those problems of practice on which they are going to focus their scarce time and energy? However, before answering this question it is necessary to define the term 'a problem of practice'.

What is a problem of practice?

Mintrop (2016) defines a problem of practice as 'a problem for which a remedy is urgently sought that can be locally implemented' (p. 23). However, a major challenge for school leaders is to try to avoid spending all their time focusing on the urgent. Nevertheless, school leaders need to spend a good proportion of their time focusing on the 'non-urgent but important', for as Drucker (2001) states: 'effective people do not make a great many decisions. They concentrate on the important ones' (p. 183). As such, and for the rest of this book, the term 'problem of practice' will be viewed 'an important problem for which a remedy is sought and that can be locally implemented'. Accordingly, evidence-based practice is probably best reserved for those 'problems of practice' that are deemed important, non-urgent and can be locally resolved.

By using this definition, it is necessary to distinguish between the important and the urgent, whilst accepting that at times an issue may be both important and urgent. One way of defining important issues is that they have the potential to either increase or decrease the long-term capacity and capability of the department or school. Depending on how they are tackled they have the potential to improve (or not) how school leaders and their colleagues go about their work. On the other hand, urgent issues are time-bound and often have to be dealt with this minute, this hour or this day.

Taking this into account, a good starting point is for school leaders to try to identify the nature of the issue being faced and ask whether it is unique or representative of a more general issue. As Drucker (2001) states: 'the generic always has to be answered through a rule, a principle. The exceptional can be handled as such and as it comes' (p. 183). Drucker then goes on to identify four types of occurrences, which are illustrated in Table 3.2. As such, evidence-based practice is potentially best suited to those non-urgent important problems that are either truly generic or are unique to the school, but generic in nature.

Table 3.2 A classification of occurrences

Classification	Examples
The truly generic	Pupil absenteeism
Unique for the school, but generic	A LEA-controlled school being incorporated into a multi-academy trust Ofsted rating the school as 'requiring improvement'
The truly exceptional	The Dunblane shooting
The emergence of a new generic problem	Post-Brexit bullying of children of EU migrants

Source: adapted from Drucker (2001)

Identifying important problems of practice

How do school leaders go about identifying the important problems for which a remedy can be implemented within their school? Mintrop (2016) provides a useful set of questions to help school leaders identify where they could spend precious time, energy and attention:

- What are the important recurring problems in the department, key stage, faculty, school or multi-academy trust?
- What is happening right now which might be an indicator of a future recurring problem?
- What are your spheres of influence in the department, key stage, faculty, school or multi-academy trust?
- Which problem is the most relevant to the learning needs of pupils and/or colleagues?
- Which problem is the most interesting to you, colleagues or pupils?
- Which problems can be addressed within a specified timeframe associated with evidence-based practice?
- What resources – be it staff, time, expertise and finance – are available to address the problem?
- What problems are linked to the broader aims and objectives of the school or multi-academy trust?

(Adapted from Mintrop, 2016: 23)

In thinking about how to identify the most important problems within a school, there are a number of approaches. One way is to look at existing departmental plans, school development plans and high-level strategic plans, and consider which aims and objectives may lend themselves to an evidence-based approach. This approach is appropriate in situations where school leaders have a pretty good idea of what to do, and evidence-based practice is just providing you with a disciplined process in how to go about making a decision. On the other hand, school leaders may wish to adopt a more open approach and scan the environment for what is going on for pupils, staff and stakeholders (Timperley et al., 2014).

Refining the problem of practice into a question worth answering by asking 'so what?'

Having undertaken an exercise identifying important problems of practice, a school leader may have come up with a number of examples similar or otherwise to the following:

- How do we best prepare pupils for external examinations?
- What is the best way of providing opportunities for teacher professional learning?
- How can we reduce teacher workload?
- Who is best placed to undertake performance reviews and appraisals?
- Where can we find the most effective marking strategies?
- What are the benefits of having a school research champion?

Drawing on the work of Booth et al. (2016), it is necessary ask the three 'so what?' questions: Does this problem of practice really matter? What would happen if the school did not address it? Would it make a difference to: the life chances of pupils; the well-being of colleagues; and the sustainability of the school, or multi-academy trust?

Using a structure suggested by Booth et al. (2016), the problems of practice can now be amended by using the 'so what?' principle, and linking each issue with related outcomes:

- I am interested in how we best prepare pupils for external examinations so that we can maximise their chances of progressing to higher education.

- I am interested in the best way of providing opportunities for teacher professional learning because I want to reduce teacher turnover at my school.
- I am concerned about how can we reduce teacher workload because I want to identify strategies that reduce the number of NQTs leaving the teaching profession.
- I am interested in who is best placed to undertake performance reviews and appraisals so that they become a more positive experience for individual staff.
- I am interested in working on marking strategies because I want to find out the most time-effective way of carrying out marking in order to reduce unnecessary workload on teaching staff.
- I am interested in understanding the role of school research champions because I want to find out how best to access academic research because I want teaching and learning to be informed by best currently available research knowledge.

Turning problems of practice into well-formulated and answerable questions

Further work is required to turn these problems of practice into well-formulated and answerable questions. To help do this a range of techniques developed in healthcare evidence-based management and library services will be used. In doing so, it is not being suggested that these are the only ways problems of practice can be translated into well-formulated questions. However, these techniques are extremely useful in helping to make questions more precise and precision leads to a number of positive benefits when it comes to searching out evidence and data to help answer the problem of practice.

PICOT

In the first instance, to help refine the problems of practice into well-formulated and answerable questions attention will be directed onto the PICOT structure, which was developed for use in evidence-based medicine. PICOT is a mnemonic for the components of a clinical question and, adapting it for the context of schools, the PICOT acronym stands for:

P — Pupil or Problem: How would you describe the group of pupils or problem?

I — Intervention: What are you planning to do with your pupils?

C — Comparison: What is the alternative to the intervention – what else could you do?

O — Outcomes: What are you trying to achieve?

T — Time: What period of time does it take for the intervention to achieve the outcomes you are aiming for?

In much of the literature PICOT is abbreviated to PICO. However, given the nature of the school year the longer version, including time (T), is probably more useful to school leaders and teachers. The following examples show how some of the problems of practice that have been converted into 'so what?' questions can now be further transformed into PICOT questions.

- Are Year 13 pupils preparing for A-level examinations using 'modern retrieval practice techniques' more successful than pupils using traditional revision techniques?
- For experienced members of staff, how does directed compared to non-directed professional learning influence professional autonomy and subsequent decisions whether to remain with the school at the end of the academic year?
- For recently qualified teachers, are heads of department better placed than senior leaders in conducting annual performance reviews and appraisal, resulting in more appropriate professional targets and objectives?
- For staff in a large secondary school, will a single specialist research lead be more effective in supporting an annual programme of research-informed teaching and learning than a group of research leads?

Alternatives to PICOT – CIMO and SPICE

The PICOT format may not meet the needs of your school, with perhaps some colleagues thinking its implied emphasis on interventions and quantitative research does not make it suitable for use in education. To address this, consideration will now be given to two alternatives: CIMO and SPICE.

CIMO

The CIMO format has been developed by Denyer and Tranfield (2009) for use in an organisational context. They argue that well-crafted review questions need to take into account both the organisational context and the relationship between an intervention and an outcome. Adapting the work of Pawson (2006) they have developed a structured and contextual approach to developing an answerable question (CIMO) which provides a better focus on both the context and the mechanism(s) by which change is brought about:

C — Context: Which individuals, relationships, institutional settings, or wider systems are being studied?

I — Intervention: The effects of what event, action, or activity are being studied?

M — Mechanisms: What are the mechanisms that explain the relationship between interventions and outcomes? Under what circumstances are these mechanisms activated or not activated?

O — Outcomes: What are the effects of the intervention? How will the outcomes be measured? What are the intended and unintended effects?

Denyer and Tranfield (2009) provide a worked example of a question framed with these components: 'Under what conditions (C) does leadership style (I) influence the performance of project teams (O), and what mechanisms operate in the influence of leadership style (I) on project team performance (O)?' (p. 682).

Let's now develop some examples of the CIMO format in action in a school or college setting:

- Under what circumstances does a secondary school's middle manager's leadership styles influence the academic performance of students, and what are the mechanisms of middle management leadership style that affect student performance?
- Under what conditions does retaking GCSE English provide an effective mechanism for developing the English skills of 16-year-old full-time further education students, where those students previously achieved a grade D? What are the processes associated with resitting GCSE English that affect English skills?

- Is the use of flipped learning an effective mechanism for engaging Year 11 secondary school pupils and reducing the risk of non-attendance, where there has previously been a history of non-attendance in the school? What are the mechanisms of flipped learning that affect pupils' attendance?
- Under what circumstance are graded lesson observations effective in improving teachers' teaching where those teachers have previously been judged to be inadequate or requiring improvement, and what are the mechanisms of graded lesson observation that affect teacher performance?

SPICE

The SPICE framework, which has its origins in library and information services, was developed by Booth (2004). This mnemonic recognises that it is necessary to distinguish between the setting and the perspective, and recognises the importance of the views of stakeholders. It also adopts a broader definition of the term 'outcomes', to include evaluation, as this captures both the longer-term impact of an intervention, but also some of its more difficult to pin down characteristics (Cleyle and Booth, 2006). As such, the SPICE framework comprises of the following:

- **Setting** – where?
- **Perspective** – for whom?
- **Intervention** – what?
- **Comparison** – compared with what?
- **Evaluation** – with what result?

Using this framework, you can now formulate a range of different questions.

- From the perspective of a newly qualified teacher (NQT) in a secondary school, is formal coaching more effective than informal mentoring in ensuring the NQT successfully completes his or her probationary year?
- From the perspective of a newly appointed primary school headteacher in a school that 'requires improvement', is seeking to replace the existing leadership team more likely to lead to the school becoming good or outstanding?

- From the perspective of Year 11 pupils, are friendship groups more important than formal career advice in influencing the preferred choice of post-16 education?

How to ask the most important question

Having identified important problems of practice and turned them into well-formulated questions, it is necessary to consider: what is the most important question to ask for this school, right now? In the context of healthcare, Straus et al. (2011) have suggested a series of filters that could be used to identify the most important questions, and which have been adapted for use in schools:

- Which question, if answered, will be most useful for our pupils/ staff wellbeing, academic or personal?
- Which question will be most useful for subject leaders, heads of department and senior leaders in gaining a better understanding of the issues at hand?
- Which question will be most useful in helping to improve the department, school or college?
- Which question is most likely to re-occur and will need to be revisited in the future?
- Which question is most interesting to you as an evidence-based practitioner and will contribute most to your personal professional development?

Alternatively, the FINER mnemonic developed by Hulley et al. (2013) can help school leaders think through what are the most important questions to answer:

- **Feasibility:** Are there sufficient resources, within the school in terms of either capacity or capability, to adequately answer the question?
- **Interesting:** Is the question interesting to those given the task of researching the answer?
- **Novel:** Is this a recurring problem/question or something that is new to the school and may become an ongoing issue?
- **Ethical:** Have ethical issues been identified and considered?
- **Relevant:** Is it relevant to the school and is it going to influence school policy and practice?

Why take the time formulating questions clearly?

Busy school leaders may ask why bother taking the time to formulate questions clearly? Straus et al. (2011) identify seven ways in which well-formulated questions can improve evidence-based practice, by:

- Focusing scarce professional learning time on evidence that is directly relevant to the needs of pupils, school or colleagues.
- Concentrating professional learning time on evidence that directly addresses colleagues' particular knowledge requirements.
- Developing time-effective search strategies for multiple sources of evidence.
- Suggesting the forms that useful answers might take.
- Helping individuals communicate more clearly when requesting support and guidance from colleagues.
- Supporting colleagues in their own professional learning, by helping school leaders to model aspects of evidence-based practice.
- Answering well-formulated questions will potentially increase levels of job-satisfaction.

Accordingly, it would seem that developing well-formulated and answerable questions is an important task, which has the potential to increase the capacity and capability of the school to engage in evidence-based practice.

Applications

One of the challenges facing school leaders in seeking to develop the use of evidence-based practice is that many colleagues will say they do not have the time to spend on such activities (Hammersley-Fletcher et al., 2015). Taking this into account, it is important to try to integrate the development of well-formulated questions into the day-to-day working of the school. One way of doing this is to use one of the suggested question formats to help frame a short coaching conversation with a colleague. For example, a colleague may have a concern about an issue, which they are struggling to fully articulate. A school leader could quickly coach the colleague by asking:

- Who and what is the issue about?
- What would be your ideal outcome?

- How could that outcome be achieved?
- How else could this or a similar outcome be achieved?
- How would you know whether you have been successful?
- What are you going to do now?

This provides an opportunity for school leaders to model evidence-based practice, without it becoming an additional and burdensome activity. A second opportunity may come in a formal department, or school leadership, team meeting. In this instance, a colleague may identify a particular problem or issue to be addressed but there is a danger that both the question and answer are lost in the day-to-day business of the department or school. One way to capture the 'question' is through the use of an educational prescription, which records: the question, who is responsible for developing the answer and the deadline for the completion of the task. Accordingly, an educational prescription consists of the following:

- A specification of the learning or managerial problem that generated the question.
- A re-statement of the problem, as a well-formulated and answerable question.
- A clear statement as to who is responsible for answering the question.
- A deadline for answering the question, bearing in mind the learning needs of pupils, or staff, and its importance and urgency.
- A clear articulation of the steps involved in answering the question (see Figure 3.1)

To make best use of educational prescriptions it is probably best to make two or more copies, one for the member of staff undertaking the reviews, the other for the manager overseeing the process. The educational prescription should be written in a way that allows the member of staff who is tasked with answering the prescription to have meaningful discussion with colleagues who may be needed to help acquire and appraise the relevant evidence (see Chapter 4 for more detail).

Third, many schools are beginning to incorporate small-scale inquiries within an individual's performance and review objectives. Using one of the suggested structures can help colleagues develop a question that is both relevant to their needs and at the same time is consistent with the time and resources available to address it.

Pupil/Class/Year Group/other: **Member of staff:**

_____   _____

Problem: How would you describe the situation?

Intervention: What are you thinking of doing?

Comparison: What else could you do?

Outcome: What would a favourable outcome look like?

Follow-up: When will you discuss progress on the educational prescription?

Checklist for future discussions:

- How did you go about searching for multiple sources of relevant evidence?
- How did you take into account pupil/student views?
- What were the outcomes of your search strategy?
- How valid and reliable is the evidence you found?
- Can this evidence be applied to the current problem?
- How useful was this process?

Figure 3.1 Educational prescription (adapted from Straus et al., 2011: 23)

Fourth, one of the problems often associated with departmental development plans is that they consist of a long list of tasks and actions that are to be undertaken. Unfortunately, at the end of the year it is not possible to identify those actions which made a difference and those actions which didn't. One way in which departmental heads can develop more effective and efficient developmental plans is to phrase department tasks by using the PICOT or one of the other formats. Doing so will give both senior leaders and the department a well-structured activity, which can be subsequently evaluated. Indeed, it might be possible to envisage a departmental development plan that consisted of three PICOT questions, and little else.

Summary and key points

- Evidence-based school leadership can be applied to all domains of school leadership.
- Evidence-based practice is possibly best suited to important generic and non-urgent problems of practice.

- Once identified, problems of practice should be converted into well-formulated and answerable questions, by using techniques such as, PICOT, CIMO and SPICE.
- The 'so what?' and FINER techniques can help identify the most important problem(s) of practice.
- There are a number of benefits of articulating a problem of practice, for example, helping you focus your scarce professional learning time on the important needs of pupils, staff or yourself. Well-articulated problems can be incorporated into the day-to-day work of the school – be it informally or formally – through use of one-to-one coaching or the use of PICOT to develop areas of inquiry for inclusion in performance review and appraisal.

References

Booth, A. (2004) *Formulating Answerable Questions*. London: Facet.

Booth, W., Colob, G., Williams, J., Bizup, J. and Fitzgerald, W. (2016) *The Craft of Research*, 4th edn. Chicago, IL: The University of Chicago Press.

Cleyle, S. and Booth, A. (2006) 'Clear and present questions: formulating questions for evidence based practice', *Library Hi Tech*, 24 (3): 355–68.

Denyer, D. and Tranfield, D. (2009) 'Producing a systematic review', in D. Buchanan and A. Bryman (eds), *The Sage Handbook of Organizational Research Methods*. London: Sage.

Drucker, P.F. (2001) *The Essential Drucker*. Oxford: Butterworth–Heinemann.

Hammersley-Fletcher, L., Lewin, C., Davies, C., Duggan, J., Rowley, H. and Spink, E. (2015) 'Evidence-based teaching: advancing capability and capacity for enquiry', in *Schools: Interim Report*. London: National College for Teaching and Leadership.

Hulley, S.B., Cummings, S.R., Browner, W.S., Grady, D.G. and Newman, T.B. (2013) *Designing Clinical Research*. Philadephia, PA: Lippincott Williams & Wilkins.

Mintrop, R. (2016) *Design-Based School Improvement: A Practical Guide for Education Leaders*. Cambridge, MA: Harvard Education Press.

Neeleman, A.-M. (2017) *Grasping the Scope of School Autonomy: a Classification Scheme for School Policy Practice*. Stratford-upon Avon: BELMAS.

Pawson, R. (2006) *Evidence-Based Policy: A Realist Perspective*. London: Sage.

Straus, S., Glasziou, P., Richardson, S. and Haynes, B. (2011) *Evidence-Based Medicine: How to Practise and Teach It*, 4th edn. Edinburgh: Churchill Livingstone Elsevier.

Timperley, H., Kaser, L. and Halbert, J. (2014) *A Framework for Transforming Learning in Schools: Innovation and the Spiral of Inquiry*. Melbourne: Centre for Strategic Education.

4

SYSTEMATICALLY SEARCHING FOR AND RETRIEVING EVIDENCE

Chapter outline

This chapter aims first to examine the nature of various sources of evidence – be it scientific research, school data, practitioner expertise and views of stakeholders. This will be followed by a discussion of the difference between tacit and explicit knowledge. Next, the chapter explores the challenges associated with the use of the best available evidence and what criteria might be used to help identify that evidence. This in turn will lead to a discussion of how to develop an evidence search strategy for all four sources of evidence, followed by a brief examination of how to distinguish between 'good, bad and ugly evidence' found on the Internet. Consideration will then be given to understanding the components of both practitioners and stakeholders of theories of action. The chapter will then explore the range of data and evidence which is available about most schools. Finally, the chapter will look at a technique known as 'open to learning' conversations as a mechanism for acquiring stakeholder evidence.

Key words: *explicit knowledge, open to learning conversations, search strategies, tacit knowledge, theories of action*

As noted in Chapter 2, this book focuses on the use of multiple sources of evidence when seeking to make a decision based on the best available evidence. This means that any approach to acquiring the best available evidence needs to do more than just seek out the most recent systematic review or reviews (see Chapter 5) relevant to the problem of practice. Instead it will require a search strategy that also seeks to access organisational/school data, experiential evidence and the views of stakeholders. However, before discussing the development of an evidence search strategy it will be helpful to look in more detail at the nature of each of the four sources of evidence.

Scientific and academic research

For many evidence-based practitioners the first source of evidence to be obtained is from academic research published in peer-reviewed journals, with this type of evidence also being found in edited books of already published peer-reviewed journal articles. There may also be official materials published on a recognised institutional website, for example, the Education Endowment Foundation, the EPPI-Centre and Evidence for ESSA (Every Student Succeeds Act). That said, educational research is wide-ranging, with approximately 280 English language peer-reviewed journals on education being published each year, and with the number of academic journals and articles being published increasing by 3–3.5% per year (Ware and Mabe, 2015).

Given the volume of research being published annually, the temptation may be to prioritise those journals specialising in education and topics such as pedagogy, professional development, school effectiveness, school improvement and assessment. However, as noted in Chapter 2, the academic/scientific research relevant to the evidence-based practitioner covers not just teaching and learning but also a wide range of other areas (Neeleman, 2017). Hence, there is much to learn from other fields such as organisational behaviour, occupational psychology, cognitive science, knowledge management – extending also to areas such as evidence-based healthcare and evidence-based social work.

School evidence

The second source of evidence comes from the school itself. School census data provides a vast range of information about the characteristics of both the school and individual pupils. Staff absence return and financial returns also provide useful information, with this data being externally validated and audited against a range of accountability measures. Next comes data such as external examination results, aggregated behaviour data (records of punctuality, poor classroom behaviour, homework completion). However, it should be noted that the school has some control over how this information is presented and it may not always be as trustworthy as you would like. This is especially the case if a school leader is new to a role. The last source of internal data is that which comes directly from the staff, such as internal assessment data (especially at Key Stage 3 in secondary schools) and attendance to parents' evenings.

For our purposes, school data is viewed as primarily quantitative – be it related to examination results, financial outcomes or staffing recruitment and turnover. Given this focus on quantitative evidence, this section on school data will also include any available external benchmark data. School data will also include documentary evidence about the school, for example, school policies, timetables and development plans. More qualitative elements – linked to school culture – such as attitudes towards the senior team will be classified as part of stakeholder evidence. However, it again needs to be stressed that this is for ease of classification of different sources of evidence and the development of simple evidence search strategies rather than implying that qualitative data about the school is not important.

Practitioner evidence

The third source of evidence is the professional experience and judgement of those individuals who are directly involved in the decision-making process. In other words, those individuals – be it school leaders, teachers or others – whose role in the decision-making process is to recommend, agree or decide. Drawing upon the work of Blenko et al. (2010), within the decision-making process there are individuals whose role is to make recommendations about how to proceed, and could be the school research or evidence lead who acquires the information, appraises and aggregates the evidence, and makes a recommendation for action. Secondly, there are the individuals who most agree to a decision before it can be implemented. For example, managers with a responsibility for child protection may have to formally agree to the recommendation before the decision can be implemented. In other circumstances, it may be the headteacher or CEO of a multi-academy trust who may have the legal responsibility for the decision, especially finances. Finally, there is the person who makes the decision. It may be the headteacher or the CEO, or it may well be another person to whom that decision has been delegated, for example, a deputy or assistant headteacher, school research lead or head of department.

However, it needs to be made explicit that individuals who are formally part of the decision-making process – 'recommenders', 'deciders' and 'agreers' – are not the only holders of appropriate knowledge and expertise relevant to the decision-making process. Rather, this categorisation is to help differentiate between the different sources of evidence and will in the future help access the knowledge and expertise of individuals who may have an input into the decision-making process or are impacted upon by the decision, but do not have the ultimate responsibility for making the decision. As such, the professional expertise and judgement of these individuals and others who are impacted upon by the decision is viewed as part of evidence from stakeholders, and is just as important as any other source of evidence.

Stakeholder evidence

Our final source of evidence is stakeholder values, concerns and expertise. In this context stakeholders are the individuals or groups

who may be affected by your evidence-based decisions and their consequences. Internal stakeholders may include teaching assistants,
teachers, heads of department, senior leaders, parents, members of
the governing body, trustees of the multi-academy trust and pupils.
Stakeholders from outside the school may include feeder schools,
parents, the local authority, the government and the public at large.

Accessing and appraising stakeholder evidence is extremely important, for the values, preferences and expertise of stakeholders will
invariably have a major part in the decision-making process. Their values, belief and expertise will bring a particular perspective to other
sources of evidence. Indeed, the values, preferences and beliefs of
stakeholders may be a fundamental source of evidence in deciding
whether a particular course of action should be taken and the level
and scale of implementation. Certain stakeholders may well need to
be 'on-board' if a particular course of action is to be pursued.

Furthermore, gathering evidence from stakeholders is a fundamental part of the essence of evidence-based decision-making.
Referring back to the work of Sackett et al. (1996), involving patients
in making informed choices about the course of treatment to be
undertaken is a fundamental component of evidence-based medicine.
As such, attempts at evidence-based school leadership and management which did not fully engage and value the preferences, beliefs and
expertise of stakeholders, should not be seen as being consistent with
the intentions of the originators of the evidence-based movement.

Tacit and explicit knowledge

Having briefly examined the role of both practitioner and stakeholder
evidence in the process of evidence-based decision-making, it is timely
to discuss the concepts of tacit and explicit knowledge. This discussion
will provide some initial insights as to how to go about accessing the
tacit and explicit knowledge of both practitioners and stakeholders.

The concept of tacit knowledge has its origins in the work of Polanyi
(1966) who sums up the concept in the succinct and pithy phrase 'We
know much more than we can tell' (p. 4). Tacit knowledge is personally
and socially embedded, and is linked to hunches, intuitions, feelings
and images and is context-specific. Accordingly, tacit knowledge can be
broken down into two components. One component involves technical skills or 'know-how'. When dealing with difficult situations, an

experienced school leader will have a pool of expertise on which they can draw, but may not necessarily be able to express the underpinning principles behind what he or she knows. A second component consists of the mental models, assumptions and the things we take as a given, and are often particularly challenging to express. (Chapter 7 will look at the implications of this in more detail when examining the role of the ladder of inference in appraising evidence.)

On the other hand, explicit knowledge is much more precise and codified and sometimes described as 'declarative knowledge' and 'knowing that'. Explicit knowledge includes tangible information, which is codified and accessible. It can be captured in formal documentation and can easily be shared with others through the use of a range of technologies and media.

As evidence-based practice involves 'making decisions through the conscientious, explicit and judicious use of the best available evidence from multiple sources' (Barends et al., 2014: 2), then as part of the process of acquiring evidence, it is necessary to look at the interaction between tacit and explicit knowledge. Nonaka and Takeuchi (1995) identify four different modes of knowledge conversion:

1. *From tacit to tacit*: '[Socialization] is a process of sharing experiences and thereby creating tacit knowledge, such as shared mental models and technical skills' (p. 62).
2. *From tacit to explicit*: '[Externalization] is a process of articulating tacit knowledge into explicit concepts. It is a quintessential knowledge-creation process in that tacit knowledge becomes explicit, taking the shape of metaphors, analogies, concepts, hypotheses or models' (p. 64).
3. *From explicit to explicit*: '[Combination] is a process of systemizing concepts into a knowledge system. This mode of knowledge conversion involves combining different bodies of explicit knowledge. Individuals exchange and combine knowledge through such media as documents, meetings, telephone conversations or computerized communication networks' (p. 67).
4. *From explicit to tacit*: '[Internalization] is a process of embodying explicit knowledge into tacit knowledge. It is closely related to "learning by doing". When experiences through socialization, externalization, and combination are internalized into individuals' tacit knowledge bases in the form of shared mental models or technical know-how' (p. 69).

This distinction between tacit and explicit has a number of important implications for the evidence-based practitioner. First, when attempting to acquire 'knowledge' to assist in the decision-making it is important to be aware of what type of knowledge is being acquired. Second, the very process of acquiring knowledge (and evidence) may lead to that knowledge changing form, for example, from tacit knowledge to explicit knowledge. Third, acquiring evidence cannot be seen just as a desk-exercise and will involve engaging in a range of social interactions, from discussion to observation. Fourth, the very process of engaging in evidence-based practice will, if done well, create new 'local knowledge' for use in your setting. Fifth, aggregating the best available evidence will involve a process of combining both tacit and explicit knowledge.

Using the best available evidence

Evidence-based practitioners in trying to address problems of practice, will find it necessary to gather a range of evidence from a number of different sources. However, evidence-based practice is not just about the quantity of evidence, but rather involves making the most of the best available evidence (Barends et al., 2014). Accordingly, evidence-based practitioners will need to give thought as to how much weight should be given to each piece of evidence. To help do this Gough et al. (2012) have put forward four key questions, which can be adapted for use with multiple sources of evidence. First, can the evidence be trusted, is it accurate, is it understandable, is it transparent, were the purposes of the research made clear? Second, was the evidence collected in such a way as to be appropriate for answering the question or problem being investigated? Third, how relevant is the evidence to the problem of practice under investigation? Fourth, what overall weight should we give this piece of evidence in seeking an answer to a problem of practice? Answering these four questions is difficult enough when seeking to judge the quality of different types of the same source of evidence, for example, different research studies. However, evidence-based practice involves looking at the best available evidence from a range of sources, which makes the task even harder.

Nevertheless, it is important to note that evidence-based practitioners are often faced with situations where there is little or no high-quality research evidence available. In these circumstances, it may be necessary to rely on the available professional experience and preferences and values of stakeholders to come up with the most plausible solution to the problem of practice. In doing so, this may subsequently require some form of rapid implementation process – such as a pilot study and the repeated use of a Plan–Do–Study–Act cycle to test the effectiveness of a particular course of action (Langley et al., 2009). As such, it is important to recognise that the evidence base across the four sources of evidence is never going to be perfect. On the other hand, having access to the best available evidence is probably better than having access to no evidence at all.

Developing an evidence search strategy

When developing an evidence search strategy, the conventional approach is to start with developing a search strategy to identify relevant high-quality academic research. However, given the emphasis in this book on the use of multiple sources of evidence, starting with the research evidence should not be adopted as the default position. So to help develop an appropriate evidence-search strategy this section will bring together the work of Briner et al. (2009), Straus et al. (2011) and Briner and Rousseau (2011) to come up with a more comprehensive and relevant search strategy. Such a search strategy might consist of the following elements:

- Further discussion of the importance and relevance of the identified problem of practice. This may well take the form of reviewing the PICOT, CIMO or SPICE formulated question so it becomes much more precise, with a greater understanding of who is being affected by this problem of practice.
- For each potential source of evidence, identifying a range of data and information that is currently available that may help answer the problem of practice.
- Attempting to identify and articulate your current 'best answer' about how to address the problem of practice – through articulating a theory of action.
- Developing a search strategy for published research, especially systematic reviews, deciding what is going to be read and how it is going to be found.

- Developing a search strategy for quantitative school and other external benchmark data.
- Engaging with stakeholders to get their views about the problem and the strategies that could be adopted and how any solutions or interventions adopted may affect stakeholders.
- Appraising the evidence for its trustworthiness and relevance and aggregating the information so that it can inform the decision-making process (see Chapters 5, 6 and 7).

Given the extensive discussion in Chapter 3 of how to articulate a well-formulated and answerable question of practice, the following section will start with trying to identify potential sources of evidence.

Identifying potential sources of evidence

As noted in Chapter 2, one of the most common misconceptions about evidence-based practice is that it totally relies upon research evidence and excludes other sources of evidence. In order to address this problem, it is necessary to gain context-relevant evidence. Accordingly, Figure 4.1, based upon the work of Briner and Rousseau (2011), looks at some of the information that a human resources officer of a multi-academy trust will seek to find when considering problems of high levels of teaching staff turnover.

Source of evidence	Question
Research	What does the research evidence suggest are the most likely causes of staff turnover?
	Are there any systematic reviews on teaching staff turnover and the most effective interventions to reduce it?
	What evidence is there that those interventions might work in my multi-academy trust?
	Are there any new analyses which might provide an alternative 'take' on teaching staff turnover?
School/class data	What actually is the teaching staff turnover rate?
	What type of staff are leaving, NQTS, RQT mid-career or experienced?
	Are staff leaving from any particular department, stage or school?
	Is there anything going on locally in other schools or multi-academy trusts which might be impacting upon staff turnover?
	What would it cost the school to undertake any form of intervention?
	What are the average rates of teaching staff turnover in my type of multi-academy trust – primary, secondary, post-16?
	What are the average rates of teaching staff turnover in other local schools?

Source of evidence	Question
Stakeholders' views (pupils, staff, parents, community)	What do teaching staff think is happening?
	What do colleagues think about any proposed changes of practice?
	Do staff surveys give an indication as to what might be happening?
	Are there any 'outlier' views, which might provide a particular insight or different perspective?
	What alternative explanations and proposed solutions do others have?
Practitioner expertise	What do other members of the senior leadership team think is happening?
	Have I seen this before in other schools or multi-academy that I have worked in?
	What happened?
	What is my 'best current answer' about staff turnover?
	What's worked in the past in other schools that I have worked in, and why?
	What does my 'gut' or 'intuition' say is happening, and why?
	How relevant and applicable is my experience?

Figure 4.1 Staff turnover and potential sources of information

Having obtained the various sources of evidence, the human resources officer will then need to evaluate the evidence – approaches to which are explored in Chapters 5, 6 and 7. Once this evaluation has been completed, the evidence will then be aggregated and incorporated into the decision-making process, and is explored in Chapters 8 and 9.

Straus et al. (2011) argue that one of the first tasks to engage in when developing a search strategy is to articulate the current best 'off the top of your head' answer to the problem of practice. One way of doing this is to try to state the current 'theory of action'. Robinson and Lai (2005), who note that the concept of a theory of action was initially developed by Argyris and Schön (1974), provide a useful summary of the term as:

It conveys the idea that people's behaviour is embedded in a set of beliefs, values, and understandings of about how to achieve their goals under a given set of conditions. Theories of action are both guides to action because they specify how to achieve particular purposes under given conditions ... Theories of action are also powerful sources of explanation. If you can discover what people's theories of action are, you can go beyond seeing what they do to understanding why they did it. (p. 19)

From the point of view of an evidence-based practitioner, theories of action are potentially extremely helpful. First, by articulating a theory of action an evidence-based school leader will potentially develop a far greater understanding of his or her own thinking, which will allow them to challenge both underpinning assumptions and interpretation of evidence (see Chapter 7 for a discussion of how this is done in the context of the ladder of inference). Second, understanding the underpinning structure of a theory of action will enable the evidence-based school leader to assess the quality of evidence put forward by stakeholders and other interested parties. Third, in seeking to identify and implement decisions, this is much easier to do if the evidence-based school leader understands colleagues' theories of action, and the constraints under which they operate (Robinson and Lai, 2005).

Using a structure of a theory of action outlined by Robinson (2011), consideration will be given to the construction of a theory of action for increasing teacher retention (see Figure 4.2) by looking at underpinning values, beliefs, associated actions and anticipated consequences.

Component	Current best guess(es)
Beliefs and values	Experienced and effective teachers are leaving the profession (and multi-academy trust) due to a lack of flexibility in working conditions
	Working conditions are important factor in attracting and retaining teaching staff
Actions	Plan and introduce flexible working conditions
Consequences	Teachers who would otherwise leave will remain with the multi-academy trust
	Teaching-staff motivation will increase due to the more personalised working arrangement leading to increased levels of pupil learning

Figure 4.2 A theory of action for retaining teacher staff

Of course, there may be more than theory of action, for example the human resources officer may believe that teaching staff are motivated by monetary rewards, such as performance pay. As such, if you are looking to recruit and retain teaching staff it is necessary to put in place appropriate performance pay structures to reward and motivate teachers. In doing so, this is likely to lead to an increased ability to recruit staff, with other effective teaching staff remaining with the school (Miller, 2017).

So how does an evidence-based practitioner go about articulating his or her current best guess? Adapting the work of Argyris and Schön

(1996), it is possible to use a relatively simple method to help articulate a theory of action. Having already articulated the problem of practice, a theory of action, or best guess, may be revealed by answers to the following questions.

- What are your beliefs and values about the problem of practice? Why is this 'problem' a problem?
- Describe the steps you could take to solve the problem. What would you do, with whom, when and how?
- What might be your thoughts and feelings as you implement the actions?
- What are the expected outcomes of your actions?
- Is there the possibility of negative unintended consequences, if so, what are they?

However, it is important to be aware of the difference between 'espoused' theories of action, which is what people do, and 'theories-in-action', which captures what people actually do. In particular, it is necessary to remember this distinction when seeking to evaluate both your own and others' espoused theories of action.

Developing a search strategy for published research, deciding what to read and how to find it

Having identified a problem of practice and turned it into a well-formulated and, hopefully, answerable question, it should be possible to develop a strategy to access the relevant academic research. Brunton et al. (2012) note that there are five main approaches to searching for research evidence: searching specialised registers and library catalogues; hand searching; reference list checking; Internet searching; and, professional and personal contacts.

Electronic databases

There are a whole range of electronic databases which the evidence-based school leader could seek to access. These include AEI; Academic Search Elite/EBSCOhost (which includes BEI); Educational Resources Information Center (ERIC); JSTOR; Social Sciences Abstracts; Sociological Collection; Web of Science being the most useful starting points.

Hand searching

It may also make sense – time permitting – to search indexes of prominent journals such as the: *American Education Research Journal, Education Researcher, Review of Educational Research, Journal of Teacher Education, British Educational Research, Teaching and Teacher Education, School Effectiveness and School Improvement, Oxford Review of Education, Educational Management Administration and Leadership, Journal of Professional Capital* and *Impact* (the new journal from England's Chartered College of Teaching). The evidence-based school leader may also want to include journals that are closely linked to the problem of practice being investigated.

Reference list checking

Brunton et al. (2012) note that by scanning the list of citations at the end of an article or book it is possible to develop a 'snowball' search strategy. Starting from one book or article on a topic, it is possible to 'snowball' backward to older publications used by the author, or authors. On the other hand, it is possible to 'snowball' forward to more recent publications by finding out how often that work has been cited in other publications. However, care will need to be taken to maintain a focus on the most relevant references and citations to the specific problem of practice.

Internet searching

Time-pressed evidence-based school leaders are likely to start looking for research by using generic search engines, for example Google or Bing. Alternatively, Google Scholar might be used, which will assist in identifying journal articles, and where PDF versions of journal articles can be often found; this is especially useful given that many journal articles sit behind expensive paywalls. Nevertheless, Kara (2016) has made a number of useful suggestions as to how to make the most of the Internet to access research articles and peer-reviewed papers, without paying for access.

Professional and personal contacts

One way of gaining access to research, particularly if it sits behind a paywall, is to email the corresponding author and request a copy of the article. More often than not a positive reply will be subsequently received, as the author will be delighted that their work has grabbed someone's attention. Alternatively, put out a request on Twitter which includes the link to the article being sought, as people will be often be generous with their time and expertise in suggesting associated research articles.

However, as Brunton et al. (2012) note, developing an effective search strategy will take time, effort and demands specialised skills, so if possible, it will be worth contacting a librarian to help plan the search. In addition, given that being 'explicit' is a key characteristic of being an evidence-based practitioner, keeping records of how the search strategy has been conducted is an essential part of acquiring evidence.

Nevertheless, as a 'rule of thumb', Brunton et al. (2012) note it is worth starting by seeking out systematic reviews, be it meta-analysis, research synthesis, systematic narrative, or meta-ethnography, with these reviews tending to be found on the websites of review-producing organisations. Examples of specialist websites that are relevant to evidence-based school leadership include:

- The Educational Endowment Foundation
- The Institute of Effective Education – University of York
- The EPPI Centre – University College London – Institute of Education
- The Best Evidence Encyclopaedia – Johns Hopkins University
- Research Schools International – Harvard University
- The Campbell Collaboration
- The Center for Evidence-Based Management

Once sources have been accessed and acquired, they will need to be evaluated for both relevance and reliability – with the latter being particularly relevant for sources found on the Internet. To that end, Wallace and Wray (2016) provide useful guidance on how to distinguish between the good, the bad and the ugly:

Likely to be very reliable

1. Peer-reviewed journal articles that are also published in an academic journal ...
2. Peer-reviewed journal articles published in genuine electronic journals ...
3. Already published journal articles and book chapters that have been posted, usually in PDF format, on an academic's home page. Check, however, that it is the published version

4. Electronically readable materials written by subject experts
5. Official materials published on a recognized institutional website

Likely to be fairly reliable

1. Pre-peer-reviewed material as described in (3) above – but track down the published version if possible
2. Lecture or research notes on the site of an academic working at a recognized university

Likely to be unreliable

1. Material on the home pages of individuals
2. Material on organization websites that is written by enthusiasts rather than experts
3. Free-for-all-post-your-views sites
4. Web-logs (blogs), chatroom pontifications etc. (Wallace and Wray, 2016: 25)

Having made a preliminary judgement about the reliability of a source, it is now necessary to make a judgement about the relevance of the source. Furthermore, given that in all likelihood evidence-based school leaders are hard-pressed, this process will need to be as efficient as possible. Accordingly, Booth et al. (2016) suggest three strategies.

• Books: scan the index for keywords and well-known 'educational experts', look at chapters that include key words, scan the introduction and last chapter, check the reference lists for titles relevant to your problem of practice.
• Articles: read the abstract, scan the introduction and conclusion; skim read for section headings and sub-headings, read the first sentences of paragraphs, check the references for titles relevant to your problem of practice.
• Internet sources: check the 'site map' and look for keywords. If the site has a search facility, type in the keywords.

Accessing school data

An evidence-based school leader's access to school data will be, to some extent, a function of where they sit within the organisational hierarchy. All other things being equal, the higher up an evidence-based school leader is within the organisational hierarchy the greater the expected level of access to school data. However, this ability to access data may lead to being swamped and unable to identify the most important data relevant to the problem of practice. Alternatively, as data is aggregated and 'moves' through the organisation some of the nuances within the data may be lost. On the other hand, leaders at lower levels of the organisational hierarchy may find it difficult to access useful data due to the presence of organisational 'gatekeepers' who may deny them. That said, these school leaders may be in a far better position to obtain data about the specific problem of practice and what is happening in classrooms, staffrooms and the broader school community.

Nevertheless, the data that is available to school leaders will, in a large part, be a function of the school information system in use and how well it is being implemented. There are a number of systems available, for example SIMS or 4Matrix, which can be used to capture data and present information through a range of dashboards and graphics. These systems can provide a whole range of reports, tracking pupils' progress through different key stages, looking at examination performance, value-added, attendance and other factors. In addition, there are a number of external services such as ALPs and YELLIs which can help schools undertake baseline assessment and value-added reports. Indeed, an entirely separate book can be written about the use of school data.

Moreover, and probably of more importance than what data is being collected, how it is presented and what system is used, is the question: why is the data being collected in the first place? Can the data help you explain, for example, why there had been either an improvement or decline in a school's examination results? The data might say what happened, but can it help explain why it happened?

However, it would be wrong to assume that the only data and evidence available about the school comes from management information systems. There is a significant amount of data available about the school which can be quite easily found and used. One way of classifying some of the available data is to use Neeleman's (2017) classification of school leadership and management activity into three domains and 16 sub-domains (see Table 4.1).

Table 4.1 Classification of school data in Neeleman's (2017) domains and sub-domains

Domain	Sub-domain	Examples of evidence and data
Education	Pedagogical approaches	Teaching and learning policy
		Homework and assessment policy
	Educational programmes	Data relating to the various Key Stages
		Extra-curricular programmes
	Systemic pathways	Alternative provision
	Learning environment	Use of virtual learning environments and other technologies to support learning
The school as an organisation	Mission, vision, identity	School strategic plan
		Development plan
	Organisational structure	Organisation chart
	Organisation of education	Mixed ability
		Streams
	Quality assurance	Approach to lesson observations
		Internal review and evaluation reports
	Student care and support	Number of temporary exclusions and permanent expulsions
		Provision of counselling support
	Stakeholder relationships	Approach to parent/school communications
		Percentage of parents who attend parents' evenings
		Trends in pupil enrolments
	Financial resources	Percentage of pupils receiving pupil premium funding
	Facilities and accommodation	Room occupancy
		Income received from lettings
Staff	Professional autonomy and culture	Continuing Professional Development Programme
		Number of staff undertaking teacher training qualifications (+ cost)
		Number of staff undertaking part-time degree-level study (+ cost)
	Teaching and school-related assignments	Planning and preparation time
		Balance between teaching and non-teaching staff

Domain	Sub-domain	Examples of evidence and data
	Staffing policy and assessment	Number of staff receiving pay uplift each year via performance-related pay policy (+ those who do not)
	Recruitment and employment	Number of unfilled vacancies Number of applications per vacancy

Up to this point this section has focused primarily on internally available evidence. We will now focus on external school data that should be 'readily available' about individual schools in England.

Performance tables

In England, the government's school performance tables website (www.gov.uk/school-performance-tables) provides information about the number of pupils in a school, the pupils' performance, the school's most recent Ofsted inspection report, school workforce and finance data. This is summarised in Table 4.2.

Table 4.2 Summary of information available about English schools

Category	Information
Pupils	Total number of pupils on roll
	Pupils with a statement of Special Educational Needs (SEN) or educational, health or care (EHCP) plan
	Boys on roll
	Girls on roll
	Pupils whose first language is not English
	Pupils eligible for free school meals at any time in the last six years
	Overall rate of absence
	The percentage of pupils missing 10% or more of the mornings or afternoons they could attend
Performance (Primary)	Percentage of pupils at the end of primary school 'meeting the expected standard' in reading, maths and writing
	Progress – How much progress pupils at this school made in reading, writing and maths between the end of Key Stage 1 and the end of Key Stage 2, compared to pupils across England who got similar results at the end of Key Stage 1

(Continued)

Table 4.2   (Continued)

Category	Information
	Pupils achieving at a higher standard
	Average score in reading
	Average score in mathematics
Performance (Secondary)	Progress 8
	Attainment 8 – schools get a score based on how well pupils have performed in up to eight qualifications, which include English, maths, three English Baccalaureate qualifications including sciences, computer science, history, geography and languages, and three other additional approved qualifications
	Percentage of pupils gaining grade 5 or above in GCSE English and GCSE maths
	Percentage of pupils achieving EBAC at grade C/or above
	Percentage remaining in education or going on to employment
Workforce	Total number of teachers
	Number of full-time equivalent teachers
	Number of pupils per full-time equivalent
	Average salary per full-time equivalent
	Total number of teaching assistants
	Number of full-time equivalent teaching assistants
	Total number of support staff
	Number of full-time equivalent support staff
Finance	Percentage of pupils receiving free school meals
	Total income per pupil
	Total spend per pupil
	Government funding per pupil
	Self-generated income per pupil
	Spend on teaching staff
	Spend on supply staff
	Spend on education support staff
	Spend on learning resources (non-ICT)
	Spend on ICT learning resources
	Spend on bought-in professional services
	Spend on back office (including staff)
	Spend on catering (including staff)
	Spend on other staff
	Spend on energy
	Spend on miscellaneous costs

Source: www.gov.uk/school-performance-tables

A full set of the available school data can also be downloaded from the associated website. However, for schools that are either single-academy trusts or part of multi-academy trusts there is significantly less financial information available. For example, the annual report and financial statements may be much more difficult to track down.

Analyse School Performance

Furthermore, 2017 saw the introduction of the Analyse School Performance (ASP) platform, which replaced the RAISEOnline service. ASP provides secure access for leaders, teachers and governors to a wide range of data in order to ensure successful analysis of pupil progress and attainment. Some of the key features of ASP include detailed school performance data, national averages, confidence intervals, and the ability to look at pupil-level data. In particular, it allows the analysis of performance data by, for example, gender or disadvantage. The ASP also includes access to the Inspection Data Summary Report.

Education Endowment Foundation – Families of Schools Database

The Education Endowment's Families of Schools Database allows evidence-based school leaders to learn from other schools which have similar pupils, in similar contexts. The prior attainment of pupils, the percentage of pupils eligible for Pupil Premium (funding) and the percentage of pupils for whom English is an additional language are all taken in account when classifying the families of schools. In addition, while data is presented for the most recent academic year for which data is available, charts measuring performance show the average performance over three years, to ensure trends are not hidden by small cohorts of pupils. The problem of small numbers is something that will be revisited in Chapter 7.

School inspection reports

As this section comes to a close, it would be wrong not to mention that Ofsted school inspection reports may be a valuable source of information about a school. School inspection reports are publicly available (and can be found at https://reports.ofsted.gov.uk). Indeed, given the high-stakes nature of the accountability system within England, a school inspection report is possibly the most 'read' piece of evidence about a school. If it is not the most read, it is possibly the most referred to piece of evidence, with the exception of school examination results (if they are improving or already at a very high level).

Nevertheless, it is important to remember that Ofsted reports and the associated judgements can become a little 'rusty' if not out of date. Camden (2017) reports that 'more than 1200 schools in England had not had a full Ofsted inspection in seven years, with more than 100 given respite for more than a decade'. Since 2011, schools graded as Outstanding have been exempted from inspection if the data indicates there are no causes for concern. Thus it is necessary to check when the most recent inspection took place, as a 'dated' inspection report may not give an accurate picture of the performance of the school.

Engaging with stakeholders

When seeking to obtain evidence from stakeholders the temptation is to immediately think of establishing focus groups, designing a survey questionnaire or to think about interviewing staff, and ample guidance on how to undertake these activities can be found in Coe et al. (2017). However, if this has to be done as a 'special effort', it possibly suggests something is wrong with the normal channels of communication within the school and its community. This is especially the case if these forms of communication reveal something completely unexpected and surprising.

Interestingly, Argyris (1994) argues that techniques such as surveys, focus groups and 'management by walking around' – even if done well – can get in the way of organisational learning. Argyris argues that although such processes might be useful in tackling relatively straightforward problems, such as car parking or menu preferences, or provide a range of quantitative data about work processes, they do not help people reflect on 'their work and behaviour' (p. 77). Indeed, what such surveys and processes could do is to lead to a reduction in individual accountability and 'do not surface the kinds of deep and potentially threatening or embarrassing information that can motivate learning and produce real change' (pp. 77–8). So instead, attention is going to focus on the use of what Robinson (2011) describes as 'open to learning' conversations, which are also derived from the work of Argyris.

Open to learning conversations

In the context of evidence-based school leadership, 'open to learn-ing' conversations are important for several reasons. First, evidence-based school leadership is all about obtaining valid data and information with which to make a decision. As seen in Chapter 2, being explicit is one of the characteristics of being an evidence-based practitioner. Indeed, by disclosing your line of thinking, hunches and assumptions, this will allow them to be challenged and tested. This type of conversation will help the evidence-based school leader both articulate their current thinking but also get feedback on that thinking from stakeholders.

Second, as Brown et al. (2016) report in a study of 829 teachers in 43 schools, in more trusting school environments there is likely to be a greater use of research evidence by teachers. Open to learn-ing conversations have an important role in encouraging professional conversations based on trust. Third, more often than not, evidence-based school leadership is likely to involve some form of change, and as Robinson (2011) argues, this is more likely to take place when teachers (and stakeholders) are involved in 'transparent and shared processes'. Indeed, if teachers and other stakeholders have the opportunities to share their views and if evidence-based school leaders are open about their own views, then staff and other stakeholders may have a greater commitment to the successful implementation of an execution.

What do open to learning conversations look like? As Robinson (2011) notes, there are 'no rules or step-by-step guides' (p. 41) as conver-sations will develop depending upon context and the dynamic of the relationships between the individuals involved. Nevertheless, as Robinson states there are a number of key components of open to learning conversations and Figure 4.3 provides an example of these as applied by the human resources officer of a multi-academy trust who is looking into teacher retention across a number of schools.

However, as Robinson (2011) notes, open to learning conversations are not just to be used on special occasions, for example, when trying to gather evidence as part of an evidence-based decision. Rather, the model provides a basis for day-to-day school leadership practice and helping to create an organisational culture that is attuned to the use of evidence and the development of relational trust.

Key component	What you might say
Describe the problem of practice from your point of view	I'm not sure whether I'm right though it would appear there is a high level of staff turnover within your school. I'd like to hear your views on this and whether we should put in place strategy A or B or do nothing.
Describe what your point of view is based on	The reason why I am saying this is because multi-academy trust data suggest that staff turnover in your school is higher than in other trust schools, and over the last three years more than 50% of teaching staff have left the school.
Invite the other's point of view	What do you think?
	Is there anything that I've missed out?
	Is there anything that I would appear to have got wrong?
	Is there other evidence or perspectives that I/we should take into account?
Paraphrase the other's point of view and check	I hear several key points you are making (summarise – using their words where at all possible)
Detect and check important assumptions	Tell me more about …
	What evidence have you got to support your view?
	Have you got any examples?
Establish common ground	It would seem to me that I have learnt this from you
	It would seem to me that we agree on …
	It would also seem that we have different views on …
Explain the next steps in the process	If you could provide me with …
	I'm going to reflect on what you have said …
	The next stage in the evidence-gathering process is …
	It is intended to make some kind of decision as to how to proceed by …

Figure 4.3   Components of open to learning conversations and evidence-based school leadership (adapted from Robinson, 2011)

Nevertheless, it would be wrong to assume that open to learning conversations are not without potential problems. Le Fevre et al. (2015) discuss the distinction between genuine and 'pseudo-inquiry'. They describe pseudo-inquiry as something that takes place where there is not a commitment to open-mindedness and while it 'has the surface characteristics of inquiry, it is not driven by a desire to learn. Genuine inquiry requires conversations to be motivated (either consciously or unconsciously) by a desire to learn and to be driven by a stance of open-mindedness' (p. 884).

As a result, 'pseudo-inquiry' can often be indicated by the types of questions that are asked; for example, if the questions posed are designed to communicate your own point of view, in a subtle and often implied manner ('don't you agree that it would be a good idea to …'). Alternatively, a number of simple straightforward questions are asked in order to create an air of consensus, which makes it more difficult to subsequently disagree. Finally, there is a form of pseudo-inquiry where the answers to the questions are already known to the inquirer. Alongside 'pseudo-inquiry', there is also the related problem of the 'quick fix', where leaders are likely to assume that they know what the problem is about, rather than test the validity of the main assumptions they have made about their selected problem. As Robinson et al. (2015) argue, 'leaders' problem-solving typically involved gaining agreement about the existence of a problem and moving straight to a discussion of how it could be fixed, with little if any inquiry into its causes' (p. 7).

In order to tackle the problems of pseudo-inquiry and the quick fix it is important for the evidence-based school leader to adopt a number of different strategies. First they should move from being a 'heroic problem-solver' to a facilitator of the conditions that allow the development of genuine partnerships for problem-solving. In this context, the role of the evidence-based school leader may well be about developing the skills to help others unpack their assumptions and causal reasoning rather than 'selling' their own answer to a problem. Second, evidence-based school leaders may have to recognise the time commitment involved in being both a genuine inquirer and the time needed to develop these skills in others.

Open to learning conversations are not the only mechanisms by which stakeholder feedback can be obtained. Using the work of Weick and Sutcliffe (2011), who cite the work of Gary Klein, a five-step briefing protocol, known as the STICC method, will be examined. Although this method was designed for use in crises and emergency situations, it can also be used to gain feedback from stakeholders before a decision is made. The STICC method consists of the following points and is followed by a worked example.

- Situation: Here's what I think we face
- Task: Here's what I think we should do
- Intent: Here's why I think this is what we should do
- Concern: Here's what we should keep our eye on because if that changes, we're in a whole new situation
- Calibrate: Now talk to me. Tell me if you don't understand, cannot do it, or see something I do not.

(Weick and Sutcliffe, 2011: 156)

XYZ school is a Teaching School, which has 15 whole-school initiatives detailed within the school development plan. The school had its last Ofsted visit in 2011, where it was graded as Outstanding, and the senior team – and in particular the headteacher – are determined that the school leaves no stone unturned as it continually seeks to maintain its reputation at local, regional and national levels. As a result, the school is constantly taking on board new initiatives, which are loosely connected and often not supported by robust evaluation evidence.

The senior leadership team are aware this number of initiatives is placing high levels of stress onto the teaching staff, and this is now being reflected in abnormally high levels of absence, and with the first signs of an increase in staff turnover, particularly among younger and newly qualified staff. In this situation, the STICC model could be used to brief the headteacher (see Figure 4.4).

Situation: Here's what I think we face

Headteacher, we are beginning to see both high levels of staff absence and increasing staff turnover, which would appear to be linked to the number of initiatives and innovations which the school is pursuing.

Task: Here's what I think we should do

We should work with the governing body and the heads of department to identify no more than five initiatives, which are carried forward into the next academic year. In addition, no more initiatives should be incorporated into the school development plan, unless there is substantive evaluative evidence supporting its effectiveness and there is a clear school need to be met.

Intent: Here's why I think this is what we should do

The reason I am making this recommendation, is that I am concerned with the impact of the large number of initiatives on staff absence, morale and culture, which may lead to us losing some of our very best staff, particularly in shortage subject areas. In addition, by taking on too many initiatives we are at risk of spreading ourselves too thinly and not doing things as well as we should.

Concern: Here's what we should keep our eye on because if that changes, we're in a whole new situation

Of course, we will need to look out for new initiatives that we will need to take in response to any changes in legislation or any new problems or issues that have emerged in the school. We will also need to work with colleagues, so we can demonstrate the rationale for the reduction in the number of initiatives, and will need to support colleagues who 'own' initiatives and which are no longer supported.

Calibrate: Now talk to me. Tell me if you don't understand, cannot do it, or see something I do not

Tell me if my analysis is incorrect. Are there some things I have missed out or have got wrong? Are there areas of agreement? Am I recommending something we can't or should not do?

Figure 4.4   An example of a STICC briefing

Having identified a comprehensive strategy to acquire appropriate evidence, the next tasks for the evidence-based school leader is to engage in a critical appraisal of evidence. In Chapter 5 the focus will be on how to appraise research evidence. Chapter 6 continues to focus on research evidence and the challenges of using quantitative data. Chapter 7 will then engage in a wide-ranging discussion of how to appraise school data, practitioner expertise and stakeholder views and preferences.

Summary and key points

- Decisions should be made using the best available evidence and evidence that has been obtained from multiple sources.
- Evidence can be drawn from a range of sources – be it scientific or academic research, school quantitative data, stakeholders and practitioner expertise.
- Using the best available evidence requires you have a clear understanding as to: whether the evidence can be trusted; how the evidence was collected; whether the evidence is relevant to the problem of practice; and what weight, if any, to give to each source of evidence in the decision-making process.
- Acquiring the most appropriate evidence to answer your problem of practice requires a carefully thought out evidence search strategy.
- By identifying a range of questions this will help you identify potential sources of evidence to your problem of practice.
- However, one of the first tasks in developing an evidence search strategy is to articulate a theory of action.
- There are a number of ways to access peer-reviewed research articles and directly contacting the author(s) is often a very successful means of accessing research.
- When searching out research evidence a good place to start is to look for systematic reviews relevant to the problem of practice.
- If accessing information found on the Internet it will be necessary to have a clear strategy for distinguishing between the good, the bad and the ugly.
- There is a wide range of school data available for use, ranging from school census data, school examination results and teachers' assessment of pupils.

- Open to learning conversations are both a very useful way of gaining evidence from stakeholders and at the same time creating the conditions for the development of relational trust.
- When engaging in open to learning conversations, evidence-based school leaders need to ensure they are engaged in genuine rather than pseudo-inquiry.

References

Argyris, C. (1994) 'Good communication that blocks learning', *Harvard Business Review*, 72 (4): 77–85.

Argyris, C. and Schön, D.A. (1974) *Theory in Practice: Increasing Professional Effectiveness*. San Francisco, CA: Jossey-Bass.

Argyris, C. and Schön, D.A. (1996) *Organizational Learning II: Theory, Method and Practice*. Reading, MA: Addison-Wesley.

Barends, E., Rousseau, D. and Briner, R. (2014) *Evidence-Based Management: The Basic Principles*. Amsterdam: Center for Evidence-Based Management.

Blenko, M.W., Mankins, M.C. and Rogers, P. (2010) *Decide and Deliver: 5 Steps to Breakthrough Performance in Your Organization*. Boston, MA: Harvard Business Press.

Booth, W., Colob, G., Williams, J., Bizup, J. and Fitzgerald, W. (2016) *The Craft of Research*, 4th edn. Chicago, IL: The University of Chicago Press.

Briner, R. and Rousseau, D. (2011) 'Evidence based I–O psychology: not there yet', *Industrial and Organizational Psychology*, 4 (1): 3–22.

Briner, R., Denyer, D. and Rousseau, D. (2009) 'Evidence-based management: concept cleanup time?', *Academy of Management Perspectives*, 23 (4): 19–32.

Brown, C., Daly, A. and Liou, Y.-H. (2016) 'Improving trust, improving schools: findings from a social network analysis of 43 primary schools in England', *Journal of Professional Capital and Community*, 1 (1): 69–91.

Brunton, G., Stansfield, C. and Thomas, J. (2012) 'Finding relevant studies', in D. Gough, S. Oliver and J. Thomas (eds) *An Introduction to Systematic Reviews*. London: Sage. pp. 93–122.

Camden, B. (2017) 'Ofsted ignores more than 100 schools for a decade', *Schools Week*, 6 January 2017. https://schoolsweek.co.uk/ofsted-ignores-more-than-100-schools-for-a-decade/ (accessed 3 May 2018).

Coe, R., Waring, M., Hedges, L. and Arthur, J. (2017) *Research Methods and Methodologies in Education*, 2nd edn. London: Sage.

Gough, D., Oliver, S. and Thomas, J. (2012) *An Introduction to Systematic Reviews*. London: Sage.

Kara, Helen (2016) *Ten Ways to Get Hold of Academic Literature*. https://helenkara.com/2016/01/06/ten-ways-to-get-hold-of-academic-literature/ (accessed 7 August 2017).

Langley, G.J., Moen, R., Nolan, K.M., Nolan, T.W., Norman, C.L. and Provost, L.P. (2009) *The Improvement Guide: A Practical Approach to Enhancing Organizational Performance*. San Francisco, CA: John Wiley & Sons.

Le Fevre, D., Robinson, V. and Sinnema, C. (2015) 'Genuine inquiry: widely espoused yet rarely enacted', *Educational Management Administration & Leadership, 43* (6): 883–99.

Miller, L. (2017) 'Performance related pay will solve teacher retention crisis', *Times Educational Supplement,* 20 November.

Neeleman, A.-M. (2017) *Grasping the Scope of School Autonomy: a Classification Scheme for School Policy Practice.* Stratford-upon Avon: BELMAS.

Nonaka, I. and Takeuchi, H. (1995) *The Knowledge-Creating Company: How Japanese Companies Create the Dynamics of Innovation.* New York: Oxford University Press.

Polanyi, M. (1966) *The Tacit Dimension.* New York: Doubleday.

Robinson, V. (2011) *Student-Centered Leadership.* San Francisco, CA: John Wiley & Sons.

Robinson, V. and Lai, M. (2005) *Practitioner Research for Educators: A Guide to Improving Classrooms and Schools.* Thousand Oaks, CA: Corwin Press.

Robinson, V., Meyer, F., Le Fevre, D. and Sinnema, C. (2015) *Leaders' Problem-Solving Capabilities: Exploring the 'Quick Fix' Mentality.* Auckland: The University of Auckland.

Sackett, D., Rosenberg, W., Gray, J., Haynes, R. and Richardson, W. (1996) 'Evidence based medicine: what it is and what it isn't', *BMJ, 312* (7023): 71–2.

Straus, S., Glasziou, P., Richardson, S. and Haynes, B. (2011) *Evidence-Based Medicine: How to Practise and Teach It,* 2nd edn. Edinburgh: Churchill Livingstone Elsevier.

Wallace, M. and Wray, A. (2016) *Critical Reading and Writing for Postgraduates,* 3rd edn. London: Sage.

Ware, M. and Mabe, M. (2015) *The STM Report: An Overview of Scientific and Scholarly Journal Publishing.* The Hague: International Association of Scientific, Technical and Medical Publishers.

Weick, K. and Sutcliffe, K. (2011) *Managing the Unexpected: Resilient Performance in an Age of Uncertainty,* 2nd edn. San Francisco, CA: Jossey-Bass.

5

APPRAISING RESEARCH EVIDENCE

Chapter outline

This chapter aims to help non-experts know when to trust expert advice. Focus will then turn to the notion of the hierarchy of evidence and the nature of both systematic reviews and randomised controlled trials, which are often at the pinnacle of various hierarchies of evidence. Next, the chapter will identify the components of an argument – the claim and associated warrant – and how these can be used to appraise the quality of research. Consideration will then be given to how to make the most of research, the use of abstracts and the writing of critical appraisals of research. Finally, the chapter will look at an overarching framework to help judge the usefulness of research evidence.

Key words: *abstracts, claim, hierarchy of evidence, randomised controlled trials, systematic reviews, warrant*

When to trust expert advice?

A major challenge facing the evidence-based practitioner is knowing when so-called expert advice – often based on research – can be trusted. This is a real problem, as it is highly unlikely that evidence-based school leaders will have the required level of expertise to critically examine the claims that are being made. To help get round this problem of a lack of expertise and increase the chances of being able to judge the credibility of evidence, Willingham (2012) has provided a 'work-around' which consists of four steps.

First, 'strip it', get rid of the fluff surrounding the idea and get right to the heart of the claim being made. What specific intervention, strategy or actions is the school leader being asked to adopt and what outcomes, for student learning or achievement, staff well-being or other outcomes are being promised? Second, 'trace it', where did the idea come from? Is the idea supported by a leading educational authority? Unfortunately, in education this can be a weak indicator of validity and reliability. Do other 'experts' support the idea? Third, 'analyse it', what are you – the evidence-based school leader – being asked to believe? What is the evidence to support the claims being made? How does this evidence relate to your experience as a school leader? Fourth, 'should I do it?' Is it something which is already being done? Is it an old idea wrapped in new language and terminology? Has it worked previously in other settings with other students? Has it failed previously in other settings with other students? What are the opportunity costs – the things necessary to give up or forgo – in pursuing this intervention or strategy? Nonetheless, as Willingham (2012) states, it is important to remember this heuristic 'is not a substitute for a thoughtful evaluation by a knowledgeable scientist. Rather, it's a workaround, a cheat. As such, it is imperfect. The great advantage is that it does not require a knowledgeable scientist' (p. 136).

Willingham goes on to argue that something like this happens when the evidence-based practitioner decides to believe an educational researcher, expert or consultant. Suppose the evidence-based school leader does not understand the research behind an idea or claim made by an educational researcher, expert or consultant, but they believe that the educational researcher, expert or consultant does. The evidence-based school leader knows that the researcher, expert or consultant is saying the research evidence supports the idea or claim being made. Therefore, the evidence-based school leader, without understanding the underpinning research, trusts that the evidence supports the claim being made. In other words, as the educational expert is an authority on the evidence, when they say something about the evidence, the greater the chance the evidence-based school leader is going to have faith in what they say.

However, Willingham (2012: 78) identifies a number of situations when this line of argument can go wrong.

1. What we take to be signs of authority can turn out not to be very reliable, if the person is not, in fact, scientifically knowledgeable.
2. We might arrive at a false belief if we misunderstand the position taken by the expert.
3. The person might be a good scientist or researcher, but be in error because he or she takes a position on a topic outside their own area of expertise.
4. Two people with equally good claims to authority might disagree on an issue, leaving it unclear which to believe.

To illustrate how easily it is to fall foul of relying on an authority let's look at an example. In oft-cited research, Robinson et al. (2009) found that when looking at different dimensions of school leadership that leading and participating in teacher learning had almost twice the impact on pupil learning as any other dimension of school leadership. Included in these other dimensions were establishing goals and expectations, resourcing strategically, ensuring teaching quality, and ensuring a safe and orderly environment. As a result, these findings have been used by Fullan (2014) to encourage principals and headteachers to promote and lead discussions about teaching and learning, provide instructional advice, and participate in teacher learning and development. However, this is a classic example of where a correlation between a particular leadership practice and pupil outcomes have been interpreted as cause and effect. Unfortunately, using this research to say what headteachers should be doing is flawed advice, as the research details the impact of different types of leadership practice on outcomes, rather than the impact of headship. This is in part due to there being insufficient studies to do separate meta-studies on school leadership and headship/principalship (Robinson, 2016).

With research open to being misunderstood or misinterpreted, what is the evidence-based practitioner to do? The answer to this question is best summarised by F. Scott Fitzgerald (1936), who said: 'The test of a first-rate intelligence is the ability to hold two opposed ideas in mind at the same time and still retain the ability to function.' In this case the two opposing ideas are: I do not possess the expertise of an educational researcher, so I need to rely on those who do, on the other hand, just because someone would appear to be a credible expert there are plenty of reasons not to believe such experts and authorities.

So how do we reconcile these competing ideas? Unfortunately, and there's no other way around it, evidence-based practitioners will need to evaluate the strength of the evidence for themselves. This does not mean evidence-based practitioners have to become instant experts in educational research, but it does mean they need have to have a list of questions which can help them critically appraise research.

The hierarchy of evidence

When asking questions about the quality of research evidence a useful place to start is with the research design, as this will allow research to be located within a 'hierarchy of evidence'. One of the commonly

Table 5.1   A summary of different types of research and their place in the hierarchy of evidence

Hierarchy of evidence	Type	Description
Top	Systematic review	A review of existing research using explicit, accountable rigorous research methods.
	Randomised controlled trial	A trial of a particular educational programme or intervention to assess whether it is effective; it is a controlled trial because it compares the progress made by those children taking part in the programme or intervention with a comparison or control group of children who do not and who continue as normal; and it is randomised because the children have been randomly allocated to the groups being compared

(Continued)

Table 5.1 (Continued)

Hierarchy of evidence	Type	Description
	Cohort studies	A cohort study is a research programme investigating a particular group with a certain trait or characteristic, and takes place over a period of time
	Case–control studies	A case–control study involves the identification of individuals with a condition being matched with individual controls without the condition
	Cross-sectional surveys	Cross-sectional research is used to examine one variable in different groups that are similar in all other characteristics
Bottom	Case study	An empirical inquiry that investigates a contemporary phenomenon within its real-life context; when the boundaries between phenomenon and context are not clearly evident; and in which multiple sources of evidence are used (Yin, 1984)

used hierarchies of evidence was developed by Petticrew and Roberts (2003) and is illustrated in Table 5.1.

To some extent this hierarchy explains the emphasis the Education Endowment Foundation and others have placed on randomised controlled trials and systematic reviews, as being likely to provide high-quality evidence as to 'what works'. As such, it is appropriate to look in more detail at both systematic reviews and randomised controlled trials. However, it needs to be remembered that there are limitations with the concept of the hierarchy of evidence, which will be explored later in this chapter.

Systematic reviews

Evidence-based school leaders seek to obtain the best available evidence to answer a problem of practice and to subsequently make a decision. Systematic reviews appear at the apex of a hierarchy of evidence and so should be one of the first sources of research evidence that an evidence-based school leader turns to, as they provide a comprehensive summary of what is currently known about a question or issue. In contrast, individual studies may be limited in scope or may be flawed in design. A systematic review should therefore provide a more robust overview of the research than any one individual research study.

Gough et al. (2017) define a systematic review as 'a review of existing research using explicit, accountable rigorous research methods' (p. 2). They then go on to state that systematic reviews involve four main activities: 'clarifying the question being asked; identifying and describing the relevant research ("mapping" the research); critically appraising the research reports in a systematic manner, bringing together the findings into a coherent statement, known as a synthesis; and establishing what evidence claims can be made from the research' (p. 4). Very helpfully, Gough et al. (2017) have provided a definition for each of the key terms:

> **Systematic**: undertaken according to a fixed plan or system or method
>
> **Review**: a critical appraisal or analysis
>
> **Explicit**: a clear understandable statement of all the details
>
> **Accountable**: answerable, responsible and justified
>
> **Map** (systematic): a systematic description and analysis of the research field defined by a review question
>
> **Synthesis:** creating something new from separate elements
>
> **Systematic reviews:** a review of existing research, using explicit, accountable and rigorous research methods
>
> **Evidence claim**: the statements can be justified in respect of answering the review question(s) from the research evidence reviewed.
>
> (Gough et al., 2017: 5)

So how do systematic reviews differ from a traditional literature review? Briner and Walshe (2014) have produced a summary of the main differences between the two approaches and the consequences of these differences (see Table 5.2).

Given these limitations of traditional literature reviews, Gough et al. (2017) argue that it is 'not possible to interpret the meaning of the review findings' (p. 5). Nevertheless, despite the apparent strengths of systematic reviews, it is important to be aware of their limitations; this is especially so given the emphasis placed on them by the Education Endowment Foundation in developing their Teaching

Table 5.2   The main differences between traditional and systematic literature reviews

Traditional or narrative literature reviews	Systematic literature reviews
Do not usually focus on specific or practice relevant questions	Always focus on specific, usually practice-relevant questions
Have diverse aims, purposes	Have similar aims, purposes: all focus on answering specific questions
Adopt a wide variety of approaches and structures	Adopt similar approaches, structure based on set of broad principles
Do not use particular methods or do not explicitly state methods to conduct the review	Use particular, explicitly stated methods to: • Search for, identify relevant literature • Make decisions about what research to include, exclude • Judge the quality and relevance of the research • Integrate or synthesize findings
Are more prone to bias e.g. because authors can select studies that support their views, ignore those that do not	Are less prone to bias, because e.g. decisions about to include, exclude are made explicitly
Are less likely to identify best available evidence	Are more likely to identify the best available evidence
Do not aim to be comprehensive by including all relevant, available research	Aim to be comprehensive by including all relevant, available research within explicitly stated boundaries or constraints
Are not replicable or easy to update	Are replicable and are easy to update

Source: Briner and Walshe (2014)

and Learning Toolkit. Many of these limitations have been identified by Gough et al. (2017) and include:

- It is challenging to combine results from different research paradigms – be it qualitative or quantitative.
- There is an absence of agreed terminology to describe the method and process of systematic reviews.
- Systematic reviews are major pieces of work and require a significant investment of resources – be it time, money or other resources.

- Organisations may lack the specialist skills and expertise to undertake systematic reviews.
- Practitioners lack the capacity to read, understand, interpret and apply reviews.
- Systematic reviews are often seen as an attempt to impose an empiricist research paradigm, with this being particularly the case in education.
- Systematic reviews can have a narrow perspective – and can focus on bringing together results of randomised controlled trials – rather than taking into account the experience of research subjects.
- Systematic reviews may only include a few studies, as much other relevant research may not meet the search or inclusion criteria.
- Government may use systematic reviews to attempt to impose a 'managerialist' agenda on the conduct of research.

Gough et al. (2017) subsequently go on to identify a number of criteria that can be used for appraising the quality of the systematic review. For example, AMSTAR (A Measurement Tool to Assess Systematic Reviews) provides a list of questions that can be used to judge the quality of review, and these include:

1. Was an 'a priori' design provided?
2. Was there duplicate study selection and extraction?
3. Was a comprehensive literature research performed?
4. Was the status of publications (for example grey literature, such as conference proceedings, theses, reports and commercial documentation) used as an inclusion criterion?
5. Was a list of studies (included and excluded) provided?
6. Were the characteristics of the included studies provided?
7. Was the scientific quality of the included studies assessed and documented?
8. Was the scientific quality of the included studies used appropriately in formulating conclusions?
9. Were the methods used to combine the findings of the studies appropriate?
10. Was the likelihood of publication bias assessed?
11. Was conflict of interest included?

(Gough et al., 2017: 256)

In addition, there are some very specific limitations of a particular form of systematic review known as 'meta-analysis' – and this will be covered in Chapter 6.

So, what are the implications of this discussion for an evidence-based practitioner? First, systematic reviews provide a very useful starting point when looking for a summary of the research evidence on a particular issue. Second, it is necessary to recognise that some systematic reviews may have a particularly narrow focus, resulting in some research not being included, so additional research evidence will need to be acquired and appraised. Third, developing the skills necessary to read and interpret systematic reviews will help the evidence-based school practitioner become more skilled in aggregating multiple sources of evidence. Fourth, by evidence-based school practitioners modelling in their own work the processes associated with systematic reviews, it will be easier to ensure that evidence-based decisions are explicit, with colleagues being able to see what evidence has been used to inform decisions.

Randomised controlled trials (RCTs)

Given both the prominence organisations involved in education research – for example the Department for Education and Education Endowment Foundation in England and the Institute of Education Science in the United States – give to RCTs and the status of the RCT within the hierarchy of evidence, it seems sensible to examine RCTs in more detail. The rest of this section will: first, examine the nature of RCTs; second, consider both benefits and limitations of RCTs; third, consider what can go wrong with RCTs; finally, provide some guidance as to how to evaluate RCTs.

What is an RCT?

Connolly et al. (2017) describe an RCT as:

> a trial of particular educational programme or intervention to assess whether it is effective; it is a controlled trial because it compares the progress made by those children taking the programme or intervention with a comparison or control group of children who do not and who continue as normal; and it is randomised because the children have been randomly allocated to the groups being compared. (p. 4)

What are the arguments for the use of RCTs?

As Slavin (1989), Willingham (2012) and others have noted, those working in education are faced with a constant barrage of educational fads and fashions, many of which have little or no evidence available to support their introduction. Connolly et al. (2017) argue that the use of RCTs provides the opportunity to develop a 'cumulative body of knowledge and an evidence base around the effectiveness of different practices, programmes and policies' (p. 11) and which supports the naturally occurring experimentation and innovation that takes place within schools and classrooms. Furthermore, Connolly et al. argue that there is a moral imperative to test the effectiveness of programmes; first, to prevent the unnecessary waste of resources; second, to prevent children and others being subject to programmes and interventions that may be doing more harm than good.

Although RCTs are often referred to as the 'gold standard' of educational research, there are major concerns about their limitations and weaknesses, with Hanley et al. (2016) identifying three broad areas of debate about the use of RCTs. First, there are concerns as to whether interventions can be standardised or students 'blinded' to the effects of the intervention. There are also concerns as to the external validity – and generalisability – of RCTs and whether they can be used to make recommendations as to changes in classroom practice. Second, there are questions about whether the rise of the use of research evidence in education represents a decline in teacher professional autonomy and an attempt to impose 'managerialist' control on schools. Third, some of the concerns are 'reminiscent of the paradigm wars between quantitative and qualitative research' (p. 290).

There is also an ethical concern in that by conducting an RCT potentially one group of pupils are being favoured over another, with one group of pupils experiencing the potential benefits of the intervention, whereas the 'control group' do not experience such benefits. Nevertheless, as stated in Coe et al. (2013): 'ethical evaluations start from a position of "equipoise", where we do not know for certain what works best, it can be argued that it is unethical not to try and establish which is more effective, particularly if the intervention is going to be repeated or rolled-out more widely' (p. 9).

What can go wrong with RCTs?

Even if you do not accept the objections to use of RCTs in education, it is still important to note that things can quite easily go wrong with them. As Gorard et al. (2017) state:

> they often do not address key issues, and are frequently so small or have so many treatment groups that they have no practical value. They may test complex or vaguely defined approaches so that even when a trial shows an approach is successful, it is unclear what that means. They are often poorly reported, missing key information such as the amount of missing data or even the basic results such as the outcome scores for each group. They too often use outcome measures created by the researchers or intervention developers, which are well known to produce more favourable results than standardised tests and official qualifications. (p. 18)

The challenges of what can go wrong with RCTs have been reported by Ginsburg and Smith (2016), who when they reviewed 27 RCTs that met the minimum standards of the What Works Clearinghouse based in the United States, found that 26 of the trials had serious threats to their usefulness. Their list of what can go wrong with RCTs includes:

- **Developer associated:** In 12 of the 27 RCT studies (44 per cent), the authors had an association with the curriculum's developer.
- **Curriculum intervention not well implemented:** In 23 of 27 studies (85 per cent), implementation fidelity was threatened because the RCT occurred in the first year of curriculum implementation. The NRC study warns that it may take up to three years to implement a substantially different curricular change.
- **Unknown comparison curricula:** In 15 of 27 studies (56 per cent), the comparison curricula are either never identified or outcomes are reported for a combined two or more comparison curricula. Without understanding the comparison's characteristics, we cannot interpret the intervention's effectiveness.

- **Instructional time greater for treatment than for control group:** In eight of nine studies for which the total time of the intervention was available, the treatment time differed substantially from that for the comparison group. In these studies, we cannot separate the effects of the intervention curriculum from the effects of the differences in the time spent by the treatment and control groups.
- **Limited grade coverage:** In 19 of 20 studies, a curriculum covering two or more grades does not have a longitudinal cohort and cannot measure cumulative effects across grades.
- **Assessment favors content of the treatment:** In 5 of 27 studies (19 per cent), the assessment was designed by the curricula developer and likely is aligned in favor of the treatment.
- **Outdated curricula:** In 19 of 27 studies (70 per cent), the RCTs were carried out on outdated curricula.

(Ginsburg and Smith, 2016: ii)

So where does this leave the evidence-based school leader trying to make sense of RCTs? Well, a useful starting point is to take the work of Ginsburg and Smith (2016) and Gorard et al. (2017) to develop a checklist of things to look out for:

1. Does the study design match the nature of the research question?
2. Is the developer of the intervention associated with the evaluation team?
3. Over what period of time was the new intervention implemented?
4. Is there evidence of 'drop-outs' from the research, and how does this impact upon the findings?
5. Is it clear what comparison curricula or interventions were used?
6. How were participants allocated to the 'control' and 'treatment' groups – have they been randomly allocated or have cases been matched between groups (non-random)?
7. Did the control group and intervention group receive the same amount of teacher/instructional time?
8. Is it a longitudinal study and shows how impact of the intervention accumulates or dissipates over time?
9. Is the assessment designed by the developer of the intervention (likely to favour the intervention)?

Nevertheless, RCTs are probably better than many other attempts to measure the effectiveness that do not use control groups, and as Nevill (2016) states: 'RCTs are rarely perfect, but we should not let the best become the enemy of the good.'

Limitations of hierarchies of evidence

Hierarchies of evidence are based on the study design, and as Gorard et al. (2017) argue research designs which appear to be at the top of the hierarchy are not necessarily the 'gold-standard' as the quality of study depends upon the research questions being asked. Indeed, Nutley et al. (2013) identify a number of challenges to hierarchies based on research design, which include:

- Hierarchies based on study design neglect too many important and relevant issues around the evidence;
- Hierarchies based on study design tend to underrate the value of good observational studies;
- Using such hierarchies to exclude all but the highest ranking studies from consideration can lead to the loss of useful evidence;
- Hierarchies based on study design pay insufficient attention to the need to understand what works, for whom, in what circumstances and why (programme theory);
- Hierarchies based on study design provide an insufficient basis for making recommendations about whether interventions should be adopted.

(Nutley et al., 2013: 11)

Given the limitations of hierarchies of evidence, how is the evidence-based school leader going to make informed judgements about research claims? One way of doing this has been suggested by Gray (2001) and adapted by Petticrew and Roberts (2003), who suggest the use of a typology to help make judgements about how different types of research can help answer certain types of research questions. Sharples (2017) shows how a matrix originally developed for the healthcare setting can be adapted for use in education. Figure 5.1 illustrates that there are different hierarchies of evidence and which depend upon the nature of the questions being asked. Accordingly, Petticrew and Roberts (2003) suggest that typologies of research question may be more useful than hierarchies when seeking to judge the strengths and weakness of different research methods

Figure 5.1 The right research tool for the job (Nutley et al., 2013)

Research question	Qualitative research	Survey	Case-control studies	Cohort studies	RCTs	Quasi-experimental studies	Non-experimental studies	Systematic reviews
Does doing this work better than doing that?					+	++	+	+++
How does it work?	++	+					+	+++
Does it matter?	++	++						+++
Will it do more good than harm?	+		+	+	++	+	+	+++
Will service users be willing to or want to take up the service offered?	++	+			+	+	+	+++
Is it worth buying this service?					++			+++
Is it the right service for these people?	++	++						++
Are users, providers, and other stakeholders satisfied with the service?	++	++	+	+				+

Critically appraising research

One thing is inescapable, if evidence-based school leaders are going to critically appraise research they are going to have to read, or at least skim-read, the research with a purpose. To help school leaders do this, the next section will make use of the work of Wallace and Wray (2016) to: understand the components of an argument; make good use of research abstracts; and show how to write a critical synopsis of a text.

Understanding the components of an argument

Wallace and Wray (2016) state:

> an argument consists of a conclusion (comprising one or more claims that something is, or should be, the case) and its

warranting (the justification for why the claim or claims in the conclusion should be accepted). The warranting is likely to be based on the evidence from the author's research or professional experience, or it will draw upon others' evidence as reported in the literature. (p. 36)

An example of an argument that is increasingly accepted within English schools is Coe's (2014) view of graded lesson observations, which can be summarised as follows: 'graded lesson observations should not be used for high stakes accountability purposes [conclusion] as there are substantive issues with both the reliability and validity of lesson observation grades [warranting]'.

There are other examples of where it is possible to identify the conclusion and warranting of current educational arguments.

- When using effect sizes to judge the effectiveness of an innovation it is necessary to take into account the age of the pupils as research shows that pupils' rate of progress slows down as they get older.
- School accountability systems should take into account the socio-economic background of the parents of a school's pupils as research evidence shows that children of poorer parents tend to perform less well academically than children of wealthier parents.

Having identified the components of an argument, the evidence-based school leader will need to work out whether the argument is flawed through, for example, drawing conclusions without sufficient evidence or insufficient warranting for the conclusion. Figure 5.2 gives examples of a range of flaws in arguments, which a critical consumer or end user of research will need to be on the look-out for.

For a more detailed and challenging account of the components of a good argument, turn to *The Craft of Research* by Booth et al. (2016), which forensically examines the making of claims, assembling reasons and evidence, acknowledgement and responses and warrants.

Making good use of abstracts

There are a number of reasons why it is important for the evidence-based school leader to make good use of the abstracts that are usually found at the beginning of published papers. First, the full text of the majority of peer-reviewed published papers is behind

Type of flaw in an argument	Example
Conclusion without warranting	The best teachers make the best heads of department.
Potential warranting without a conclusion	In-house research shows that many parents often sign 'consent' forms without reading them. School correspondence to parents can be confusing.
Warranting leading to an illogical conclusion	Early career teachers are not very experienced. This indicates that they are not very good teachers.
Conclusion not explicitly linked to warranting	Evidence shows that our KS3 pupils are spending insufficient time on homework. KS3 pupils should be set more homework.
Conclusion with inadequate warranting	Experienced teachers learn more effectively when they are given positive feedback. An in-house school survey of teachers over the age of 50 indicated that the vast majority said they preferred praise to criticism.

Figure 5.2 Identifying flaws in arguments derived from different sources of evidence (adapted from Wallace and Wray, 2016)

paywalls, which makes it expensive for the evidence-based school leader to access research. Abstracts provide a summary of the paper, indicating the topics covered, the approach adopted and the main claims made, without the expense of paying for access to the full paper. Second, because so much research is published and abstracts are very short, often no more than 150–200 words, the skilled reading of research abstracts makes it much easier to keep up with the latest research in your area of interest. Finally, as Wallace and Wray (2016) note, the very brevity of an abstract encourages the development of critical reading. The relative lack of information in an abstract will facilitate the development of your skills as a critical reader by forcing you to ask questions about what additional information is required to be convinced by the argument underpinning the research.

Now it may well be that when reading, all the questions are answered. On the other hand, it may be that a few questions remain unanswered. Wallace and Wray (2016) argue that you are more likely to identify these unanswered questions when looking for answers. Furthermore, as the questions reflect current levels knowledge, skills and expertise, then it is likely that these questions are extremely relevant to the problem of practice and associated well-formulated and answerable question. Wallace and Wray go on to suggest that the best way of illustrating how to critically read an abstract is through a worked example (see Figure 5.3)

Text	Comments
Source: *Educational Management Administration and Leadership* 2015; 43 (2): 198–213	This journal focuses on educational leadership, with original contributions from educational researchers from around the world
Title: Value(s)-driven decision-making: the ethics work of English headteachers within discourses of constraint	What does the author mean by value(s)-driven decision-making? What is the 'ethics work' of headteachers? What sector(s) are the headteachers drawn from?
Author: Linda Hammersley-Fletcher, Institute of Education, Manchester Metropolitan University, Crewe Green Road, Crewe, Cheshire, CW1 5DU, UK	What's the author's main purpose in writing the paper?
This article considers the experiences and perceptions of practising English headteachers and the tensions that they face when juggling government prescription and government initiatives, which may be antagonistic to their educational values and beliefs.	How long have the headteachers been practising? What are the tensions arising from government prescription and initiatives? What do we mean by educational values and beliefs? How might these values and beliefs be at odds with government initiatives?
Managerial control over teachers' work has been particularly acute and destructive to 'human flourishing'.	What is meant by managerial control? What is the work of teachers? What is meant by 'human flourishing'?
Headteachers have a moral and ethical responsibility for the welfare and education of pupils.	What are the moral and ethical responsibilities of headteachers? Is there a difference between the education and welfare of pupils?
Such professional ethics oblige the professional to seek the good of the pupil and therefore good is viewed as intrinsic to the work of an educator.	Is there a difference between professional and educational ethics? Is the intrinsic role of headteachers confined to seeking the good of the pupil?
Thus headteachers are directly involved in negotiating between sometimes contradictory imperatives and drivers.	What sort of imperatives are there? Do these imperatives change over time? What scope do headteachers have to negotiate contradictory pressures?
How then does the headteacher cope with what the author refers to as 'situated ethics work'?	What is meant by 'situated ethics work'? What coping strategies do headteachers adopt?
This article presents data derived from written responses from 10 headteachers that begin to open up this question.	How were the headteachers selected? Were the headteachers given a pro-forma to respond to? How were the written responses analysed?
I argue that it is not uncommon for people to weaken in their values-driven stance when under great pressure.	How frequent is 'uncommon'? What types of pressure are headteachers under? How does the pressure change the decision-making of headteachers? What other decisions would they be taking?

Text	Comments
It is, however, important to recognise the extent to which educational values are constrained by neo-liberal value-based market agendas in order to continually question and re-evaluate what is happening within education re-articulating this for the benefit of pupils.	What are neo-liberal value-based market agendas?
	How are headteachers re-evaluating what is happening?
	In what ways are these values being rearticulated to the meet the needs of pupils?

Figure 5.3 Critically reading an abstract

It should be noted that the list of questions in Figure 5.3 is fairly eclectic and could be added to or subtracted from depending on your particular problem of practice. As such, this list of questions should not be seen as definitive, rather it should be seen as an initial stimulus to develop critical thinking.

Writing a critical synopsis

Given the wide-ranging responsibilities of a school leader, it is important to develop strategies to make the most of the relatively scarce amount of time that school leaders may have available for reading. Wallace and Wray (2016: 48) suggest five questions that should act as a starting point whenever reading and summarising research evidence, and which may contribute to the answering of a problem of practice and associated well-formulated and answerable question (see Chapter 3). In addition, these five questions can form the basis for producing a written summary of research evidence, which has the benefit that it can easily be shared with colleagues, and may aid their own evidence-based practice.

Wallace and Wray's five critical questions are:

1. Why am I reading this?
2. What are the authors trying to achieve in writing this?
3. What are the authors claiming that is relevant to my work?
4. How convincing are these claims, and why?
5. In conclusion, what use can I make of this?

Each question is supported by a number of sub-questions, which have been amended to ensure a specific focus on the needs of the evidence-based practitioner:

1. *Why am I reading this?*
   o Is this reading going to help me gain a better understanding of the problem of practice?
   o Am I still trying to develop a well-formulated and answerable question?
   o Is the reading to assist with making an evidence-based decision or for the purpose of academic study?
   o Is the purpose of this reading to help develop my skills as an evidence-based practitioner?

2. *What are the authors trying to achieve in writing this?*
   The authors may have a range of differing purposes including:
   o Reporting on their own research activities
   o Synthesising and evaluating the work of others
   o Contributing to the development of theory
   o Suggesting changes to practice
   o Criticising both policy and practice

3. *What are the authors claiming that is relevant to my work?*
   o What is the text actually about and what do the authors say about it?
   o How does the text relate to my own interests and the problems of practice?
   o Is the text directly linked to the problem of practice?
   o Is the text indirectly related to the problem of practice?
   o Does the text provide an alternative perspective on the problem of practice?

4. *How convincing are these claims, and why?*
   o Are there any underpinning assumptions, which have not been made explicit?
   o Are the conclusions of the study supported with evidence?
   o Is the evidence used to support an illogical conclusion?
   o Does the evidence suggest other conclusions?

5. *In conclusion, what use can I make of this?*
   o Does this research contribute to my understanding of the problem of practice?
   o Is the research relevant to my context?
   o Is there any evidence to suggest that the 'intervention' might work in my school?
   o Does the research influence any decisions I need to make?
   o Is this research worth sharing with colleagues?

o   Should I undertake further reading?
o   Should I seek further sources of contrary evidence, particularly if the research is consistent with my own values and experiences?

Using a template provided by Wallace and Wray (2016), a critical synopsis of a text is best illustrated by the development of a worked example (see Figure 5.4).

Author, date, title, publication details: GODFREY, D. Leadership of schools as research-led organisations in the English educational environment: Cultivating a research-engaged school culture. *Educational Management Administration and Leadership*, 2016; 44: 301–21

Why am I reading this?

I am trying to find out more about the conditions necessary for the long-term development and sustainability of the evidence-based school.

What is the author trying to achieve in writing this?

The author is trying to explain the conditions for growth and expansion of research-engaged schools. In doing so, the author is trying to make a contribution to theory development. At the same time, the author's article is informed by his own research into the development of a school's research culture.

What is the author claiming that is relevant to my work?

The author provides a biological analogy for understanding the development of the research-engaged school movement. As such, nourishing factors such as a systemic connectedness, leadership for knowledge creation, teaching as a research-informed practice, and the school as a learning organisation need to be taken into account. To make the most of the research-informed school requires a long-term and sustainable school improvement strategy.

How convincing are these claims, and why? Within the conceptual framework used the argument is convincing. However, a particularly narrow view is taken of 'evidence-based practice' and the term 'research-informed practice' is used instead. As such the nature of 'evidence-based practice' is misrepresented, which undermines the quality of the article as a whole. In addition, with the use of a biological analogy, it is surprising that there is no reference to both the decline and 'death' of a research culture.

In conclusion, what use can I make of this?

The paper is useful as an overview of the development of research-informed/engaged schools.

It also has a number of suggestions for strategies for what a research-engaged school could look like, and how a school's culture might change over time.

Figure 5.4   A critical synopsis: a worked example

However, when seeking to answer a problem of practice by appraising the quality of research evidence more than one framework could be used. Professor Steve Higgins of Durham University has developed a framework based on the '6As of the usefulness of research' which can help you do this. Is the research: accessible, accurate, applicable, acceptable, appropriate and actionable? To help make a judgement as to the usefulness of research in answering a problem of practice, a 'fleshed-out' version of Higgins's 6As has been developed, which draws upon both Wallace and Wray (2016) and the TAPUPAS framework developed by Pawson et al. (2003) and is illustrated in Figure 5.5.

Factor	Sub-question
Accessible	Physical: Google scholar Chartered College of Teaching and the EBSCO database, Open source journals
	Direct contact with the author(s)
	Who is the audience: practitioners, policymakers or researchers?
	Aim: How and why are the authors making this contribution?
	Is it a contribution to policy, theory or practice?
	What do the authors assume about the knowledge of the readers?
	What about other issues of intellectual accessibility – easy to read, jargon-free, clear messages?
Accurate	How robust is the evidence?
	Are the methods used suitable for the research aims?
	To what extent are the claims made supported by others' work?
	What evidence that challenges their claims is not mentioned?
	Does the knowledge generated meet the specific standards of that type of knowledge?
Applicable	What groups of learners might benefit from the findings?
	What degree of certainty do the authors make for their claims?
	How generalisable are their claims?
	Context: System, age, phase, type of school, subject, content
	Level of use: Teacher, head of department, business manager executive head, CEO, board of trustees, governing body, policymaker
Acceptable	What values stance is being adopted – are they implicit or explicit?
	How might the values stances taken by the authors affect their claims and acceptability by colleagues?
	To what extent are the claims consistent with your experience?
	Is the research relevant to the problem which is the most interesting to you and your colleagues?
	Are there any ethical issues arising from the research?
	Conduct
	Subsequent implementation
Appropriate	Is the research relevant to the most recurring problems in your department, key stage, school or multi-academy trust?
	Is the research related to a problem within your sphere of influence/most relevant to your sphere of influence?
	Is the research relevant to problems for which resources – be it staff, time, expertise and finance – are available?
Actionable	Does the research specify causal statements – If this ... then ...?
	Are concrete behaviours specified to bring about the intended outcomes?
	Do the teaching staff have the skills required/or can they be taught the skills required to put the research into effect?

Figure 5.5 The 6As framework for evaluating the usefulness of research: a worked example

Source: Based on Higgins, 2017

To help show how this framework could be applied, a worked example is provided in Figure 5.6 which looks into a study of the
management of teachers' non-directed time in a secondary school
(Holmes, 2017).

Author, date, title, publication details: HOLMES, B. The management of teachers' non-directed time in a secondary school. *Management in Education*, 2017; 31 (1): 39–42. doi:10.1177/0892020616685287

Abstract

This article describes a study that investigated the motivations behind why teachers dedicate non-directed time to school-related tasks and the extent to which managers understand and harness these motivations. Data was collected through three case studies within one secondary school. Three heads of department (HoDs) and three teachers were interviewed, and questionnaires were given to all the teachers in the three departments. A questionnaire was developed using ideas from the voluntary sector with the premise that teachers give their time out of their 'own free will'. This was used to assess what motivates teachers to dedicate their non-directed time to school-focused tasks and the attitudes of their managers towards this. A common finding from all case studies was that teachers are motivated by the idea that they are 'doing it for the students'. At the same time, it was reported that 'motivators' such as performance-related pay had little effect on teachers' motivation to dedicate their non-directed time to school-focused activities but could increase teachers' work pressure and stress. The implications for educational managers from this research are that an understanding of teachers' motivation is imperative if they are to be managed well, especially in terms of the monitoring of non-directed time, and that a reduction of pressure from extrinsic motivators may be of benefit to teachers' well-being and job satisfaction. One way in which this could be achieved is through a more collaborative style of management and shared departmental goals.

Accessibility

The article was published in *Management in Education*, which is a peer-reviewed journal and sits behind a pay-wall. However, the journal is freely available if you are a member of the British Educational Leadership Management and Administration Society.

The article is written in a clear and accessible style, which should make it understandable to any existing or aspiring school leader.

Accuracy

This is a descriptive piece, which does not make any claims about causality. It would appear from the acknowledgement that it has its origins in work undertaken to complete a Masters degree at the University of Warwick. In addition, the article has been published in a journal that requires two blind peer reviews. As such, the article should be deemed to be of an appropriate level for the journal.

Nevertheless, there appear to be several concerns re. the rigour or otherwise of the article. First, it is not clear whether the research has been conducted by an 'insider' and how that may have influenced the data collected.

Second, the use of 'volunteerism' – one who enlists or offers their services to the organisations of their own free will, and without expecting remuneration' Getz (1997) – as underpinning framework is potentially flawed, as teachers are paid and are not volunteers. As such, theoretical frameworks associated with 'discretionary effort' may have been more appropriate. Furthermore, there is an emphasis on the place of extrinsic motivation, with teachers being judged on how well pupils meet aspirational target grades in teacher decision-making about number of hours chosen to be worked.

(Continued)

Figure 5.6 (Continued)

Third, there is no description of how the questionnaire used to gain teachers' views was developed, with the results not fully reported. There are also issues re the reliability of self-reports on what factors influence motivations, with possible reluctance to express less intrinsic motivations.

Fourth, the findings are reported in such a way to suggest a uniformity of responses, which is unlikely and suggests weaknesses in the research instruments, data analysis and subsequent discussion.

Applicable

The research involved 24 teachers – in three departments – in a single secondary school in England, which had been rated as Outstanding in all areas by Ofsted (March 2015). This does not mean the research is generalisable to every secondary school in England, who each may be facing different internal or external pressures to improve.

Acceptable

Given existing concerns about teacher workloads, well-being and teacher retention, research into teacher motivation is extremely timely. However, the approaches advocated would fit with many teachers' and senior leaders' concerns about workload and teacher well-being.

Appropriate

This depends upon the context of your school and whether there are any pressing problems of practice relating to teacher retention, well-being, performance-related pay or the level of discretionary effort currently being made available.

Actionable

The research concludes: 'This study has shown that teachers in this school are predominantly working for their students in their non-directed times. Perhaps more of a focus on the intrinsic reasons why teachers teach, rather than creating extrinsic pressures may be a more positive move for the health and well-being of students.' Unfortunately, this does meet any of the criteria of effective advice laid out by Argyris (2000) – for example, it does not lay out the detailed concrete behaviours necessary to bring about the intended outcomes.

In conclusion, what use can I make of this?

The research raises awareness about the issues impacting upon teacher discretionary effort. However, it provides little guidance on how best to proceed to address any associated issues.

Figure 5.6 A worked example – Using the 6 As

Having now briefly looked at the some of the key issues in seeking to appraise research evidence, Chapters 6 and 7 will consider the challenges of appraising statistical research evidence, along with other sources of evidence, such as school data, stakeholder views and practitioner expertise.

Summary and key points

- A simple workaround to evaluate research evidence is to 'strip it, trace it, analyse it, and ask "should I do it?"'.
- In judging the quality of research a useful place to start is to consider the research design and where that places the research in the hierarchy of evidence.

- Both systematic reviews and randomised controlled trials sit towards the apex of the hierarchy of evidence.
- Nevertheless, different types of research question lend themselves to be answered by different types of research evidence.
- An argument consists of two components – a claim and a warrant.
- Research abstracts are extremely useful in making a quick appraisal of the usefulness and relevance of research.
- There are a number of frameworks available to help you judge the usefulness of research in addressing a problem of practice.

References

Argyris, C. (2000) *Flawed Advice and the Management Trap: How Managers Can Know When They're Getting Good Advice and When They're Not*. Oxford: Oxford University Press.

Booth, W., Colob, G., Williams, J., Bizup, J. and Fitzgerald, W. (2016) *The Craft of Research*, 4th edn. Chicago, IL: The University of Chicago Press.

Briner, R. and Walshe, N. (2014) 'From passively received wisdom to actively constructed knowledge: teaching systematic review skills as a foundation of evidence-based management', *Academy of Management Learning and Education*, 13 (3): 415–32.

Coe, R. (2014) 'Classroom observation: it's harder than you think'. Blog post, 29 January 2014. http://cem.org/blog/414/ (accessed 3 May 2018).

Coe, R., Kime, S., Nevill, C. and Coleman, R. (2013) *The DIY Evaluation Guide*. London: Education Endowment Foundation.

Connolly, P., Biggart, A., Miller, S., O'Hare, L. and Thurston, A. (2017) *Using Randomised Controlled Trials in Education*. London: Sage.

Fitzgerald, F. Scott (1936) *The Crack-Up*. London: Alma Classics.

Fullan, M. (2014) *The Principal: Three Keys to Maximizing Impact*. San Francisco, CA: John Wiley & Sons.

Getz, D. (1997) *Event Management and Event Tourism*. New York: Cognizant Communication Corporation.

Ginsburg, A. and Smith, M.S. (2016) 'Do randomized controlled trials meet the "gold standard"'? American Enterprise Institute. Available at: www.carnegie foundation.org/wp-content/uploads/2016/03/Do-randomized-controlled-trials-meet-the-gold-standard.pdf (accessed 18 March 2016).

Gorard, S., See, B. and Siddiqui, N. (2017) *The Trials of Evidence-Based Education*. London: Routledge.

Gough, D., Oliver, S. and Thomas, J. (2017) *An Introduction to Systematic Reviews*, 2nd edn. London: Sage.

Gray, J. (2001) *Evidence-Based Healthcare: How to Make Health Policy and Management Decisions*. London: Churchill Livingstone.

Hanley, P., Chambers, B. and Haslam, J. (2016) 'Reassessing RCTs as the "gold standard": synergy not separatism in evaluation designs', *International Journal of Research & Method in Education*, 39 (3): 287–98.

Higgins, S. (2017) My own take on necessary conditions for effective research use [online]. Twitter. 6th March. Available: http://twitter.com/profstig/status/838768634919006208 (accessed 30 July 2018).

Holmes, B. (2017) 'The management of teachers' non-directed time in a secondary school', *Management in Education, 31* (1): 39–42.

Nevill, C. (2016) 'Do EEF trials meet the new "gold-standard"?'. https://education endowmentfoundation.org.uk/news/do-eef-trials-meet-the-new-gold-standard/ (accessed 24 January 2017).

Nutley, S., Powell, A. and Davies, H. (2013) *What Counts as Good Evidence?* St Andrews: Alliance for Useful Evidence.

Pawson, R., Boaz, A., Grayson, L., Long, A. and Barnes, C. (2003) *Types and Quality of Social Care Knowledge. Stage Two: Towards the Quality Assessment of Social Care Knowledge.* ESRC Centre for Evidence Based Policy and Practice: Working Paper.

Petticrew, M. and Roberts, H. (2003) 'Evidence, hierarchies, and typologies: horses for courses', *Journal of Epidemiology & Community Health, 57* (7): 527–9.

Robinson, V. (2016) *Personal correspondence.*

Robinson, V., Hohepa, M. and Lloyd, C. (2009) 'School leadership and student outcomes: identifying what works and why', *Best Evidence Synthesis Iteration [BES].* Wellington, New Zealand: Ministry of Education.

Sharples, J. (2017) 'My vision for an evidence-based education system – or some things I'd like to see'. *Evidence-Based Education podcast,* posted 8 August 2017. https://evidencebased.education/podcast-jonathan-sharples/ (accessed 3 May 2018).

Slavin, R. (1989) 'Pet and the pendulum: faddism in education and how to stop it', *Phi Delta Kappan, 70* (10): 752–8.

Wallace, M. and Wray, A. (2016) *Critical Reading and Writing for Postgraduates,* 3rd edn. London: Sage.

Willingham, D. (2012) *When Can You Trust the Experts? How to Tell Good Science from Bad in Education.* San Francisco, CA: John Wiley & Sons.

Yin, R. (1984) *Case Study Research: Design and Methods.* Beverly Hills, CA: Sage.

6

APPRAISING RESEARCH AND STATISTICS

Chapter outline

This chapter will provide a brief introduction to becoming a critical reader of quantitative educational research evidence. In the first part of the chapter, attention will focus on: what is meant by an 'effect size'; how effect sizes are calculated; and how to interpret the 'size' of an effect size. The chapter will then go on to examine meta-analyses and their limitations. Following on, the chapter will focus on correlation and how this is often confused with cause and effect. Subsequently, the chapter will briefly explain the terms: p-values, confidence intervals, statistical significance and highlight some of the challenges in their use. Finally, the chapter will provide a checklist of questions to be asked when seeking to interpret the quality of quantitative educational research findings.

Key words: *confidence intervals, correlation, effect sizes, meta-analyses, p-values, statistical significance*

Effect sizes

In simple terms, an effect size is a 'way of quantifying the difference between two groups' (Coe, 2017: 339). To illustrate how an effect size is calculated, Coe (2002) makes reference to the work of Dowson (2002), who attempted to demonstrate the time-of-day effects on children's learning, or in other words: do children learn better in the morning or afternoon? Thirty-eight children were included in the intervention, with half being randomly allocated to listen to a story and respond to questions at 9.00am, whereas the remaining 19 students listened to the same story and questions at 3.00pm. The children's understanding of the story was assessed by using a test where the number of correct answers was measured out of 20. The morning group had an average score of 15.2, whereas the afternoon group had an average score of 17.9, a difference of 2.7. Coe then poses the question: 'How big a difference is this?' However, given that in this example the effect of the intervention cannot be measured by, say, the impact on GCSE grades, what are we to do? One way is to look at the standard deviation (SD), i.e. a measure of the spread of values – within the two groups. Coe notes that in Dowson's experiment the SD of the combined groups is 3.3, so the effect size can be calculated by using the following formula:

> Effect size = (Mean of experimental group) – (Mean of the control group)/Standard Deviation

Putting the results of Dowson's experiment into this formula, the effect size of the intervention is:

$(17.9–15.2)/3.3 = 0.8$ SD.

So far, so good. Yet as Wiliam (2016) notes, a major problem with using effect sizes is that they are not particularly intuitive, and it is not clear how to interpret any values generated by a calculation of effect sizes. Wiliam goes on to ask whether effect sizes of, say, 0.25 and 0.14 are respectively large or small. Or do they tell us nothing of value at all?

To help interpret effect sizes, a useful starting point is the work of Cohen (1992), who describes a small effect size as something that is only visible through careful inquiry. On the other hand, a 'medium' effect size is something that you should be able to see 'with the naked eye' and is substantial. Accordingly, Cohen defines small, medium and large effect sizes as 0.2, 0.5 and 0.8 respectively. Yet, it should be noted that these effect sizes were being used to identify the sample size required to give yourself a reasonable chance of detecting an effect size of that size, if it existed. In other words, Cohen's scale of effect sizes was developed to help with research design rather than the size of the impact of the intervention. As such, 0.2, 0.5 and 0.8 should not be used to interpret the magnitude of an effect size.

The most well-known interpretation of the magnitude of effect size has been put forward by Hattie (2008), who having reviewed over 800 meta-studies argues that the average effect size of a range of educational strategies is 0.4 SD and which was deemed to be the equivalent of a year's worth of progress. Alternatively, Higgins et al. (2013a) provide some guidance on the interpretation of effect sizes (−0.01 to 0.18 low, 0.19 to 0.44 moderate, 0.45 to 0.69 high, 0.7+ very high) with effect sizes being converted into months of progress, as illustrated in Figure 6.1.

Months' progress	Effect size from	To	Description
0	−0.1	0.01	Very low or no effect
1	0.02	0.09	Low
2	0.1	0.18	Low
3	0.19	0.26	Moderate
4	0.27	0.35	Moderate
5	0.36	0.44	Moderate
6	0.45	0.52	High
7	0.53	0.61	High
8	0.62	0.69	High
9	0.70	0.78	Very High
10	0.79	0.87	Very High
11	0.88	0.95	Very High
12	0.96	> 1.0	Very High

Figure 6.1 Converting effect size to months' progress (Higgins et al., 2013a)

When looking at the relationship between effect sizes and GCSE grades, Coe (2002) notes the distribution of GCSE grades in compulsory subjects (such as maths and English) as having standard deviations of between 1.5 and 1.8 grades. An improvement of one GCSE grade therefore represents an effect size of 0.5–0.7. Using this as a starting point, a teaching intervention which led to an effect size of 0.6 would lead to each pupil improving by approximately one GCSE grade. Or another way of putting this, is that if in a school 50% of pupils were gaining five or more A*–C grades, then if you have a 0.6 effect size across the cohort and all subjects, this would lead to an increase from 50% to 73% (Coe, 2017).

However, Slavin (2016) has published an analysis of effect sizes which challenges these interpretations as to what is a large effect size. Slavin argues that what is a large effect size depends on two factors: sample size and student assignment to treatment or controlled groups (was it done randomly or through a matching process). According to this analysis, average effect sizes would appear to range from between 0.11 and 0.32 SD, which suggests any judgement about the size of an effect size will require careful reading of the original research to consider issues such as study design and sample size.

Meta-analyses

In recent years there has been an increase in attempts to aggregate effect sizes through the use of meta-analysis so as to make judgements about the impact of educational interventions (Hattie, 2008; Higgins et al., 2013b; Marzano et al., 2001). Figure 6.2 provides examples of the average effect sizes of a range of interventions.

However, before going further into examining how to interpret meta-analysis it is important to define the following terms: meta; meta-evaluations; meta-analysis; review of reviews. Very helpfully, Gough et al. (2017: 10) provide the following definitions:

- Meta: about, above to beyond something
- Meta-evaluations: evaluation of evaluations. These can be systematic reviews, alternatively they can be formative or summative evaluations of evaluations. Including standards for such evaluations.
- Meta-analysis: the term has been used in the past to refer to all forms of reviews, but does not usually refer to the statistical meta-analysis of data from primary research studies.
- Review of reviews: a review of previous reviews. This contrasts with reviews that only review primary research studies.

Intervention	Effect size
After-school programmes: Services offered during term time and at the end of the school day where children or young people are involved in planned activities which are supervised by adults	+0.16
Ability-grouping: Pupils with similar attainment levels are grouped together either for specific lessons on a regular basis (setting or regrouping) or as a class (streaming or tracking)	−0.06 to 0.12
Assessment for learning: AfL is based on the idea that students need a clear understanding of what it is that they need to learn and evidence about their current level of performance, so they can close this gap	0.32
Arts participation: Participation in artistic and creative activities, including dance, drama, music, painting, sculpture etc., both in terms of performance and creation	0.05
Block scheduling: An approach to school timetabling in secondary schools. It typically means that pupils have fewer classes (4–5) per day, for a longer period of time (70–90 minutes)	−0.02 to 0.15
Early intervention: Approaches where the aim is to ensure that young children have educationally based pre-school or nursery experience to prepare them effectively for school	0.45
Feedback: Information given to the learner and/or the teacher about the learner's performance relative to the learning goals which then redirects or refocuses either the teacher's or the learner's actions to achieve the goal	0.73
Homework: Tasks given to pupils by their teachers to be completed outside of class, with the normal expectation that it will be completed at home	0.36
Individualised instruction: Based on the idea that all learners are different and therefore have different needs, so an individualised or tailored approach to instruction ought to be more effective	0.10
Metacognitive strategies: Teaching approaches that make learners' thinking about learning more explicit in the classroom	0.67

Figure 6.2 Examples of average effect sizes for different interventions (adapted from Higgins et al., 2013b)

Nevertheless, the use of meta-analysis is not without its problems. Simpson (2017) argues there are two key assumptions associated with meta-analysis and meta-meta-analysis. First, larger effect sizes are associated with greater educational significance. Second, two or more different studies on the same interventions can have their effect sizes combined to give a meaningful estimate of the intervention's educational importance. However, Simpson identifies three reasons – different comparator groups, range restrictions, and measure design – as to why these assumptions do not hold.

Unequal comparator groups

Say you are looking at comparing the effect sizes of a couple of studies on the impact of written feedback. In one study the results of a group of pupils who receive written feedback is compared with the results of pupils who receive verbal feedback. Let's say that gives us an effect size of 0.6. A second study, in which the results of pupils who receive written feedback are compared with pupils who receive only group feedback, has an effect size of 0.4. Now it is tempting to add the two effect sizes together to find out the average effect size of written feedback, in this case 0.5. However, that would not allow us to make an accurate estimate as to the effect size of providing written feedback. This would require a study where the results of written feedback is compared to pupils who receive no feedback whatsoever. As such, it is simply not possible to accurately combine studies that have used different types of comparator groups.

Range restrictions

This time we are going to undertake the same two interventions but in this example we are going to restrict the range of pupils used in the studies. In the first study, only highly attaining pupils are included. Whereas in the second study, pupils involved in the intervention are drawn from the whole ability range. As a result, and for at least two reasons, this may lead to a change in the effect size of receiving written feedback. First, it will take out from the study pupils who may not know how to respond to the feedback. Second, it may well be that highly attaining pupils have less 'head-room' to demonstrate the impact of either type of feedback. As a result, the effect size is highly likely to change. The consequence of this is that the different ranges of pupils used in interventions will influence the impact of an intervention and influence the effect size. As such, unless the interventions combine studies that use the same range of pupils, the combined effect size is unlikely to be an accurate estimate of the 'true' effect size of the intervention.

Measure design

Finally, we are going to look at the impact of measure design on effect sizes. Simpson (2017) argues that researchers can directly influence effect size by choices they make about how to measure the effect. For example, if researchers design an intervention and the measure used is specifically focused on measuring the effect of that intervention, this will lead to an increase in effect size. Let's say you are undertaking an intervention looking to improve algebra scores. Now you could choose to use a measure that is specifically designed to 'measure' algebra or you could choose to use a measure of general mathematical competence, which includes an element of algebra. In this situation, the effect size of the former will be greater than the latter, due to the sensitivity of the measure used.

Other considerations

It is important to note that there are considerations regarding the limitation of effect sizes and meta-analysis. Wiliam (2016) identifies a number of limitations of 'meta-analyses' which include: first, the intensity and duration of the intervention will have an impact on the resulting effect size. Second, the 'file drawer' problem, this is a phenomenon where studies with large and/or statistically significant effects, relative to studies with small or null effects, have a greater chance of being published. It is not known how many similar interventions have been carried out that did not generate statistically significant results, and as a result have not been published. Indeed, Polanin et al. (2016) found when reviewing 383 meta-analyses that published research yielded larger effect results than those from unpublished studies, and provides evidence to support the notion of publication bias. Third, there is the age dependence of effect size. All other things being equal, the older the pupils the smaller the effect size, which is a result of a greater diversity in the population of older pupils compared to younger pupils. Fourth, Wiliam raises the issue of the generalisability of the studies. One of the problems of trying to calculate the overall effect size of an intervention is that much of the published research is undertaken by psychology professors in laboratories on their own undergraduate students. As such, these students will have little in common with, say, Key Stage 2 or Key Stage 3 pupils, and will have a substantial impact on the generalisability of the findings.

Implications of effect sizes and meta-analyses for the evidence-based practitioner

First, it should be pretty clear from above that 'effect sizes' and associated 'meta-analyses' are not without their limitations. Second, league tables of educational interventions based on effect size may well be flawed and provide little guidance in prioritising interventions relevant to a school. Third, it is necessary to be wary of researchers, experts and consultants who offer up both simplistic interpretations of effect sizes and subsequent recommendations for action. Fourth, the relevance and importance of effect sizes and meta-analyses largely depends on the problem of practice being addressed. Finally, effect sizes are just one piece of the evidence jigsaw that evidence-based practitioners need to put together before making a decision.

Correlation

Correlation is an alternative way of thinking about effect size. Quite simply, correlation addresses questions about the 'relationship between two or more variables and the extent to which they co-vary' (Gorard, 2017: 139).The correlation coefficient seeks to quantify both the strength and direction of a relationship between two variables. The correlation coefficient (r) can range from +1, where there is perfectly positive correlation, to −1, where there is a perfectly negative correlation. A value of 0 would suggest that there is no relationship between the two variables. Normally, the correlation coefficient will generate a range of intermediate values, between −1 and +1.

A range of r values are illustrated in Figures 6.3, 6.4 and 6.5

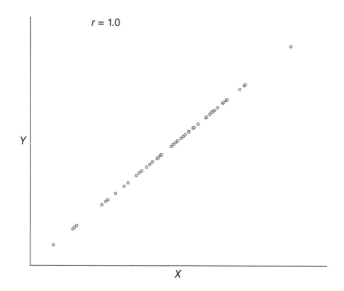

Figure 6.3   r equals 1

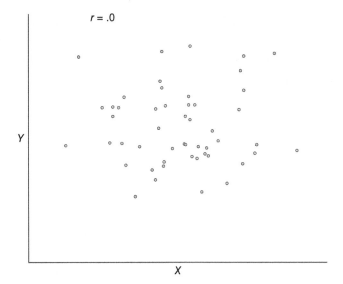

Figure 6.4   r equals 0

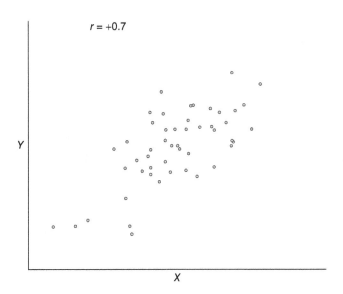

Figure 6.5   r equals +0.7

Cumming and Calin-Jageman (2017) argue that when interpreting an r value, of say 0.7, which hints at some positive relationship between two variables X and Y, a number of different things could be going on.

- There may be a causal link between X and Y so that changes in X lead to changes in Y, or changes in Y are leading to changes in X.
- Something else may be going on, with other variables impacting on either X or Y or both.
- There are no causal links, and what we are seeing is what Cumming and Calin-Jageman describe as 'seeing a face in the clouds' (2017: 216).

As such, Cumming and Calin-Jageman note that all that correlations do is give us some form of guidance as to what to investigate further. The r values may suggest what and where to look, however, it needs to be made clear that correlation does not imply causation. In other words, just because X *appears* to be linked with changes in Y, this does not mean that changes in X are causing changes in Y. For example, the appointment of a new head of department may be linked with improved pupils' results, but that does not mean the change in departmental leadership caused the change in pupils' results.

With this in mind, different r values have been put forward by statisticians as a way of interpreting the size of a correlation coefficient, see for example the guidance provided by Hinkle et al. (2003) for interpreting the correlation coefficient (Figure 6.6).

Size of correlation	Interpretation
0.90 to 1.00 (−0.90 to −1.0)	Very high positive (negative) correlation
0.70 to 0.90 (−0.70 to −0.90)	High positive (negative) correlation
0.50 to 0.70 (−0.50 to −0.70)	Moderate positive (negative) correlation
0.30 to 0.50 (−0.30 to −0.50)	Low positive (negative) correlation
0.00 to 0.30 (0.00 to −0.30)	Little if any correlation

Figure 6.6 Rules of thumb for interpreting the size of a correlation coefficient (Hinkle et al., 2003)

As an alternative, Cohen (1988) has suggested the following guidelines for the interpretation of r values, where an r value of 0.1 indicates a small positive correlation, 0.3 represents a medium correlation, 0.5 represents a large correlation, and 0.7 represents a very large correlation. However, Cumming and Calin-Jageman (2017) argue that r values need to be interpreted in context, as correlation is used in such a wide-ranging number of ways and settings that reference values for r provide little help in interpreting the data. Indeed, Cummings and Calin-Jageman argue that an r value of 0.3 may suggest there is a relationship between two variables, even though when graphed the data looks like a 'shotgun blast'.

However, in trying to identify the strength of the association between the two variables it is necessary to use the coefficient of determination – r squared – which gives you the proportion of shared variance. In other words, how much of the variability in one variable can be caused or explained by its relationship to another factor. If we have two variables (X the independent variable and Y the dependent variable) and we have a correlation coefficient of +0.5 then our coefficient of determination will be 0.25, which can be interpreted as:

- A might cause B 25% of the time OR
- B might cause A 25% of the time OR
- C causes them both (and is not present all of the time) OR
- It is a pure coincidence OR
- It is some of the above in some unknown combination.

Let's now look at an example of how both the correlation coefficient and the coefficient of determination can be used to interpret research findings.

A correlation case study: Daniel Goleman, emotional intelligence and organisational climate

Goleman (2000) argues that leaders often mistakenly assume that their leadership is a function of their personality, rather than something that can be chosen to meet the needs of a specific circumstance. Goleman claims that successful leaders have strengths in five emotional intelligence competences: self-awareness, self-regulation, motivation, empathy and social skill. Moreover, these components of emotional intelligence can be combined in different ways which reflect six basic styles of leadership: coercive, authoritative, affiliative, democratic, pace-setting and coaching. Furthermore, the very best leaders are not wedded to one particular approach and can change approaches depending upon the demands of the situation.

Based on research interviews with nearly 4000 executives out of a database of 20,000 executives worldwide, Goleman goes on to demonstrate the impact that different leadership styles have on the organisational climate (working atmosphere). Using the correlation coefficient (r), Goleman seeks to quantify both the strength and direction of a relationship between leadership style and organisational climate. Goleman's research indicates that the relationship between leadership style and organisational climate reflects a range of intermediate values between −1 and +1. Table 6.1 shows the relationship between different styles of leadership and aspects of organisational climate. So looking at the table we can see that the coercive (−0.26) and pace-setting (−0.25) styles have a negative overall correlation with organisational climate. Whereas, the authoritative (+0.54), affiliative (+0.46), democratic (+0.43) and coaching (+0.42) styles have a positive correlation with organisational climate. However, Goleman notes that all styles can have their uses, and no one style should be relied upon nor excluded, when seeking to tackle the ranges of circumstances that are faced by leaders.

We can now turn Goleman's correlation coefficient into the coefficient determinant and interpret what it means for the relationship between leadership style and organisational climate, and this is illustrated in Table 6.1. This suggests that for both the coercive and pace-setting styles relatively small amounts of variances in leadership style and organisational climate appear to be shared (+0.07 and +0.06, respectively) As for the relationship between an authoritative style and organisational climate, the data suggests that at best only 29% of the total variance between the two variables is shared.

Table 6.1 Leadership style, organisation climate, correlation coefficient and correlation coefficient determinant

Leadership style	Correlation coefficient r	Coefficient determinant r squared
Coercive	−0.26	+0.07
Authoritative	+0.54	+0.29
Affiliative	+0.46	+0.21
Democratic	+0.43	+0.18
Pace-setting	−0.25	+0.06
Coaching	+0.42	+0.18

Source: based on Goleman, 2000

Implications in using correlations

It would seem that there are a number of implications in using correlations when making recommendations about leadership and management.

- Correlation does not mean there is a causal link between two variables –just because you have a positive correlation that does not mean the changes in leadership style have caused the change in organisational climate. Indeed, it may be the change in organisational climate could cause the change in leadership style.
- It is important to have some rules of thumb for interpreting the size of the correlation coefficient. In this example the largest correlation coefficient (authoritative 0.54) is around the borderline between positive and low correlation. In other words, just because this is the largest correlation coefficient in your study this does not mean that the size of correlation coefficient is large.

If you are looking to make judgements about the strength of the relationship between two variables, then you need to calculate the coefficient of determination. Again, in this example we have two values (coercive 0.06 and pace-setting 0.07) that are close to zero, which suggests there is very little of the variance in leadership style and organisational climate which seems to be shared.

P-values, significance testing and confidence intervals

When seeking to understand quantitative educational research effect sizes, correlations and meta-analyses are not the only terms needed to be understood. It is also useful to understand terms such as p-values, significance testing and confidence intervals. However, when seeking to understand these terms there are a number of major problems, and as Greenland et al. (2016) state: 'There are no interpretations of these concepts which are at once simple, intuitive, correct, and foolproof' (p. 337). Greenland et al. go on to illustrate their point by providing 25 examples of common misconceptions and interpretation of these terms.

Not only are these concepts exceedingly difficult for the layperson to grasp, they are even difficult for professional academics to get right. Gorard et al. (2017) give numerous examples of p-values, confidence intervals and significance testing being misinterpreted and misapplied in peer-reviewed journal articles. As such, and given the complexities involved, this section will provide only a brief introduction to p-values, confidence intervals and significance testing. To gain a deeper understanding it is advisable to refer, amongst others, to: Coe et al., 2017; Connolly et al., 2017; Cumming and Calin-Jageman, 2017; Ellis, 2010; Gorard et al., 2017.

P-values

Evidence-based school leaders seek to make decisions using the best available evidence. In doing so, evidence-based school leaders are going to be looking to find interventions and strategies that have the potential to have a favourable impact on the outcomes experienced by the intended beneficiaries of the decision – be it pupils, colleagues or the school community at large. However, when looking at whether an intervention 'works', it is necessary to be aware that some of the difference produced by the intervention may be down to chance or some random variation in the intended beneficiaries – be it pupils or staff – of the intervention.

Imagine reading the work of an educational researcher who is interested in testing the hypothesis that a certain teaching strategy will lead to improvements in scores on a particular maths test. On the one hand, there is what is called the 'null hypothesis' which states that the teaching intervention will have no effect on pupils' maths test scores. On the other hand, there is the 'alternative hypothesis' which states that the teaching strategy will lead to improvement in the maths test scores.

The educational researcher will now collect data about the intervention in maths, and calculate what is known as the p-value, which can be thought of as a 'statistical summary of the compatibility between the observed data and what we predict or expect to see if we know the entire statistical model (all the assumptions used to compute the p-value) were correct' (Greenland et al., 2016: 339). The smaller the p-value, the more unlikely are our results if the null hypothesis (and test assumptions) hold true. Whereas, the larger the p-value, the less surprising are our results, given the null hypothesis (and test assumptions) hold true. In other words, as Greenland et al. state:

> the P value simply indicates the degree to which the data conform to the pattern predicted by the test hypothesis and all the other assumptions used in the test (the underlying statistical model). Thus P = 0.01 would indicate that the data are not very close to what the statistical model (including the null hypothesis) predicted they should be, while P = 0.40 would indicate that the data are much closer to the model prediction, allowing for chance variation. (p. 340)

The next step is to compare the p-value with the significance level. For reasons largely to do with custom and practice, the significance level is often chosen to be 0.05, in other words a 95% level of significance. Now if the p-value calculated from the data is less than 0.05, this casts doubt on the null hypothesis that the teaching intervention has no impact, and we can say we have a statistically significant result. On the other hand, if our p value is greater than 0.05, it could be said there is a statistically non-significant result.

However, as Ellis (2010) notes, p values and significance testing are not without difficulties. First, null hypothesis significance testing (NHST) involves dichotomous thinking – the results are either statistically significant or they are not. Using a 0.05 p-value to determine significance is purely arbitrary; why not choose 0.04 or 0.06? Second, it would be mistaken to assume just because the p-value is greater than 0.05 that there is not an underlying effect. The p-value is not a measure of the size of an effect, but rather is a measure of surprise, with a smaller p-value suggesting the greater the surprise. Indeed, the p-value is a function of both the size of the effect and the size of the sample. As such, it is possible to get a statistically significant p-value from either a large effect or large sample or both. In other words, there may be a very small effect and a large sample leading to a statistically significant result, or there might be a very large effect and a small sample leading to a statistically insignificant result. As a consequence, significance testing tells you very little about the usefulness of a study's research results, rather the interest is in whether the study's results are practically significant. Or more strongly, as Gorard et al. (2017) state: 'significance tests just do not work' (p. 28).

Practical significance

As Willingham (2012) states: '"practical significance" refers to whether or not that difference is something you care about' (p. 203). To help illustrate this point, Ellis (2010) cites the work of Kirk (1996), who tells a story about a researcher who believes that a certain treatment will bring about an increase in the IQ of patients suffering from Alzheimer's disease. Although the results were not statistically significant, there did appear to be some evidence that the treatment may have been having a positive impact on patients' IQ – and would be something to care about. In the context of education, there may be an intervention that is having a positive effect on pupils' learning with an effect size of 0.8 but would appear not to be statistically significant. Yet this result may be far more interesting and useful than an intervention with an effect size of 0.01 but is statistically significant (Higgins et al., 2013a).

As a consequence, evidence-based practitioners need to make a judgement call about the relevance and usefulness of research findings, which are never easy when you are not an expert. Nonetheless, Willingham (2012) suggests that evidence-based practitioners should consider whether the practical significance of the research relates to your problem of practice, what you are trying to achieve. Is the improvement, or intervention, that is being suggested consistent with your objectives and the resources available to achieve them?

From this discussion, it should be clear it is very easy to misinterpret p-values. As such, at this stage it might be worth looking at some recent guidance provided by the American Statistical Association on the interpretation of p-values (ASA, 2016), which is summarised in Figure 6.7.

Principle	Explanation
P-values can indicate how incompatible the data are with a specified statistical model	'The smaller the *p*-value, the greater the statistical incompatibility of the data with the null hypothesis, if the underlying assumptions used to calculate the *p*-value hold. This incompatibility can be interpreted as casting doubt on or providing evidence against the null hypothesis or the underlying assumption' (p. 131)
P-values do not measure the probability that the studied hypothesis is true, or the probability that the data were produced by random chance alone	'It is a statement about data in relation to a specified hypothetical explanation, and is not a statement about the explanation itself' (p. 131)

Principle	Explanation
Scientific conclusions and business or policy decisions should not be based only on whether a p-value passes a specific threshold	'Practices that reduce data analysis or scientific inference to mechanical "bright-line" rules (such as "p <0.05") for justifying scientific claims or conclusions can lead to erroneous beliefs and poor decision-making. A conclusion does not immediately become "true" on one side of the divide and "false" on the other. The widespread use of "statistical significance" (generally interpreted as "p ≤0.05") as a license for making a claim of a scientific finding (or implied truth) leads to considerable distortion of the scientific process' (p.131)
Proper inference requires full reporting and transparency	'P-values and related analyses should not be reported selectively. Researchers should disclose the number of hypotheses explored during the study, all data collection decisions, all statistical analyses conducted, and all p-values computed. Valid scientific conclusions based on p-values and related statistics cannot be drawn without at least knowing how many and which analyses were conducted, and how those analyses (including p-values) were selected for reporting' (p. 131–2)
A p-value, or statistical significance, does not measure the size of an effect or the importance of a result	'Smaller p-values do not necessarily imply the presence of larger or more important effects, and larger p-values do not imply a lack of importance or even lack of effect. Any effect, no matter how tiny, can produce a small p-value if the sample size or measurement precision is high enough, and large effects may produce unimpressive p-values if the sample size is small or measurements are imprecise. Similarly, identical estimated effects will have different p-values if the precision of the estimates differs' (p. 131)
By itself, a p-value does not provide a good measure of evidence regarding a model or hypothesis	'Researchers should recognize that a p-value without context or other evidence provides limited information. For example, a p-value near 0.05 taken by itself offers only weak evidence against the null hypothesis. Likewise, a relatively large p-value does not imply evidence in favor of the null hypothesis; many other hypotheses may be equally or more consistent with the observed data. For these reasons, data analysis should not end with the calculation of a p-value when other approaches are appropriate and feasible' (p. 132)

Figure 6.7 Summary of American Statistical Association guidance on the interpretation of p-values (based on Wasserstein and Lazar, 2016)

Confidence intervals

In order to address some of the issues associated with statistical significance and p-values, note that academics such as Cumming (2014) suggest the use of confidence intervals (CIs). As Ellis (2010) notes, 'a confidence interval is a range of plausible values for the index or parameter being estimated' (p. 17). Although we should add, this assumes that all the other assumptions made in the statistical model are correct and hold true (Greenland et al., 2016).

To help understand the notion of CIs let's turn to an example developed by Cumming and Calin-Jageman (2017) and imagine there is an opinion poll on whether there is support for a particular proposition in a referendum.

> Public support for Proposition A is 53%
>
> Due to issues with the poll design and sampling from the population there is an estimated 2% margin of error
>
> As such the suggested support for Proposition A is 53% ffl 2%
>
> This gives us a 95% CI between 51% and 55%

What does this mean? Again as Greenland et al. (2016) note, CIs are subject to a number of misconceptions. For example, a common misconception would be that the 95% CI presented by the poll has a 95% chance of containing the 'true' number of people who intend to support Proposition A. However, this is not the case, and merely refers to how often a 95% CI computed from a number of polls would contain the 'true' number intending to support Proposition A 'if all the assumptions used to compute the intervals were correct' (Greenland et al., 2016: 343).

It should also be noted that the appropriateness of the use of CIs is challenged by Gorard et al. (2017), who argue CIs say 'nothing about the quality of the study, cannot account for missing data, apply only to complete random samples' (p. 32). Indeed, it could be argued that as many measures of school performance in England use CIs, their use is totally inappropriate as pupils are not randomly allocated between schools and there is missing data due to pupils 'leaving' before the end of the school year. Furthermore, this is compounded by the Department for Education using a technically incorrect definition of a confidence interval (Kime, 2017).

Judging the trustworthiness of statistical research

Given the challenges associated with the application and interpretation of many key statistical terms used in educational research, how is the evidence-based school leader to go about judging the trustworthiness of research findings? A useful starting point might be to ask the following questions (Higgins, 2017):

- Does the research design indicate a causal effect or is there an association or just a description?
- Was the research conducted in schools or other realistic contexts?
- Was the sample reasonably large? (e.g. over 100 pupils, or at least more than 50)
- What were the measures used to evaluate its impact? (standardised tests, national tests or examinations, or perceptions and beliefs)
- Can you tell how important the impact is?
- In addition, you may want to take into account the extent to which there is missing data, with pupils having dropped out of the intervention (Gorard et al., 2017).

Application

The chapter ends by seeking to apply some of the insights generated to a piece of research into the use of Lesson Study in US elementary schools. In doing so, Higgins's 6As framework (see Chapter 5) will be used to give some structure to the analysis, and is illustrated in Figure 6.8.

Author, date, title, publication details: LEWIS, C. and PERRY, R. Lesson study to scale up research-based knowledge: a randomized, controlled trial of fractions learning. *Journal for Research in Mathematics Education*, 2017; 48 (3): 261–99.

Abstract

A randomised controlled trial of Lesson Study supported by mathematical resources assigned 39 educator teams across the United States to locally managed Lesson Study (LS) supported by a fractions LS resource kit or to one of two control conditions (One – use of LS with no focus on fractions or use of resources; Two – professional learning 'business as usual' with no use of LS or focus of professional learning on fractions).

The effect of the LS plus mathematical resources on educators' fractions knowledge was statistically significant with an effect size of 0.19.

The effect on pupils' fractions knowledge was also statistically significant with an effect size of 0.49 for those pupils taught by teachers engaged in LS and using the resources pack.

The research suggests that 'integrating research-based resources into LS offers a new approach to the problem of "scale-up" by combining the strengths of teacher leadership and research-based knowledge.'

(Continued)

Figure 6.8 (Continued)

Accessibility

Physical

Unfortunately Lewis and Perry's work sits behind a 'paywall'. Moreover, the *Journal for Research in Mathematics Education* is not included in the 2000 journals you can access via your membership of the Chartered College of Teaching. Although a summary of the research findings was available on Twitter, the paper was ultimately obtained by direct email contact with the corresponding author.

Intellectual

Lewis and Perry provide a very clear theoretical map showing the relationship between LS with resource kits and changes in teacher and pupil learning. However, the statistics used in the paper are advanced, and would not necessarily be accessible even to colleagues who hold advanced degrees in education. Nevertheless, anyone who has an understanding of effect sizes should be able to judge the claims being made, i.e., LS combined with an appropriate resource pack would appear to lead to increases in both teachers' and pupils' knowledge of fractions.

Accurate

Given the statistical complexity of the paper it is difficult for the 'non-expert' to judge whether the paper is accurate or not. However, it is possible to identify a number of 'weaknesses' which may impact on the study's accuracy.

Time

The amount of time involved varied between the intervention group and the control groups, with the teachers in intervention participating for approximately 40% more time than the control group. As such, it is not possible to separate the effects of the intervention curriculum from the effects of the differences in the time spent by the treatment and control groups.

Comparator groups

There are two quite different control groups – whose results are combined when making comparison with the intervention group, which Simpson (2017) notes raises all sorts of issues about validity of any measure of effect size.

Effect size

The effect size of the impact of the intervention on pupils' knowledge of fractions was 0.49. However, Simpson argues that researchers can directly influence effect size by choices they make about how to measure the effect. This study uses an 'instrument' to 'measure' algebra whereas a measure of general mathematical competence, which includes an element of algebra, could have been chosen. As such, the effect size of the former will be greater than the latter, due to the sensitivity of the measure used. This is particularly important given the 0.49 effect size would be deemed to be above average.

Applicable

The research was conducted mainly in elementary schools in the United States, with volunteer staff, of whom the majority had previous experience of LS. As such, this does not mean the research is generalisable to a secondary school in England, where there is little or no experience of LS and is being adopted as a mandatory school-wide approach to professional learning.

Acceptable

Given that LS has in recent years become a widely adopted form of professional learning, the research would appear to be outwardly consistent with current views and beliefs re. teacher professional learning. However, teachers may have concerns about the amount of time required to engage with such an intervention.

Appropriate

This will depend upon the needs of school, staff and pupils, and whether there is a need to develop teachers' and pupils' knowledge of fractions. Within the school, there may be other, more pressing problems of practice. Accordingly, we need to ask : What is the current problem of practice that LS is the answer to? Nevertheless, fractions are notoriously difficult to teach well, so the approach may be relevant to many schools, teachers and pupils.

Actionable

There would appear to be two inter-related issues as regards whether the research is actionable or not. First, the model of LS used in the research is extremely resource-intensive, with individual teachers committing up to 42 hours to the intervention. As such, there are questions as to whether in the current climate of austerity schools have the resources to support the implementation of LS.

Second, even if schools have the capacity to support LS, the effectiveness of LS with mathematical resources does not mean that LS will be effective without such resources (Lewis and Perry, 2017). Thus whether this research is actionable depends upon whether appropriate specialist resources are available to support its implementation.

In conclusion, what use can I make of this?

On balance, Lewis and Perry's work is a welcome contribution to the evidence base on the effectiveness of LS.

Figure 6.8   The 6As framework – Lewis and Perry (2017) and Lesson Study

Summary and key points

- There is no agreement over the 'size' of an effect size and care should be taken with simplistic interpretations.
- Meta-analyses are often used as a way of bringing together information about interventions, though they are not without limitations such as the 'file drawer problem' and effect size being age-dependent.
- A correlation between two variables does not mean there is a direct causal relationship between the two variables as other factors, such as confounds, may be at work.
- Great care should be taken when interpreting p-values as there are a number of common misconceptions.
- A p-value or statistical significance, does not measure the size of an effect or the importance of a result.
- Decisions to proceed or otherwise with an intervention should not be based on whether the 'intervention' passes some arbitrary notion of statistical significance.
- When evaluating research results, the practical significance of the outcomes of research for your problem of practice are more important than statistical significance.

- A confidence interval does not necessarily include the true value of an effect size.
- Given the challenges associated with interpreting the results of quantitative educational research it is necessary to asks questions, such as 'is there missing data?', 'have random samples been used?' and so on.

References

ASA (2016) *American Statistical Association Releases Statement on Statistical Significance and P-Values Provides Principles to Improve the Conduct and Interpretation of Quantitative Science.* Alexandria, VA: American Statistical Association.

Coe, R. (2002) 'It's the effect size, stupid: what effect size is and why it is important'. Paper presented at the British Educational Research Association annual conference, Exeter, 12–14 September 2002.

Coe, R. (2017) 'Effect size', in R. Coe, M. Waring, L. Hedges and J. Arthur (eds), *Research Methods and Methodologies in Education*, 2nd edn. London: Sage. pp. 368–77.

Coe, R., Waring, M., Hedges, L. and Arthur, J. (2017) *Research Methods and Methodologies in Education.* London: Sage.

Cohen, J. (1988) *Statistical Power Analysis for the Behavior Science.* Hillsdale, NJ: Lawrence Erlbaum Associates.

Cohen, J. (1992) 'A power primer', *Psychological Bulletin, 112* (1): 155.

Connolly, P., Biggart, A., Miller, S., O'Hare, L. and Thurston, A. (2017) *Using Randomised Controlled Trials in Education.* London: Sage.

Cumming, G. (2014) 'The new statistics why and how', *Psychological Science, 25* (1): 7–29.

Cumming, G. and Calin-Jageman, R. (2017) *Introduction to the New Statistics: Estimation, Open Science, and Beyond.* Abingdon: Routledge.

Dowson, V. (2002) *Time of Day Effects in Schoolchildren's Immediate and Delayed Recall of Meaningful Material.* Durham: CEM.

Ellis, P.D. (2010) *The Essential Guide to Effect Sizes: Statistical Power, Meta-Analysis, and the Interpretation of Research Results.* Cambridge: Cambridge University Press.

Goleman, D. (2000) 'Leadership that gets results', *Harvard Business Review, 78* (2): 4–17.

Gorard, S. (2017) 'Statistical and correlational techniques', in R. Coe, M. Waring, L. Hedges and J. Arthur (eds), *Research Methods and Methodologies in Education.* London: Sage. pp. 119–24.

Gorard, S., See, B. and Siddiqui, N. (2017) *The Trials of Evidence-Based Education.* London: Routledge.

Gough, D., Oliver, S. and Thomas, J. (2017) *An Introduction to Systematic Reviews*, 2nd edn. London: Sage.

Greenland, S., Senn, S., Rothman, K., Carlin, J., Poole, C., Goodman, S. and Altman, D. (2016) 'Statistical tests, P values, confidence intervals, and power: a guide to misinterpretations', *European Journal of Epidemiology*, *31* (4): 337–50.

Hattie, J. (2008) *Visible Learning: A Synthesis of over 800 Meta-Analyses Relating to Achievement*. London: Routledge.

Higgins, S. (2017) *Personal correspondence*.

Higgins, S., Katsipataki, M., Kokotsaki, D., Coe, R., Elliot Major, L. and Coleman, R. (2013a) *Teaching and Learning Toolkit: Technical Appendices*. London: Sutton Trust Education Endowment Foundation.

Higgins, S., Katsipataki, M., Kokotsaki, D., Coleman, R., Major, L.E. and Coe, R. (2013b) *The Sutton Trust Education Endowment Foundation Teaching and Learning Toolkit Manual*. London: Sutton Trust Education Endowment Foundation.

Hinkle, D.E., Wiersma, W. and Jurs, S.G. (2003) *Applied Statistics for the Behavioral Sciences*, 5th edn. Belmont, CA: Cengage Learning.

Kime, S. (2017) 'Progress 8: beware confidence intervals!', *Schools Week*, 23 January. https://schoolsweek.co.uk/progress-8-beware-confidence-intervals/ (accessed 3 May 2018).

Kirk, R.E. (1996) 'Practical significance: a concept whose time has come', *Educational and Psychological Measurement*, *56* (5): 746–59.

Lewis, C. and Perry, R. (2017) 'Lesson study to scale up research-based knowledge: a randomized, controlled trial of fractions learning', *Journal for Research in Mathematics Education*, *48* (3): 261–99.

Marzano, R.J., Pickering, D. and Pollock, J.E. (2001) *Classroom Instruction that Works: Research-Based Strategies for Increasing Student Achievement*. Alexandria, VA: ASCD.

Polanin, J.R., Tanner-Smith, E.E. and Hennessy, E.A. (2016) 'Estimating the difference between published and unpublished effect sizes a meta-review', *Review of Educational Research*, *86* (1:) 207–36.

Simpson, A. (2017) 'The misdirection of public policy: comparing and combining standardised effect sizes', *Journal of Education Policy*, *32* (4): 450–66.

Slavin, R. (2016) *What Is a Large Effect Size*. Huffington Post. www.huffingtonpost.com/robert-e-slavin/what-is-a-large-effect-si_b_9426372.html (Accessed 23 April 2017).

Wasserstein, R. and Lazar, N. (2016) 'The ASA's statement on P-values: context, process, and purpose', *The American Statistician*, *70* (2): 129–33.

Wiliam, D. (2016) *Leadership for Teacher Learning: Creating a Culture Where All Teachers Improve So that All Students Succeed*. West Palm Beach, FL: Learning Sciences International.

Willingham, D. (2012) *When Can You Trust the Experts? How to Tell Good Science from Bad in Education*. San Francisco, CA: John Wiley & Sons.

7

APPRAISING SCHOOL DATA, STAKEHOLDER VIEWS AND PRACTITIONER EXPERTISE

Chapter outline

This chapter will look at ways of appraising different sources of evidence. First, the chapter will look at some of the difficulties associated with using 'organisational facts' to inform decision-making. Second, consideration will be given to the problems associated with appraising stakeholder feedback: including the difficulties associated with empathy; the ladder of inference; how to know when you are receiving good advice; and, what to do when you disagree with others. Finally, the chapter will examine both experience and intuition, and consider the limits of expertise and whether intuition can be used as a trusted source of evidence.

Key words: *advice, empathy, experience, intuition, ladder of inference, organisational facts, small numbers*

School data and organisational facts

In the context of this book, when discussing organisational facts, reference is being made to quantitative rather than qualitative evidence. Schools have masses of data that looks at a range of variables and outcomes – be it number of pupils, pupil progress, number and type of staff, external examination results, income and expenditure. In addition, there is externally published data such as school census data, school performance tables, financial statements and inspection reports. This being the case, it is important to remember that thinking about school data and organisational facts involves more than just considering pupils' learning and achievement. Consideration is also given to a whole range of evidence, which reflects the diversity of the work of the school leader (Neeleman, 2017). However, it needs to be emphasised that qualitative school data is not being discounted, but rather for the purposes of analysis it is included within the 'stakeholder' source of evidence.

Using the work of Donaldson (2012), this section examines some of the common sources of error – small numbers, measurement error, range restrictions and confounds – to be wary of when interpreting organisational facts. The section will also explore strategies that can be adopted to try to reduce the probability of making these errors.

Small numbers

A major challenge for the evidence-based school leader is the necessity to often make decisions on the basis of a relatively small number of observations. However, whenever dealing with small numbers, there is a very real issue that any changes in results from year to year may be the product of chance and random variations.

Let's imagine you are the chief executive of a multi-academy trust, which has seven very small village primary schools under its control, all of which have 10 or fewer full-time teaching staff, and is looking at trying to make meaningful comparisons between the schools on staff absence rates. However, absence rates within any one particular school may be influenced by a range of random factors, such as an outbreak of illness, which may lead to the individual school having a 'spike' in their absence rate, with that school's absence rate being seen as an outlier. As such, in this case, when trying to assess absence rates, it might be better to aggregate the absence rates across all the schools.

In addition, it might be worth looking at rolling averages, which look at a three- to five-year period of time.

The impact of random variation in pupils on GCSE examination results has recently been examined by Crawford and Benton (2017b), who argue that a school's results will vary from year to year – even if approaches to teaching and learning remain unchanged. Crawford and Benton (2017a: 1) argue results change because:

- You never know what grade a student will get before they take a test (as it depends upon what a student does on the day)
- This year's class is different than last year's class (as seen by their results in other subjects).

Crawford and Benton's analysis of GCSE maths (relative to grade C) results suggests that if all we know about students is the year they took the examination and the school attended, then 67% of the variation in students' results is unexplainable. However, if we then take into account how well the students performed in other qualifications taken at that time, then 63% of the performance variation can be explained. Indeed, only around 2.7% of the remaining variation is correlated with the school attended.

Measurement error

Measurement error presents a real difficulty when trying to interpret quantitative school data. These errors occur when the response given differs from the real value. These mistakes may be the result of: the respondent not understanding what is being asked of them; how and when the data is collected; or how the school holds the data. These errors may be random, although they can lead to systematic bias if they are not random. Indeed, Christodoulou (2017) argues that much of the pupil assessment data generated by schools may indeed be rubbish.

For example, within post-16 education a school or college leader may be trying to predict how many pupils will successfully complete their programme of study. Now in this context, success means not only are the learners retained until the end of academic year, but they also pass any coursework or examination requirements. Twice a year personal tutors are asked to predict both whether they think a pupil is at risk of not completing his or her programme of study and, if they were to stay to the end of the academic year, whether they would pass the end course/programme of study. Figure 7.1 shows that at the end of December it is predicted that 95% of pupils will complete the academic year, with 90% of those pupils being projected to achieve the course requirements, resulting in a projected success rate of 85%. Whereas in the following March the projected success rate falls to 82.8%.

	Projected completion rate	Projected achievement rate	Projected success rate
December	95%	90%	85.5%
March	92%	90%	82.8%

Figure 7.1 Projected completion, achievement and success rates for post-16 students within a college

However, the accuracy of these results will depend upon a range of different factors. (In this case not whether they actually predict the levels of completion and achievement, but rather whether they are an internally reliable measure of expected completion and achievement.) So how might these measures not be an accurate measure of expected completion, achievement rates and success rates? For a start, individual personal tutors may have different interpretations of what is meant by the risks of non-completion or failure. Are the risk factors mainly academic or are social factors taken into account? Secondly, the tutor or teacher making the judgement may apply different interpretations of risk to different individuals within the same group. Thirdly, the personal tutor may have a different level of knowledge of personal circumstances facing individual students. Indeed, this different level of knowledge may apply to different personal tutors, with some who know their students well and some less so. Unfortunately, in this situation reliance is being placed on there being an equal number of overestimates of completion and success as there will be underestimates. In other words, it is hoped the errors will even themselves out.

Nevertheless, measurement error is not restricted to internally generated data it can also be found in centrally produced data. Allen (2017), when looking at retention rates in sixth form colleges, found that figures produced by the Department for Education overstated retention rates by over 13%, with this being the result of counting students as retained even if they left after completing Year 12 having decided further study is not for them.

Range restriction

This occurs when a variable in the data has less than the range it possesses in the population as a whole and is often seen when schools use A-level examination results for marketing purposes. On many occasions, schools or sixth form colleges publicise A-level pass rates of 98%, 99% or 100%. However, what this information does not disclose is how many pupils started A-levels and subsequently either did not complete their programme of study or were not entered for the examination. Nor does it state how many pupils gained the equivalent of three A-levels. So, if attention is focused on the number of pupils gaining three A-levels or their equivalent, then a completely different picture of pupil success at A-level or its equivalent may emerge.

Indeed, by taking into account pupils' prior attainment it is apparent that the chances of gaining three A-levels or their equivalent changes quite significantly. For pupils who have done very well at the end of Key Stage 4 and have a profile of GCSE passes of grade A and A*, their chance of gaining three A-levels is approximately 95%, whereas pupils with an overall GCSE grade profile of Bs would have an approximately 68% chance of gaining three A-levels (Allen, 2016).

In a different context, the impact of range restriction can also be seen in the following example relating to a staff survey. To assess teachers' satisfaction with their senior leadership, a governing body conducted a survey among its 125 employees. The survey contained some demographic questions such as date of birth and job title, and five questions on employee satisfaction with their immediate line manager. The introductory letter by the chair of the governing body stated that all answers would remain anonymous. After the survey was sent out, only 12 employees responded, a response rate of less than 10%. Discussion with teaching staff indicated that they were concerned that the demographic data would make it possible to identify individuals. Given the sensitive nature of the survey's topic they therefore decided not to complete the survey. The survey and how it was reported was changed so it would not be possible to identify individual staff members.

Confounds

A confound occurs when the true relationship between two variables is hidden by the influence of a third variable. For example, the senior leadership team of a school may assume that there is a direct and positive relationship between teaching expertise and pupils' results and may interpret any decline in results as being the result of 'poor' teaching. However, there may be other variables at work. For example, the GCSE History results for a particular school are disappointing, with only 50% of pupils passing at grades A*–C compared to the school average of 75% in other GCSE subjects. Given that GCSE History was being managed by a new and inexperienced head of department and the other member of teaching staff had only two years' teaching experience, the initial concern focused on the quality of both teaching and departmental leadership. The school's senior leadership team decided to put a number of interventions in place, including regular teaching observations, a mentoring programme for the head of department, and regular governors' monitoring of the department. These actions reflected an underlying theory of action, driven by the belief that improving the quality of teaching will improve pupil outcomes.

However, further analysis of the examination results discovered that for over a third of the pupils, GCSE History was their best result, whilst the remainder achieved the same grade as their average grade in other subjects. Additional analysis showed that a smaller number than usual of high-performing pupils had opted for GCSE History at the end of Year 9, which was in large part due to teaching that year being disrupted by long-term staff absence, and long-term non-specialist cover being put in place. In the following years subject recruitment patterns returned to normal and results improved to above the school average.

To overcome the challenge of identifying confounds one approach that could be adopted is to ask the question 'why?' at least five times, to identify the root cause of a problem. The process tends to come to an end when it is no longer possible to come up with an answer to 'why' (Pojasek, 2000). Let's return to our example of a decline in GCSE History results and use the 'five whys'. Box 7.1 gives one possible outcome.

BOX 7.1   PROBLEM: GCSE HISTORY RESULTS
ARE BELOW PREVIOUS YEAR'S RESULTS

Q1: Why are examination results below the previous year's results?

A: Because this year a weaker cohort of students took the subject.

(Continued)

(Continued)

Q2: Why did a weaker cohort of students take the subject this year?

A: Because 'stronger' students who would normally take this subject chose other subjects.

Q3: Why did the stronger students choose other subjects?

A: Because in Year 9 when the students chose their 'options', they had been taught predominantly by non-specialist teachers who were adequate rather than inspiring.

Q4: Why did a non-specialist teacher deliver this subject?

A: Because all teachers had to have a full timetable.

Q5: Why did all teachers have to have a full timetable?

A: Due to financial pressures it was not viable to have teachers on 'light' timetables.

Pojasek (2000) identifies benefits and challenges which come from asking 'why?' five times. First, it's a pretty quick and easy technique to use. Second, it helps school leaders think through an issue so that you can drill down to the underlying cause of the problem. Third, it may help school leaders change their perception of the root cause of a problem. Nevertheless, there are a couple of clear challenges in using the 'five whys' and these include the need for strong facilitation skills, as the focus is on getting to the root cause of an issue rather than allocating blame. There's also the issue that there may be multiple issues in play, so it may be difficult to isolate the root cause of the problem.

Implications

It is now necessary to ask the question: what actions can the evidence-based school leader take to avoid invalid inferences being made from school quantitative data? First, when trying to avoid errors associated with small numbers one way of trying to avoid it is to use a larger number of observations. This can be done by the school aggregating its data, rather than over-relying on relatively small amounts of data gathered from individual departments. In multi-academy trusts this may involve aggregating the data from a number of schools in order to avoid the chances of sampling error. It may also involve leaders of multi-academy trusts ensuring that standard definitions of data are used across the trust, with standard procedures being used for both collecting and organising the data.

Second, in dealing with measurement error it will be necessary to identify a wide range of indicators. In the example cited, reliance would not be placed on personal tutor 'predictions' about completion and success, but these 'predictions' could be cross-referenced against a range of other indicators. These indicators could measure variables such as punctuality, attendance and timely completion of course-work or homework, or performance in mock examinations and tests. In other words, it is probably unwise to rely on a limited range of indicators when making inferences about the future based on cur-rent levels of performance. Multiple indicators are likely to give you a more balanced overall picture.

Third, when dealing with range restrictions it is important for the evidence-based school leader not to fall into the trap of only looking at data that supports existing biases. The starting point needs to be: has all the data needed been captured, or is the focus on 'winners' – pupils who passed their A levels – at the expense of 'losers' who did not successfully complete their A levels? With this in mind, it will be important to think of different ways of presenting the data, ways that may need to allow the school leader to confront the restricted range of data currently used.

Finally, when trying to confront the issue of confounding errors it is important to avoid jumping to conclusions. There is very rarely just one reason which explains what happened. Invariably, there will be a number of factors at work.

Stakeholder views

This section will look at the challenge of appraising the views of stake-holders, as taking account of the views of stakeholders is an essential part of evidence-based school leadership. The views of stakeholders are extremely valuable in helping to challenge your own thinking, and at the same time making you aware of the values, beliefs, expertise and aspirations of others. Indeed, the views of stakeholders may exert a major influence on what course of action is decided upon or the scale of implementation. At this stage, consideration is also being given to the expertise of both stakeholders and practitioners outside of the school. With that in mind, in this section we are going to focus on three aspects of appraising stakeholder views; first, the impact of empathy; second, the ladder of inference; third, how to tell good advice from bad.

Empathy

When appraising and taking into account the views of stakeholders, one of the things it is necessary to look out for is the undue impact of empathy, which Bloom (2017) argues can lead to poor decision-making. Empathy can lead to being biased in favour of people we know or are like us – and biases us against the values, needs and interests of others who are not like us, or who we don't know. Accordingly, as an evidence-based school leader it is important to: understand the difference between intellectual and emotional empathy; be aware of how some types of empathy can get in the way of evidence-based school leadership; and, identify strategies to adopt to offset the potential negative consequences of emotional empathy.

Bloom (2017) defines empathy as: 'the act of coming to experience the world as you think someone else does' (p. 16). Bloom then goes on to cite Adam Smith who – using the term sympathy – describes empathy as the ability to think about another person and 'place ourselves in his situation and become in some measure the same person as him, and thence form some idea of his sensations, and even feel something, which, though weaker in degree, is not altogether unlike them'.

However, this form of empathy, known as emotional empathy, is not the same as cognitive empathy, which is the 'capacity to understand what's going on in other people's heads, to know what makes them tick, and what gives them joy and pain, what they see as humiliating and ennobling' (Bloom, 2017: 36). In other words, with cognitive empathy we are not talking about feeling your pain, but rather the ability to recognise that the other person is in pain.

So how does emotional empathy get in the way of good decision-making? Bloom (2017) argues:

> Empathy is a spotlight focusing on certain people in the here and now. This makes us care more about them, but it leaves us insensitive to the long-term consequences of our acts as well as to the suffering of those we do not or cannot empathise with. Empathy is biased, pushing us in the directions of parochialism and racism. It is short sighted, motivating actions that might makes things better in the short-term but lead to tragic results

in the future. It is innumerate, favouring the one over the many. It can spark violence; our empathy for those close to us, is a powerful force for war and atrocity toward others. It is corrosive in personal relationships, it exhausts the spirit and can diminish the forces of kindness and love. (p.9)

If this argument is accepted, how does it impact upon the evidence-based school leader? First, just because something seems intuitively a good thing – in this case emotional empathy – does not necessarily mean that it is. Second, given the distinction between cognitive and emotional empathy, when discussing stakeholder feedback with colleagues, it is important to be in command of the terminology being used. Otherwise, discussions may become unfocused as colleagues have different understandings of the terms being discussed. Third, given that emotional empathy shines a 'spotlight' on the needs of certain individuals in the here and now, it may be that emotional empathy will steer attention in the direction of current problems of practice and the individuals who are experiencing them. On the other hand, given the scarce time and resources available to the school, it may be that there are other activities which may be more beneficial, particularly for pupils who have yet to join the school. Fourth, in working with colleagues you are more likely to empathise with colleagues who are like you. You may have been in teaching for say 5–10 years and have vivid memories of what it is like to be a newly qualified teacher, so you may cut newly qualified teachers or recently qualified colleagues some 'slack' in participating in knowledge-building activities. On the other hand, you just might not 'get' the colleague who has been teaching for 30 years and who has no apparent interest in research. As a result, you are more willing to spend your time with the NQT rather than the more experienced colleague. Fifth, there is a potential danger that when looking for problems of practice on which to focus, the focus may be on groups of pupils who may have had the same problems or issues that you experienced when you were that age. That said, there may be other pupils or colleagues for whom you have no 'emotional' connection, which means that their issues are potentially ignored.

The ladder of inference

A major challenge facing the evidence-based school leader is the constant time pressure and the need to respond to the urgent and the immediate rather than the important. However, these pressures and the 'need for speed' can have quite detrimental effects on the evidence made available on which to base a decision. Time pressure may lead to school leaders 'jumping to conclusions' with events and data, having interpreted data in quite different ways, and which may lead to serious disagreement. However, to make the most of stakeholders' feedback and evidence, it is necessary to peel back the layers of what they may be thinking; to understand their reasoning and the information and data which they are using to inform their thinking.

Initially developed by Argyris (1990) and subsequently used by, amongst others, Senge (1990), Senge et al. (1994), Stone et al. (2000) and Robinson and Lai (2005), the ladder of inference will help evidence-based school leaders to get to grips with the notion that just because 'you' see something as being a 'fact' does not mean that other people see the same 'fact' as either existing or being relevant. The ladder of inference can help both evidence-based school leaders and their colleagues understand the 'evidence' and 'logic' supporting what, for some, might be self-evident conclusions, but to others may not actually be that self-evident. Climbing the ladder of inference can help facilitate the generation of different interpretations of evidence, and, hopefully, lead to more informed and better decision-making, as is illustrated in Figure 7.2.

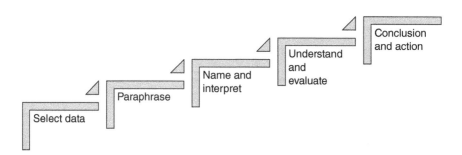

Figure 7.2 Ladder of inference

The ladder of inference has a number of distinct 'rungs', which include:

- **Select:** data is selected from the pool of all the information that is available – be it research, school data, stakeholder views or personal experience and expertise.
- **Paraphrase:** the various sources of data and evidence are summarised.

- **Name and interpret:** this is where the data is interpreted and an attempt is made to name and work out what is happening.
- **Understand and evaluate:** this is where an attempt is made to make a judgement about what is happening and identify a theory of action – if we do A then B will happen.
- **Conclusion and action:** at this stage you decide what you are going to do.

Let's look at an example where you have climbed the 'ladder of inference' and have drawn possible faulty conclusions from perceived stakeholder feedback, resulting in inappropriate actions.

- You are the school research lead and are taking the weekly staff research briefing.
- The vast majority of colleagues are actively engaged, however two colleagues appear not to be listening, with one being the head of the English department – who could be described as one of the 'usual suspects' – and the other being a senior teacher.
- At this point you make a brief announcement that the school will be submitting a bid to be included in an Education Endowment Foundation research project.
- The head of English then decides to whisper something to his or her nearest colleague, which you interpret as 'typical' and the usual cynicism from long-standing and experienced colleagues who don't want to engage in change.
- You then make an instant judgement not to put forward the English department for inclusion in the study, even though you think the staff and department may be ideally suited for the project.
- As you leave the meeting, you are making plans for which other departments, for example history, could be included in the study, and casually mention to another head of department that they should think of putting their department forward.

What has happened? You've taken some observable data, for example, stakeholder and staff engagement in the staff meetings, and have selected those two staff who seem not to be engaged. Your focus is on one of those two members of staff, the head of English, and someone who you regard as 'one of the usual suspects'. Having made your announcement, you interpret that what the head of English appears to have muttered is an example of the cynicism that you have come to expect from certain members of staff. You've concluded that if the English department is included in the study, this is likely not to reflect well on the school. You are now taking action to find other departments who wish to take part in the study. In other words, you have very quickly climbed the ladder of inference.

However, your journey up the ladder of inference may be informed by a whole range of inaccurate assumptions and subsequent interpretations. The head of English might not appear engaged because they are teaching a particularly challenging Year 9 group straight after the morning briefing ends, rather than because of some malign non-interest in the work of the school. In addition, what the head of English may have whispered to his or her colleague could have been 'this is really exciting and at last we are doing something with the EEF'. The thing is though, as we just don't know what someone else is thinking, we have to find a way of validating our conclusions. Otherwise you may end up taking actions that are not in the best interest of individual members of staff, relationships between colleagues and pupils' learning.

Evidence-based school leaders often have to reconcile and understand the views of colleagues who see 'data' in quite different ways. Indeed, one way of using the ladder of inference is to help identify duelling logics when colleagues disagree on a particular course of action (Argyris, 2000) In Figure 7.3 the duelling logics of two colleagues are explored over the merits or otherwise of introducing a journal club into the school professional learning programme.

Duelling logics

Example:

Your school is currently looking at revising your programme of professional learning. One of the things you are considering is to introduce a 'journal club' which has already been done by several local schools – including one of the area's most innovative schools. However, one school (school Y) which is very similar to your school has decided not to carry on with their journal club as they had difficulty in both accessing relevant research and finding time in their professional learning programme – this is not the first time they have dropped an innovation.

Alison decides what to do	Andrew decides what to do
We need to introduce a journal club	We don't need to introduce a journal club
Alison understands and evaluates the data	**Andrew understands and evaluates the data**
A journal club will help us become an innovative school	A journal club will be another failed innovation
Alison names the data	**Andrew names the data**
The journal club contributes to school X's success and record of innovation	The journal club has contributed to school Y's reputation as constantly introducing then 'dropping' innovations

Duelling logics	
Alison paraphrases the data	Andrew paraphrases the data
School X is an innovative and successful school which has implemented a journal club	School Y has failed in implementing a journal club due to a lack of time and resources
Alison selects the data	Andrew selects the data
I really like school X – it has been an innovative and successful school for a long-time and has introduced a journal club	Schools like us, for example Y, are coming under increasing pressure to introduce innovations – which then flop due to lack of time and resources

Figure 7.3   Duelling logics and journal clubs (based on Argyris, 2000: 201)

In this example, two colleagues have reached conclusions that cannot be reconciled, with neither colleague understanding how the other got to their conclusions, contributing to a sharp exchange of views when this topic is discussed at a senior leadership team meeting. This, of course, can have some unfortunate fallout for the senior leadership team both in the near-term – coming to an agreement on how to proceed – and in the long-term as colleagues become possibly marginalised or withdrawn from the decision-making process. However, effective use of the ladder of inference may allow you as a school leader to unpack colleagues' thinking and make explicit how they came to their conclusions.

Telling good advice from bad

One of the challenges when appraising stakeholder feedback is trying to tell good advice from bad. Advice may come from a number of sources, be it experienced teachers, members of the senior leadership team, the parents of pupils, members of the governing body, members of the community as a whole or from experienced colleagues from outside of the school. However, Argyris (2000) argues that most advice is fundamentally flawed and it is neither valid nor actionable. With this in mind, the rest of this section will consider the following questions: What is effective advice? What are the tests for the validity of advice? What are the tests for the actionability of advice? What are the implications for the evidence-based school leader?

Argyris (2000) states: 'Advice is effective to the extent to which it leads to the consequences intended in ways that persevere – but without generating ... unintended consequences that undermine the beneficial outcomes. Advice is effective to the extent that it is valid and actionable – that is, leads to effective action' (p. 7). In other words,

Argyris is arguing that when you receive effective advice, and if you act on it, you will get the outcomes anticipated, subject of course to no unforeseen circumstances. The advice is also practical in that it can be introduced and developed within the parameters of normal day-to-day working life. Furthermore, actionable advice gives clear statements as to what needs to be done to get the intended outcomes, plus it also acknowledges that individuals either have the skills or are able to be taught the skills necessary to act on the advice.

Argyris' notion of actionable advice has a number of implications for the evidence-based school leader when trying to evaluate the quality of advice. First, is the stakeholder totally clear in what they want to be done or not done? Is there a clear theory of action, if you do X then will Y happen? Do colleagues have the skills necessary to act on the advice you are receiving from other colleagues, and if not, how can they be helped to get those skills? Are there likely to be any negative consequences, which may disadvantage one group over another? Finally, is the advice being received appropriate to your context? There is no point trying to act on the advice if there are insufficient resources available to make it happen.

Another way of thinking about 'advice' and how to appraise it, is to view it as some form of espoused theory of action (see Chapter 4). To help with the task of appraising theories of action, Robinson and Lai (2005) identify four criteria – accuracy, effectiveness, coherence and improvability – that should be taken into account when evaluating theories of action. For example, the theory of action articulated in Table 7.1 details the views of 'external experts' on the merits of introducing performance-related pay for teachers within a school or group of schools.

Table 7.1   A theory of action for teacher performance-related pay

Practical Problem	How to recruit, retain and reward teachers
Constraint set	Recruit teaching staff
	Recognise teacher performance and increase motivation
	Teachers are perceived to want performance-related pay
	Commitment to continued improvements in teaching and learning by improving quality of teaching staff
Actions	Introduction of 'premium' starting salaries for newly qualified teachers (NQTs)
	Introduction of performance-related pay related to pre-set objectives

Practical Problem	How to recruit, retain and reward teachers
Consequences	High-quality teaching staff recruited
	Increases in motivation of teaching staff
	Reduced teaching staff turnover
	Improved pupil performance

Source: based on Robinson and Lai, 2005: 29

First, it is important to check for accuracy as to whether teachers actually want performance-related pay. It is also necessary to check whether 'performance pay' is the most effective way of recognising teacher performance. Second, the theory of action needs to be checked for effectiveness – does it solve the constraints associated with teacher recruitment, retention and reward? For example, does performance-related pay increase teacher motivation? Third, the theory of action needs to be checked for coherence and unintended consequences. Are there groups of staff who may decide to work fewer hours after the introduction of performance-related pay, for example working mothers? Finally, is the theory of action improvable? In other words, are there sufficient feedback loops in the process that allow changes to be made as and when circumstances change or feedback suggests something is or isn't working, for example, have premium starting salaries increased the school's ability to recruit high-quality newly qualified teachers?

Managing differences of opinion

Inevitably there will be differences of opinion between the evidence-based practitioner and stakeholders about the problem of practice which is in most need of being tackled, or the causes of the problem, and how it should be solved. To help address this issue, Dennett suggests that at times of disagreement Rapoport's Rules should be used.

1. You should attempt to re-express your target's position so clearly, vividly, and fairly that your target says, 'Thanks, I wish I'd thought of putting it that way'.
2. You should list any points of agreement (especially if they are not matters of general and widespread agreement).
3. You should mention anything you have learned from your target.

4. Only then are you permitted to say so much as a word of rebuttal or criticism.

(Dennett, 2013: p. 34)

Dennett goes on to argue that by adopting this set of rules then colleagues with whom you disagree will be far more receptive to your arguments as you will have demonstrated that you understand their position. Not only that, Dennett states you also will be seen to have already exhibited sound judgement by agreeing with them on some matters and having learnt from them on others. Indeed, the most important thing about this process is that it is likely to increase the chances of the conversation continuing.

Practitioner expertise

A major challenge for an evidence-based school leader when making a decision is how to evaluate your own expertise, experience and intuition. This section will briefly examine the nature of expertise by using the Dreyfus model of adult learning. Then the section will explore how prior experience can get in the way of making the very best decisions. Next, the nature of intuition and under what circumstances that intuition may be trusted will be examined. Finally, there will be a discussion of some of the strategies that evidence-based school leaders can adopt to ensure they make the most of experience, expertise and intuition.

A model of adult learning and skill acquisition

Dreyfus and Dreyfus (1986) developed a model of adult skill acquisition which operates at five different levels: novice, advanced beginners, competent beginner, proficient performer, and expert. However, it should be noted that depending upon the skill being acquired – guitar playing, chess, teaching, surgery and leading – not everyone progresses through each of the five stages. Let's examine each of the levels in more detail.

Stage 1: Novice

Dreyfus (2004) argues that in this situation skill acquisition commences with the teacher/tutor breaking down the task to be completed into its various component parts, which can be identified by the novice even when lacking the required level of skill. The novice is then given instruction on what to do when these features have been identified. At this stage, there is no awareness of context and the 'rules' for action are context-free. In other words, if X happens, do Y.

Stage 2: Advanced beginner

Dreyfus (2004) notes that as the novice progresses, they begin to acquire experience of having to deal with actual problems and situations, and begin to form an awareness of the importance of context. Possibly with the help of the teacher, or tutor, they begin to identify what features of the context are relevant. After a while our advanced beginner is then able to recognise these situations for themselves and the teacher/tutor suggests what to do in these contexts. Again, in other words if in X context Y happens, do Z.

Stage 3: Competent performer

As our learner gains more experience and is exposed to a range of different contexts they begin to recognise the vast range of factors that may influence the actions they may choose to take. In these circumstances, there is the risk of 'paralysis by analysis' as our learner is unable to identify those contextual factors that really matter. In this context our learner begins to devise a plan as to what to do in certain situations. They develop a framework for 'noticing' that allows them to work out the things that matter in this setting. In these circumstances and as a defence mechanism to prevent being confused by too much choice our learner may develop a limited 'repertoire' of how to proceed. However, this phase may be marked by 'failure' as not every 'plan' or 'set of rules' will work in the contexts faced. Finally, at this stage our learner becomes more and more emotionally invested in the success or otherwise of his or her actions.

Stage 4: Proficient performer

Our emotionally invested competent learner will begin to find it more and more difficult to adopt a narrowly rule-based approach. Our learner begins to replace the anxiety associated with choice, with the involvement and engagement associated with deep learning and understanding. As our learner experiences success and failure, they will begin to become able to replace his or her 'rule-based' approach with what could be described as the ability to choose actions that are fit for context. Such proficiency involves the ability to make situational judgements.

Stage 5: Expert

Whereas the proficient performer would appear to go through a process of observe, interpret, take stock and then act, the expert can see instantly what needs to be done and how to do it. This is in large part due to their experience of a range of situations which had allowed them to develop a range of responses. The expert is able to make a number of small, situational-specific adjustments, which sets them apart from the 'proficient performer'. As such, the expert is not so much a 'solver of problems' but rather someone who is a 'doer' of what works. And as Dreyfus (2004) notes, more often than not it does.

Table 7.2

Skill Level	Components	Perspective	Decisions	Commitment
Novice	Context free	None	Analytic	Detached
Advanced beginner	Context-free and situational	None	Analytic	Detached
Competent	Context-free and situational	Chosen	Analytic	Detached understanding and deciding; involved in outcome
Proficient	Context-free and situational	Experienced	Analytic	Involved understanding; detached deciding
Expert	Context-free and situational	Experienced	Intuitive	Involved

Source: Dreyfus, 2004: 81

Dreyfus (2004) summarises the five-stage process of skill acquisition as shown in Table 7.2. This shows how the model gives prominence to the roles of both experience and intuition in becoming an expert practitioner. It is therefore necessary to examine the implications of this for the evidence-based school leader.

A useful starting point is to acknowledge the limitations of experience and expertise, something known as the *Einstellung* (set) effect, which happens when the first idea or solution that comes to mind gets in the way of better or more optimal solutions being generated (Bilalić et al., 2008). Bilalić et al. demonstrate in a series of experiments involving expert chess players that attention generated by the availability of an obvious solution, such as checkmate in five moves, gets in the way of identifying a checkmate available in three moves. They go on to argue that this direction of attention to an existing solution can contribute to a wide range of cognitive biases. This being so, it is necessary to ensure experienced school leaders do not allow the first solution that comes to mind based on experience to get in the way of other more efficient and effective options.

Second, a further problem with expertise is that it can get in the way of the assessment of data and information. Tetlock and Gardner (2016), describing Tetlock's book *Expert Political Judgement: How Good Is It and How Can We Know?*, found that being a subject expert more often than not got in the way of making an accurate forecast or prediction. These experts were classified as hedgehogs as they arranged their thinking around 'big ideas' (p. 68) and were expert in one particular area and were unswerving in their commitment to their conclusions. This resulted in 'hedgehogs' being extremely reluctant to alter their opinions even if their forecasts had gone 'horribly wrong'. Indeed, hedgehogs' predictions were not as accurate as random guesses. On the other hand, Tetlock and Gardner (2016) identified another group of experts, whom they called 'foxes', who were more accurate in their predictions. They say 'foxes' know many things, they don't just know or specialise in one thing. They seek out data, information and evidence from many different sources and use a number of different ways to analyse the data. 'Foxes' on the whole, tended to be much less confident about their predictions and forecasts, and were willing to change their position and admit when they had got things wrong.

Third, the notion of skilful intuition is not without its problems. Kahneman and Klein (2009) agree on Simon's definition of skilled intuition as: 'the situation has provided a cue: this cue has given the expert access to information stored in memory, and the information provides the answer. Intuition is nothing more and nothing less than recognition' (Simon, 1992 cited in Kahneman and Klein, 2009: 520). Kahneman and Klein note that this definition is extremely useful in that not only does it help clarify what is meant by intuition, it also makes clear that intuition is not some mysterious process but instead a form of pattern recognition that can be acquired rationally.

Kahneman and Klein (2009) go on to state that this recognition model of intuition requires two conditions for intuition to be genuinely skilful: 'first, the environment must provide adequately valid cues to the nature of the situation. Second, people must have an opportunity to learn the relevant cues' (p. 520). Kahneman and Klein argue that medicine and firefighting take place in fairly 'high-validity' environments, in that there are relatively stable relationships between the observed cues and the results of a range of decisions. However, there are other procedures, such as financial and political forecasting, which take place in what Kahneman and Klein describe as zero-validity environments. As to whether education provides a 'high-validity' environment, Shulman (2004) states:

> after 30 years of doing such work, I have concluded that class-room teaching … is perhaps the most complex, most challenging, and most demanding, subtle, nuanced, and frightening activity that our species has ever invented …The only time a physician could possibly encounter a situation of comparable complexity would be in the emergency room of a hospital during or after a natural disaster. (p. 504)

So what role does intuition have in the decision-making processes of the evidence-based leader? In Kahneman and Klein (2010), Kahneman argues that there may be circumstances when the evidence-based practitioner may need to trust his or her gut intuition, especially if the matter is urgent and there are pressing time constraints. That said, Kahneman states that intuition should never be taken at 'face value' and should always be subject to scrutiny. In a similar vein, Klein states 'If you mean, "My gut feeling is telling me this; therefore, I can act on it and I don't have to worry," we say you should never trust your gut' (p. 1). Nevertheless, Klein argues that intuition and gut feeling should be seen as a valuable source of data, which you should evaluate rigorously.

Summary and key points

- Interpreting school quantitative data is not without its challenges, be it from the problem of small numbers, measurement error, range restrictions and confounds. Accordingly strategies such as aggregating data or taking a medium- to long-term view should be adopted.
- The analysis and interpretation of stakeholder views needs to be done with care and vigilance as being emotionally empathetic to

the needs of some stakeholders may come at a cost, especially in being unempathetic to people who are not like us.

- When interpreting feedback from others, it is necessary to be mindful of moving up the 'ladder of inference' and the need to ensure that assumptions and interpretations are continually challenged.
- In trying to appraise feedback from stakeholders it is necessary also to take into account whether it meets the criteria of effective advice and whether it is actionable.
- If there is disagreement, Rapoport's Rules provide a useful way of trying to maintain an ongoing conversation.
- Experience may get us to become rigid in our thinking by adopting the first viable solution we come across.
- There may be some circumstances where there may be little or no choice but to rely on intuition, particularly if circumstances are urgent and time-pressured.
- Nevertheless, schools are not the ideal environment for the development of skilled intuition and evidence-based school leaders should always be looking to find evidence to challenge their intuition.

References

Allen, N. (2016) *Snowblind: The Understanding Performance in Sixth Form Colleges Project Report 2016*. London: Sixth Form Colleges Association.

Allen, N. (2017) *Known Knowns, Known Unknowns and Unknown Unknowns: The Six Dimensions Project Report 2017*. London: Sixth Form Colleges Association.

Argyris, C. (1990) *Overcoming Organizational Defenses*. Boston, MA: Allyn and Bacon.

Argyris, C. (2000) *Flawed Advice and the Management Trap: How Managers Can Know When They're Getting Good Advice and When They're Not*. Oxford: Oxford University Press.

Bilalić, M., McLeod, P. and Gobet, F. (2008) 'Why good thoughts block better ones: the mechanism of the pernicious Einstellung (set) effect', *Cognition*, 108 (3): 652–61.

Bloom, P. (2017) *Against Empathy: The Case for Rational Compassion*. London: Penguin Random House.

Christodoulou, D. (2017) 'Garbage in – garbage out: is this the reality of school data?', *TES London*, 13 November.

Crawford, C. and Benton, T. (2017a) *Volatility Happens. Why? Infographic*. Cambridge: Cambridge Assessment.

Crawford, C. and Benton, T. (2017b) *Volatility Happens: Understanding Variation in Schools' GCSE Results: Cambridge Assessment Research Report*. Cambridge: Cambridge Assessment.

Dennett, D. (2013) *Intuition Pumps and Other Tools for Thinking*. London: Allen Lane.

Donaldson, L. (2012) 'Evidence-based management (EBMgt) using organizational facts', in D. Rousseau (ed.), *The Oxford Handbook of Evidence-Based Management*. Oxford: Oxford University Press. pp. 249–61.

Dreyfus, S. (2004) 'The five-stage model of adult skill acquisition', *Bulletin of Science, Technology & Society*, *24* (3): 177–81.

Dreyfus, H. and Dreyfus, S. (1986) *Mind over Machine: The Power of Human Intuition and Expertise in the Era of the Computer*. Oxford: Free Press.

Kahneman, D. and Klein, G. (2009) 'Conditions for intuitive expertise: a failure to disagree', *American Psychologist*, *64* (6): 515–26.

Kahneman, D. and Klein, G. (2010) 'Strategic decisions: when can you trust your gut', *McKinsey Quarterly*, *13*: 1–10.

Neeleman, A.-M. (2017) *Grasping the Scope of School Autonomy: a Classification Scheme for School Policy Practice*. Stratford-upon-Avon: BELMAS.

Pojasek, R.B. (2000) 'Asking "why?" five times', *Environmental Quality Management*, *10* (1): 79–84.

Robinson, V. and Lai, M. (2005) *Practitioner Research for Educators: a Guide to Improving Classrooms and Schools*. Thousand Oaks, CA: Corwin Press.

Senge, P. (1990) *The Fifth Discipline: the Art and Practice of the Learning Organization*. London: Century Business.

Senge, P., Roberts, C., Ross, R., Smith, B. and Kleiner, A. (1994) *The Fifth Discipline Fieldbook*. New York: Bantam Doubleday Dell.

Shulman, L. (2004) *The Wisdom of Practice: Essays on Teaching, Learning and Learning to Teach*. San Francisco, CA: Jossey-Bass.

Stone, D., Patton, B. and Heen, S. (2000) *Difficult Conversations: How to Discuss What Matters Most*. London: Penguin Books.

Tetlock, P. and Gardner, D. (2016) *Superforecasting: the Art and Science of Prediction*. London: Penguin Random House.

8

AGGREGATING SOURCES OF EVIDENCE

Chapter outline

This chapter will look at how to go about aggregating different sources of evidence. First, consideration will be given to relatively simple ways of aggregating research evidence through the use of tables. Next, the challenge of how different sources of evidence – be it school data, stakeholders' views, practitioner expertise and research – can be aggregated will be explored. This will lead on to a discussion of how logic models can help aggregate the available evidence. Finally, the chapter will suggest a number of techniques the evidence-based school leader can use when judging both the quality of the aggregation and synthesis of the evidence.

Key words: *aggregation, systematic reviews, logic model, theory of change critically appraised topics*

Putting the evidence together

For the evidence-based school leader the prospect of aggregating and summarising evidence and data may, at first, appear to be quite daunting. Nonetheless, there are a range of relatively straightforward methods that can be used to aggregate both evidence of the same type or evidence that has been drawn from a number of different sources. Probably the easiest way of using tables to aggregate and appraise evidence is suggested by Willingham (2012), who suggests the use of a simple scorecard to keep track of research findings (see Figure 8.1).

The research	What was measured?	Comparison	How many kids?	How much did it help?
Article 1	Written feedback	Verbal feedback	50	0.4 effect size
Article 2	Written feedback	Group feedback	40	0.6 effect size
Article 3	Written feedback	No feedback	30	0.7 effect size

Figure 8.1 Summarising research evidence (based on Willingham, 2012: 200)

In Figure 8.1, the findings of three pieces of research on the impact of written feedback to pupils are compared. Each of the research studies has used a different comparator when trying to judge the effectiveness of written feedback, involved different numbers of pupils and had differing impacts on pupil learning. However, any attempt to work out the average effect size should be resisted. For a full explanation of the reasons why it would be unwise to average the effect size, refer to Simpson (2017) and the discussion in Chapter 6.

It is also possible to develop summary tables, which include far more detail about individual pieces of research. Figure 8.2 provides a simple example of a comparison of two Education Endowment Foundation studies on how the use of research evidence could be encouraged in schools. In this example, the two reports are compared side by side against the following categories: nature of the intervention, the participants, setting and context, outcomes, results, methods and other comments. This structure will hopefully allow the evidence-based school leader to 'eyeball' any obvious similarities or differences in the two studies.

Reference	Griggs, J. Speight, S. and Cartagena Farias, J. (2016) Ashford Teaching Alliance Research Champion Evaluation report and executive summary May 2016, Education Endowment Foundation	Speight, S. Callanan, M., Griggs, J. and Cartagena Farias, J. Rochdale Research into Practice Evaluation report and executive summary May 2016, Education Endowment Foundation
Intervention	Research lead based at teaching school worked with the school's research leaders and senior leaders to promote the use of research evidence in teaching and decision-making. Involved • Audit • Research symposia • Twilight forums • Bespoke research brokerage	Senior Continuing Professional Development (CPD) consultant based at one of the schools and involved the following strands • CPD sessions – 3 full days and 4 half-day sessions • School visits by the CPD leads • Ongoing implementation • Ongoing email and phone advice and guidance by CPD lead • Collaborative CPD and professional learning conversations • Engagement with senior leadership
Participants	Teachers from five schools	Teachers from ten primary schools
Setting context	Schools in Ashford Teaching School Alliance	Rochdale area, all of which are members of the Inspirational Professional Learning Community Network (IPLCN)
Outcomes	Teachers use of research evidence in teaching	Teachers use of research evidence in teaching
Results	There was no evidence that teachers' attitudes towards research, or their use of research evidence, changed during the intervention Teachers found the research symposia and twilight events valuable Participation was occasionally low due to time pressures faced by teachers A greater commitment from senior leadership teams to fully support staff likely to be necessary for success	Some positive changes in teachers' attitudes towards research during the course of the pilot No evidence that teachers were more likely to use research to inform their teaching practice after being involved in the pilot The project was very well received by teachers Overall the requirements of the programme were feasible
Methods – Quality	Quantitative/qualitative Survey of teachers at participating school In-depth interviews and observations at training events	Quantitative/qualitative Teachers surveys In-depth interviews and observations at training events
Other notes	Study did not provide evidence or promise of readiness for further pilot. Mixed view as to whether pilot feasible	Before a trial is considered, further thought should be given as to which elements of the project are essential for its efficacy, and whether a trial should test the project *structure* as a model for research dissemination or both the *structure* and *content* of the project as piloted

Figure 8.2   Research champions: a comparison of two Education Endowment Foundation studies

Having brought together summaries of two research reports, it now is possible to cast the net a little wider and look at how research is aggregated in many systematic reviews (see Chapter 5). To help us do this, it is useful to refer to the work of Godfrey and Seleznyov (forthcoming), who have undertaken a systematic review on Lesson Study. In this review the authors identify seven critical features of Lesson Study and identify which of the 97 studies they reviewed included those features, as illustrated in the excerpt shown in Figure 8.3. Nevertheless, it should be remembered that although this approach is very useful when trying to compare the basic elements of a number of studies, it has limitations when trying to review the finer detail of the studies, particularly some of the more qualitative elements.

Bringing together different sources of evidence

So far, attention has focused on aggregating academic research evidence. However evidence-based school leadership should involve aggregating four different sources of evidence. Again, making use of a tabular format, this can be done relatively simply, with Figure 8.4 providing a summary of the different sources of evidence regarding the adoption, or otherwise, of a teacher journal club. Such a table allows the evidence-based school leader to compile a short summary of each source of evidence, with a brief description of where the evidence came from, the year the evidence became available, the setting from which the evidence was drawn, who provided the evidence, along with some form of summative commentary about the individual sources of evidence.

The use of tables is not the only way to summarise our four sources of evidence and there are other techniques which can be used. For example, we might want to summarise the evidence in the form of a fishbone diagram, which helps us to visually represent the different sources of evidence. In a fishbone diagram (see Figure 8.5), each major 'bone' represents one of the four sources of evidence, with each smaller bone representing the supporting data and evidence. Figure 8.5 illustrates the use of a fishbone diagram to help us summarise the evidence for introducing a teachers' journal club.

Study	Critical feature 1: Identify focus	Critical feature 2: Collaborative planning	Critical feature 3: kyozai kenkyu as part of planning	Critical feature 3: Research lesson with live observation	Critical feature 4: Post-lesson discussion	Critical feature 5: Repeated cycles of research	Critical feature 5: Repeated cycles but no repeat teaching of a revised lesson	Critical feature 6: Outside expertise	Critical feature 7: Mobilising knowledge	Location
Benedict, A. et al. (2013)	Y	Y	N	Y	Y	Y	N	N	N	USA
Black, P. (2010)	Y	Y	N	Y	Y	Y	N	N	Y	USA
Budak, A. (2012)	N	Y	N	N	Y	Y	N	N	N	Turkey
Buono, A. (2012)	Y	Y	N	Y	Y	Y	N	Y	Y	USA
Burghes, D. and Robinson, D. (2010)	Y	Y	N	Y	Y	Y	Y	N	Y	UK
Cajkler, W., Wood, P., Norton, J. et al. (2014)	Y	Y	N	Y	Y	Y	Y	N	N	UK
Cajkler, W. et al. (2015)	Y	Y	Y	Y	Y	Y	Y	Y	N	UK
Carpenter, J. (2009)	Y	Y	N	Y	Y	Y	N	N	Y	USA
Cerbin, W. and Kopp, B. (2006)	Y	Y	N	Y	Y	N	N	N	N	USA
Cheng, L. and Lee, P. (2011)	Y	Y	N	Y	Y	Y	N	Y	Y	Singapore
Chokshi, S. and Fernandez, C. (2004)	Y	Y	N	Y	Y	Y	Y	N	N	USA
Chokshi, S. and Fernandez, C. (2005)	Y	Y	N	Y	Y	Y	Y	N	N	USA
Chong, W. and Kong, C. (2012)	N	Y	N	Y	Y	Y	N	Y	Y	Singapore
Clevenger, M. et al. (2009)	N	Y	N	Y	Y	Y	N	Y	N	USA
Corcoran, D. (2009)	N	Y	N	N	Y	N	Y	Y	N	Ireland
Demir, K., Czerniak, C. and Hart, L. (2013)	Y	Y	N	Y	Y	Y	Y	Y	N	USA
Doig, B. and Groves, S. (2011)	Y	Y	Y	Y	Y	Y	Y	N	N	Australia
Dotger, S. (2015)	Y	Y	Y	Y	Y	Y	Y	N	Y	USA
Droese, S. (2010)	Y	Y	N	Y	Y	Y	Y	Y	N	USA
Dudley, P. (2005)	N	Y	N	Y	Y	Y	Y	N	N	UK
Dudley, P. (2008)	N	Y	N	Y	Y	Y	N	N	N	UK
Dudley, P. (2011)	N	Y	N	Y	Y	Y	N	Y	Y	UK

Figure 8.3 Review of Lesson Study literature: critical features

Source: Seleznyov, forthcoming

Author/sources	Description	Year	Setting	Who	Commentary
Research literature	Sims, Moss and Marshall	2017	Two mixed 11–18 schools Ofsted – Outstanding	10 teachers in school A and 7 teachers in school B	The research finds that journal clubs are a viable, scalable model of teacher-led professional development, capable of creating sustained increases in evidence-informed practice
School data (quantitative)	Professional Learning Programme	2018	The school	All staff	Some space in professional learning calendar for half-termly journal clubs
Stakeholder views	School staff meeting	2018	The school	All teaching staff including teaching assistants	General acceptance of idea in principle, though suggested it should be trialled with a group of 7–10 volunteers
Practitioner expertise	Senior Leadership Team	2018	The school	HT, 2 DHs and School Research Lead	No direct experience though School Research Lead has attended sessions on journal clubs at researchED and is aware of available resources

Figure 8.4 Aggregating different sources of evidence: journal clubs – a worked example

However, it is also possible to provide a textual summary of the evidence by producing something that is typically described as a critically appraised topic. For use by evidence-based school leaders, a critically appraised topic has a number of elements: the question that is being addressed; an overall summary of the evidence; summaries of each of the four sources of evidence; questions for consideration; references; who produced the document; and finally, when further information might become available (see Figure 8.6 for a worked example).

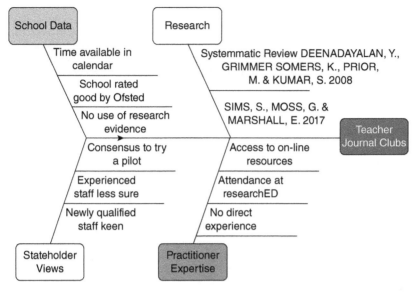

Figure 8.5   Example of a fishbone diagram

Title	Journal Clubs
Background question	How can teacher journal clubs contribute to teacher professional learning and the use of evidence-based practice?
Summary	Teacher journal clubs appear to have the potential to contribute to the increased use of evidence-informed practice. Initial discussions with stakeholders suggest there is support for piloting a journal club within the school. Although, no one within the school – be it teaching assistants, teachers and senior leadership – has experience in running journal clubs, adequate resources are available on the Internet to support their introduction.

Description of the best available evidence

Research	Although there appear to be no systematic reviews in educational settings about use of teacher journal clubs, a systematic review in a health setting (Deenadayalan et al., 2008) provides guidance on how to run a successful journal club. This guidance suggests: *regular and anticipated meetings, mandatory attendance, clear long- and short-term purpose, appropriate meeting timing and incentives, a trained journal club leader to choose papers and lead discussion, circulating papers prior to the meeting, using the Internet for wider dissemination and data storage, using established critical appraisal processes and summarising journal club findings.* (from abstract)
	Recent research in education (Sims et al., 2017) involving two 11–18 mixed secondary schools (Ofsted – Outstanding) indicates that journal clubs are a viable, scalable model of teacher-led professional development, capable of creating sustained increases in evidence-informed practice.

(Continued)

Figure 8.6 (Continued)

School/class data	The school is a mixed 11–18 school and is currently rated by Ofsted as Good. The school has an extensive programme of professional learning – though little or none is focused on research use. The school has recently recruited a number of new staff who are at the beginning of their career. However, there are also a number of staff who have been at the school for over 20 years. Although in recent years the professional learning budget has been squeezed – there is still sufficient time in the programme for half-termly journal clubs.
Stakeholders' views (pupils, staff, parents, community)	A number of teachers within the school are active on Twitter and are aware that the school currently provides few opportunities for teachers to engage in research evidence. Successful schools in the locality have introduced journal clubs and it is perceived that this has contributed to those schools' reputation for innovation. However, there are other teachers who do not see the value of educational research and are aware of schools which have introduced journal clubs – and then have quietly dropped them after a year. Nevertheless, there is a general consensus amongst the teaching staff that it may be worth undertaking a small pilot with volunteers.
Practitioner expertise – key leaders	None of the major decision-makers within the school – the HT, 2 DHTs and the newly appointed School Research Lead (SRL) – have experience of running or participating in a journal club. However, the SRL has attended a number of researchED events and has seen presentations on how to successfully run a journal club. The SRL is also aware of resources available on the Internet and produced by teachers – which give clear advice on how to ensure a journal club is successful. In addition, the SRL is currently studying for a post-graduate degree in education.
Questions for consideration	• Can we access suitable research journals? • How do we recruit volunteers for the pilot? • Do teachers have the capacity and capability to understand and apply research findings? • Do we have someone of sufficient knowledge and expertise to lead the journal club? • Can desired changes in teaching practice be identified? • Is sufficient time available for the implementation of a journal club? • How will the impact of the journal club be measured?
References and resources	• Deenadayalan et al. (2008) • Sims et al. (2017) • www.edujournalclub.com
Appraiser/author	• School Research Lead
Dissemination	• To be shared by email and to be discussed at the next staff meeting • Prior discussion of paper at departmental meetings
Update and review	• When is it likely that new relevant evidence be available? • During 2018 as reports on the efficacy of research learning communities and the school research leads are published by the EEF • End of the academic year

Figure 8.6 Critically appraised topic: journal clubs – a detailed example

Producing some form of critically appraised topic has a number of potential benefits for the evidence-based school leader. First, it helps summarise and bring together learning about the topic. Second, as mentioned in Chapter 3, many types of problems are generic and the critically appraised topic provides a summary of learning which may be used in the future. Third, by sharing the critically appraised topic with colleagues, this may contribute to the development of an open professional learning community. Finally, by writing a critically appraised topic this will help the evidence-based school leader hone and develop the skills of appraising and aggregating evidence (Straus et al., 2011).

Using levels of impact as way of aggregating evidence

As evidence-based school leadership is about making decisions so as to bring about favourable outcomes for the intended beneficiaries of those decisions, it makes sense to aggregate evidence at the level of impact. A useful starting point is Thomas Guskey's five-stage model for evaluation of professional development (Guskey, 2000) which looks at: participants' reactions, participants' learning; organisational support and change; participants' use of knowledge and new skills; and, students' learning outcomes. An example of how this has been done can be found in Godfrey and Seleznyov (forthcoming) in their systematic review of Lesson Study (see Figure 8.7).

Exploring the relationships within the evidence using logic models

Up to this point, the aggregation of data and evidence could be described as being preliminary in that the focus has been on drawing the data and evidence together – primarily by text, listing, tabulating – into some kind of coherent summary. Accordingly, consideration will now be given to exploring how to use logic models to undertake both a more dynamic aggregation of the evidence and a future framework for evaluation (see Chapter 10).

Study	1. Teachers' reactions: Attitudes and enjoyment	2. Teachers' professional learning: Subject knowledge, pedagogical content knowledge, confidence	3. The organisation's professional development model: Time, structure, resourcing; Networking beyond the school	4. Teacher use of new knowledge and skills: Changes in practices	Within or beyond research lessons	5. Pupil learning outcomes: Attitudes and progress	Sample size: teachers	Sample size: schools	Location
Black, P.J. (2010)	Y	Y	N	Y	Within	N	14	3	USA
Budak, A. (2012)	Y	Y	N	N		N	2	2	Turkey
Buono, A.G. (2012)	N	Y	N	N		Y	8	1	USA
Burghes, D. and Robinson, D. (2010)	Y	Y	N	Y	Within		?	?	UK
Cajkler, W., Wood, P., Norton, J. et al. (2014)	N	Y	N	Y	Beyond		4	1	UK
Cajkler, W., Wood, P., Norton, J. et al. (2015)	Y	Y	N	Y	Within		7	1	UK
Cheng, L.P. and Lee, P.Y. (2011)	N	Y	Y	Y	Beyond	Y	6	1	Singapore
Chong, W.H. and Kong, C.A. (2012)	Y	Y	N	N		Y	10	1	Singapore
Droese, S. (2010)	Y	Y	Y	Y	Beyond	Y	3	3	USA
Fernandez, C. (2005)	Y	Y	N	N	Within		4	1	USA
Groth, E. (2011)	Y	Y	N	Y	Beyond		4	1	USA
Gutierez, S. (2016)	Y	Y	N	Y	Beyond		30	?	Philippines
Hadfield, M., Jopling, M. and Emira, M. (2011)	N	N	Y	N			?	?	UK
Halvorsen, A.L. and Kesler Lund, A. (2013)	Y	Y	N	N	Within	N	20	?	USA
Hart, L. (2009)	N	Y	N	Y	Within		8	6	USA
Hixon, M. (2009)	Y	Y	N	Y	Within	Y	8	1	USA
Hunter, J. and Back, J. (2011)	Y	Y	N	Y	Within		19	4	UK
Inoue, N. (2011)	N	Y	N	Y	Beyond		6	?	USA
Kratzer, C.C. and Teplin, A.S. (2007)	Y	Y	N	N		N	128	16	USA
Kriewaldt, J. (2012)	Y	N	N	N		N	10	4	Australia
Lawrence, C. and Chong, W. (2010)	Y	Y	N	Y	Beyond	Y	10	1	Singapore
Lee, A.T. (2012)	N	N	N	Y	Beyond	Y	6	1	USA
Lee, J.F. (2008)	Y	Y	N	N		N	7	?	Hong Kong
Lewis, C., Perry, R. and Hurd, J. (2009)	Y	Y	N	Y	Within		6	5	USA
Lewis, C., Perry, R., Hurd, J. et al. (2006)	N	Y	Y	Y	Beyond	Y	22	1	USA

Figure 8.7 Review of Lesson Study literature: impact evidence

Source: (Seleznyov, in draft)

Logic models

Put simply, a logic model graphically illustrates the components of an intervention or programme in terms of: inputs (resources), activities (implementation), outputs and outcomes. A simple example is shown in Figure 8.8.

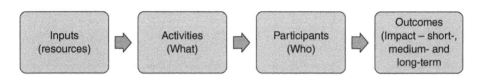

Figure 8.8 A simple logic model

This logic model can now be used to aggregate evidence relating to an intervention.

- What does the evidence suggest about the resources – time, money and skilled facilitation – required for a successful intervention?
- What does the evidence suggest about the activities required for a successful intervention?
- What does the evidence suggest about the outputs of such interventions?
- What does the evidence suggest about this intervention and changes to participants' knowledge, understanding and skills relevant to their work?
- Do participants subsequently skilfully apply that knowledge and understanding acquired from the intervention in their work setting?
- Are there any improvements in pupil outcomes or changes in the schools' capacity and culture resulting from the intervention?

By asking these questions, the evidence-based school leader will then be in a position to summarise the evidence by completing a table like the one illustrated in Figure 8.9.

Component	Sub-component	Evidence
Input		
Output	Activities	
	Participants	
Outcomes	Short-term	
	Medium-term	
	Long-term	

Figure 8.9 Elements of a logic model

Indeed, logic model frameworks have particular value for the evidence-based practitioner who in using a PICO formation is seeking to make a comparison between an intervention and a comparator (see Figure 8.10) as it facilitates a side-by-side analysis of each component of the respective logic models.

Component	Sub-component	Intervention	Comparator
Input			
Output	Activities		
	Participants		
Outcomes	Short-term		
	Medium-term		
	Long-term		

Figure 8.10 Comparing logic models of the intervention and comparator

Furthermore, it is also possible to add additional elements to the logic model – i.e., a description of the context, what's the problem of practice for which a solution is being sought, an articulation of underpinning assumptions and associated causal mechanisms – to turn it into something known as a 'theory of change' (ToC). Accordingly, the evidence-based school leader may well ask the following questions (adapted from Brown, 2017).

Context

What is the context of the school, group of schools, federation, multi-academy trust or local education authority in which the problem of practice is situated? This should include data and information on aspects such as:

- The percentage of pupils using English as an additional language
- The percentage of pupils entitled to free school meals, or other measures of poverty
- The percentage of pupils with special educational needs
- Relevant accountability measures or scores
- Relationships between the school or setting and the wider community
- Issues with staff recruitment or retention
- Any specific policy issues or drivers faced by the school(s), federation, multi-academy trust or local education authority concerned and that need to be responded to?
- Are there other factors that need to be taken into account, e.g. changes in the senior leadership team?

Problem

What is the problem of practice being faced?

- Who does it affect?
- How long has it been going on for?
- What do you know about any underlying causes?
- Conversely, what is the motivation to solve/address the problem of practice?
- What are the drivers for the intervention?
- To what extent are there external and internal pressures to solve the problem of practice?
- Are these internal or external drivers?
- Are there any barriers to change which need to be overcome?

Assumptions

What are the underpinning beliefs about the problem, the people involved and how it can be addressed? This can be illustrated by use of the teacher journal club example:

- It assumes that there is at least one individual available who has the skills to facilitate a journal club meeting.
- It assumes that it is possible to identify suitable research.
- It assumes that it is possible to access suitable research and journals.
- It assumes that teachers are motivated to attend the journal club meetings.
- It assumes that time can be found in the school calendar for journal club meetings.

- It assumes that teachers can find the time to attend journal club meetings.
- It assumes that there are no other commitments/priorities that get in the way of the journal club.
- It assumes that teachers can understand the research.
- It assumes that by reading research that teachers may change their classroom practice.
- It assumes that research is applicable to classroom practice.
- It assumes that changes in classroom practice will lead to change in pupil outcomes.

Finally, do the various sources of evidence that have been gathered together support the validity of these assumptions?

One of the main benefits of using either a logic model or a theory of change to help aggregate the available evidence is that it creates an initial framework for any subsequent evaluation of the intervention within the school or other setting. How a logic model and associated theory of action can be used to evaluate the success or otherwise of a decision will be explored in more detail in Chapter 10.

A template for a theory of change is provided by Taylor-Powell et al. (2003) and is illustrated in Figure 8.11.

Assessing the robustness of the aggregation and synthesis of the evidence – critical reflections

Having begun the processes of aggregating and synthesising our four sources of evidence and developing a logic model and/or theory of change, it is now necessary to look at how to go about judging the robustness and quality of the aggregation and synthesis. One way of doing this is to use a very simple table to help inform the evidence-based school leader of the quality of the different sources of evidence. As shown in Table 8.1, using a very simple scale the available evidence from each of the four sources is judged to be: Red – little or no evidence available; Amber – some evidence available; Green – comprehensive evidence available; Dark green – comprehensive, systematic, explicit and critical evidence available. However, the figure does not provide any guidance as to how to weight the different sources of evidence.

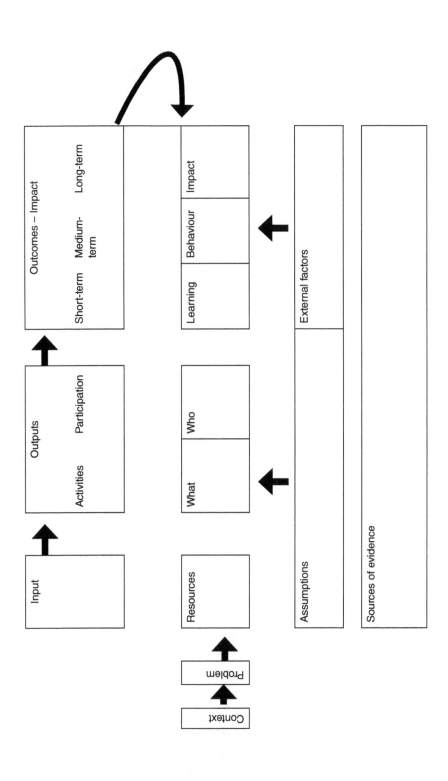

Figure 8.11 Theory of change template (based on Taylor-Powell et al., 2003)

Source: Copyright of the Board of Regents of the University of Wisconsin System. Used with permission.

Table 8.1 Aggregation and evaluation of sources of evidence

Source of evidence	RED Little or no evidence available	AMBER Some evidence available	GREEN Comprehensive evidence available	DARK GREEN Comprehensive, systematic, explicit and critical
Research	Background information/ Expert opinion	Cohort data/ case studies/ randomised controlled trial	Multiple randomised controlled trials	Systematic reviews of RCTs, best evidence syntheses
School data	Little or no school data available – mainly anecdotal	Some data available – 1 year – but data mainly available from departments – reliability and validity issues	Valid and reliable school-wide data available for three years	Valid and reliable school-wide data available for 5 years and which has been subject to review and audit
Stakeholder views	Some views expressed from a small range of stake-holders	Views obtained from the majority of stakeholders	Comprehensive range of views expressed and gathered from multiple sources	Comprehensive, systematic collection of diverse range of views – gathered from multiple sources
Practitioner expertise (decision-makers)	Novice – with little or no knowledge or experience of issue at hand	Advanced beginners with internal professional challenge and support	Competent with internal professional challenge and support – some external support	Expert with extensive internal and external professional challenge and support

Popay et al. (2006) suggest one way of checking your interpretation of research is to contact the author or authors of the original research. It is highly likely that a report's authors will be delighted if you contact them and check out your interpretation of their work. Normally, this is not too difficult as most research articles include the email address of the primary author.

A potentially more sophisticated approach is identified by Popay et al. (2006), who cite the work of Busse et al. (2002) and argue that any aggregation of results requires some form of summary discussion. Items that could be included in some form of discussion of the quality are shown in Figure 8.12

Nevertheless, it should be remembered that aggregating evidence will not in itself provide the answer to your well-formulated question and problem of practice. Rather, the process of aggregating the data may help you see how various parts of the answer fit together. Indeed,

Criteria	Possible questions to be asked
How has the evidence been collected?	Is it a comprehensive summary of evidence, or has a restricted range of evidence been included?
Evidence used (quality, validity, generalisability)	How relevant is the evidence for your key stage or type of school?
	Are recommendations arising from the evidence 'strong' or are they at best 'provisional'? (see Chapter 9)
	Are the 'costs' and 'benefits' of any intervention/decision clear?
	How are these 'costs' and 'benefits' shared between intended beneficiaries?
Assumptions made	What assumptions have you made in selecting the evidence to be aggregated?
	What assumptions have you made when interpreting types of evidence?
	Have you given primacy to one type of evidence over others?
	What assumptions have been made about staff capability and capacity?
Discrepancies and uncertainties identified	Are there any discrepancies, within and between, different types of evidence?
	Are there areas where insufficient evidence is available?
	How are these 'costs' and 'benefits' shared between intended beneficiaries?
	What other evidence might be required?
Expected changes (technology and evidence)	Are we expecting any new reports from the Education Endowment Foundation?
	Since you started with the review, has new evidence been created which is not included in your review?

Figure 8.12 Appraising the quality of the evidence

the aggregation process in itself may lead to a greater understanding of the problem of practice resulting in the development of an explicit logic model and theory of change. In doing so, this will aid the next steps in the process of being an evidence-based school leader: acting on the evidence and assessing the outcomes of the decision. However, there is little if no research evidence available about how school leaders combine these different sources of evidence.

Summary and key points

- Aggregating different sources of evidence may at first appear daunting though it can be aided by the use of simple tabular formats.
- The summarising of research does not require the writing of a long literature review, tables can be used to summarise research findings as used in systematic reviews.
- The summarising of evidence is not limited to tables and a variety of graphical forms can be used, for example, fishbone diagrams.
- The use of a critically appraised topic format will assist in developing a text-based summary of the evidence.

- The process of aggregating the data can be assisted by the use of logic models and theories of change which will help both the categorisation of evidence and future evaluations.
- It is important to use some kind of framework that takes into account, for example, how the evidence was collected, assumptions made and possible future evidence, to help judge the quality of the aggregation and synthesis.

References

Brown, C. (2017) *Measuring Impact and the Scale-up of Educational Innovations: A Working Paper*. London: UCL Institute of Education, Centre for Knowledge Exchange and Impact in Education.

Busse, R., Orvain, J., Velasco, M., Perleth, M., Drummond, M., Jørgensen, T., Jovell, A., Malone, J., Alric, R. and Wild, C. (2002) 'Best practice in undertaking and reporting health technology assessments', *International Journal of Technology Assessment in Health Care*, 18 (2): 361–422.

Deenadayalan, Y., Grimmer-Somers, K., Prior, M. and Kumar, S. (2008) 'How to run an effective journal club: a systematic review', *Journal of Evaluation in Clinical Practice*, 14 (5): 898–911.

Godfrey, D. and Seleznyov, S. (forthcoming) *Lesson Study: What, Why and How. A Review of the Literature (draft)*.

Guskey, T. (2000) *Evaluating Professional Development*. Thousand Oaks, CA: Corwin.

Popay, J., Roberts, H., Sowden, A., Petticrew, M., Arai, L., Rodgers, M., Britten, N., Roen, K. and Duffy, S. (2006) *Guidance on the Conduct of Narrative Synthesis in Systematic Reviews*. A product from the ESRC methods programme Version. 1. b92. Available at: www.lancaster.ac.uk/shm/research/nssr/research/dissemination/publications/NS_Synthesis_Guidance_v1.pdf (accessed 4 May 2018).

Seleznyov, S. (forthcoming) *Lesson study: An exploration of its impact beyond Japan*.

Seleznyov, S. (in draft) *Lesson study: An exploration of its translation beyond Japan*.

Simpson, A. (2017) 'The misdirection of public policy: comparing and combining standardised effect sizes', *Journal of Education Policy*, 32 (4): 450–66.

Sims, S., Moss, G. and Marshall, E. (2017) 'Teacher journal clubs: how do they work and can they increase evidence-based practice?', *Impact*, 1. https://impact.chartered.college/issue/issue-1-assessment/ (accessed 4 May 2018).

Straus, S., Glasziou, P., Richardson, S. and Haynes, B. (2011) *Evidence-Based Medicine: How to Practise and Teach It*, 4th edn. Edinburgh: Churchill Livingstone Elsevier.

Taylor-Powell, E., Jones, L. and Henert, E. (2003) 'Enhancing program performance with logic models'. *University of Wisconsin Extension Services online course*. https://fyi.uwex.edu/programdevelopment/files/2016/03/lmcourseall.pdf

Willingham, D. (2012) *When Can You Trust the Experts: How to Tell Good Science from Bad in Education*. San Francisco, CA: John Wiley & Sons.

9

APPLYING EVIDENCE TO THE DECISION-MAKING PROCESS

Chapter outline

This chapter will explore issues relating to both the decision-making process and the implementation of any subsequent decision. Consideration will be given to a simple rule of thumb to be used when making a decision on whether to act or not. Next, some of the challenges in identifying some of the costs associated with a decision, and how educational research has paid insufficient attention to side-effects, will be discussed. This will lead on to a discussion that considers some of the issues associated with decision-making and cognitive biases. Following on from this, the chapter will begin to explore the issues associated with implementing the decision Plan–Do–Study–Act (PDSA) cycle. Attention

(Continued)

(Continued)

will focus on some of the many challenges associated with trying to implement successfully an intervention or innovation on a large scale. Finally, the chapter will look at the Education Endowment Foundation's guidance on making use of evidence.

Key words: *side-effects, cognitive biases, pre-mortem, Plan–Do–Study–Act (PDSA), strength of recommendation, implementation*

Making a decision – should you do nothing?

Having articulated a well-formulated and answerable question, accessed multiple sources of evidence and then aggregated the evidence, the evidence-based school leader will be faced with a decision about how to proceed. However, just because the evidence base appears to be sound, that in itself is not a good enough reason to adopt the intervention or change. As Drucker (2001) states, 'one alternative is always the alternative of doing nothing' (p. 195).

Drucker argues that decision-making invariably sits between two ends of a spectrum: at one end, it is necessary to make a decision otherwise the situation will deteriorate if no action is taken; at the other end, if nothing is done the situation will resolve itself. However, the vast majority of decisions will take place in circumstances where, if nothing is done, the situation will not deteriorate to the extent that the very survival of the organisation is threatened. If, on the other hand, a decision is taken to act, hopefully this will lead to some form of improvement. Or as Drucker puts it: 'if we do not act, in other words, we will in all probability survive. But if we do act, we may be better off' (p. 196). To aid the evidence-based school leader with this task, Drucker provides a useful 'rule of thumb' to be applied when incorporating evidence into the decision-making process, which is: 'act if on balance the benefits greatly outweigh cost and risk' (p. 196).

However, it is not always easy to identify the costs associated with what works. Zhao (2017) identifies four reasons why educational research has largely ignored the potential harms arising from what works. First, given that education is perceived as a good thing, this leads to individuals potentially ignoring negative unintended consequences as education is not routinely linked with unfavourable consequences. Second, the negative unintended consequences may take some time to emerge, which makes it challenging to report on side-effects. Third, if a narrow definition of success is adopted, then it becomes much more difficult to observe unintended consequences, as they may be deemed to be out of the scope of any evaluation of the intervention. Finally, there may be a range of pressures – be it political, commercial or economic – which may lead to wilful blindness towards the side-effects.

Bearing in mind all the different factors that evidence-based leaders need to take into account when making a decision, it will be useful to have some kind of checklist or template that brings the evidence together in a way that supports decision-making. Helpfully, in the context of healthcare and inadequacies in the decision-making process Alonso-Coello et al. (2016) have developed a framework for a systematic and transparent approach to making evidence-informed decisions. They argue that

> often the process that decision-makers used, the criteria that they considered and the evidence that they used to reach their judgments are unclear. They may omit important criteria, give undue weight to some criteria, or not use the best available evidence. Systematic and transparent systems for decision-making can help to ensure that all important criteria are considered and that the best available research evidence informs decisions. (Alonso-Coello et al., 2016: 1)

If as evidence-based school leader you adopt such an approach, then there are a number of benefits which may accrue, and these include:

- having an improved understanding of the advantages and disadvantages of the various actions being proposed;
- ensuring all important criteria in the decision-making process are included;
- providing a concise summary of all the best available evidence – be it research evidence, school data, stakeholder views or practitioner expertise;
- helping colleagues to be in a better position to understand the decisions by senior leadership teams and the evidence supporting those decisions. (adapted from Alonso-Coello et al., 2016)

As discussed in Chapter 2, an evidence-based school leader makes explicit the criteria they use to make a decision. In the context of a school or multi-academy trust, these criteria may well change depending on what domain and sub-domain of school leadership and management you are concerned with (Neeleman, 2017). The criteria for making decisions about teaching and learning may well be different from the criteria applied to those involving financial decisions. In addition, the evidence-based school leader may want to take into account whether criteria are adjusted for different parts of the organisation. As such, the criteria being applied at, say, the level of the board of a multi-academy trust may well be different to how the criteria are applied at Key Stage 1 in a primary school. Using Alonso-Coello et al. (2016) as a starting point, let's look at some of the criteria that could be applied to decision-making (see Figure 9.1).

Element	Criteria
Priority of the problem	Is the issue an important problem for which a remedy is sought and that can be locally implemented?
Logic model	Is there a clear logic model – detailing the relationship between inputs, outputs and outcomes?
Benefits	How substantial are the desirable anticipated effects?
Costs	How substantial are the undesirable anticipated effects?
Certainty of the evidence	How robust and secure are the different sources – research, practitioner expertise, stakeholder views and school data – of evidence?
Balance	Does the balance of the desirable and undesirable effects favour the intervention or the comparator?
Resource use	How large are the resource requirements – attention, time, money, professional learning?
	Does the balance of costs and benefits favour the intervention or the comparator?
Equity	What impact does the decision have on educational equity? Will it help close gaps in attainment?
	Are there important ethical issues which need to be taken into account?
Acceptability	Are there key stakeholders – teachers, parents, trustees – who would not accept the distribution of the benefits, harms and costs?
	Would the intervention adversely affect the autonomy of teacher, department, school or multi-academy trust?

Element	Criteria
Feasibility	Are there important barriers that are likely to limit the feasibility of implementing the intervention (option) or require consideration when implementing it?
	Is the intervention or strategy sustainable?
Additional comments and recommendation	

Figure 9.1 Evidence to decision template

Making a recommendation

Having gathered the evidence together, appraised the evidence and assessed the evidence against a range of criteria, a recommendation is now needed on how to proceed. But before making a recommendation, it is worth remembering that recommendations come with differing levels of strength. For example, you may have a strong recommendation where it appears that the benefits of the intervention clearly outweigh the risks; there is strong and consistent supporting research evidence and associated practitioner expertise; there are high levels of stakeholder support; and resources are available to implement the intervention. On the other hand, where it appears to be touch and go whether the benefits outweigh the costs and there is inconsistent research evidence with little or no local expertise, this would result in a weak recommendation – if any recommendation at all – to adopt the proposed intervention (see Table 9.1).

Table 9.1 Strength of recommendation

Benefits vs Risks	Grade of recommendation	Strength of supporting evidence
Benefits clearly outweigh risks or vice versa	Strong recommendation, high-quality evidence	Consistent supporting evidence from research evidence, practitioner expertise, school data and stakeholders – without major limitations
Benefits clearly outweigh risks or vice versa	Strong recommendation, moderate quality evidence	Consistent supporting evidence from research evidence, school data, stakeholders and practitioner expertise – though with some limitations

(Continued)

Table 9.1 (Continued)

Benefits vs Risks	Grade of recommendation	Strength of supporting evidence
Benefits clearly outweigh risks or vice versa	Strong recommendation, low-quality evidence	Consistent supporting evidence from research evidence, practitioner expertise, school data and stakeholders – though with significant limitations
Benefits closely balanced with risks and burden	Weak recommendation, high-quality evidence	Consistent supporting evidence from research evidence, practitioner expertise, school data and stakeholders – without major limitations
Benefits closely balanced	Weak recommendation, moderate-quality evidence	Consistent supporting evidence from research evidence, practitioner expertise, school data and stakeholders – though with some limitations
Uncertainty in estimates of benefits and costs	Weak recommendation, low-quality evidence	Some supporting evidence from research evidence, practitioner expertise, school data and stakeholders – though with major limitations

Source: adapted from Guyatt et al., 2012

Cognitive biases and decision-making

Chapter 1 included a brief discussion on the problem of cognitive biases and how this contributes to the need for evidence-based school leadership. Accordingly, it is worth taking some time to reflect on whether the decision-making process has been 'hijacked' by a particular individual, group or groups and their associated biases. To help do this Kahneman et al. (2011) have identified a number of specific biases, questions and actions which could be used to improve the rigour of decision-making (see Figure 9.2).

Preliminary questions		
Check/Confirm for		Action
Self-interested biases	Is there any reason to suspect that the team of individuals making the recommendation are making errors motivated by self-interest, for example, opportunities for promotion or enhanced status?	Review the proposal with care, looking out for whether only one realistic option is put forward.
Affect heuristic	Has the senior leadership or other team fallen in love with its proposals and cannot see any of the downsides associated with the proposal?	Apply the checklist and examine whether biases may have impacted upon the people making the recommendation.

Preliminary questions		
Groupthink	Were there dissenting opinions, from different stakeholders, and were these opinions fully explored?	Discretely obtain dissenting views from a range of interested parties. Watch out for absence of dissent, especially if the issue is complex.

Challenge questions		
Saliency bias	Could the diagnosis be overly influenced by an analogy to a memorable success, for example, does the intervention look similar to an intervention that has been successful in the past?	Are there other analogies? How similar are this and other analogies to the current situation?
Confirmation bias	Are credible alternatives included with the recommendation?	Request that additional options be provided.
Availability bias	If this decision was to be made again in a year's time, what information would you want and can you get more of it now?	Develop checklists of available information for different types of decision.
Anchoring bias	Do you know where the evidence came from – are there unsubstantiated numbers – have they been extrapolated from historical data?	Check the figures against other models, are there alternative benchmarks which can be used for analysis?
Halo effect	Is the team assuming that a person, organisation or innovation which is successful in one area – department, phase or school – will be just as successful in another?	Eliminate false inferences – seek alternative examples where the innovation has worked in similar contexts.

Ask about the proposal		
Overconfidence, planning fallacy, optimistic biases, competition neglect	Is the base case overly optimistic? Are the likely benefits overstated, are the associate costs understated (see Table 9.1)?	Have outside – either internal or external – views been taken into account? What would an external third-party think?
Check for disaster neglect	Is the worst case bad enough? Could this project have substantive unintended negative consequences?	Conduct a premortem to work out what could go wrong (see Box 9.1).
Check for loss aversion	Is the recommending team overly cautious? Is there a fear of failure?	Realign incentives to share responsibility for the risk or remove the risk.

Figure 9.2 Avoiding biases and making better decisions: a checklist (adapted from Kahneman et al., 2011)

So how can the checklist help school leaders make decisions based on the best available evidence? Kahneman et al. (2011) identify four key considerations. First, the process should be reserved for use with 'important yet recurring decisions'. For example, this might include approving expenditure on a new IT system or a decision as to whether to expand the multi-academy trust by adding another school or schools. Second, the review should be conducted ensuring the decision checklist is applied by a member or members of staff who are both sufficiently senior within the school and are not part of the group making the recommendation. The separation between recommenders and decision-makers is desirable and has implications for governance and leadership. Third, the checklist must be used in whole and not in parts and not be 'cherry-picked' to legitimate a decision. Finally, consider whether using the checklist is a good use of everyone's time and effort; is there an appropriate balance between due diligence and speed of action?

BOX 9.1 PREMORTEMS

Klein (2007a), who devised the approach, describes a premortem as:

> the hypothetical opposite of a postmortem. A postmortem in a medical setting allows health professionals and the family to learn what caused a patient's death. Everyone benefits except, of course, the patient. A premortem in a business setting comes at the beginning of a project rather than the end, so the project can be improved rather than autopsied. Unlike a typical critiquing session, in which project team members are asked what might go wrong, the premortem operates on the assumption that the 'patient' has died, and so asks what did go wrong. The team members' task is to generate plausible reasons for the project's failure. (p. 1)

In the context of a school or multi-academy trust a project premortem comes at the beginning of a new initiative – say a new timetabling system or uniform policy – and works out why the new initiative has not delivered the desired results and has created a number of negative unintended consequences. In other words, you have imagined the initiative has failed, and is to be withdrawn.

How to conduct a premortem

Klein (2007b) usefully provides the following outline process for conducting a premortem.

Prior to the final decision to proceed with a project or policy, a group of people who are knowledgeable about the project – including both the project leader and sponsor – get together for a meeting lasting approximately 45–60 minutes and go through the following.

Step 1: Preparation. Team members take out sheets of paper and get relaxed in their chairs. They should already be familiar with the plan, or else have the plan described to them so they can understand what is supposed to be happening.

Step 2: Imagine a fiasco. When I conduct the premortem, I say I am looking into a crystal ball and, oh no, I am seeing the project has failed. It isn't a simple failure either. It is total, embarrassing, devastating failure. The people on the team are no longer talking to one another. Our company is not talking to the sponsors. Things have gone as wrong as they could. However, we could only afford an inexpensive model of the crystal ball so we cannot make out the reasons for the failures. Then I ask, 'What could have caused this?'

Step 3: Generate reasons for the failure. The people on the team spend the next three minutes writing down all the reasons why they believe the failure occurred.

Step 4: Consolidate the lists. When each member of the group is done writing, the facilitator goes around the room, asking each person to state one item from his or her list. Each item is recorded on a whiteboard. The process continues until every member of the group has revealed every item on their list. By the end of this step, you should have a comprehensive list of the group's concerns with the plan at hand.

Step 5: Revisit the plan. They can address two or three items of greatest concern, and then schedule another meeting to discuss the ideas for avoiding or minimising the other problems.

Step 6: Periodically review the list. Some project leaders take out the list every three or four months to keep the spectre of failure fresh, and to resensitize the team to problems that may just be emerging.

Source: Klein, 2007b: 99–100

Implementation

It is necessary to decide upon the scale of implementation within the department, school or multi-academy trust. In particular, thought will have to be given to the organisational context within which the intervention or change will take place. Indeed as Bryk et al. (2015) argue, one of several reasons why educational interventions/ innovations often fail is that insufficient thought is given to the organisational context into which the intervention is to be introduced.

As an evidence-based school leader you will already have gathered evidence from multiple sources – research evidence, school data, stakeholder views and practitioner expertise – and should already have a sense of the scale of implementation which is right for the school's context. It may be that there is little know-how, capacity, or capability, and commitment towards the intervention, so this may mean either the intervention is abandoned or a small number of volunteers are sought. On the other hand, there may well be extensive know-how on how to make something work, sufficient resources to support the implementation, and wide-scale teacher commitment to the intervention, which might justify a whole-school roll-out. And, of course, there may be levels of intervention which lie in between these two extremes – such as at the departmental, year group or key stage level (see Figure 9.3).

Sizing up a context		Participants will be		
		Resistant	Indifferent	Ready
Extant know-how limited	Limited capacity	Very small-scale	Very small-scale	Very small-scale
	Good capacity	Small-scale test	Small-scale test	Moderate-scale test
Substantial know-how exists	Limited capacity	Small-scale test	Moderate-scale test	Large-scale test
	Good capacity	Moderate-scale test	Large-scale test	System-wide implementation

Figure 9.3 A framework for analysing the institutional context for improvement (Bryk et al., 2015)

Given the previous discussion about the problems associated with educational research (see Chapter 5) in identifying what works, for whom, in what context, to what extent, for how long and why – Bryk et al. suggest this is likely to locate most interventions in the top left-hand corner of Figure 9.3. So in the context of a school within a multi-academy trust, a very small test of an intervention may be with just a few volunteers. A small-scale test may be with a couple of departments in different schools, whereas a moderate-scale test may involve a key stage in two or more schools. A large-scale test may involve one or more schools adopting the intervention at the level of the school. Finally, a system-wide implementation may reflect intervention being adopted within all of the schools of the multi-academy trust. Of course, these interpretations of scale of implementation can be adjusted to take into account different settings.

This framework indicates most decisions are more likely than not going to be implemented with either a very small-scale or a small-scale test, leading Bryk et al. to put forward a number of guiding principles. First, learn 'quickly and cheaply'. Second, some interventions will fail, so try to minimise the negative consequence for both pupils, staff or stakeholders. Third, at all times gather data to inform future iterations of the intervention. Bryk et al. go on to argue that a number of benefits accrue from adopting these principles. The original idea may well be developed in such a way that it now actually works and is scalable. Those colleagues involved in the very small-scale and small-scale test will gain expertise in the intervention, which makes the rolling out of the intervention to others that much easier. The final benefit is that a successful initial test will create 'champions' for the intervention, as those colleagues will have seen benefits for their pupils, or experienced benefits for themselves.

Plan–Do–Study–Act

At this stage, the evidence-based school leader will begin to think about putting together an action plan. So the next step of the evidence-based practice process is to connect the knowledge and understanding which has emerged from the first four steps (As) of the evidence-based practice process , and turn that knowledge and understanding into action and rapid learning. Bryk et al. (2015), drawing upon the work of Langley et al. (2009), suggest the use of the Plan–Do–Study–Act (PDSA) cycle to help with this task. Although the PDSA cycle is relatively simple, to make the most of it will require time, attention and perseverance. Figure 9.4 provides an explanation of what makes up each stage of the cycle.

In the context of evidence-based practice, the PDSA cycle has the potential to incorporate another part of the evidence-based practice process – assessing and evaluating the outcome of the decision taken. However, in this context it is likely that several PDSA cycles will be undertaken before completing a substantive evaluation of the intervention. An appropriate analysis of your organisational context is more than likely to start off with either a very small-scale or a small-scale test. However, Bryk et al. (2015) do note that if the capacity and know-how is present in the organisation then under the right conditions, for example, the support of important stakeholders, then whole-school or multi-academy trust-wide implementation may be appropriate.

Let's now illustrate the PDSA cycle by returning to the example of a teacher journal club.

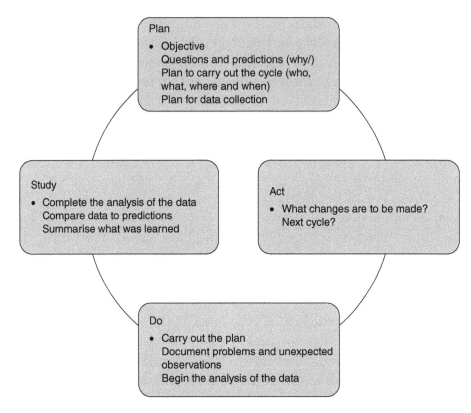

Figure 9.4 The Plan–Do–Study–Act cycle (based on Langley et al., 2009: 97)

The plan: A decision was made to incorporate a teacher journal club into the school's programme of professional learning and it was to be led by the recently appointed School Research Lead (SRL). A piece of reading was chosen. It was predicted that the session would last 45 minutes, and that the eight staff who volunteered would all turn up, having read the suggested reading. The teachers would be able to understand the reading and the key terms there would be a basis for a discussion about the key messages of the book extract or article read. Ideally, this would lead to some suggestions about how to improve practice, which the participant teachers might incorporate into their own teaching. The participant teachers would feel energised and become advocates for the use of 'research' to inform professional practice.

What happened?: Unfortunately, only six of the eight staff who had been invited turned up, with the other two members of staff being called away for urgent departmental meetings on student progress. Of the six staff who had turned up, two had not had time to read the suggested reading, two had skimmed through the reading and only two had completed the reading, with one taking extensive written notes. Rather than focus on discussing the reading, much of the conversation was spent on talking about the difficulties of finding time to undertake the reading and whether research was relevant to their teaching practice. One participant who admitted to not having done the reading, stated they had had a go but had not been able to understand much of the language used. Finally, the session was held at the end of the working day and refreshments had not been made available.

Analysis: The chosen text had been at the wrong level and was also too long for the time the majority of the teachers had available to participate in this activity. There was a lack of structure to the discussion and no series of prompts or a framework for analysing the chosen text. However, it was recognised in the post-session feedback that it was important to have another go and to make a teachers' journal club work.

Next steps: A much shorter piece of reading would be found, which could be read in the session. In addition, it was agreed to provide a 'reading framework' to help tease out the main issues. The next session was scheduled for a 'protected' block of time in the next half-term's professional learning programme, with suitable refreshments being provided.

Of course, after the next session we can go through the same PDSA cycle on a number of different occasions, and as Langley et al. (2009) note this creates an 'iterative, trial and learning approach to improvement' (p. 102). We can start small to reduce the impact of getting things wrong and as we learn we can slowly scale up the activity so that, as in this example, more and more staff can become involved in teacher journal clubs. Figure 9.5 shows how a teacher journal club can develop over several cycles.

Implementing an intervention on a large scale

In this next section, consideration will be given to some of the challenges associated with implementation at scale. To help do this, the work of Robert I. Sutton, one of the intellectual forefathers of evidence-based management, and Huggy Rao will be examined to help identify useful strategies as we attempt to scale up what is hoped are necessary, important and valuable interventions.

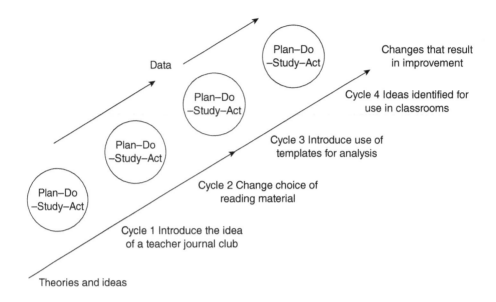

Figure 9.5 Repeated use of PDSA cycle to develop a teacher journal club (based on Langley et al., 2009: 103)

Sutton and Rao (2014), drawing upon case studies that ranged from firms based in the Silicon Valley to non-profit and third sector organisations, identify a number of generic lessons that evidence-based school leaders need to be aware of if they wish to have new interventions or programmes adopted widely. First, it is not enough to make a rational argument for an intervention or change, it is necessary to connect to people's emotions in ways that lead to substantive and positive action. Sutton and Rao talk about connecting 'hot causes to cool solutions' (p. xii). Second, scaling is not about rolling out more of the same, with a rigidly prescriptive and standard way of doing things being adopted across a school or multi-academy trust. Rather it involves 'relentless restlessness' where new and improved ways are found to do things, across all aspects and functions of the school or multi-academy trust. Third, those leaders who are particularly good at scaling up excellence 'talk and act as if they are knee-deep in a manageable mess' (p. xiv). On the one hand, they believe by acting in the correct way and using their knowledge, skills and experience and with the support of others that they can have some control over the future. On the other hand, they recognise in scaling excellence they will often be faced with what at first glance seem insurmountable problems. That said, the best leaders find a way to 'muddle-through' (p. xiv) and enjoy the uncertainty and ambiguity. Finally, scaling up excellence 'starts and ends with individuals – success depends on the will and the skill of people at every level of the organisation' (p. xv). Indeed, the only way excellence can be spread across an organisation is through the commitment, determination and dynamism of individuals throughout the organisation – or in our case the department, school or multi-academy trust. As a result, many changes will come about because skilled and dedicated individuals have identified a problem and set about solving it, with those individuals being found all across the organisation not just in the school senior leadership team or trust executive group. Sutton and Rao (2014) then go on to identify a number of key considerations when seeking to scale up excellence and these are summarised in Figure 9.6.

Aspect	Commentary
It's a ground war, not just an air war: Going slower to scale faster (and better) later	PowerPoint presentations, inspirational speeches and staff training are not enough, rather each individual, team, department instead 'make one small change after another in what they believe, feel, or do' (p. 4)
Buddhism versus Catholicism: Choosing a path	What is our goal? 'Is it like Catholicism where we try and replicate preordained beliefs and practices. Or is it more like Buddhism, where an underlying mindset guides people to do certain things – but the specifics of what they (*individual, team, department or school*) do can vary wildly from person to person and place to places' (p. 33)
Hot causes, cool solutions: Stoking the scaling engine	It's not enough to appeal to individuals' and groups' 'rational side' it's also necessary to appeal to emotions: 'stoke the scaling engines by targeting beliefs, behaviour, or both at once. The key is creating and fuelling a virtuous circle' (p.70)
Cut cognitive load: But deal with necessary complexity	You can't keep adding things to workloads – unnecessary tasks need to be eliminated to create the 'headspace' to think things through. However, rules and processes are sometimes necessary to make things easier to process
The people who propel scaling: Build organizations where 'I own the place and the place owns me'	Recruiting talented individuals is not enough, you need to recruit individuals 'who feel compelled to act in the organisation's best interests' (p. 139)
Connect people and cascade excellences using social bonds to spread the right mindset	Discover or (create) 'pockets of excellence and connect the people who have it, and their ideas and expertise to others. Where all goes well a chain reaction is created where excellence flows from one person, team or place to the next' (p. 175)
'Bad is stronger than good': Clearing the way for excellence	'the outcome of spreading excellence depends on the process that enables people to eliminate destructive attitudes, beliefs, and behaviours' (p. 231)

Figure 9.6   A summary of the key aspects of scaling up excellence (adapted from Sutton and Rao, 2014)

What does this mean for the scaling up of an intervention within your school or multi-academy trust? Returning to our teacher journal club example, by using Sutton and Rao (2014) model of scaling of excellence, it's possible to show how a small intervention could be spread across a multi-academy trust. First, there would need to be a recognition that a one-off presentation exhorting the potential of research to bring about improvements in teaching and learning is not enough. Opportunities need to be created for teams, departments and schools to make small changes. Second, there will need to be a decision or decision(s) about how the journal clubs will be run. Will they have to be conducted in the same way – with the same basic agenda – with everyone reading the same articles or books? Or can people be given the opportunity to identify their own problems of practice and associated reading material and how they will go about reading that material? Third, it will not be enough to say to teachers that journal clubs will lead to increases in teacher knowledge and expertise and therefore will result in improvement in pupils' outcomes. It will be necessary to appeal to individual's professional beliefs and values about what it is to be a teacher, and how research can play a role. Fourth, it is unwise to keep asking colleagues to do 'new stuff' and other things will need to be eliminated from the workload of teachers so that they have the time and space to fully participate in and engage with the journal club. Fifth, when looking to recruit individuals to run the journal clubs, focussing on individuals who have a post-graduate degree and who may be research literate is not enough. Whoever runs the journal club needs to have a genuine commitment to do what it is necessary to support colleagues to improve, not just in their own school but across the multi-academy trust. Sixth, as small-scale pilots of journal clubs are tried out, where there is success, make sure these individuals are connected to others in the school or multi-academy trust. However, don't focus just on internal school/multi-academy trust connections – make use of a wider professional network to find examples of where journal clubs have worked well and learn from them. Finally, make sure the basics are attended to, ensuring any unnecessary disruptors or inhibitors are removed. If meetings take place at lunch times or after school make sure there are suitable refreshments available. Make sure colleagues can access the reading and it is of an appropriate level and if they need help they are supported.

An alternative way of thinking about implementation

The preceding sections in this chapter have mapped out just one of many ways of going about the decision-making and implementation process. At this stage, it might make sense to actively seek out other approaches to implementation, which can be used to cross-reference and check whatever action plan has been developed. One such approach to implementation has been put forward in the Education Endowment Foundation's *Putting Evidence to Work: A School's Guide to Implementation* and which has been used as the basis of putting together the following checklist (see Figure 9.7).

Recommendation	Key questions
Treat implementation as a process, not an event; plan and execute it in stages	Do we implement changes across the school in a structured and staged manner?
	Is adequate time and care taken when preparing for implementation?
	Are there opportunities to make fewer, but more strategic, implementation decisions and pursue these with greater effort?
	Are there less effective practices that can be stopped to free up time and resources? (p. 11)
Create a leadership environment and school climate that is conducive to good implementation	Does our school have a climate that is conducive to good implementation?
	Does the school leadership team create a clear vision and understanding of expectations when changing practices across the school?
	Do staff feel empowered to step forward and take on implementation responsibilities?
	How do day-to-day practices affect the motivation and readiness of staff to change? (p. 13)
Define the problem you want to solve and identify appropriate programmes and practices to implement	Are we confident we have identified a strong school improvement priority that is amenable to change?
	What are we looking to achieve by adopting a new programme or practice?
	Have we systematically identified the right approach to achieve these goals?
	Is there reliable evidence it can have the desired impact, if implemented well?
	Is it feasible within our context? (p. 17)
Create a clear implementation plan, judge the readiness of the school to deliver that plan, then prepare staff and resources	Is there a logical and well-specified implementation plan?
	Do we have a clear and shared understanding of the active ingredients of our intervention and how they will be implemented?
	Have we selected the right set of implementation strategies, in the right order?
	Are we able to capture the desired (and undesired) changes in practices?
	Have we honestly appraised our capacity to make those changes?
	Are staff and the school practically ready to adopt the new approach? (p. 30)

(Continued)

Figure 9.7 (Continued)

Recommendation	Key questions
Support staff, monitor progress, solve problems and adapt strategies as the approach is used for the first time	Are we able to respond to challenges that arise during the initial stages of using a new approach?
	Can we use existing structures and processes or are novel solutions required?
	Is appropriate follow-on support available to embed new skills and knowledge developed during initial training, in the form of coaching, mentoring, and peer-to-peer collaboration?
	Is the intervention being implemented as intended?
	Are the active ingredients being observed in day-to-day practice?
	Does implementation data suggest we need to adapt our implementation strategies? (p. 34)
Plan for sustaining and scaling an intervention from the outset and continuously acknowledge and nurture its use	Do we have a stable use of the intervention, as intended?
	Is it achieving the desired outcomes?
	Have we created contingency plans for any changes across the school that may disrupt successful implementation?
	Is it appropriate to extend the use of the approach to additional staff? What is required to achieve this?
	How can the existing capacity and resources be best used to support scale-up? (p. 37)

Figure 9.7 An implementation checklist (adapted from Sharples et al., 2018)

Whilst this is an extremely useful checklist, it does have a number of limitations. First, the term 'school climate' is used as a major component of one of the recommendations. Unfortunately, this is problematic as there is no consensus as to how to define the term school climate (Thapa et al., 2013). Second, within the guidance there is an implicit assumption that the intervention should be scaled-up. Some attention has been be paid to how to make a decision to 'stop' the intervention and admit that it has not worked. So with that in mind it seems sensible to examine a process for disengaging from strategies and interventions that appear not to be working. McGrath (2011) has identified a disciplined process for getting out of projects, which includes these steps:

- Decide in advance on periodic checkpoints for determining whether to continue or not.
- Evaluate the project's upside against the current estimated costs of continuing. If it no longer appears that the project will deliver the returns anticipated at the outset, it may be time to stop.
- Compare the project with other candidate projects that need resources. If this one looks less attractive than they do, it may be time to stop.

- Assess whether the project teams may be falling prey to escalation pressures (all will be OK as long as we make the project bigger).
- Involve an objective, informed outsider in the decisions about whether to continue, instead of leaving it up to the project team members.
- If the decision is made to stop, spell out the reasons clearly.
- Think through how capabilities and assets developed during the course of the projects might be recouped.
- Identify all who will be affected by the project's terminations; draw up a plan to address disappointments or 'damage' they might suffer.
- Use a symbolic event – a wake, a play, a memorial – to give people closure.
- Make sure that the people involved get a new, equally interesting opportunity.

(McGrath, 2011: 8)

Given these two reservations, it is appropriate that the next two chapters look at how to assess the outcomes of a decision (Chapter 10) and how to lead the evidence-based school (Chapter 11).

Summary and key points

- Act only if, on balance, the benefits outweigh the costs.
- The costs associated with an intervention are often extremely difficult to identify.
- Making a recommendation whether to act or not depends on a range of factors not just the quality of the available research.
- There are various levels of recommendation – from strong to weak – as to whether on the basis of the evidence you should proceed with an intervention.
- Undertake a rigorous process to try to minimise the impact of cognitive biases.
- A project premortem is extremely useful in identifying what could go wrong with an intervention by providing individuals with an opportunity to challenge consensus.
- The scale of implementation of an intervention will depend on a local analysis that takes into account levels of available expertise, resources and support.

- When undertaking the intervention or action – the PDSA cycle provides a useful framework for what needs to be done.
- Ideally, the PDSA cycle will be undertaken rapidly with a number of iterations.
- When seeking to scale up excellence there are a number of factors that can create the conditions for success.

References

Alonso-Coello, P., Oxman, A.D., Moberg, J., Brignardello-Petersen, R., Akl, E.A., Davoli, M., Treweek, S., Mustafa, R.A., Vandvik, P.O., Meerpohl, J., Guyatt, G.H. and Schünemann, H.J. (2016) 'GRADE evidence to decision (EtD) frameworks: a systematic and transparent approach to making well informed healthcare choices. 2: Clinical practice guidelines', *BMJ* 2016;*353*:i2089 (accessed 4 May 2018).

Bryk, A.S., Gomez, L.M., Grunow, A. and LeMahieu, P.G. (2015) *Learning to Improve: How America's Schools Can Get Better at Getting Better*. Cambridge, MA: Harvard Education Press.

Drucker, P.F. (2001) *The Essential Drucker*. Oxford: Butterworth–Heinemann.

Guyatt, G., Norris, S., Schulman, S., Hirsh, J., Eckman, M., Akl, E.A. and Schünemann, H.J. (2012) *Methodology for the Development of Antithrombotic Therapy and Prevention of Thrombosis Guidelines: Antithrombotic Therapy and Prevention of Thrombosis*, 9th edn. Chest. 141. (2 Suppl), 53S–70S.

Kahneman, D., Lovallo, D. and Sibony, O. (2011) 'Before you make that big decision', *Harvard Business Review, 89* (6): 50–60.

Klein, G. (2007a) 'Performing a project premortem', *Harvard Business Review, 85* (9) 18–9.

Klein, G. (2007b) *The Power of Intuition: How to Use Your Gut Feelings to Make Better Decisions at Work*. Crown Business.

Langley, G.J., Moen, R., Nolan, K.M., Nolan, T.W., Norman, C.L. and Provost, L.P. (2009) *The Improvement Guide: a Practical Approach to Enhancing Organizational Performance*, 2nd edn. San Francisco, CA: Jossey-Bass.

McGrath, R. (2011) 'Failing by design', *Harvard Business Review*, April: 77–83.

Neeleman, A.-M. (2017) *Grasping the Scope of School Autonomy: a Classification Scheme for School Policy Practice*. Stratford-upon-Avon: BELMAS.

Sharples, J., Albers, B. and Fraser, S. (2018) *Putting Evidence to Work: A School's Guide to Implementation. Guidance Report*. London: Education Endowment Foundation

Sutton, R.I. and Rao, H. (2014) *Scaling Up Excellence: Getting to More Without Settling for Less*. London: Crown Business.

Thapa, A., Cohen, J. Guffey, S. and Higgins-D'Alessandro, A. (2013) 'A review of school climate research', *Review of Educational Research, 83* (3): 357–385.

Zhao, Y. (2017) 'What works may hurt: side effects in education', *Journal of Educational Change, 18* (1): 1–19.

10

ASSESSING AND EVALUATING THE OUTCOME OF THE DECISION TAKEN

Chapter outline

To help evidence-based school leaders to evaluate the outcome of any decision taken, this chapter will provide the following. First, basic definitions of the terms evaluation, merit and worth. Second, a brief explanation of how a range of techniques, such as After Action Review, logic models, theories of change and contributions analysis, can be used to help evaluate the outcomes of a decision. Third, an examination of how to learn from successful decisions, intervention and changes, which will be accompanied by a review of how to learn from failure. Finally, a checklist to help school leaders self-assess their performance as evidence-based practitioners.

Key words: *After Action Review, contribution analysis, evaluation, improvement, merit, logic model, theory of change, worth*

Evaluation – a definition

Stufflebeam and Coryn (2014) use a basic definition of evaluation developed by the Joint Committee (a standing committee that was established in 1975, with members drawn from 15 professional societies in the United States and Canada that are concerned with improving evaluation in education) in 1994 which describes evaluation as 'the systematic assessment of the worth or merit of an object' (p. 8). Stufflebeam and Coryn go on to argue that given that evaluation's root term is value, then evaluations inevitably involve some form of value judgement. In the context of leading the evidence-based school, it is important to recognise the role of values – be it personal, school, social – in influencing the evaluation of the decision taken. Moreover, given the financial constraints under which many, many schools operate it is essential to ensure any benefits arising from a decision are not outweighed by their financial costs.

Distinguishing between merit and worth

As Stufflebeam and Coryn (2014) note, when discussing a decision's merit, the interest is in whether that decision led to what it is supposed to do, in other words did the decision lead to the intended outcomes. Merit, in other words, can be seen as intrinsic merit in the absence of costs. Worth, on the other hand, does not just limit itself to the intrinsic value of a decision it also includes reference to the outcomes of the decision and its associated costs. In other words, merit is a necessary but not sufficient condition for the outcomes of a decision to be of worth.

It is possible to illustrate the distinction between merit and worth by using the Education Endowment Foundation's Teaching and Learning Toolkit, which evaluates the impact of interventions in relation to their costs. One-to-one tuition would appear to have merit, with learners advancing by five months through its use. However, it may not be worth it as the intervention is associated with high costs, whereas feedback may advance pupil learning by eight months with very low associated costs, and as such may have both merit and worth. Indeed, the EEF Teaching and Learning Toolkit identifies a number of interventions, for example, repeating a year, setting and streaming, aspiration interventions – which either have a negative or zero impact on pupil learning – and as such, would appear to have neither merit nor worth.

However, the concept of 'evaluation' is not just limited to notions of merit and worth and Stufflebeam and Coryn (2014) have provided an extended definition of evaluation, which they describe as: 'the systematic process of delineating, obtaining, reporting, and applying descriptive and judgmental information about some subject's merit, worth, probity, feasibility, safety, significance, and or equity' (p. 14).

In the context of the evidence-based school these terms could be interpreted as the following.

- **Probity** – was the decision a product of a 'conscientious, explicit and judicious' process? Was the decision implemented ethically and with probity?
- **Feasibility** – does the intervention or change use up more resources than available or are there 'political' considerations regarding certain stakeholders which make the intervention 'impractical'.
- **Safety** – are those engaging with the intervention – be it pupils, staff or stakeholder vulnerable to harm, for example, physical or psychological.
- **Significance** – what is the potential of interventions and its importance within the context of an individual department or school? On the other hand, some decision interventions have a relevance far beyond department or school and may apply in other settings. As such, a key question for the evidence-based school leader when evaluating the outcomes of a decision is whether the associated intervention is scalable and could it work in other, quite different, situations.
- **Equity** – this can include: provision to all; access for all; equal participation; impact on different groups. Are only certain groups going to benefit from the decision or intervention?

Conducting an evaluation

In this section a number of approaches to conducting an evaluation will be examined. First, the section will look at an approach known as After Action Review (AAR). Second, consideration will be given to how logic models and theories and action can be used as the basis for conducting an evaluation. Third, how 'contribution' analysis may be particularly helpful in the complex environment of a school.

After Action Reviews

Initially developed by the US Army, an After Action Review (AAR) is a group process which is designed to provide a systematic procedure to review incidents, events and projects, and identify the lessons to be learned. Indeed, anything can be evaluated that has some basis on which it can be evaluated – the induction process for new staff, the transition arrangements for new Year 7 pupils – using the AAR process. The AAR consists of four steps:

1. What did we set out to do?
2. What actually happened?
3. Why did it happen?
4. What are we going to do next time?

What are the key features of an AAR?

The key features of an AAR can be seen in Figure 10.1, which has been devised by adapting and amending materials developed by the National Institute for Health Research (see Bray et al., 2013).

AAR Action	Outcomes
When	AAR should be performed after each identifiable event within a project or process, for example, the introduction of department-wide approaches to retrieval practice
How	Often AARs can be conducted informally and take around 15–30 minutes. On other occasions, it may be desirable to bring someone in to help facilitate the process, say another head of department
Participants	It should involve, if at all possible, everyone who was involved in the project – teachers, classroom assistants and other support staff
What the AAR aims to do	Find out what worked, find out what didn't work and identify suggestions as to what could be done differently next time
What it is not	AAR is not about solving things, or assigning blame
Ground rules	AAR should take place in a 'safe-environment' where individual participants are confident they can make a full contribution to the review
What is suitable for an AAR?	Basically, anything that involves a project or event and has some basis on which it can be evaluated, e.g. a scheme of work; a new type of CPD event; or process for recruiting staff
Outcomes of an AAR	These can be informal, for example, on-the-spot learning for those involved in the AAR. Or it can be more formal, with the AAR being documented and shared with others within the school

Figure 10.1 How to conduct an After Action Review (adapted from Bray et al., 2013)

Having detailed how to conduct an AAR, it is important to emphasise the following points. An AAR should not be overly time-consuming and should be able to be completed within 15–30 minutes. AARs also need to be conducted in a 'safe-environment' that allows colleagues to be open about what worked and what did not work, without having a concern that they will be blamed. Ideally, everyone who was involved in the project or intervention should take part in the review as this will provide access to a diverse range of perspectives. Finally, it is possible to use AARs for a range of projects, for example, a one-day staff development event or an evaluation at the end of an academic year of a major school-wide or multi-academy trust policy. Figure 10.2 provides a provisional AAR template which could be used to both frame the discussion and capture the outcomes of that discussion.

Event/Project

Participants

Date

AAR led by AAR Questions

- *What did we set out to do?*
- *What was the project leader's intent?*
- *What was the plan?*
- *Was there anything missing?*

- *What actually happened?*
- *What took place?*
- *Who was involved?*
- *Where did it happen?*
- *When did it happen?*
- *How did it happen?*

- *Why did it happen?*
- *What worked?*
- *What didn't work?*

- *What are we going to do next time?*
- *What worked this time that might not work next time?*
- *What didn't work this time that might work next time?*
- *What are we going to do differently instead?*
- *How are we going to share our learning with others*

Figure 10.2 After Action Review template

Making the most of an AAR

To ensure lessons learned from an AAR are disseminated within the organisation (school or multi-academy trust), Weick and Sutcliffe (2011), drawing upon the work of the Wildland Fire Lessons Learner Centre, suggest the following questions are asked in what they call an AAR 'rollup':

1. What was the most notable success at the incident that others may learn from?
2. What were the most difficult challenges faced and how were they overcome?
3. What changes, additions or deletions are recommended to wildland fire training curriculums?
4. What issues were not resolved to your satisfactions and need further review? Based on what was learned, what is your recommendations for resolution.

(Weick and Sutcliffe, 2011: 145)

As such, AARs are an attempt to support the development of more mindful action, through the use of systematic processes to review projects and identify lessons. When used well, AARs have the potential to bring about in a time-effective manner a range of marginal gains across the school, which hopefully will benefit pupils, staff and other stakeholders. Indeed, there is some evidence that AARs can improve group effectiveness. Tannenbaum and Cerasoli (2013) undertook a systematic review of the use of After Action Reviews with individuals and groups in a number of diverse settings. From 46 samples ($N = 2136$) Tannenbaum and Cerasoli found that, on average, debriefs improve effectiveness over a control group by approximately 25% ($d = .67$). Average effect sizes were similar for teams and individuals, across simulated and real settings, for within- or between-group control designs, and for medical and non-medical samples. However, the important thing to note is that this 20–25% improvement in individual and team performance requires properly conducted debriefs.

Evaluation and contribution analysis

Chapter 8 examined how logic models and theories of change could be used to help aggregate different sources of evidence. Attention now turns to how evidence-based school leaders can use both logic models and theories to help them evaluate the outcome of a decision. To help with the task, this section will draw upon of the work of Mayne (2012), who has developed the notion of 'contribution analysis' (CA). Mayne states that:

> CA is based on the existence of, or more usually, the development of a postulated theory of change for the intervention being examined. The analysis examines and tests this theory against logic and the evidence available from results observed and the various assumptions behind the theory of change, and examines other influencing factors. The analysis either confirms – verifies – the postulated theory of change or suggests revisions in the theory where the reality appears otherwise. (p. 271)

Mayne (2012) goes on to argue there are three different – and non-mutually exclusive – levels at which a CA can be undertaken: minimalist contribution analysis; contribution analysis of direct influence; and, contribution analysis of indirect influence.

Minimalist contribution analysis: At this initial level there is an attempt to further refine the logic model, whilst at the same time confirming the 'expected outputs were delivered' (Mayne, 2011: 85). In other words, were the resources made available; did the planned-for activities occur; and did the target audience attend and participate, with the anticipated outcomes simply being stated as a given? For example, after extensive consultation a school introduces a new homework and marking policy, which is largely designed to reduce teacher workload. Policy statements and guidance documents are produced, training sessions are held with relevant school staff. At the end of the year it is assumed that the new policy has led to the desired reduction in workload.

Contribution analysis of direct influence: Building upon a minimalist analysis, evidence is sought that the anticipated results in the realm of the direct influence of the theory of change have been observed. As such, evidence is sought that the intervention was directly responsible for bringing about those results, as well as what other influencing factors may have been at work. In other words, at the end of the year there may be a survey of teacher workloads that seeks to find out whether the changes in the homework and marking policy and supporting activities led to new knowledge and skills *vis-à-vis* assessment practice. Did these changes in knowledge and skills lead to changes in behaviour which resulted in actual evidenced reductions in teacher workload? Evidence is also sought as to what other factors were at work in influencing teacher workload.

Contribution analysis of indirect influence: As Mayne (2011) notes, at this level the indirect factors impacting upon our theory of change are explored. The anticipated intermediate outcomes of the theory of change, alongside whether the assumptions underpinning the theory of change are scrutinised. Were new knowledge skills acquired, were new behaviours exhibited? It is also necessary to check out the influence of other factors. For example, factors other than homework and assessment policy can impact upon teacher workload and these could vary from the appointment of new members of staff to the senior team, relatively poor examinations results in the previous year, changes in syllabuses.

However, it needs to be noted that contribution analysis should be conducted in a way that is consistent with the principles of evidence-based practice in being conscientious, explicit and judicious. As such it should be clear that as Mayne (2011) states: 'Contribution analysis is not about finding convenient evidence to back pet theories' (p. 87) and that the attributes of a credible contribution statement would include:

- a well-articulated context of the intervention and discussion of other influencing factors;
- a plausible theory of change (no obvious flaws) which is not disproved;
- a description of the implemented activities, resulting outputs and observed outcomes;
- the results of the contribution analysis;
- the evidence in a support of the assumptions behind the key links in the theory of change;
- a discussion of the roles of the other influencing factors; and
- a discussion of the quality of the evidence provided, noting weaknesses.

(Mayne, 2011: 87)

Making the most of success

Gino and Pisano (2011) argue that very many leaders fail to get a deep understanding of what has contributed to a success. Ironically, and as Gino and Pisano argue, success can be the forerunner of failure by getting in the way of learning at both the organisational and individual level. First, successful leaders can attribute the success to their skills, knowledge and expertise rather than acknowledge the role of circumstances or just plain luck. Second, success can lead to overconfidence and that all that is needed to remain successful is to continue to do what has always been done. Third, people in general have a predisposition not to look into the causes of good performance.

Gino and Pisano (2011) go on to identify five ways in which organisations (schools) can avoid some of these problems. These are:

- 'Celebrate success but examine it' – so if there is an unexpected improvement in examination results, investigate what happened with the same attention to detail as you would apply if examination results had unexpectedly fallen.
- 'Use the right time horizon' – make sure you are clear about the lag between cause and effect, between action and reaction. For example, the benefits of Lesson Study for teacher professional learning and subsequent changes in practice may take several cycles or years to become evident.
- 'Recognise that replication is not learning.' For example, just because something has worked within one school within a multi-academy trust – say a homework policy – does not mean that by trying to replicate that in other schools it will be a success. It is necessary to identify those factors that contributed to the success which are 'controllable' and those which are 'outside of your control'. As Gino and Pisano (2011) state 'if the chief lessons of a successful project is a list of things to do the same the next time, consider the exercise the failure' (p. 74).
- 'If it ain't broke, experiment' – in the context of schools this can be challenging. On the one hand, by experimentation we check out our underpinning assumptions and theories of action about what we need to do to bring about favourable outcomes. On the other hand, by conducting experiments we potentially place pupils at risk of achieving less favourable learning outcomes.

- 'Institute systematic project reviews' – after each project, intervention or innovation undertake a systematic review which looks at the desired outcomes and the reasons for those outcomes, in order to make recommendations for the future (see previous section on After Action Reviews).

Learning from failure

Unfortunately, not every decision, intervention or change will be a success, although as already noted success may be its forerunner. Sometimes, it will be necessary to acknowledge that an innovation has not been successful and has failed. Whilst the temptation is to luxuriate in successes and forget failures, it is important to have structured processes in place to help learn from failure (or relative lack of success). As Birkinshaw and Haas state, 'one of the most important and most deeply entrenched reasons why established companies struggle to grow is fear of failure ... [with] a risk-averse culture as key obstacle to innovation' (2016: 90).

To aid individuals and companies with the task of learning from failure, Birkinshaw and Haas (2016) have outlined a three-step approach which can be easily adopted for use at departmental, school or multi-academy trust level to help evidence-based school leaders learn from failure. 'First, study individual projects that did not pan out and gather as many insights as possible from them. Second, crystallise those insights and spread them across the organisation. Third, do a corporate-level survey to make sure that your overall approach is yielding all the benefits it should' (p. 90).

The first step involves getting colleagues to look back on interventions and innovations which have not been successful. Birkinshaw and Haas (2016) argue that for many organisations (and individuals) this does not come naturally, with colleagues expressing a preference to look to the future and not back to the past. To offset this problem, Birkinshaw and Haas have developed a worksheet which identifies all the sources of costs and benefits that might come about from a failed project or intervention, which has been amended so that it sits more easily within a school context (see Figure 10.3).

Birkinshaw and Haas (2016) argue that the real organisational (school or multi-academy trust) benefit from failure comes when the learning from that failure is shared across the organisation. As such, it is argued that this requires the organisation (department, school or

---

THE PROJECT REVIEW WORKSHEET

Briefly describe a recent failed project or activity you were involved in:

Benefits	**Costs**
What have we learned about our pupils', pupils parents', staff's needs and preferences and our current school context?	What were costs of the project – staffing, materials, financial and time?
Should we change any of our assumptions?	
What insights have we gained into the future of the school?	What were the external costs?
How should we adjust, if at all, our school development plan?	Did we damage the school's reputation in the local area, regionally or nationally?
	Have we weakened our position to attract pupils, staff and funding?
What have we discovered about the way we work together?	What were the internal costs?
How effective are our school processes, structure, and culture?	Did the project damage school/team morale or cost too much attention at the expense of other projects?
	Was there any cultural fallout?
	Were relationships unnecessarily undermined?
How did we grow our skills individually and as a team?	
Did the project increase relational trust and goodwill?	
Were any developmental needs highlighted?	
Key insights and takeaways	

Figure 10.3 A project/intervention review worksheet to learn from failure (adapted from Birkinshaw and Haas, 2016: 92)

multi-academy trust) to allow lessons from failure to contribute into existing processes, such as the departmental or school development plan. Furthermore, by having difficult but positive conversations about failure this creates the conditions to generate relational trust, which is so important for school improvement (Bryk and Schneider, 2002). This also creates the conditions by which colleagues may wish to be involved in more difficult and challenging projects. Birkinshaw and Haas argue that organisational leaders need to be brought together on a regular basis to discuss their failures, and they suggest the use of what they call the Triple F process. Birkinshaw and Haas state: 'These reviews work best when they are fast and to the point; take place frequently, through good times and bad; are forward looking, with an emphasis on learning' (p. 92).

Birkinshaw and Haas (2016) stress that the final step involves stepping back to see whether the organisational approach to failure is making the most of the opportunities for learning. Is the department, school or multi-academy trust learning from every new innovation which it has introduced over the last year (or academic year)? Is the department, school or multi-academy trust learning from every unsuccessful intervention or innovation? Have the lessons from failure being shared across the department, school or multi-academy trust? Are these interventions delivering improved pupil outcomes – cognitive or affective – or enhanced staff well-being?

However, to make the most of the Birkinshaw and Haas (2016) process it essential that evidence-based school leaders create a psychologically safe environment which allows colleagues to speak up about existing or pending failures. Edmondson (2011) identifies a number of practices that leaders could adopt which are likely to promote a psychologically safe environment. These practices include:

- Frame the work accurately – there needs to be both a common understanding of the types of failure and why the learning from failure is important.
- Embrace messengers – reward those who come forward with bad news about projects and ask them to work out what can be done to resolve the situation.
- Acknowledge limits – be open about what you think you know and don't know. State how you have contributed to mistakes and accept responsibility for your actions.
- Invite participation – actively seek the views of stakeholders and others involved. Encourage individuals to undertake small 'Plan–Do–Study–Act' experiments, which have multiple iterations.
- Set boundaries and hold people accountable to be clear about what is acceptable and what is not – so reporting on when things have gone wrong is acceptable, reckless conduct or breach of professional codes of conduct is not.

(Edmondson, 2011: 50)

Assessing your performance as an evidence-based practitioner

The next stage of assessing and evaluating the outcome of the decision is to consider how well you have performed as an evidence-based practitioner. In Chapter 11 there will be a separate discussion about how to engage in a self-assessment of how well the school is doing in using evidence.

In undertaking a self-assessment of performance as an evidence-based practitioner there are six basic questions:

1. How well am I doing at translating a practical issue or problem into answerable questions?
2. How well am I doing at systematically searching for and retrieving the evidence?
3. How well am I doing at critically judging the trustworthiness of and relevance of the evidence?
4. How well am I doing at weighing and pulling together the evidence?
5. How well am I doing at incorporating the best available evidence into the decision-making process?
6. How well am I doing at evaluating the outcomes of the decision taken to increase the likelihood of a favourable outcome?

Each question is supported by a number of sub-questions, which have been informed by Straus et al. (2011) and Dawes et al. (2005).

1. How well am I doing at translating a practical issue or problem into answerable questions?
    a. Can I identify problems of practice which are best suited to being addressed through the use of evidence-based practice?
    b. Can I translate problems of practice into well-formulated and answerable questions, by using techniques such as PICOT, CIMO and SPICE (see Chapter 3)?
    c. Can I use techniques such as 'so what?' and FINER to help identify the most important problem of practice?
    d. Can I identify knowledge gaps and develop strategies to address those knowledge gaps?

2. How well am I doing at systematically searching for and retrieving the evidence?
    a. Can I develop a carefully thought out evidence search strategy to access multiple sources of evidence?
    b. Can I articulate my own current 'theory of action'?

    c. Can I use a range of techniques to access different sources of evidence?

    d. Am I becoming more efficient in my search for evidence?

3. How well am I doing at critically judging the trustworthiness of and relevance of the evidence?

    a. Can I critically appraise evidence, be it research or other sources of evidence?

    b. Am I becoming more effective in applying 'critical appraisal techniques' when reviewing the research evidence?

    c. Am I becoming more knowledgeable about some of the key terms used in educational research, for example, effect sizes and confidence intervals?

    d. Can I tell theory from dogma, and data from myth and folklore?

4. How well am I doing at weighing and pulling together the evidence?

    a. Can I use different techniques, such as tables and fishbone diagrams, and aggregate multiple sources of evidence?

    b. Can I write critically appraised summaries of the evidence?

    c. Can I use logic models and theories of change to help understand relationships between different sources of evidence?

    d. Can I assess the appropriateness of the appraised evidence to the original problem of practice?

    e. Can I give due weight to different sources of evidence?

5. How well am I doing at incorporating the best available evidence into the decision-making process?

    a. Can I identify the potential costs and benefits of a decision?

    b. Can I articulate different levels of recommendation – from strong to weak – as to whether to act on the basis of the evidence and proceed with an intervention?

    c. Am I using a rigorous process to try to minimise the impact of cognitive biases?

    d. Can I identify the appropriate scale of implementation of the intervention?

    e. Can I identify a clear and deliverable action plan to implement the decision?

6. How well am I doing at evaluating the outcomes of the decision taken to increase the likelihood of a favourable outcome?
   a. Can I identify between the merit and worth of an intervention?
   b. Can I use logic models and theories of change to help evaluate the outcomes of a decision?
   c. Do I actively seek to learn from both success and failure?
   d. Am I critically self-assessing my own performance as an evidence-based practitioner?
   e. Am I sharing my 'new' knowledge and expertise with others?

Identifying the implications of the answers to the above questions will depend very much on where you are as an evidence-based school leader in developing your own skills as an evidence-based practitioner. In addition, it will also depend upon the prevailing 'evidence-use' culture within your school. That said, the following may be worthy of consideration.

1. If you have responded to the above questions predominantly with YES answers, then great. Think about what is working and try to do more of it, and if something is not working, stop doing it and do something else instead.
2. Avoid being intimidated by the above list of questions; it is unlikely that you will have answered YES to a majority of the questions. Focus on what you can control and is within your domain of influence. Maybe start with trying to identify important but non-urgent problems of practice.
3. If you answered NO to any of the questions, then pose yourself the question: why did I answer NO? What's going on? Are there things I could stop doing which are getting in the way of my development in evidence-based practice?

Becoming expert as an evidence-based practitioner is not something that happens overnight. It will take time, effort and patience. It is not a quick fix for a current problem – but rather is an approach that needs to be embedded in day-to-day practice. So having outlined the different stages of the evidence-based practice process, it is now necessary to consider how the evidence-based school leader can go about the process of facilitating a school culture that is rich in evidence use and is embedded in the day-to-day work of the school.

Summary and key points

- At its simplest, evaluation involves the systematic assessment of the merit and worth of a decision.
- However, an evaluation could be extended to include notions of probity, feasibility, safety, significance and equity.
- After Action Reviews provide a structured way to conduct an evaluation of a decision.
- Contribution analysis provides a way of using logic models and theories of change to help distinguish between different levels of contribution to change: minimal, direct influence and indirect influence.
- There is no guarantee that success will lead to learning, so appropriate strategies need to be put in place, for example, choosing the right time horizon.
- It is also important that relevant and suitable strategies are put in place to help learn from failure.
- To make the most of being an evidence-based practitioner requires a structured process of self-assessment.
- To become both skilled and wise in the use of evidence-based practice will take time, effort and commitment.

References

Birkinshaw, J. and Haas, M. (2016) 'Increase your return on failure', *Harvard Business Review*, *94* (5): 88–93.

Bray, K., Laker, L., Ilott, I. and Gerrish, K. (2013) 'After Action Review: an evaluation tool'. *Bridging the gap between knowledge and practice: Your starter for 10: No. 9.* CLAHRC for South Yorkshire, NHS National Institute for Health Research. Available at: www.cebma.org/wp-content/uploads/Starter-for-10-No-9-Final-05-03-2013.pdf (accessed 4 May 2018).

Bryk, A. and Schneider, B. (2002) *Trust in Schools: A Core Resource for Improvement.* New York: Russell Sage Foundation.

Dawes, M., Summerskill, W., Glasziou, P., Cartabellotta, A., Martin, J., Hopayian, K., Porzsolt, F., Burls, A. and Osborne, J. (2005) 'Sicily statement on evidence-based practice', *BMC Medical Education*, *5* (1): 1.

Edmondson, A.C. (2011) 'Strategies for learning from failure', *Harvard Business Review*, *89* (4): 48–55.

Gino, F. and Pisano, G. (2011) 'Why leaders don't learn from success', *Harvard Business Review*, *89* (4): 68–74.

Mayne, J. (2011) 'Contribution analysis: addressing cause and effect', in K. Forss, M. Marra and R. Schwartz (eds), *Evaluating the Complex: Attribution, Contribution, and Beyond*. London: Routledge. pp. 53–97.

Mayne, J. (2012) 'Contribution analysis: coming of age?', *Evaluation*, 18 (3): 270–80.

Straus, S., Glasziou, P., Richardson, S. and Haynes, B. (2011) *Evidence-Based Medicine: How to Practise and Teach It*, 2nd edn. Edinburgh: Churchill Livingstone Elsevier.

Stufflebeam, D.L. and Coryn, C. (2014) *Evaluation Theory, Models and Applications*, 2nd edn. San Francisco, CA: Jossey–Bass.

Tannenbaum, S.I. and Cerasoli, C.P. (2013) 'Do team and individual debriefs enhance performance? a meta-analysis', *Human Factors*, 55 (1): 231–45.

Weick, K. and Sutcliffe, K. (2011) *Managing the Unexpected: Resilient Performance in an Age of Uncertainty*, 2nd edn. San Francisco, CA: Jossey–Bass.

11

LEADING THE EVIDENCE-BASED SCHOOL

Chapter outline

The chapter starts by examining different types of school culture regarding evidence use. This is followed by a brief look at the research on the use of research evidence in decision-making and the importance of capability, motivation and opportunity (Langer et al., 2016). The chapter then draws upon the work of Brown (2015) to devise a checklist that school leaders can use to help create an evidence-based culture within their school. Next, the chapter explores a number of aspects of the checklist, including: promoting a vision of the research and evidence-based school; how to be consensual and engage in shared decision-making; how to stop doing some things; continuing to support the importance of teachers' expertise; and, how to help people develop the right set of skills to support the use of research and evidence. Finally, the chapter will look at a number of ways in which a school can assess its readiness to engage in evidence-based practice.

Key words: *research, quality improvement, evidence-based practice, vision, consultation*

Differences in the use of evidence

A recent report sponsored by the Department for Education in England suggests there is a significant difference between the rhetoric and reality of evidence-informed teaching within schools, with a number of schools appearing to adopt the rhetoric of evidence-informed teaching, whilst at the same time not embedding research and evidence into their day-to-day practice (Coldwell et al., 2017). Of the 23 schools involved in the report, only six could be described as having a whole-school approach to research and evidence, with another seven schools where the head and senior leadership were proactive in their approach to a culture supporting the use of research and evidence. Finally, there were 10 schools having an unengaged research evidence culture. This finding was particularly surprising given the attention to creating a balanced sample of schools who said they were engaged with research evidence. The difference between unengaged and highly engaged research evidence cultures is illustrated in Table 11.1.

Table 11.1 Categorisation of school evidence cultures

Weak evidence culture	School leadership evidence culture	Whole-school evidence culture
No dedicated time to engage with research evidence	Dedicated time for senior leaders	Evidence engagement embedded within time allocated for school improvement practices
Narrow culture focused on immediate imperatives		Open learning culture, focusing on longer-term goals

(Continued)

Table 11.1 (Continued)

Weak evidence culture	School leadership evidence culture	Whole-school evidence culture
Inconsistent and/or low level of engagement with research evidence across the school	Senior leaders filter research evidence	Senior leaders filter research evidence, staff engage with this critically
Few staff motivated, skilled and confident in engaging with evidence	Senior leaders motivated, skilled and confident in engaging with evidence	Some staff in other groups motivated, skilled and confident in engaging with evidence; staff expect to engage with research to improve practice
Support structures – reading groups, research projects, learning communities – limited or unavailable	Support structures in place – reading groups, research projects, learning communities – that all staff are invited to engage in	Research evidence is part of routine processes, meetings, CPD and school improvement practices of the school
No or very limited informal policies and guidance on engaging with research evidence	Few informal policies and guidance on engaging with research evidence	Some informal policies and guidance on engaging with research evidence
Few or no research-related relationships with other schools and external organisations	School leader research-related relationships with other schools and external organisations	Research-related relationships with other schools and external organisations beyond the SLT in place in some cases

Source: Coldwell et al., 2017: 61

In order to help the evidence-based school leader to either close the 'rhetoric reality' gap or never let it emerge in the first place, the next part of the chapter will look at two separate though linked ways of thinking about how to lead and develop the research and evidence-based school. First comes a systematic review of the research on the use of research evidence in decision-making undertaken by Langer et al. (2016). This review is extremely useful as it provides a model of behaviour change and it also identifies a range of mechanisms that promote the use of evidence. Second, an analysis of a checklist for leading research and an evidence-informed school which was derived by Brown (2015) is explored.

The science of using science: researching the use of research evidence in decision-making – a systematic review

Langer et al. (2016) found that if research evidence is going to be used by individuals and teams, three conditions have to be met. Individuals and teams need to have the necessary skills and knowledge – i.e. capability – to engage with the research. Individuals and teams need to be motivated to engage with the research. Finally, individuals and teams will be need to have the opportunity to engage with the research. Accordingly, evidence-based leaders who attempt to promote a whole-school culture of evidence use will have to address all three conditions.

Langer et al. (2016) go on to identify six mechanisms (which they categorise as M1 to M6) that appear to be 'driving' interventions and bringing about behaviour change in the use of evidence:

- *M1 Awareness building*: Awareness for, and positive attitudes toward, evidence-informed decision-making (EIDM).
- *M2 Agree*: Building mutual understanding and agreement on policy-relevant questions and the kind of evidence needed to answer them.
- *M3 Communication and access*: Interaction between decision-makers and researchers.
- *M4 Interact*: Providing communication of, and access to, evidence.
- *M5 Skills*: Supporting decision-makers to develop skills in accessing and making sense of evidence.
- *M6 Structure and process*: Influencing decision-making structures and processes.

Combining these six mechanisms with Michie et al.'s (2011) model of the components of behaviour change – capability, motivation and opportunity – allowed Langer et al. to create the logic model shown in Figure 11.1.

For evidence-based school leaders this models show how different interventions, which may incorporate a single or number of mechanisms, influence evidence use. Designing leadership interventions and strategies that incorporate these mechanisms may lead to

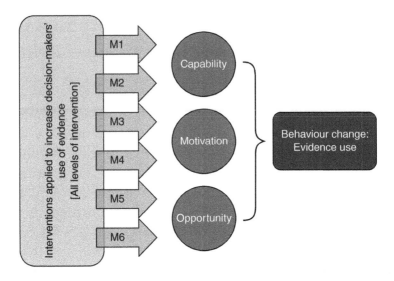

Figure 11.1 Logic model (Langer et al., 2016: 8)

changes in the capability, motivation and opportunity to use evidence, which then facilitates evidence use.

The main benefit of this logic model for the evidence-based school leader is that it focuses the mind on those actions and mechanisms which are going to impact upon the capacity, motivation and opportunity to use evidence. As such, developing and maintaining a whole-school culture of evidence requires a laser-like focus on developing colleagues' capacity, motivation and opportunity to use evidence – with a recognition that no one mechanism is going to bring about the desired result.

Accordingly, it may be useful to map the various elements of a whole-school evidence culture with the components of Michie et al.'s (2011) behaviour change model, which is illustrated in Table 11.2.

Table 11.2 Figure mapping a whole-school evidence culture against mechanisms, capability, opportunities and motivation-behaviour

Element	Mechanism	COM-B Components
Evidence engagement embedded within time allocated for school improvement practices	M6 Structure and process	Opportunity
Open learning culture focus on longer-term goals	M2 Agree M6 Structure and process	Motivation Opportunity

Element	Mechanism	COM-B Components
Senior leaders filter research, staff engage with this critically	M1 Awareness M4 Interact	Capability Motivation
Some staff in other groups motivated, skilled and confident in engaging with evidence, staff expect to engage with research	M6 Structure and process	Capability Motivation
Research evidence is part of routine processes, meetings, CPD and school improvement practices	M6 Structure and process M5 Skills	Opportunity Capability
Some informal policies and guidance on engaging with research evidence	M6 Structure and process	Opportunity Capability
Research-related relationships with other schools and external organisations beyond the SLT in place in some cases	M3 Communication and access	Opportunity Capability

Source: Based on Michie et al., 2011 and Coldwell et al., 2017

From this very brief analysis, it would appear that those school leaders who have created a whole-school evidence culture have used the full range of mechanisms identified by Langer et al. (2016), with these mechanisms appearing to come together to change colleagues' capacity, motivation and opportunity to engage with and use evidence.

Leading the use of research and evidence in schools – a checklist

Brown (2015) has produced a very useful checklist for school leaders wishing to develop a research and evidence-informed school culture. In this checklist Brown distinguishes between factors and overarching sub-actions which are 'transformational' in nature and enable research and evidence to be a core component of the work of the school. These 'transformational' actions are contrasted with those which are pupil-centred and focus upon using research and evidence to improve teaching and learning. These themes, factors and sub-actions are summarised in Figure 11.2.

Theme	Factor	Sub-action
Transformational	Does your approach to research and evidence demonstrate your own commitment as well as facilitate the efforts of others?	Promote a vision of a research- and evidence-informed school
		Make resources available
		Design and implement support structures
		Create time and space for such work
		Make it part of everyone's work (especially leaders)
		Model the use of research and evidence in decision-making
		Develop an enquiry habit of mind – look for new perspectives
		Seek out new information
		Explore new ways to tackle old problems
	Does your approach to research and evidence use have buy-in throughout the school?	Adopt a distributive approach to leadership
		Attend to the informal aspects of the school organisation
		Identify and influence key-opinion formers and shapers
		Seek to be consensual
Teaching and learning	Does your approach to research and evidence use 'start with the end in mind' and ensure that progress towards this end is tracked?	Articulate what success would look like
		Consider what will need to be done differently
		Question how things will be different for pupils and teachers
		How will you know things are different?
		Evaluate impact of any changes
		Engage in learning conversations – develop theories of action and develop and trial new actions
		Constantly refine processes and actions
		Stop doing some things
	Does your approach to research and evidence have teacher learning and practice at its core?	Continue to emphasise the importance of teacher-expertise
		Use data to help teachers refine their practice
		Create opportunities for collaborative learning both inside and outside of the school
		Continually focus on evidence
		Draw in external experience and knowledge/theory
		Develop protocols and ways of working
		Create facilitative arrangements
	Does your approach to research and evidence ensure that the right people are in the room?	Develop middle leaders who are interested in evidence-informed practice
		Identify research and evidence champions
		Involve people with the right mix of skills to support the use of research and evidence

Figure 11.2 Leading research and evidence use in schools – themes, factors and sub-actions (derived from Brown, 2015)

As useful as this checklist is; from the perspective of the evidence-based school leader it is important to acknowledge its limitations. First, as argued in Chapter 2, evidence-based school leadership is not limited to issues related to pedagogy and teaching and learning but extends to all aspects of the school. Second, Brown's checklist has been derived from a relatively narrow view of what is meant by evidence-informed practice (see Chapter 2). Third, the checklist does not make specific reference to ethical issues associated with evidence-based practice nor does it ensure any actions you take as a school-leader are right for your school and context. Finally, any checklist is only as good as the knowledge, skills and situational understanding which are used to implement it. That said, Brown's work provides a very handy starting point for school leaders wishing to initiate, implement and sustain an evidence-based school culture.

Each of the main factors and an associated sub-factor are now examined in more detail.

1: Does your approach to research and evidence demonstrate your own commitment as well as facilitate the efforts of others?

Promoting a vision of a research- and evidence-informed school

When promoting a vision of research and the evidence-informed/based school it is important that the evidence-based school leader is clear in his or her own mind of the distinction between research, quality improvement and evidence-based practice. By doing so, it will make it much easier to articulate to colleagues both the intended direction and how to get there. So, without wishing to get into the scientific paradigm wars, the following definitions are offered up to help get some critical purchase on what is meant by each term.

- *Research* can be defined as the process of creating new generalisable knowledge, and which could include both the generation and testing of hypotheses.
- *Quality improvement* can be defined as systematic, data-guided activities designed to bring about immediate improvements in local settings (Lynn et al., 2007).

- *Evidence-based practice* can be defined as the making of decisions through the conscientious, explicit and judicious use of the best available evidence from multiple sources in order to increase the likelihood of a favourable outcome. (Barends et al., 2014)

Accordingly, in the context of schools these terms could be repurposed to read something like: quality improvement seeks to improve the individual school or multi-academy trust, research generates new knowledge, and evidence-based practice allows educators to have, and use, the best available evidence when making a decision (Hicks, 2016: 1). The operational differences between these terms are summarised in Figure 11.3 using examples of typical activities that might be found in a research- or evidence-based school.

Type of activity	Examples
Research – the process of creating new generalisable knowledge, and which could include both the generation and testing of hypotheses	Participation in an Education Endowment Foundation randomised controlled trial in mathematics
	Working with a university department of education on a study into teachers' use of new technology
	Individual member of staff conducting doctoral research under the supervision of a higher education institution
Quality improvement – systematic, data-guided activities designed to bring about immediate improvements in local settings	Interviewing a range of colleagues about examination performance in a particular department and production of an associated action plan
	Making changes in pupil enrolment systems
	An internally devised school-based trial on a new approach to providing individual support prior to external examinations
Evidence-based practice – the making of decisions through the conscientious, explicit and judicious use of the best available evidence from multiple sources in order to increase the likelihood of a favourable outcome	Undertaking a review of existing evidence – research, school, stakeholders, personal experience – on graded lesson observations and making a decision on whether to move to a non-graded approach
	Undertaking a review of existing evidence – research, school, stakeholders, personal experience – on the effectiveness of marking homework and adopting a new school-wide policy

Figure 11.3 Examples of research, quality improvement and evidence-based practice

However, it should be abundantly clear that there are overlaps between the various terms. In England, the Education Endowment Foundation's *The DIY Evaluation Guide*, which uses the language of research (for example, interventions, measures, pre-tests, post-tests, random allocation, matched control groups, effect-sizes, analysis and reporting of results), is probably more akin to quality improvement than research. In the United States, Bryk et al. (2015), writing about the application of improvement science to education, state: 'Improvements typically entail a sequence of inquiries, where the results from each test of change offer guidance for the next test. Formally each test is akin to a small experiment; the overall arch of activity is an improvement investigation' (p. 16).

These overlaps between research, quality improvement and evidence-based practice have a number of ethical implications for how to go about being an evidence-based school leader. That said, at this stage it is enough to be aware of the differences between research, quality improvement and evidence-based practice and to be able to articulate them.

2:Does your approach to research and evidence use have buy-in throughout the school?

Seek to be consensual

School leadership and evidence-based practice are fundamentally about the same thing: decision-making (Collins and Coleman, 2017). Regardless of what decision is made, the decision-making process will add (or possibly subtract) to what Hargreaves and Fullan (2012) describe as the school's decisional-capital, which is:

> the capital that professionals acquire and accumulate through structured and unstructured experience, practice and reflection – capital that enables them to make wise judgments in circumstances where there is no fixed rule or incontrovertible evidence to guide them. Decisional capital is enhanced by drawing on the insights and experiences of colleagues in forming judgements over many occasions. In other words, in teaching and other professions social capital is actually an integral part of decisional capital, as well as an addition to it. (p. 93)

Accordingly, a major challenge for the evidence-based school leader is to try to establish how they will engage with colleagues in order to increase the decisional capital of the school. To do this, it will be necessary to be clear about the approach to be adopted towards evidence-based practice, decision-making and engagement with colleagues.

Amending the work of Senge et al. (1994) on building a shared vision, it is possible to come up with five strategies which the evidence-based school leader could use in engaging with colleagues. The five strategies are:

- **Telling** – the school leader knows what the evidence is and subsequent solution, and the school is going to have to agree with them.
- **Selling** – the school leader knows what the evidence is, but needs the school to 'buy-in' to the proposed solution.
- **Testing** – the school leader has an idea of what evidence is needed to address a problem of practice, but wants to check out the school's reaction.
- **Consulting** – the school leader has an idea about what the 'evidence' is, but wants input from the school stakeholders – internal and external – before proceeding.
- **Co-creating** – the school leaders and school stakeholders go through a collaborative process to appraise, access and assess the evidence and then come to a collective decision.

The continuum of these various strategies is illustrated in Figure 11.4. adapted from Senge et al (1994)

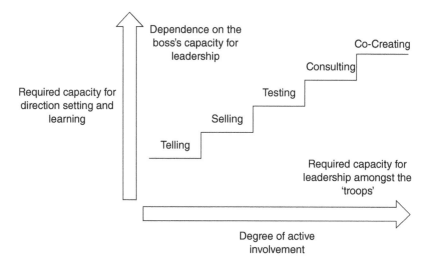

Figure 11.4 Decision-making strategies and the engagement of staff – amended from Senge et al (1994)

This continuum of engagement should help evidence-based school leaders think through how to engage in the decision-making process. Using the typology of engagement in decision-making should help evidence-based school leaders to be explicit about the decision-making process, and also allow colleagues who participate in the process to be clear in their expectations about their involvement. If expectations are aligned this is likely lead to an increase in the stock of decisional capital, rather than a decrease. It also means the rhetoric of evidence-based practice is likely to match the day-to-day reality in a school.

Furthermore, in the context of evidence-based school leadership it is possibly only the 'consulting' and 'co-creating' strategies that would appear to be consistent with the original meaning of evidence-based medicine. In the pioneering work of Sackett et al. (1996) there is an emphasis on shared decision-making, which prioritises the role of patients' rights, preferences, values and predicaments when making decisions about the care they are to receive. As such, an approach to school leadership and management that is based upon evidence-based practice requires the evidence-based school leader to actively engage with the holders of professional expertise and the views and preferences of stakeholders. Indeed, authentic evidence-based school leadership is not consistent with a general approach to decision-making, which involves school leaders telling or selling colleagues both the evidence and the solution.

It is now necessary to ask the question: what competences will the evidence-based school leader need to demonstrate in order to engage in shared decision-making? To help answer this question, attention will focus on the work of Edwards et al. (2004), who have developed a very useful checklist for general practitioners to display when making shared decisions with patients. This checklist has subsequently been amended to identify the competences an evidence-based school leader needs to display if they are to truly engage in evidence-based practice and is illustrated in Figure 11.5.

There are three aspects of the competences which are worthy of further consideration, and which if practised may lead to an increase in the school's decisional capital. First, the competences provide an easily amended checklist which can be used to engage with colleagues or others in shared decision-making. In particular, the competences make explicit the need to: define the problem; identify options;

Competence	Description
Define the problem	Clear specification of the problem of practice that requires a decision
Portray equipoise	Leaders and decision-makers may not have a clear preference about which option is best in the context
Portray options	One or more interventions and the option of no change if relevant
Provide information in preferred format	Information provided to other parties involved in the decision-making process in a way that is aligned to their preferences
Check understanding	Shared understanding of the range of options and information provided about them
Explore ideas, concerns and expectations	About the problem of practice, possible interventions, the alternatives and outcomes
Check role preference	That others involved in the decision-making accept the process and identify their decision-making role preference
Decision-making	Involving others to the extent to which they desire to be involved
Deferment if necessary	Deferring the decision and resulting action, if appropriate
Review arrangements	A specified time to review the decision

Figure 11.5 Competences required for shared decision-making (adapted from Edwards et al., 2004: 347)

explore the implications of the decision; check shared understanding of the situation; involve colleagues in the decision-making process; and, then, make follow-up arrangements. The list of competences required for shared decision-making thus provides a useful tool to reflect upon the decision-making processes and identify areas for development. As such, it has the potential to provide a mechanism to help engage in the deliberate practice of decision-making.

Second, the notion of equipoise is central to the process, in terms of maintaining a sense of balance, if not neutrality, when outlining the different options available and their respective advantages and disadvantages. By displaying authentic equipoise, this should lead to increased levels of engagement by colleagues in shared decision-making, leading to increased levels of decisional capital emerging, as colleagues feel they have an authentic part to play in the decision-making process.

Third, given the increasing emphasis within England on pupil voice and engaging with pupils, understanding the nature of shared decision-making and the associated processes may be an essential first step in helping a school develop opportunities for 'genuine' pupil voice. Indeed, this notion of accessing pupil voice is an essential component of processes that an evidence-based school leader needs to engage in.

3:Does your approach to research and evidence use 'start with the end in mind' and ensure that progress towards this end is tracked?

Stop doing some things

One of the barriers that you will face when trying to engage colleagues with evidence-based practice is that it can be perceived as 'just another thing to do' (DeLuca et al., 2017). So it is important to ensure that when introducing 'research and evidence-based' approaches an attempt is made to stop doing other things. Indeed, there is a 'rule of thumb' that could be adopted which states that for every 'new' thing which is introduced into a school, the school should 'stop' doing at least one other existing practice. Indeed, it could be argued that schools will need to stop doing at least two or three other things, as introducing and implementing new things will invariably be a time-consuming process.

So then, what does the school stop doing? It is tempting to come up with a list of the top ten things a school should stop doing. However, that is a judgement that only the leaders of a school can take and is situated within the circumstances of the school. That said, there are a number of analytical tools that can be used to help prioritise those things that make a difference and identify those things that do not. One such tool is the RAMMP matrix developed by General Electric (Ulrich et al., 2002) which can help identify actions that are making little difference to pupil learning, staff well-being or the sustainability of the school or multi-academy trust.

- Reports – is this report to the senior team, governing body or board of trustees necessary?
- Approvals – does this decision need to be approved by so many people, or can people have a delegated budget?
- Meetings – why are we having this meeting and do we need it? If so, who needs to attend the meeting, do they need to attend it for the whole meeting?

- Measures – what performance measures have you in place, do they contribute to bringing about improvement?
- Policies and practices – do processes such as lesson observations or CPD events help people to improve, or do they just get in the way?

As such, the RAMMP process could be applied at most levels of the school and is illustrated in Figure 11.6.

	Department	Key Stage	School	MAT	Could it be
Reports					A. Eliminated
Approvals					B. Partially eliminated
Meetings					C. Done less often
Measures					D. Delegated downward
Policies					E. Done in a less complicated manner
Practices					F. Other

Figure 11.6 Application of the RAMMP method to schools (adapted from Ulrich et al., 2002)

To make the most of the RAMMP method and bring together colleagues from different functions of the school – be it teaching or support and who are at different levels of the school's hierarchy – we need to ask the following question: do we need to keep doing these tasks in the same old way? (Senge et al., 1999). However, it is essential that this is done in a 'safe' environment, where no personal blame is attached to the tasks that would appear to have run their course.

4:Does your approach to research and evidence have teacher learning and practice at its core?

Continue to emphasise the importance of teacher expertise

Throughout this book there has been an emphasis on evidence-based practice being not just about teaching and learning. However, it would be wrong not to consider the relationship between research evidence and different practices of teaching. As Hargreaves and Stone-Johnson (2009) state: 'The practice of teaching is complex. It is not mechanical or predictable. Nor does it follow simple rules. Indeed, teaching is an assemblage of many practices, each affecting, drawing on, or intersecting with the others. Each of these practices relates to evidence in its own distinctive way' (p. 91).

These different practices of teaching and their relationship to evidence for educational improvement are summarised in Figure 11.7.

Practice of teaching	Description	Role of evidence in evidence-informed change
Technical	Teaching involves the mastery and employment of a technical skill	Evidence can show how differing teacher behaviours and practices – wait-time, pacing and coverage of content – impact on the classroom learning challenge of teachers' work. Teacher development should be based on scientific evidence.
Intellectual	Teaching involves increasingly complex work that is highly cognitive and intellectual	'Evidence, rather, becomes a source for improving student learning through enhancing teacher learning about effects of their teaching; strengths and needs of their students; and alternative strategies that have externally validated record of success' (p. 94).
Experiential	Teacher understandings of their problems are deeper than offered by theorists	'Scientific evidence provides a legitimate and at the same time, imperfect base for professional judgment and knowledge' (p. 95). As such, it is necessary to combine knowledge-for-practice with knowledge-in-practice to create knowledge-of-practice.
Emotional	Teaching is an embedded practice that produces emotional alteration in the stream of experience – giving emotional culmination to thoughts, feelings and actions (amended from Denzin, 1984: 96)	Evidence-based changes need to include emotional goals and processes of learning (empathy, resilience, self-esteem) as well as emotional conditions for learning (safety and security). Evidence-based education must go through authentic rather than superficial processes, with authentic processes strengthening the relationships of the groups and communities that produce it.
Moral and ethical	Teaching is never amoral – it always involves ethical and moral practices, either in a good or bad way. Teachers promote and produce virtues such as justice, fairness, respect and responsibility	Requires judgement about how evidence is produced, used and interpreted in relation to the moral nature, the moral duties and obligations of teachers. Colleagues to hold others to account within professional learning communities for the integrity of their practice and the evidence supporting their work.

(Continued)

Figure 11.7 (Continued)

Practice of teaching	Description	Role of evidence in evidence-informed change
Political	Teaching always in some measure involves a relationship of power	Given selective use of evidence by government, it is essential that teachers have the professional capacity to review, critique, make informed decisions and adapt the evidence accordingly.
Situated	Teaching varies in what is taught, who is taught and how learning is assessed	For evidence-based improvement to be effective contextual contingencies need to be embraced, which acknowledge situational challenges alongside realistic timelines for change.
Cultural	As teaching practices become ingrained and accepted, they form part of the professional culture of teaching, i.e. the attitudes, beliefs, values and the patterns of relationship between teachers	'Evidence-based educational initiatives require significant investment in the culture building process. They can also push collaborative teacher cultures to focus more persistently on the student learning needs, especially when this might create professional discomfort for teachers themselves. A systematic connection between culture and evidence-based inquiry in caring and trusting relationships of ethical integrity is at the heart of one of the most powerful principles of implementing evidence-based improvement: professional learning communities' (p. 103).

Figure 11.7 The relationship between different practices of education and the role of evidence in evidence-informed change (based on Hargreaves and Stone-Johnson, 2009)

So, what are the implications of these different conceptions of the practices of teaching for evidence-based school leadership? First, given the variety of practices of teaching it is important to reflect on which of these practices most closely mirrors your own view of teaching and reflect on how that view will impact upon on your approach to developing evidence-informed practice within your school. In particular, it is essential to challenge your own 'practice of teaching' and its relationship with evidence and acknowledge the inherent weaknesses of your approach.

Second, although focused on teaching, these different practices of teaching also have implications for leading the school. For example, do you regard leadership as a form of 'technical practice' where you just have to do what the research evidence tells you? Or do you regard leading a school as a moral and ethical endeavour, where doing the right thing is valued over and above doing things right? In other words, the various practices of teaching can be used as a framework to think about your own practice of leadership.

Third, given that within your school there will be a diverse range of views on the practice of teaching and leading, it may be necessary to do the following: identify which model or models colleagues are using to describe their practice and then adapt your use of 'evidence' to one that is consistent to that paradigm. In doing so, this may provide you with the opportunity to engage in ongoing dialogue rather than engage in the 'dialogue of the deaf'. If you do this, you will keep the conversation going and hopefully each of you will learn from one another.

Finally, leading evidence-based change is clearly a complex and challenging task that will require a significant personal investment of time, no little skill, and large dollops of patience. As such, given the challenges and complexities of evidence-based, or evidence-informed change it would be wrong to expect evidence-based practices to provide 'wonder-cures' for all of a school's ailments.

5:Does your approach to research and evidence ensure that the right people are in the room?

Developing middle leaders who are interested in evidence-informed practice within your school

In seeking to support and develop an evidence-based culture within your school, you may be tempted to appoint an individual to the role of the school research champion or research lead. Recently, Bennett (2016) looked in some detail at the different roles of the school research lead, be it gatekeeper, consigliere, devil's advocate, auditor or project manager. Bennett goes on to identify a number of factors that appear to be essential for the success of the school research lead. First, the school leader must be genuinely committed to the use of evidence and research within their school. Appointing a School Research Lead (SRL) just because the school down the road has done so is not going to create the conditions for success. Second, the SRL must be given time to do the role; it's not enough for it to be bolted on to the role of an already heavily burdened colleague. Protected time should be allocated to support the role. Third, it is necessary to ensure that the work of the SRL is given sufficient status and profile, with research and evidence being appropriately prioritised in both the school's development plan and the school's day-to-day business. Finally, it is essential to appoint the right person as the SRL. Just because someone is keen and enthusiastic or has just done a postgraduate degree does not make them automatically suitable. Indeed, the SRL will need to be able to deploy a mix of generic and specific skills to support the use of research and evidence within the school.

So, in looking to appoint someone to the role of the SRL in your school it would be worthwhile to try to identify both the generic and specific skills necessary to be successful in the role. However, given the relative newness of the role within schools, there is little, if any, research on what it takes to be a successful SRL. With this in mind, the work of Kislov et al. (2016) on knowledge brokers in healthcare is extremely helpful as they identify three roles for knowledge brokers (school research leaders): information management; linkage and exchange; and, capacity building and the development of associated skills. Table 11.3 summarises aspects of the knowledge brokering role and the skills required for their realisation.

Table 11.3 The roles and skills required for knowledge brokering

	Information management	Linkage and exchange	Capacity building
Generic skills	Understanding the cultures of both the research and decision-making environments		
	Ability to establish credibility		
	Ability to assess the context of implementation		
	Communication skills		
	Problem-solving skills		
	Project management skills		
Specific skills	Searching and retrieving evidence	Mediation skills	Teaching skills
	Appraising evidence	Negotiation skills	Mentoring skills
	Synthesizing evidence	Networking skills	Facilitation skills
	IT skills	Interpersonal skills	Change management skills
	Tailoring resources to local needs	Stakeholder management and influencing skills	Improvement skills

Source: Kislov et al., 2016: 108

It should be immediately apparent that it will not be enough for the SRL to be 'research literate', they will also need to have good pedagogical knowledge to understand how the research impacts on the work of teachers. They will also have to have excellent people management skills, as they will need to link different people within the school, be it teaching assistants, teachers, heads of department and members of senior leadership teams. The SRL will also have to be aware of the context and have 'situational' knowledge and be able to identify the 'school as it is' rather than the 'school they would want'. In other words, the SRL will need to be aware of the willingness of others to participate in knowledge management and which priorities of the school at the time lend themselves to a significant use of research evidence.

In addition, is it reasonable to expect any one individual to have all the skills necessary to be a successful school research champion, cope with the different types of knowledge, build connections both within and outside of the school, and at the same time maintain their credibility with diverse audiences – be it researchers, senior leadership or teachers? So rather than have a school research lead it may be necessary to have a number of people engaged in the process of knowledge brokering and mobilisation within your school. If the school decides that rather than having an SRL it wishes to have a number of people engaged in knowledge brokering, there are a number of questions that need to be taken into account as the team of knowledge brokers is put together.

- Does the team have the combination of skills required for information management, linkage and exchange and capacity building?
- What skills are currently lacking and how can their development be supported?
- What incentives can be provided to support the engagement of a school, department, or multi-academy trust chain in capacity-building activities?
- What arrangements are in place to ensure knowledge mobilisation turns into actual changes in practice?
- How will research and other evidence be integrated into existing ways of doing things within a school or multi-academy trust?
- How can an adequate mix of research, school data, stakeholder views and practitioner expertise and other forms of knowledge be achieved in the team?

234 EVIDENCE-BASED SCHOOL LEADERSHIP AND MANAGEMENT

- Does the team have credibility with teachers, support staff, managers, leaders, governors, trustees and external researchers?
- How can individuals already playing the role of informal school research leads be identified and engaged?
- Are the interests of all stakeholder groups taken into account in the process of gathering and generating evidence?
- What procedures are in place to support the recognition, promotion and career development of school research leads?
- What arrangements are in place for accessing the knowledge and experience of existing school research leads in other schools?
- What social support structures (professional learning communities, peer support groups, mentorship groups) are available? (Adapted from Kislov et al., 2016: 110)

Involve people with the right mix of skills to support the use of research and evidence

As well as making sure that you involve school staff with the right mix of skills to support the use of research, it is important to also consider the extent to which external support is necessary for success. The involvement of external partners in helping shape your evidence-based practice is important for two reasons; first, not all research is easily accessible – physically or intellectually – and external support may be necessary to help you access and interpret the research; second, recent work on how continuous professional development contributes to great teaching suggests that external partners have an important role to play in most forms of effective professional learning (Higgins et al., 2015).

If we now focus our attention on how you can make the most of partnerships between schools and universities to ensure that you have access to the right mix of skills and supports, some helpful guidance is provided by Greany and Brown (2015), who looked at the relationships between teaching schools and universities. They argue that there are at least four things you should give consideration to. First, on the one hand be clear with the university partner on what help you need, whilst on the other hand be clear what it is that you have to offer the university. Second, once you have created a partnership with a university it is necessary to empower leaders and others to create a 'third-space' so that colleagues from each institution can come together and engage in processes of inquiry. Third, the building of a trusting relationship between your school and university partner will take time. Just because you have made some kind of formal link with a university, doesn't automatically mean this will lead to research influencing the evidence used in the decision-making process within the school. However, you will need to look out for when the relationship has become too 'cosy' and provides insufficient challenge to either party. Indeed, if this is the case, this may be doing more harm than good to evidence-based decision-making. Fourth, focus on impact, but be prepared for unexpected outcomes. Evidence-based practice is all about making decisions that will hopefully lead to favourable outcomes. However, the net benefits from deep and embedded relationships with a university partner may be extremely difficult to demonstrate, particularly in times of austerity.

And finally, are you and your school ready for evidence-based school leadership?

As has been demonstrated throughout this book, evidence-based school leadership involves more than just reading the latest research or finding evidence to justify a decision that has already been made. Evidence-based school leadership involves a conscientious, explicit and judicious process of making a decision through the use of the best available evidence. So before seeking to introduce evidence-based school leadership into your school it makes a lot of sense to undertake some form of audit or self-assessment of you and your school's current state of readiness. At the end of Chapter 10 there is a brief self-assessment tool as to your personal practice as an evidence-based practitioner. Accordingly, this chapter will conclude by providing a self-assessment checklist to help understand your current behaviour in leading evidence-based practice. It will also direct you to resources that will help you assess the school's readiness to engage with evidence.

How well am I doing in supporting evidence-based practice?

The following is a list of questions that could be posed to try to get some kind of snapshot of where you are as an evidence-based school leader. The questions listed are by no means the only questions that could be asked. Nevertheless, hopefully, these questions and others they may stimulate you to ask, will provide a basis for working through some of the things you need to do to develop your own practice as an evidence-based school leader.

1. Am I constantly communicating a vision for evidence-based practice within the school?
2. Am I clear in my own mind about the relationship between evidence, practice and outcomes?
3. Am I modelling the integration of the best available evidence within my own decision-making practice?
4. Am I challenging myself to constantly develop my own skills and practice by developing an inquiry habit of mind?
5. Am I making appropriate resources available be it time, money and attention to support the development of evidence-based practice?
6. Am I constantly seeking feedback – to challenge my understanding of my performance as an evidence-based school leader?
7. Am I teaching and modelling the integration of pupils' and other stakeholders' preferences within my own leadership practice?
8. Am I working to create mutually supportive yet challenging relationships with colleagues within the school?
9. Am I incorporating the asking of well-formulated questions in the day-to-day work of the school?
10. Am I leading and modelling research skills in seeking out the best available current evidence, be it academic research, school data, practitioner expertise or stakeholders' views?
11. Am I facilitating ease of access within the school to multiple sources of evidence?
12. Am I leading, teaching and modelling the development of critical appraisal skills in order to be able to identify high-quality evidence?
13. Am I teaching and modelling the creation of critical summaries of the best available evidence?
14. Am I teaching and modelling how to analyse the local setting?
15. Am I developing evidence implementation plans which are suitable for the school's context?
16. Am I working to create a mutually supportive yet self-critical network of colleagues in both school and other settings?

17. Am I developing new ways of evaluating the effectiveness of my leading of evidence-based practice?
18. Am I aware of the ethical imperative to engage in evidence-based school leadership?

Is the school ready for evidence-based practice?

As for the school as a whole, there are other audit tools that could be used. Stoll et al. (2018) have developed a self-assessment tool, which is derived from Coldwell et al. (2017) to help school leaders judge their present degrees of interaction with evidence in terms of awareness, engagement and use. Alternatively, the National Foundation for Education Research have developed an online self-review tool for research engagement in schools and other providers, which looks at a range of dimensions of research use including: leadership and vision; learning and participation; management of resources; setting priorities; rigorous methodologies; impact; embedding and sustaining; and working collaboratively.

Summary and key points

- A whole-school evidence-use culture requires the use of evidence to be embedded into the day-to-day work of the school.
- To encourage evidence use it is necessary to ensure staff have the appropriate capability, motivation and opportunity to do so.
- Evidence-based school leaders need demonstrate their own commitment to research and evidence use as well as facilitate the efforts of others.
- It is important to be clear about the differences between research, quality improvement and evidence-based practice.
- Your approach to research and evidence use must have buy-in throughout the school.
- It is important to be clear in how both stakeholders and others are to be engaged in evidence-based practice.
- Before starting to introduce research and evidence use it is important if not essential to identify actions or tasks to stop doing.
- It is important to remember there are different views about the importance of research evidence to school improvement and the evidence-based school leader needs to challenge his or her own views.

- It is essential to develop middle leaders in the use of research evidence by understanding both the generic and specific skills necessary to be an effective school research lead.
- There are various approaches to self-assessing both your own and the school's readiness to engage in evidence-based practice.

References

Barends, E., Rousseau, D. and Briner, R. (2014) *Evidence-based Management: The Basic Principles*. Amsterdam. Center for Evidence-Based Management.

Bennett, T. (2016) *The School Research Lead*. Reading: Education Development Trust.

Brown, C. (2015) *Leading the Use of Research and Evidence in Schools*. London: IOE Press.

Bryk, A.S., Gomez, L.M., Grunow, A. and LeMahieu, P.G. (2015) *Learning to Improve: How America's Schools Can Get Better at Getting Better*. Cambridge, MA: Harvard Education Press.

Coldwell, M., Greany, T., Higgins, S., Brown, C., Maxwell, B., B, S., Stoll, L., Willis, B. and Burns, H. (2017) *Evidence-informed Teaching: An Evaluation of Progress in England Research Report*. London: Department for Education.

Collins, K. and Coleman, R. (2017) 'Evidence-informed policy and practice', in P. Earley and T. Greany (eds), *School Leadership and Education System Reform*. London: Bloomsbury.

DeLuca, C., Bolden, B. and Chan, J. (2017) 'Systemic professional learning through collaborative inquiry: examining teachers' perspectives', *Teaching and Teacher Education*, 67: 67–78.

Denzin, N. (1984) *On Understanding Emotion*. San Francisco, CA: Jossey-Bass.

Edwards, A., Elwyn, G., Hood, K., Atwell, C., Robling, M., Houston, H., Kinnersley, P., Russell, I. and Group, S.S. (2004) 'Patient-based outcome results from a cluster randomized trial of shared decision making skill development and use of risk communication aids in general practice', *Family Practice*, 21 (4): 347–54.

Greany, T. and Brown, C. (2015) *Partnerships between Teaching Schools and Universities: Research Report*. London: IOE.

Hargreaves, A. and Fullan, M. (2012) *Professional Capital: Transforming Teaching in Every School*. New York: Teachers College Press.

Hargreaves, A. and Stone-Johnson, C. (2009) 'Evidence-informed change and the practice of teaching', in J. Bransford, D. Stipek, N. Vye, L. Gomez and D. Lam (eds), *The Role of Research in Educational Improvement*. Cambridge, MA: Harvard Education Press. pp.89–110.

Hicks, R.W. (2016). 'Maintaining ethics in quality improvement', *AORN journal*, 103: 139–141.

Higgins, S., Cordingley, P., Greany, T. and Coe, R. (2015) *Developing Great Teaching: Lessons from the International Reviews into Effective Professional Development*. London: Teacher Development Trust.

Kislov, R., Wilson, P. and Boaden, R. (2016) 'The "dark side" of knowledge brokering', *Journal of Health Services Research and Policy*, 22 (2): 107–12.

Langer, L., Tripnet, J. and Gough, D. (2016) *The Science of Using Science: Researching the Use of Research Evidence in Decision-Making*. London: EPPI Centre, Insitute of Education.

Lynn, J., Baily, M.A., Bottrell, M., Jennings, B., Levine R.J., Davidoff, F., Casaretti, D., Corrigan, J., Fox, E. and Wynia, M.K. (2007). 'The ethics of using quality improvement methods in health care', *Annals of Internal Medicine*, 146: 666–73.

Michie, S., Van Stralen, M.M. and West, R. (2011) *The Behaviour Change Wheel: A New Method for Characterising and Designing Behaviour Change Interventions*. Implementation Science, 6. 1. 42.

Sackett, D., Rosenberg, W., Gray, J., Haynes, R. and Richardson, W. (1996) 'Evidence based medicine: what it is and what it isn't', *BMJ, 312* (7023): 71–2.

Senge, P., Roberts, C., Ross, R., Smith, B. and Kleiner, A. (1994) *The Fifth Discipline Fieldbook*. New York: Bantam Doubleday Dell.

Senge, P., Kleiner, A., Roberts, C., Ross, R., Roth, G. and Smith, B. (1999) *The Dance of Change: the Challenges of Sustaining Momentum in Learning Organisations*. London: Nicholas Brealey Publishing.

Stoll,L., Greany, T., Coldwell, M., Higgins, S., Brown, C., Maxwell, B., Stiell,B., Willis, B. and Burns, H. (2018) *Evidence-Informed Teaching: Self-assessment for Schools*. London: Chartered College of Teaching.

Ulrich, D., Kerr, S. and Ashkenas, R. (2002) *The GE Work-Out: How to Implement GE's Revolutionary Methods for Busting Bureuacracy and Attacking Organisational Problems Fast*. New York: McGraw–Hill.

12

SOME CONCLUDING THOUGHTS

Chapter outline

This final chapter looks at the varying roles that practitioners, policy-makers and researchers can play in supporting the development of evidence-based school leadership. The chapter ends by setting out an agenda for evidence-based school leadership.

Practioners, policy-makers and researchers

School leaders

There is no easy way of putting it other than to say that head-teachers, executive heads and multi-academy trust chief executive officers have an absolutely critical role in implementing and sup-porting evidence-based practice within schools. Without school leaders' full commitment and engagement to fully embed evidence-based practice within the decision-making processes, then evidence-based education will be seen as nothing more than the latest fad. Indeed, unless school leaders have a real and last-ing commitment to 'genuine inquiry' and openness of mind to get past both the immediate and possibly superficial, then it is probably best not even to pay lip service to the notion of being an evidence-based school.

Researchers

Researchers into evidence-based education need to ensure that they do all they can to learn from other related fields, such as, evidence-based healthcare, evidence-based nursing, evidence-based social work and knowledge mobilisation. In researching for this book, there have been too many occasions where I have found educational researchers to have been broadly dismissive or unaware of work con-ducted in other disciplines. Yet many of the problems faced in education in trying to close the 'research–practice' gap have been experienced elsewhere, and promising strategies and innovations have been developed. For example, evidence-based education has much to learn from both improvement and implementation sciences. There is also much to be learnt from approaches such as 'realistic evaluation', which takes into account the interaction between the context and the intervention.

Research funders

In 2017, the Education Endowment Foundation published the results of a number of interventions where the outcomes could be described as disappointing (Murphy et al., 2017; Worth et al., 2017). Indeed, it could be argued these interventions were 'doomed to fail' as they had not taken into account what we know about the conditions needed for research-use and behaviour change (see Cuckorova and Luckin, 2018). So what are research funders to do? First, research funders need to insist that the logic models or frameworks which inform any research proposals are thoroughly 'stress-tested' and, in doing so, become robust theories of change, with assumptions and the condi-tions for success fully explored. Second, having created a robust theory of change a risk-management strategy should be created which identifies mitigating actions that could or should be taken

Providers of leadership development training for aspiring and current leaders

Providers of leadership development training for aspiring and current leaders need to ensure that the programmes they put together do more than promote the latest managerial or pedagogic fads. They should help aspiring and current school leaders develop the skills to be able to distinguish between innovations that have realistic chances of bringing about improvement in schools and those innovations which are little more than 'snake-oil'. Furthermore, it is not enough for leadership development training providers to say their programmes are evidence-based. The designers and providers of leadership development programmes should also provide multiple sources of evidence to support the claims they make about the effectiveness of their programmes.

Providers of initial teacher training

The vast majority of school leaders still 'come through the ranks' having entered the profession as prospective teachers. This being so, the nature and quality of the initial teacher training that new entrants will receive will form a significant role in shaping future leaders' professional DNA. Accordingly, it is essential providers of initial teacher training design programmes have evidence-based practice at their very core. New and aspiring teachers need to be supported so that they can become both research-literate and be able to incorporate multiple sources of evidence into their day-to-day work as teachers. With this in mind, Teach First's recent report *Putting Evidence to Work: How Can We Help New Teachers Use Research Evidence to Inform Their Teaching*? is to be welcomed (Teach First, 2017).

Professional bodies

Professional bodies have a pivotal role in shaping the environment in which school leaders operate. In England, the Chartered College of Teaching has done some excellent work by making academic research easily available to its members and by holding a wide range of events to help teachers and leaders engage with evidence. In addition, the professional bodies representing school leaders can play a vital role in articulating the professional values that should inform school leadership. As argued in Chapter 1, evidence-based school leadership is fundamentally an ethical endeavour, and school leadership practices that are not ethically driven are not consistent with real evidence-based leadership. The use of practices within schools such as 'off-rolling', i.e. the removal by one means or another of pupils from a school's roll in order to manipulate a school's examination results, has no part to play in evidence-based school leadership. The creation by the Association of School and College Leaders of an Ethical Leadership Commission is therefore to be applauded.

Accountability bodies

As Brown and Greany (2017) state: 'evidence-informed practice is now viewed by educational policymakers in England as a driver of school and system self-improvement' (p. 18). However, the work of Coldwell et al. (2017) would suggest that there are significant differences between schools in the way in which evidence is used, with many schools having what could only be described as a weak evidence-use culture. Indeed, Brown and Greany go on to argue that evidence informed self-improvement within England's schools needs to be underpinned by external accountability and inspection processes, with Ofsted's inspection framework being suitably amended.

However, it is not enough for accountability bodies such as Ofsted to amend their inspection framework to pay explicit attention to evidence-informed practice. Ofsted and other bodies need to ensure that their own processes are suitably based or informed on solid research evidence. For as Professor Rob Coe states in Niemtus (2018): 'there have been changes, but it's still a pretty amateurish business. Ofsted may not make individual gradings for lessons any more, but the processes they use [to judge teaching and learning] are not in line with the best evidence.'

Teachers

If leadership decisions within schools are going to be 'evidence-based' then teachers have a central role to play in ensuring the success of such an approach. First, the views of teachers and their practical expertise form an integral part of the evidence base on which decisions are made. As such, teachers need to recognise their importance within the decision-making process. Second, given that evidence-based school leaders need to be 'conscientious, explicit and judicious' then teachers have an essential role of 'calling-out' leaders who do not meet such standards. This will not always be easy, and in many instances may not even be 'safe' given the leadership and management culture of a school. Third, teachers need to demand better evidence from the leaders of their schools to show both the direct impact of current practices and the potential impact of future interventions. Being a teacher is hard enough, without spending unnecessary amounts of time on practices that just do not make any kind of positive impact. It's not enough for an intervention or practice to have merit, it needs to be 'worth it'.

Governing bodies and boards of trustees

Given that the board is the accountable body – be it of a school or a multi-academy trust – it is the key decision-maker within a school and although decisions may be delegated to executive leaders, committee or individual, the board as the body corporate remains responsible and accountable for all decisions made (DfE, 2017b). What is clear from the Governance Handbook, subsequent guidance on competences required by governors and trustees (DfE 2017a) and the National Governance Association guidance (NGA, 2017) is the essential role of evidence-based school leadership within the decision-making framework of a school or multi-academy trusts. These documents make it clear that governors need to take into account multiple sources of evidence – research, school data, practitioner expertise and stakeholders – in the decision-making process. Furthermore, that these decisions should be taken where: viable options are identified; personal interests are set aside; free and frank discussion takes place; a range of perspectives are valued; assumptions are rejected with nothing taken for granted; decisions are made impartially, fairly and on merit using the best evidence and without discrimination or bias; transparency in decision making is encouraged; the board is willingly answerable to, and open to challenge from, those with an interest in decisions made (DfE, 2017a). In other words, unless boards are using principles, practices and processes that are consistent with evidence-based school leadership, then the board of governors is highly likely to be in breach of its statutory responsibilities.

Government

This brings us to the role of government in supporting the development of evidence-based school leadership. In many ways governments have a critical role in creating the context in which evidence-based practice will either flourish or fade away like other educational fads. First, governments have a responsibility to engage in evidence-based policy-making and ensure that new policies are informed by evidence and not based on 'zombie ideas' (Quiggin, 2012) such as grammar schools. Second, governments need to create the conditions in which school leaders can develop both the opportunities and skills to engage in evidence-based school leadership. This needs to be done through the provision of both appropriate leadership development programmes and in-school resources to provide the time and the space to make the best use of evidence. Third, governments have a responsibility to ensure that accountability schemes hold school leaders to account for their use of research and evidence. In other words, school leaders need to have both intrinsic and extrinsic motivation to engage in evidence-based school leadership. Finally, the government's use of data when providing information about the 'performance' of schools needs to be done in such a way that it actively discourages 'gamefication' of results. The reality of school improvement and evidence used needs to match the rhetoric.

And finally

This book concludes with an agenda for real evidence-based education. Any reader who has reached the end of this book will not be surprised to find that this agenda has been heavily influenced by developments within evidence-based medicine. As such, the following is informed by the work of Greenhalgh et al. (2014), who developed an agenda for real evidence-based medicine. Amended for an educational context, an agenda for real evidence-based school leadership might look this:

- Makes the ethical leadership and management of school its top priority
- Demands multiple sources of evidence in a format that governors, school leaders, teachers, support staff, parents and pupils can understand

- Is characterised by expert judgement rather than mechanical rule following
- Involves shared decision-making between governors, leaders, teachers, pupils, parents and other stakeholders
- Builds on the fundamentally human aspect of education to foster mutual respect between everyone within a school community
- Applies these principles to all aspects of the work of the school.

References

Brown, C. and Greany, T. (2017) 'The evidence-informed school system in England: where should school leaders be focusing their efforts?', *Leadership and Policy in Schools, 17* (1): 115–37.

Coldwell, M., Greany, T., Higgins, S., Brown, C., Maxwell, B., Stiell, B., Stoll, L., Willis, B. and Burns, H. (2017) *Evidence-Informed Teaching: An Evaluation of Progress in England Research Report*. London: Department for Education.

Cuckorova, M. and Luckin, R. (2018) 'The sweet smell of success: how can we help educators develop a "nose" for evidence they can use in the classroom?' IOE London Blog, posted 8 February. https://ioelondonblog.wordpress.com/2018/02/08/the-sweet-smell-of-success-how-can-we-help-educators-develop-a-nose-for-evidence-they-can-use-in-the-classroom/ (accessed 15 February 2018).

DfE (2017a) *A Competency Framework for Governance: the Knowledge, Skills and Behaviours Needed for Effective Governance in Maintained Schools, Academies and Multi-Academy Trusts January 2017*. London: Department for Education.

DfE (2017b) *Governance Handbook: For Academies, Multi-Academy Trusts and Maintained Schools January 2017*. London: Department for Education.

Greenhalgh, T., Howick, J. and Marskey, N. (2014) 'Evidence based medicine: a movement in crisis', *BMJ* 2014;*348* g3725 (accessed 1 May 2018).

Murphy, R., Weinhardt, F., Wyness, G. and Rolfe, H. (2017) *Lesson Study Evaluation Report and Executive Summary November 2017*. London: Education Endowment Foundation.

NGA (2017) *Model Procedures: Code of Conduct Legislation, Policies and Procedures*. Birmingham: National Governance Association.

Niemtus, Z. (2018) 'The fact is, teaching is just a difficult thing to judge', *TES London*, 16 February.

Quiggin, J. (2012) *Zombie Economics: How Dead Ideas Still Walk Among Us*. Princeton, NJ: Princeton University Press.

Teach First (2017) *Putting Evidence to Work: How Can We Help New Teachers Use Research Evidence to Inform Their Teaching?* London: Teach First.

Worth, J., Sizmur, J., Walker, M., Bradshaw, S. and Styles, B. (2017) *Teacher Observation*. Evaluation Report and Executive Summary November 2017. London: Education Endowment Foundation.

INDEX